FORGING THE STAR

FORGING THE STAR

The Official Modern History of
the United States Marshals Service

David S. Turk, Historian, U.S. Marshals Service

Denton, Texas

Published in 2016 by the University of North Texas Press

All rights reserved.
Printed in the United States of America.

10 9 8 7 6 5 4 3 2 1

Permissions:
University of North Texas Press
1155 Union Circle #311336
Denton, TX 76203-5017

Library of Congress Cataloging-in-Publication Data

Names: Turk, David S., author.
Title: Forging the star : the official modern history of the United States Marshals Service / by David S. Turk.
Description: Denton, Texas : University of North Texas Press, 2016. | Includes bibliographical references and index.
Identifiers: LCCN 2016013241| ISBN 9781574416541 (cloth : alk. paper) | ISBN 9781574416626 (ebook)
Subjects: LCSH: United States. Marshals Service--History. | Law enforcement--United States--History.
Classification: LCC HV8144.M37 T87 2016 | DDC 363.28/20973--dc 3
LC record available at http://lccn.loc.gov/2016013241

The electronic edition of this book was made possible by the support of the Vick Family Foundation.

TABLE OF CONTENTS

LIST OF PHOTOS

ACKNOWLEDGMENTS

This book is a result of thirteen years (2002–15) of research and writing. In such a large span of time, there are many to thank for their efforts and assistance. If any name is omitted here, it is not because of ingratitude, but the fact that I couldn't possibly remember every name who deserves credit—the listing would take more space than allowed for publication.

I would first thank those who were internally critical supporters of this endeavor. This would not be possible were it not for the support of former U.S. Marshals Service Director Stacia A. Hylton, Acting Director David Harlow, Associate Director for Administration David Musel, Associate Director for Operations William Snelson, former Chief of Staff Donald O'Hearn, Chief of Staff Sophia Edwards, Executive Officer Maureen Pan, and Chief of the Office of Congressional and Public Affairs William Delaney. I also thank all our assistant directors, past and present, for their contributions and leadership. In the Department of Justice, I thank Assistant Attorney General for Administration Lee J. Lofthus, Chief Counsel Arthur Gary, Nia Smith, and the Justice Management Division's Paula Scholz and Doug Cohn.

Although the Office of Public Affairs has employed me as historian since the closing months of 2001, my direct leadership was a great part of this success. Public Affairs Chief Drew J. Wade started in the U.S. Marshals Service before I did, in 1989—and returned to the agency of his youth. He has been steadfast in supporting our historical heritage. His vision for the 225th anniversary of the U.S. Marshals as a law enforcement entity made this book's completion a reality. Former Public Affairs Chief Donald Hines (2001–05) saw the trials and tribulations of bringing on a new historian, yet took a chance on me. Other past chiefs and deputy chiefs must also be commended for their tolerance and patience in this long wait: Bill Licotovich, Larry Cooper, Michael Kulstad, Jeff Carter, Steve Blando, and Donna Sellers.

I also must thank those who coordinated the "big vision." Robert X. Marcovici is the solid rock of ethics law, and I truly appreciate his good counsel. His bosses, Gerald Auerbach and Lisa Dickinson, must also be commended. Retired Assistant Director Carl Caulk has been vital for the review of this work, but also for his contributions towards the forthcoming U.S. Marshals Museum. Chief Deputies Tom Morefield and John Svinos both reviewed large portions of the manuscript and gave their input.

My co-workers are likewise dedicated and talented people who achieve good deeds on a daily basis. Deputy Chief Donna Sellers keeps us aligned. Information Specialist Nikki Credic excels in numerous arenas —but particularly shines in outreach functions. Specialist David Oney understands Hollywood and related media like few others. Former co-worker Carolyn "CeCe" Gwathmey could probably multi-task in her sleep. Specialist Lynzey Donahue interfaces with the public more than anyone in Public Affairs and adeptly handles the publicity of seized assets cases big and small. Our recently-retired administrative officer, Rose Griffin, kept us all running smoothly for years. Last, but not least, is Photographer Shane McCoy. Dedicated to the artistry and design of the still picture, poster, or video, he contributes to this work. Some of the Public Affairs crew who have moved on were instrumental in the development of the book: Mavis DeZulovich, Bill Dempsey, Dave Sacks, Bob Leschorn, and

Dave Turner. I would be remiss to not mention Amy Osborne, who has been posting my historical accounts on the web for years.

Others in the U.S. Marshals Service, past and present, contributed to the success of this account. In addition to Director Hylton, former Directors Bill Hall, Stanley Morris, Henry Hudson, the late Eduardo Gonzalez, John Marshall, Benigno Reyna, and John F. Clark were all extraordinary sources in my endeavors and gracious with their time; I also thank former Acting Director Louie McKinney, who led us when the tragedy of 9/11 struck the nation; former Associate Director Howard Safir; former Enforcement Chief Chuck Kupferer; former U.S. Marshal Roger Arechiga; former Chief for International Affairs Billy Sorukas; retired Inspectors Henry Ohrenburger and Mark Shealey; former Associate Director Gary Mead; former Acting Deputy Director and Witness Security Chief Eugene Coon; former Assistant Director Sylvester Jones; former Assistant Director Don Horton; former Chief Deputy John Cleveland; Tactical Operation's Mike Pyo, Jeff Cahall, and Jeff Stine; Information Technology's Harry Scott; Office of Internal Affair's John Noory; Witness Security's Anthony Corbitt; the Office of Congressional Affair's Christie Dawson and Natalie Brown; the Directors' Office staff former and present, including Vicky Smith and Claudia Peacock; former warehouse supervisor Carleton Parish; Procurement Officer Elizabeth Howard; former Property Management Chief Nick Prevas; former EEO chief Joseph Tolson; former Chief of Printing and Publications Larry Mogavero, and present staff; the former "closer" in the Seized Assets Division, Jim Herzog; Chief Deputies Rick Long, Rich Knighten, John Svinos, Tom Morefield, Mike Ferstl, Bob Christman are to be thanked among the many who held this rank.

Some of those I thank from the old Enforcement Division days include former Chief of Staff and Assistant Director Arthur Roderick, former Acting Enforcement Chief Don Ward, Bill Hufnagel, and Robert "Buck" Leschorn.

I could not have written this book without numerous dedicated retirees from our ranks. Some have passed on before publication of this book.

Clarence "Al" Butler was like a grandfather to me, and the consummate deputy U.S. marshal of his time. He worked directly with his boss, Chief U.S. Marshal James J.P. McShane, and alongside equally stalwart deputies and administrators like Donnie Forsht, Ellis Duley, Frank Noe, and Jack Cameron. This group was the leadership engine for the Civil Rights Era, and served on the front lines during the Ole Miss riots and many other missions of the time. It was Al who coined the phrase—"you put on the badge, you do the job." His widow Pat and son Greg are great friends.

I would be remiss to not mention my other friends from this time —the late Denzil "Bud" Staple, of Washington State, a deputy whose positive attitude could cut through the tear gas at Oxford; the late Ernie Mike of Kentucky; Charlie Burks of Indiana; Bill Banta and Rod Taubel of Wisconsin; Charles Burrows of California; Donnie Forsht of Florida; Ronnie Messa and Rufus Campbell of Louisiana; Lloyd Caldwell of Missouri; the late Willard McArdle of Oregon; William Dunn of Texas; the late Graham "Gene" Same of Indiana; and Herschel Garner of Arkansas.

I appreciate the help of Michael McShane, son of James and a great man himself. His insights really enlightened me about his father—and he is every bit like him! Larry Palmer was helpful in studying his father, Chief U.S. Marshal Clive Palmer. William Neptune was a key official in the Executive Office of the U.S. Marshals during the turbulent 1968-69 years, and vital to my understanding of it. I also appreciate James Meredith, his son John, and his sister Hazel Hall. I also appreciated the help of late U.S. Marshal Marvin Lutes, who was the "hidden hand" behind the success of the movie *The Fugitive*.

Perhaps the most detailed assistance came from the pen of the late Jack Cameron. He served many roles in our agency. His meticulous recordkeeping brought some of the most obscure details into the light. His son Bill must be thanked for forwarding his papers long ago. I worked with the National Archives, Civil Reference Division and retired Archivist Fred Romansky; the Library of Congress Manuscript Division; the Department of Justice Libraries' former Director Blaine Dessy, current Director Dennis Feldt, retired Librarian Jim Higgins; and former Librarian David Mendoza; preservationist Rick Parker; Arkansas Parks' Richard Davies, Tony Perrin, and Linda Goza; great researchers like Robert Ernst, George Stumpf and the late Ronald Van Raalte; former employee William Reinkens; and fellow historians John Fox and Sean Fearns, respectively of the Federal Bureau of Investigation and the Drug Enforcement Administration.

The U.S. Marshals Museum, which will honor our personnel past and present, will be in Fort Smith, Arkansas. Other than this book, it is probably the longest endeavor I have worked on as historian. Any initiative such as this takes many hands to build. Former Assistant Director Michael A. Pearson guided the launch of the process; Claude Legris, the experienced commerce man; former U.S. Marshal Richard O'Connell; Judge James Spears; CEO James Dunn and his staff. Behind them, pushing the whole thing forward, were U.S. Senators and Congressman, particularly Senator John Boozman.

Last, but not least, I thank my family. They have endured me through this long journey. Janet and son Ryan, a writer himself; my mother Ann and friend Van Napper; my father Howard, a writer before me, and my stepmother Karen; my sister Suzanne, brother-in-law Bruce Napper, and niece Corinne; stepbrother Brian Ray; and my cousin with the heart of gold, Billy Bayne, wife Angie, and three daughters Elaine, Olivia, and Allison. I also thank friends such as Dave Edwards, Juan Ray, Anthony Corbitt, Todd Yeatts and his gal Cindy, Carolyn and Steve Sederwall, and Sallie Chisum Robert, as well as the many friends and cousins not named.

History has been my life, and I am grateful for being allowed to work in it. When I began my apprenticeship under the first U.S. Marshals Historian, Ted Calhoun, he mentioned "bringing out the ghosts." That always stuck with me. If we are to bring out the ghosts, and make them speak, then we are the stewards of those ghosts. May those gentle or restless spirits, as well as the flesh and blood readership, find solace and understanding in these pages of a great law enforcement agency.

Forging the Star

INTRODUCTION

People often ask the question—"What is the U.S. Marshals Service?" The answer is tied to the agency's storied history. The U.S. Marshals were founded with the Federal Courts in Sections 27 and 28 of the Federal Judiciary Act of September 24, 1789. The overall legislation was Senate Bill No. 1, in the initial United States Congress. This bedrock measure provided our organizational baseline, and explains our many changing missions to this day. It's fair to say the Judiciary Act of September 24, 1789, inaugurated the U.S. Marshals alongside the development of the nation.[1]

The specific text of Sections 27 and 28 was instrumental in those changes. The first provides for a political appointee as U.S. marshal for each judicial district, and to delegate powers to deputy U.S. marshals.

> *And be it further enacted,* That a marshal shall be appointed in and for each district for a term of four years, but shall be removable from office at pleasure, whose duty it shall be to attend the district and circuit courts when sitting therein, and also the Supreme Court in the district in which that court shall sit.(b) And to execute throughout the district, all lawful precepts directed to him, and issued under the authority of the United States, and he shall have the power to command all necessary assistance in the execution of his duty, and to appoint as shall be occasion, one or more deputies...[2]

Several highlights should be noted from Section 27 of the Federal Judiciary Act of September 24, 1789. This legislation provided for one political appointment as "United States Marshal," and civilian "deputy

United States marshals." Long careers were not envisioned at this early date, as U.S. Marshals served a four-year term or at the pleasure of the President of the United States. Most deputies worked briefly. Even as career deputies were employed longer, some service by deputies was abbreviated by event or established term period. Eventually, this necessitated the rank of "special deputy U.S. marshal." From this concept developed the role of the posse in the Old West, and later non-agency personnel in modern-day task forces. It also allowed for hybrid service—a cross-deputation in certain cases. For example, Lincoln County Sheriff Patrick Garrett, the famed pursuer of the outlaw Billy the Kid in Territorial New Mexico, was cross-deputized as a special deputy U.S. marshal.[3]

The organizational model for the U.S. Marshal was based on the colonial British vice-admiralty courts. This enabled the U.S. Marshal authority to enforce federal law across some jurisdictional lines to deal with issues such as coastal piracy and the custody of prisoners from other districts.[4] This wide-ranging authority is explained in Section 28 of the Federal Judiciary Act. The article addresses the power to execute process and writs, sworn personnel, and continuity in office. While Section 27 defined the office, Section 28 was the fuel for effectively accomplishing the job.[5]

Original duties comprised many functions over which we no longer maintain responsibility. Many of these are currently done by others—such as taking the Federal Census until 1870 and pursuing counterfeiting operations until the advent of the Secret Service in 1865. The U.S. Marshals Service has acquired many formal functions, including the Witness Security Program, and the Seized Assets Management Program. Other commitments with judicial protection, prisoner transportation, service of process, and maintaining order during civil disturbances continue from those early days. It is the multitude and diversity of these functions that characterize the agency today.

Equally complicated was the historical supervision of the U.S. Marshals. If asked, many people assume the U.S. Attorney General managed them throughout their existence. In fact, the organization wandered from the initial purview of the State Department, followed by just over a decade of hybrid supervision that included the Interior Department, before they arrived under the general jurisdiction of the Attorney General in 1861. In 1870, the founding of the Department of Justice gave the U.S. Marshals a permanent home.[6]

The public perception of the deputy U.S. marshal changed over the course of time. They were most often seen in the federal territories of the West. The absence of state authorities amplified their presence. Territorial events that involved deputy U.S. marshals include the gunfight near Tombstone's OK Corral (Arizona Territory, October 1881), the Lincoln County War (New Mexico Territory, 1878–79), and the major gunfight with the Doolin Gang at Ingalls (Oklahoma Territory, September 1893). Bold personalities such as Wyatt Earp and his brothers, Wild Bill Hickok, Bass Reeves, and "Catch 'Em Alive Jack" Abernathy provided a small sample of legendary deputies in the American story. As territories became states, their visibility lessened.[7]

The six-shooter-carrying U.S. Marshals were placed on a shelf at the closing of the Old West, with a few exceptions. New federal law and regulatory enforcement agencies appeared, such as the Bureau of Narcotics, the Federal Bureau of Investigation, and the Internal Revenue Service. The new agencies and their missions reduced the duties formerly carried out by U.S. Marshals, like taking the Federal Census and shutting down illicit whiskey stills. As the new entities chipped away at their mission areas, the deputies still kept careful watch over existing federal territories. In addition, they continued important duties in the Consular Courts overseas in China, the Panama Canal Zone, and the Ottoman Empire. Overall, the presence of deputies diminished steadily with the changes, and the U.S. Marshals went from enforcing federal laws with a broad range of powers to primarily court-bound tasks, like service of process. Protecting the federal judiciary was important and seen as an honorable duty. However, it lacked the romantic visions invoked by the likes of Special Deputy U.S. Marshal and Lincoln County Sheriff Pat Garrett chasing Billy the Kid through the arid valleys of New Mexico.[8]

As America moved into a new age, the image of the deputy U.S. marshal came from other sources. In 1915, former Deputy U.S. Marshal William Tilghman filmed himself and some living legends and villains in *The Passing of the Oklahoma Outlaws*. The new medium of film brought law and order to the screen. People could see their heroes and villains, or at least the actors that played them. Films allowed audiences to have their own memories. Western films and books romanticized the Old West. In fact, during the 1920s and '30s, many legends of the Old West were still alive.[9] Other legends wrote their own story. Bat Masterson, a deputy U.S. marshal in 1905, was an aged sports writer in New York. The legendary Wyatt Earp lived in San Francisco. Retired U.S. Marshal Evett D. Nix of Oklahoma still lived too. They wrote memoirs and magazine articles around the same time popular new texts on Billy the Kid and Jesse James were published.[10]

However, movies and books could not assign new duties to the U.S. Marshals. By the 1920s, U.S. attorneys began looking to the Federal Bureau of Investigation, under Director J. Edgar Hoover, for investigative and enforcement support. In October 1935, Special Assistant to the Attorney General Alexander Holtzoff went so far as to state the duties of the U.S. Marshals were police powers "limited to the court room and its immediate vicinity."[11]

Perhaps Holtzoff's short-sighted views foreshadowed future developments, but they were incorrect in large part. Deputies during that time still performed other functions, like registering aliens during World War I, working on Prohibition cases, as well as providing court protection.[12]

The name "United States Marshal" looms large. Some of that is reputation—whether this happened in the Old West, Civil Rights Period, or in catching sex offenders and "the worst of the worst." Perhaps less known is the fact the agency is small in number. In 2013, there were only a little over 5,600 total employees, almost 4,000 of these operational deputies and criminal investigators. There are 94 presidentially appointed U.S. Marshals—one in each federal court district. Districts are not only in states, but part of the flexibility of the agency is the ability to transcend rigid borders between U.S. protectorate, commonwealth, territory, and state. To have a deputy U.S. marshal in a multi-jurisdictional force of state and local police enhances its reach to catch criminals. Indeed, part of the reason the U.S. Marshals Service succeeds is due to its small, adjustable work force.[13]

The U.S. Marshals Service has the advantage of its own heritage. The organization has survived and prospered because of its professional administrative and operational employees. Personnel understand the value of their heritage. The U.S. Marshals are the oldest federal law enforcement organization in the United States and handle dangerous situations, regardless of how unpopular they might be. This repetitive fact is woven into our mission's historical fabric.

The demarcation of the origins for the United States Marshals' modern history is as difficult to explain as that general question of what the organization does. The current term "service" did not officially exist in the name until the late 1960s. In December 1956, the official formation of headquarters came through another name—the "Executive Office for United States Marshals." Until then, true functionality was in the districts, and each U.S. Marshal "called the shots." The Executive Office provided for a separate identity, even providing oversight in the form of a Chief United States Marshal.[14] However, 1956 was not really the year that marked the beginning of the modern period for the U.S. Marshals. It was a gradual shift and the need for unification that created headquarters. By 1941, a nationally issued badge appeared. The decision of badge design previously rested with each district's U.S. Marshal. Further change toward a centralized publication brought about the *United States Marshals Bulletin* five years later. The new handout was a neatly packaged report, primarily containing information on regulations and financial matters. In addition, the *Bulletin* included historical facts and personal achievements.

However, the *Bulletin* was an independent publication only meant for internal personnel. With these two initial unifying features, the modern history of the U.S. Marshals truly began.[15]

By 1941, the U.S. Marshals wandered the frontiers of bureaucratic reform for some time, but still sought a solid independent identity. No one really knew the organization would be expanding its responsibilities. By 1956, limited autonomy started the road to growth. By the late 1960s, it was apparent the missions of the Executive Office for U.S. Marshals had outgrown its borders. The United States Marshals Service had several brushes with bureau status before finally receiving it permanently. Even then, the undefined tug-of-war between a burgeoning headquarters and the districts was inevitable. As the current agency matured, the process was not unlike a child becoming an adult. There were growing pains, great achievements, and times nerves were tested. Each passing decade brought a new direction.

The historical period between 1941 and 2002 was a wide swath of change. Neither date marks a full beginning or end—much happened before and after this time period. However, between these dates people glimpsed the modern structure. The many generations of deputies in those 61 years were the common strands in "forging the badge" with adherence to duty and each other through some of the rockiest roads possible. It can be summed up in a statement from United States Marshals Service Director Stacia A. Hylton, who served from December 2010 through July 2015.

> It's the heart and soul of the Marshals Service. I will always believe that any law enforcement dedicated to that badge—both operational and administrative...you just have to be a part of the organizational mission. The heart and soul... to build the relationships in an organization that lasts a lifetime. I think we bond together.[16]

SECTION ONE—Origins
of a Modern Agency

CHAPTER 1

THE THIRTIES AND FORTIES: ROOTS OF DISPARATE DUTIES

THE EMERGENCE OF OVERSIGHT

Societal changes during the 1930s proved dangerous for deputy marshals. As an example, Deputy U.S. Marshal William Raoul Dorsay, a four-year veteran of the Northern District of California, sought information about a fugitive who had stolen an automobile on November 25, 1937. Accompanied by two policemen, he came to the home of 73-year-old William Pierce in Oakland, California. The man was not a suspect but a former landlord of the fugitive. He was also partially blind and deaf. The lawmen pounded heavily on the front door. Pierce pulled out a double-barrel shotgun because he believed that Deputy Dorsay and the two officers were robbers. As the lawmen prepared to force an entry, Pierce fired the shotgun. The blast struck Dorsey in the neck, cutting his jugular vein. He fell to the walk, bleeding to death. The two others apprehended Pierce, who was tried and later sent to a mental hospital. Deputy Dorsay, the native Kentuckian who wrote poetry in his spare time, was given a hero's funeral with full military honors at age 41.[1]

The organizational structure of the U.S. marshals had remained unchanged since 1789. Each U.S. Marshal controlled his own district, including his preference for badge design. The President of the United States appointed each U.S. Marshal, so each possessed equal authority to lead the district. Congressional representatives viewed the patronage positions as political plums in their home districts, so the vestiges of unilateral, autonomous management perpetuated for generations. Perhaps politics prompted the changes to the structure of the U.S. Marshals starting the 1930s. By then, news coverage of deputies paled in comparison to coverage of the burgeoning Federal Bureau of Investigation. J. Edgar Hoover's keen grasp of the public eye boosted the profile of his agents and their fugitives, while U.S. Marshals received little of the spotlight. Additionally, from its inception the FBI had a centralized internal structure that the U.S. Marshals lacked in the 1930s. After recognizing the need for centralization and observing the efficiencies gained by other agencies with a core command structure, the U.S. Marshals eventually followed suit and established a central office, which would eventually become its headquarters in 1956.[2]

Until the establishment of headquarters, only occasional conferences brought together the appointed U.S. marshals or career deputy U.S. marshals from different districts and representatives from the Department of Justice. Continuously since 1861, each U.S. marshal turned to the Office of the Attorney General for both guidance and accountability. The Attorney General represented a distant boss to most deputies in the field, and was rarely involved in any district issue. In 1935, New Jersey native Salvatore A. Andretta joined the Justice Department. He was the first person charged with centralization of the U.S. marshals, and to improve their financial accountability. Justice officials tasked Andretta with managing and reconciling all expense accounts for the myriad U.S. marshals offices. The uneven flow of money between Justice and the district offices became a regular concern to the Department of Justice. With the Great Depression impacting the nation, federal budgets and expenses desperately needed oversight. The use of automobiles, investigative expenses, and rising living costs made fiscal discipline a critical issue. With only a secretary to assist him, Andretta became the central point person to authorize travel expenses for the large number of district offices.[3] Furthermore, in 1939, Attorney General Frank Murphy announced his intention to call a conference to discuss "improvements." It was actually a way for Murphy to "raise the bar" and remind all personnel of their specific duties.[4]

Still, the general notion of federal marshals being merely an extension of the courtroom stemmed from a decision in 1937 to replace bailiffs in the federal court with deputy U.S. marshals. Traditionally, bailiffs had been hired by the U.S. Marshals as a guard-type position. In fact, the old bailiff system was being phased out, but legislation from the 1930s and early 1940s inadvertently reinforced a stereotype that deputy U.S. marshals served as bailiffs. Largely based on the Appropriations Act of 1937, the hard-scrabble image of the Old West deputy marshal riding on his horse in the search for his quarry suffered as a result. The fact that federal bailiffs served long careers in a single court provoked the stereotype of aged deputy marshals well into the 1950s.[5]

While the image of the U.S. Marshals continued to develop with society's changes, the common strands of their core duties provided continuity. Patterned after the court system, U.S. Marshals' authority was spread over the many districts throughout the country. This began changing after World War II, with a trend towards greater workforce professionalization and more oversight of district activity. Eventually, these early efforts at centralized organization led to "headquarters."

One primary function of the deputy marshals that stood the test of time was "hooking and hauling." It is a term of workplace lexicon, which means shackling and transporting prisoners to and from court. Deputies have brought federal defendants and prisoners from cells to the court as a principal duty. For example, in 1931, U.S. Marshal Henry C.W. Laubenheimer brought Al Capone to court, under arrest for tax evasion. Photographers snapped numerous images as Capone—accompanied by the deputy marshal—entered the courthouse. In fact, the "perp walk" became a publicity, and sometimes political, duty for federal marshals when bringing a high-profile defendant to face justice. It was their way to let the world know "the feds got their man." The practice has since fallen out of favor.[6]

Overseas

Since the 1860s, deputies served in Constantinople (later Istanbul), Seoul, and other key courts around the world. By treaty, these courts handled the legal and criminal matters of American citizens in specific countries. By 1900, because of the competing national interests among a number of western countries, the U.S. likewise kept a strategic economic presence in China. Starting in June 1906, the U.S. Marshals maintained a constant presence in China through the Consular Court system. By Executive Order 6166, dated June 10, 1933, administrative supervision of the U.S. Court for China moved from the State to the Justice Department. The following year saw the arrival of U.S. Marshal Edward L. Faupel in Shanghai. Only 36 years old, Faupel learned much of war simply by being in the post.[7] The Sino-Japanese War almost led to the evacuation of personnel. By September 1937, U.S. Marshal Edward Faupel toyed with the idea of fleeing as he watched bombs drop on nearby Chinese military encampments. He wrote Salvatore Andretta, who maintained fiscal oversight of the U.S. marshals at Justice:

> At present there are only three of us remaining to carry on the work of the Court, Judge Helmick, Deputy Marshal Peterson and myself, with occasional gratis help from outside in matters concerning the District Attorney and Clerks offices. I find my position, both officially and otherwise, most interesting, and I might say entertaining, preferring not to leave this area until, and if, general evacuation becomes imperative.
>
> From the top of my apartment am able to observe frequent bombings of the Chinese positions which are so close to the settlement

boundry [*sic*] one may observe the bombs leave the planes, follow them to the ground and see the broken bodies fly into the air when satisfactory hits are made.

As acting Coroner, during this emergency, was at the scene of the bombings at the Cathay and Palace Hotels, Avenue Edward VII and Sinceres Department Store a few moments after the actual bombings occurred....[8]

Faupel would later depart Shanghai, leaving a vacancy at the Consular Court in June 1938. Californian Gordon Campbell, a young man who had recently returned from the Pacific theatre, was offered the job by his Congressman despite little experience in police work. Given that Campbell needed a regular salary, he accepted.[9]

U.S. Marshal Campbell's office was in a busy section of Shanghai. There was regular contact with other foreign offices in the city. He had few deputies, four at one point. One was stationed in the city of Tientsin, while the remainder stayed closer to Shanghai. No one actually explained his job to him, Campbell recalled years later. The former Attorney General of New Mexico, Milton Helmick, was the judge at the Consular Court. Like other U.S. marshals, Campbell carried civil and criminal process papers. In a rare case, he located a fugitive American attorney who had attempted escape on a cruise ship.[10]

He took off and went aboard an ocean liner and received his cabin for the trip, and was taking off for some foreign spot, I know not which. I had to go and commandeer the ship and hold it up until we got hold of him, which took place. We got him and brought him back to shore, and the ship went off and he was left to work out his troubles.[11]

While Marshal Campbell was greatly assisted by the Chinese citizens, the issue of jurisdiction arose. Shanghai was divided into international sections known as "concessions." On occasion, jurisdiction became murky. In one case, Deputy U.S. Marshal Arthur Peterson, a retired petty officer, called Campbell early one morning and stated that a murder had been committed at a bar on the border of American, British, and French jurisdictions—"on the corner of Blood Alley and Avenue Edward VII."[12]

> I went on down to investigate, because the owner of the bar was a chief petty officer of our navy who was living out there also. His name was Smell Bad Shelton. He [a patron] was dead, all right, from a meat cleaver. But he got his name from the fact that the night soil of the city was dumped in the river just across the street from his bar... On top of that, this was the time of Franklin Roosevelt in this country. He was carrying out his New Deal and getting lots of publicity. The New Deal Bar, that was its name. In a quick investigation, I found that Smell Bad was not connected with the murder and released him. That was the end of the case... When I found that Smell Bad didn't have any connection, I turned it over to the French *gendarmes*, and they took it from there.[13]

Other than the occasional excitement, his duties proved routine. Interaction with occupying Japanese forces was limited, even though they surrounded Shanghai and posted soldiers at the city limits. The judge held court sessions routinely, a clerk worked administrative tasks, and monies were handled by the U.S. Marshal's office. Appeals passed to the 9th Circuit Court in San Francisco.[14]

U.S. Marshal Campbell served until 1940. Once Japanese pressure increased in the region, the judge removed with the court to the city of Chungking, where it remained for the duration of World War II. He returned to the United States, serving alongside Secretary of Defense James Forrestal in Washington. Later, Campbell became a judge.[15]

WARTIME

In 1941, the Department of Justice eliminated one of the prerogatives of the presidentially appointed U.S. marshals. The Department took away each marshal's discretion to hire deputies as a way of achieving some centralized, fiscal restraint. However, this decision handicapped the appointed marshals' ability to carry out duties in the district offices, and appeared to them as a reversal of fortunes. Although later reversed, the move turned out to be one of the first seeds of centralization.[16]

Ties to the Department of Justice increased that same year with the issuance of a nationwide badge and credential to replace the slew of badges issued at the district level, creating some order and uniformity. Prior to this, official badges were a mixture of bronze, silver, enamel, copper, and even gold emblems, and came in a variety of shapes—most commonly a circle cut-out star or shield. The identification on the existing badges differed, with some designating the district or territory and others simply naming the wearer as a federal officer. The new, nationally issued badges were numbered and recorded for accountability. The first nationwide U.S. marshal's badge was shield-shaped, with an eagle on top. On the face in large type was the title "U.S. Marshal" or "Deputy U.S. Marshal" with the words "Dept. of Justice" included.[17]

Highlighting the impact of the centralization efforts was a memo from U.S. Marshal James E. Mulcahy of the Southern District of New York to T.D. Quinn, Administrative Assistant to the Attorney General, dated October 23, 1941. U.S. Marshal Mulcahy, after just six months on the job, made an official plea to block issuance of national badges to chief deputies. He stated "there are approximately 1,050 deputy marshals, including 94 chief deputies" and cited the increased costs of extra die casts. Quinn received the recommendations on November 1, but rejected outright the Marshal's point on chief deputy badges. As a side note, he also turned down Mulcahy's suggestion that confiscated vehicles be used by the districts instead of personal vehicles which required a reimbursement process.[18]

Even with a distinct badge to highlight semi-autonomy, finances were not independent. Andretta, Quinn, and the Chief of Division Accounts Eugene J. Matchett held a firm fiscal line on the Marshals. When irregularities were discovered in individual accounts, Matchett informed Andretta. In turn, Andretta issued a memorandum providing corrective instructions to a specific U.S. marshal. The irregularities were not always fiscal in nature. Andretta wrote Marshal Mulcahy in March 1946 that one of his deputies appeared to show preferred treatment of certain inmates—for example, by allowing certain prisoners to ride with him in the front seat of his van. Andretta requested the Marshal demand the resignations of the offending deputies, citing the civil service rules should they refuse.[19]

During World War II, while other agencies focused elsewhere, the U.S. marshals became internal guardians. Deputies transferred detainees to federal internment camps, regulated the internal movement of alien nationals, and caught "draft dodgers." In Utah, one deputy faced down a set of brothers who used religion as their defense for not reporting for duty. In this case, he simply gave them a choice: join your camp or go to jail. Chief Deputy Helen Crawford of the Eastern District of Texas was given the dangerous job of bringing in the commander and crew of a captured German U-Boat in the waters outside Beaumont, Texas. Although the U-Boat was disabled and helpless, the commander refused to surrender to a woman—even a gun-wielding one. Chief Crawford, with several deputies, leveled her gun and made it clear he had no choice.[20]

However, even busy with wartime tasks, "hooking and hauling" still dominated the work of the deputy U.S. marshals. A deputy typically tracked his activities and expenses in a logbook with gold-stamped lettering on the binding, often referred to as a "standard diary," in which year-by-year entries were made. One such diary, from the Northern District of New York, noted a typical day in the life of a deputy in January 1944.

> Jan 25—Arrested John E. Towse at the Conn Office and Brought [sic] him to Marsh Office and Took Finger Prints and Took to Madison Co Jail Ed. Breen as gard [sic] Contract Taxi co 55 yrs Old Lives [sic] at 300 Slocum 675 Syracuse[21]

All tasks were meticulously recorded. Any reimbursement of expense needed names and dates for verification. Interestingly, one diary has a slip pasted on the back—as a reminder of the process. It reads:

> I hearby [sic] Certify and return I received Within Warrant at Syracuse NY, on [ ] 1944 and herewith return it unexecuted as requested By the F.B.I. Agent [ ] Who States the Within Named Defendant is not believed to Be Within the Northern Dist of New York.[22]

Deputy U.S. marshals escorted in handcuffs to and from court many famous persons in the 1940s. Photographers captured Tokyo Rose, Ezra Pound, and Charlie Chaplin in the custody of deputies. Federal trials for Chaplin and Pound began in 1946 and put largely anonymous deputies in the headlines. Chaplin was a famous playboy whose fame went far beyond the movies that made his reputation. One of his girlfriends, Joan Barry, dragged him into court over the paternity of her child. The papers made much of the charge.[23] Chaplin's case dated from 1942. Chaplin had allegedly promised Joan Barry a major part in an upcoming film he planned, but he reneged. This triggered a very public federal case, no doubt fueled by his prior legal woes. Federal prosecutors charged him with transporting a minor over state lines, in violation of the Mann Act. In the press, headlines claimed Chaplin fathered Barry's child. The courts agreed and ordered Chaplin to make child support payments until the child was 21 years of age. The deputies took the actor to and from hearings throughout this period.[24]

Ezra Pound had lived abroad in Italy during the war. He found himself in hot water over views he expressed on public radio from the 1930s through World War II. On one such occasion, an Italian network had invited him to speak and he expressed muted criticism of America. However, he did not exhibit restraint regarding a "Jewish conspiracy" about which he felt the world knew little. He believed his only audience was a local one in Florence, but word reached the Allies. The Idaho-born poet turned self-imposed exile was arrested and confined at the Military

Disciplinary Center near Pisa in October 1945. Pound was extradited to the District of Columbia in November. Deputy U.S. marshals took him from the jail to his hearing before Judge Bolitha J. Laws. Fearing the death penalty, his defense was insanity. After examination, doctors agreed. For 13 years, Ezra Pound was confined to St. Elizabeth's Hospital until his contemporaries convinced medical authorities to re-examine and release him in 1958.[25]

NATIONAL ASSOCIATION OF DEPUTY UNITED STATES MARSHALS

At the end of World War II, deputy marshals had no national organization or place of meeting to gather and share ideas aside from assignments that occasionally crossed state or district lines. While the Presidentially appointed U.S. Marshals met sparingly, usually at a conference or meeting with the Attorney General, the career deputies missed these occasions unless they were acting for their bosses.

In 1946, the National Association of Deputy U.S. Marshals became the first forum for deputies to discuss common issues and practices. According to the existing newsletters of the organization, the first of which was dated January 1947, the group boasted 679 deputy U.S. marshals from nine national regions in its initial membership. The first gathering occurred in Washington, D.C., in December 1946 with Deputy U.S. Marshal Hayden Saunders as its first president. Formation of the association was not an independent effort. It enjoyed the full support of Attorney General Tom C. Clark. The newsletter, *Deputy United States Marshals' News*, initially appeared monthly in an attractive glossy format. Early membership included key personnel in the Justice Department.[26]

The Association worked hard to find high-profile speakers for their annual conventions. From the Olympic Hotel in Seattle, Washington, Training Officer Roy H. Webb wrote President Harry S. Truman on July

6, 1947. By that time, the membership had swelled to nearly 800 members. Truman could not attend, but sent a letter commending the effort.[27]

In addition to the annual convention, early efforts in training were part of the Association's goals. U.S. Marshal Ted Ranson of the District of Nevada wrote a small article for the *Nevada Peace Officer*. He reported that after attending a department-wide training school in Reno in August 1947, the National Association of Deputy United States Marshals intended to create its own permanent school. The agreed-upon location was Arkansas, with future goals of hosting a school on each coast of the United States. Marshal Ranson stated that Reno was the site for the western school. The idea was that "each person now on the job would be required to attend the academy at least ten days out of each 18 months and all new employees would be required to attend the academy not less than 60 days prior to reporting for duty."[28]

At least once, in 1950, they issued a yearbook identifying members from around the nation. It featured glossy photographs of their leaders, and a national pledge to uphold the mission of the U.S. marshals. Its constitution provided for different types of membership, and listed active administrative or operational personnel in good standing and retired personnel. U.S. Marshals were allowed to join the National Association, but could not hold office.[29]

Although total membership in the National Association of Deputy United States Marshals declined later in the 1950s, the group remained active and hosted a conference every year until 1975. It later developed into the Retired U.S. Marshals Association, and later still into the current United States Marshals Association.[30]

Regardless of the changes, the adaptability of the U.S. Marshals during the 1940s showed the true potential of its personnel. In faraway lands and on our own shores, deputies continued to carry out their duties in a time of unprecedented change.

CHAPTER 2

THE FIFTIES: SIGNS
OF A COMING ERA

Unlike the previous decade, the 1950s tested the U.S. Marshals with challenges from both internal and external sources. Internally, the organization improved its training to adjust to escalating racial tensions in the South. The first existence of a headquarters office appeared. Externally, the presence of deputies was heightened with one of the most publicized federal executions in American history—that of Julius and Ethel Rosenberg. Likewise, they made national headlines guarding anarchists and suspected communists. Senator Joseph McCarthy's Committee on Un-American Activities heightened the spotlight on these fears. In U.S. history, this period was known as the "Red Scare."

U.S. Marshals were often seen in the newspapers during the many arrests during this period, including wire photographs taken around the activities of Puerto Rican nationalist Oscar Collazo in November 1950. In the unsuccessful plot to kill President Harry Truman, Collazo succeeded in slaying policeman Leslie Coffelt outside Blair House, a residence frequented by politicians for events near the White House. Two other officers were wounded as Collazo and his fellow conspirator fought police to gain entry. Griselio Torresola, a second nationalist, was killed in the gunfire. Collazo was left to face two death penalty charges and further counts for attempted murder. For 10 days, a wounded Collazo lay in Gallagher Hospital in Washington, D.C., under the general custody of the U.S. Marshals. A hatted Deputy U.S. Marshal Charles Cranford graced the pages of almost every major newspaper, when he transferred his infamous prisoner to the District of Columbia Jail. Cranford did not appear thrilled by the attention, but the "perp walk" was a public relations tool.[1]

After WWII, the fears of communism and its potential discovery of the United States' nuclear secrets fueled insecurities and increased the visibility of federal law enforcement. Alger Hiss became a prisoner of deputy marshals. Hiss, once a State Department diplomat, was found guilty of perjury. Emerging with deputies, he was handcuffed to another prisoner, who saw fit to hide his face with a hat.[2]

In this flurry of activity in Washington, nothing connected the U.S. Marshals closer to the "Red Scare" than the high-profile Rosenberg case. Many newspaper accounts show convicted spies Julius and Ethel Rosenberg in handcuffs and led by federal marshals during and after their trial. The lengthy proceedings that led to the execution of both Julius and Ethel Rosenberg took a winding legal path for U.S. Marshal William A. Carroll of the Southern District of New York. The original trial lasted from March 6 to 29, 1951, before U.S. District Judge Irving R. Kaufman. Largely driven by evidence presented by Ethel's brother, David Greenglass, the Rosenbergs were sentenced to die in the electric chair the week of May 21, 1951, by Judge Kaufman. Six days after the trial, U.S. Marshal Carroll transferred the couple to Warden Wilfred L. Denno of Sing Sing Prison in Ossining, New York, "Pursuant to Judgment and Sentence Imposed by the Hon. Irving R. Kaufman, United States District Judge."[3]

It took two years longer to carry out the federal execution of Julius and Ethel Rosenberg. When their appeals ran out, Judge Kaufman again set the execution for January 1953. President Harry S. Truman, departing office days afterward, passed the clemency petition to incoming President Dwight D. Eisenhower. While he could not grant clemency, Pope Pius XII appealed several times in early 1953. Delays necessitated setting a third execution date, this time in March.[4] This constant activity concerned Marshal Carroll. He had the unenviable job of overseeing the execution and granting access in response to requests from the press. Each written request to the Marshal was answered by a letter that echoed the ticket system of old western executions. The "invitation" to the planned January 1953 execution read in part:

> Dear Sir:
>
> In accordance with the Regulations of the Department of Justice, you are hereby invited to be present as a witness at the execution by electricity of
>
> JULIUS and ETHEL ROSENBERG
>
> which will occur at Sing Sing Prison on January 14, 1953. The hour of 11:00 p.m. has been designated for such execution and you will arrange to be at the office of the Warden not later than 10:30 p.m.... Under no circumstances is this invitation transferable.[5]

Nine appeals had lapsed when the final sentence was carried out at Sing Sing Prison on June 20, 1953. Three Marshals personnel were certainly there: U.S. Marshal Carroll, Chief Deputy U.S. Marshal Thomas M. Farley, and Matron Helen Evans. Numerous reporters were expected, each having to obtain permission from Marshal Carroll. The couple spent the afternoon of that day together, separated by a mesh screen between cells in the women's wing of the prison, but they learned President Eisenhower did not grant clemency at about 7:20 p.m. Mr. Rosenberg's brother attempted to see Julius, but was escorted out after reaching the prison's administration building. At 8:04 p.m., Julius Rosenberg was taken to the chamber containing the electric chair. Rabbi Irving Kaslowe walked ahead of him, reading the 23rd Psalm out loud. Wearing dark brown trousers and a white shirt, Julius sat in the chair without a word. A black mask was placed over his head. Upon receiving word from Marshal Carroll, three jolts of electricity were applied. Mrs. Evans, who was assigned as Mrs. Rosenberg's matron, clasped her hand to comfort her. As if to thank her, Mrs. Rosenberg kissed her caretaker. They spoke to each other as she was strapped to the chair. Ethel Rosenberg died at 8:16 p.m.[6]

Because President Dwight Eisenhower sought his resignation after the execution, U.S. Marshal Carroll felt he was a political victim during this ordeal. "I've done their dirty work for them, and they won't have my resignation." However, U.S. Marshals serve at the will of the President, so Carroll had to step down.[7]

The related duties of U.S. Marshals in federal executions remained constant through history. The organization received intense coverage by the media in the mid-1900s leading up to federal executions. By 1963, when U.S. Marshal Covell Meek of Iowa nodded and gave the sign for execution of Victor Feuger, the number of enacted executions had decreased significantly. After Feuger, the next federal execution would not be until June 2001, of Timothy McVeigh, the Oklahoma City Bomber.[8]

Despite the checks on power with individual U.S. Marshals, the roots of relevance and self-determination came through a societal change: civil rights. Attorney General Herbert Brownell and his Deputy Attorney General, William P. Rogers, provided the first impetus to return some discretion to the U.S. Marshals. President Eisenhower decided to deal with the issue of civil rights after the landmark Supreme Court decision of *Brown v. Board of Education* in May 1954. As civil rights was an area of previous experience for the U.S. Marshals during the Reconstruction period that followed the Civil War, the Justice Department called on them. However, they lacked uniformity. At first, Rogers realized the broader issue as presented by Andretta: "The problem is providing for the effective supervision and direction of the United States Marshals offices."[9]

Brownell and Rogers learned of the problem in a report prepared by Sal Andretta in June 1956, "calling to the need for more frequent examinations of the district offices" and "the difficulty he has had in getting qualified men to fill existing vacancies in the Examiner's Section."[10] This Section, located in the Department of Justice, was responsible for the timely review and reimbursement of vouchers and expenses for each district office. Andretta believed the shortage of personnel assigned to the Section impeded its proper functioning. Brownell asked Rogers for recommendations—and even inquired if the General Accounting Office or auditors could perform the fiscal duties. The creation of the Executive Office for U.S. Attorneys had been a "considerable" undertaking and proved successful in providing a robust oversight function of the U.S. attorneys. The idea of a complementing executive office for U.S. Marshals seemed prudent to DOJ officials. Andretta envisioned that the centralized structure would expedite the filling of vacancies. However, the Deputy Attorney General would still need to maintain supervision over both executive offices. In the end, Andretta lost three positions when the Executive Office for U.S. Attorneys was formed despite his direct hand in formulating the idea.[11]

A six-page report by Andretta argued for creating the Executive Office of the U.S. Marshals. He claimed that "little supervision has been exercised over the Marshals," and while capable of self-policing, the appointed marshals had no first-line supervision. He further noted that "lack of staff, and probably lack of interest" left the U.S. marshals largely on their own. Andretta felt the Administrative Division of the Department was "the natural place for the Marshals to go for advice and assistance in the absence of any other place to answer their questions."[12]

Andretta commented on the framework for such an organization. He noted that training programs, such as the inter-agency departmental pistol competition, held in November 1953 in El Paso, Texas, benefitted the Marshals. He went on to recount the responsibilities of oversight from the Department of Justice, and recommended supervision and coordination of the office delegated with new positions. For the staffing of the Executive Office for the U.S. Marshals, Andretta recommended that 15 employees be supervised by an Assistant Deputy Attorney General with three primary assistants. Four executive assistants were available from the Department's Administrative Division: Eugene Matchett, George Miller, Homer H. Henry, and R.A. Miller. Andretta also recommended a deputy marshal as a training officer.[13]

Attorney General Brownell agreed with the recommendations, as the lack of oversight had been "debated for a number of years and has been analyzed by various units of the Department of Justice as well as outside independent analysts employed at the suggestion of Congress."[14] He supported Andretta's recommendations, and approved the implementation "at the earliest practicable time."[15]

The Department of Justice issued a press release dated December 17, 1956, about the creation of the headquarters for U.S. Marshals. It read, in part:

> Attorney General Herbert Brownell, Jr., announced today the establishment of an Executive Office for United States Marshals as a part of the office of the Deputy Attorney General. The office will be supervised by Mr. Clive W. Palmer, assistant to Deputy Attorney General William P. Rogers.
>
> Explaining the purpose of the new office which will begin functioning immediately, Mr. Rogers said:
>
> A major goal of the Deputy Attorney General's office is to insure teamwork between the Washington divisions and the field offices of the Department. For this purpose the Executive Office for United States Attorneys was established in April 1953, thus meeting the need for closer liaison between the Department and the United States Attorneys' offices. The Attorney General has now issued an order creating a similar office to insure closer and more effective relationships with the United States Marshals' offices.[16]

The Executive Office for U.S. Marshals had an organizational structure similar to other federal entities requiring centralization. While control of expenses was an immediate goal, the need to streamline functions was evident. To this end, the Executive Office for U.S. Marshals established a supervisory role beyond the fiscal one performed by Andretta.

Clive W. Palmer was a bespectacled, heavyset man, and hardly the image of a policeman. However, he possessed a wealth of institutional knowledge and organizational skills. The Frederick County, Maryland, native had started working at age 19, in 1920. By 1928, the attorney had been admitted to the Maryland and Virginia state bars. He entered federal government service as a clerk in the Department of Commerce, and then joined the Department of Justice as a special assistant to the Attorney General in 1941. After a stint in the Army during World War II, Palmer returned to the Department of Justice. Eugene Matchett joined him in the newly-formed executive office, along with several other assistants.[17]

Palmer had unique access to the Deputy Attorney General, and consulted him on many matters in establishing the Executive Office for United States Marshals. In January 1957, Palmer reported to Rogers:

> As you know I finally had a conference with Mr. Andretta today and arrangements have been made to transfer certain personnel on detail in order that the Executive Office for United States Marshals can get started.
>
> Since the Order creating this office has been distributed I have had a number of visits as well as a number of telephone calls from United States Marshals during which I took the opportunity of consulting them concerning their views with respect to those things which are of most importance to them. In almost every case I found the Marshals very much pleased with the fact that there would be an office here to which they could come for a solution to their problems; and without exception they all expressed the hope that someone other than Examiners would now be coming to see them giving them an opportunity to discuss their problems in their own offices. I also took the occasion to ask them their views concerning regional conferences at which some twenty to

thirty of the Marshals could be brought together at a central point without expense...[18]

Palmer's non-threatening strategy of collaboration and conference forums served as a key element in the formation of a central headquarters. Palmer felt Atlanta, Chicago, Denver, El Reno, Oklahoma, and Danbury, Connecticut, would be ideal locations for the first regional conferences. He acquainted himself with the appointed U.S. Marshals, but his primary goal was "to try to determine during these meetings what sort of training would be most helpful in the various offices."[19]

In 1958, Palmer started bringing together the appointed Marshals in national meetings on a regular basis. Up to that point, marshals had experienced little "interference" from Washington, D.C. Any notable power shift would have caused discontent. Palmer found it necessary to appoint an official who could bridge differences between DOJ and the districts. He found a stalwart in John W. "Jack" Cameron. A Navy seaman during World War II and a 1951 law school graduate from George Washington University, Cameron, age 30, was the youngest assistant on Palmer's staff. He served as a judicial examiner, but had an engaging personality and a remarkable administrative talent that brought people together. Another notable administrator was Homer H. Henry, a holdover from the early Andretta days.[20]

Palmer wasted little time with his plans. In mid-1957, he submitted a summary report on the regional conferences with the districts. U.S. Marshals generally welcomed him as an official to solve potential conflicts, and they also revealed concern about the constant presence of examiners sent from Washington. Some U.S. Marshals felt distrusted about the handling of their duties, and hoped Palmer might stave off some pressure. In addition to calming the waters, Palmer made use of his site visits to lobby for the effectiveness of regional conferences.[21]

Next, Palmer wanted a nationwide training program for the U.S. Marshals and their deputies. To avoid bureaucratic obstacles and Marshals' objections, he recommended ample advance analysis of benefits to personnel before implementation. Brownell and Rogers agreed to Palmer's recommendation.[22]

On December 29, 1958, the Department of Justice announced via a news release that the U.S. Marshals conducted a nationwide training program. The training curriculum and agenda were determined by handpicked employees and attorneys—as well as local police officers trained in specialized areas. The two-week course included training in fingerprinting techniques, judo, prisoner handling, first aid, firearms qualification, and physical fitness. New qualifications required deputy marshals to possess previous police experience and successfully complete fitness standards annually.[23]

At the time of the news release, 125 deputies had completed the course. By the next year, the executive office formalized the program with a training manual and requisite coursework. The office noted four younger employees—Al Butler, Don Forsht, Ellis Duley, and Jack Cameron—as architects of the courses. Deputy U.S. Marshal Frank Noe later joined the team. From 1959-60, courses were held at the Federal Reformatory at El Reno, Oklahoma, Washington, D.C., and other locations.[24]

Not all of the appointed U.S. Marshals had state or local law enforcement experience. One example was Archie M. "Jake" Meyer, appointed to replace a Marshal who had held the office for 18 years in the District of Arizona. The scholarly, bespectacled Meyer had served 31 years as chief attendance officer for Tucson Public Schools.[25] His friends wasted no time ribbing him about his new position. One, the president of a San Diego bank, wrote, "You sure aren't going to get me across the line so long as you're the U.S. Marshal. And if you want a drink of good scotch, you've got to come to San Diego.... Congratulations! Jake, in spite of the fact that I think you make a louzy [sic] Marshal..."[26]

U.S. Marshal Carlton Beall served as the U.S. Marshal for the District of Columbia from 1954 through early 1959; he had been a former tobacco farmer and Prince George's County, Maryland, sheriff. He served as the catalyst for key reforms through his participation in the Advisory

Committee to the Executive Office. He trimmed duplication of duties in the district and re-fashioned the paperwork process to speed up efficiency. He departed in 1959 to become postmaster of the District of Columbia.[27]

Hired by Beall in 1956, retired Deputy Robert Haislip recalled, "it was my understanding that no one could be hired that did not have either education or experience, or a combination of both. I didn't know of hardly any, too many individuals that weren't hired on this basis."[28] Haislip had experience in various law enforcement schools, plus years of criminology classes at the University of Maryland. He noted the enormous backlog of court orders and warrants as a primary reason the deputy marshal's routine duties changed in the late 1950s. In the District of Columbia, Beall organized a warrant squad to whittle down the approximate 2,600 outstanding cases. Haislip said, "We averaged, I think, around was it, I'd say at least 30-35 arrests a week."[29]

Frank Vandegrift, hired as a deputy U.S. marshal just after the 1957 military intervention to integrate Little Rock Central High School, explained that Beall was "brought in... to, if you would, revamp the D.C. office."[30] He continued, "[Beall] started bringing in people that he knew. People that had worked for him. His Chief Deputy Ellis Duley, was brought in to head up the newly established Warrants Squad. Donny Forsht, Al Butler, I was hired during that period. We were all called Carlton's Boys, I guess, because the few older deputies that remained, I guess just didn't like the change."[31]

Haislip noted that the district's eight- to ten-hour workday for deputies was atypical in those days. In the District of Columbia, the U.S. Marshal pushed his deputies hard to turn around the image of its personnel. "What he would do is periodically... he'd call everybody together and have a meeting and say, hey look, you know, things are starting to pile up again, we're going to have to work a little harder so, you know, get in and do it... Plus we were young and ambitious."[32]

By 1960, U.S. Marshals and their deputies became more professional through training programs, and deputies took on new responsibilities and "thought outside the box." Retired Deputy Bud Staple recalled that he went alone to execute an arrest warrant rather than bother his aged partner. In time, the younger deputies who began their service in the 1950s grew apart from their predecessors because their expectations were greater.[33]

Still, the deputies and the Executive Office for U.S. Marshals were largely unconnected. In fact, Deputy Vandegrift admitted that there was "very little contact with them. As a matter of fact, I think I was probably in the Service for two or three years before I knew they existed."[34]

LITTLE ROCK

In 1954, the Supreme Court's decision in *Brown v. Board of Education* directly challenged the "Jim Crow" system and sparked persistent resistance to change in the South.[35] Politics hardened on both sides of the educational and civil rights issue. Intellectuals and leaders with differing philosophies about resistance to the Supreme Court decision vied for influence.

U.S. Marshal Beal Kidd of the Eastern District of Arkansas submitted a "report of special activities" that served as a summation of tactics and experiences that resulted from his efforts to integrate schools in Little Rock. Because of the impact of his experiences, the report became a training manual of sorts for deputies involved in similar efforts.[36]

In August 1958, nervous officials in Washington summoned U.S. Marshal Kidd to confer on his efforts to carry out orders to racially integrate schools in his district. After attending conferences on civil disturbance over two days, he gave recommendations on the "approach" to school integration at Little Rock. This was a two-pronged approach with political and law enforcement angles. Arkansas Governor Orval Faubus was a popular politician for his stance and tactics against integration. Although the federal government had used military forces to ensure the safety of African-American students to integrate Little Rock the previous year, Governor Faubus would not back down.[37] Also, the Posse Comitatus Act forbade the use of military against civilians, so the Marshals were brought in to enforce the federal rule.

The Little Rock situation presented problems unusual in the normal daily experience of a U.S. Marshal's office. Among those functions of interest to other offices confronted with a similar task were recruiting, training, administration, special equipment, planning, and public relations.[38]

Attorney General William P. Rogers, appointed in October 1957, authorized Kidd to form a special unit of up to 120 special deputies to carry out integration orders at Little Rock the following year.[39] According to Kidd's report, he recruited deputies for the assignment with unusual confidentiality—literally by word of mouth. He formed a core force of 47 deputy U.S. marshals, drawn from districts throughout the country, who gathered in the city. Additional citizen applicants trickled in, and some 100 prospects went through screening for three weeks. The press found out about the interviews. Kidd was horrified when several news articles on the secret efforts appeared. However, the unintended exposure created a silver lining. More applicants from around the country stepped up, willing to undertake what would be a dangerous assignment.[40]

Two early recruits were retired military officers from Major General Edwin Walker's staff. Walker's men had carried out the original court orders in 1957 to integrate students into Little Rock's Central High School. Lt. Colonel George H. Williams, Jr., who served as Walker's operations officer, agreed to form a master plan and training framework. Major Ralph A. Boatman, a former supply staff officer with Walker, signed on to help with logistics. The U.S. Attorney in Little Rock, Osro Cobb, kept a daily line of communication with Marshal Kidd and the Department of Justice policy point man, Assistant Attorney General Malcolm R. Wilkey.[41] The officials fleshed out a comprehensive riot control program:

> The concept of the basic plan called for the accomplishment of several tasks. These were: The security and protection of students

entering and leaving Central High School; The containment and dispersal of crowds in the immediate vicinity of Central High School; The preservation of law and order in the immediate vicinity of Central High School.[42]

The deputies and recruits met on Friday, September 12, 1958. After administering the oaths of office, assignments were made. At least one deputy was to accompany every five special deputies in the area around Central High School. Most of the experienced deputies were held back in emergency reserve. Governor Faubus closed down the schools the following Monday, so training resumed at the Albert Pike Hotel. Although citizen recruits trained and assembled several times, the Department of Justice terminated all but two of them by mid-November, as the schools remained closed.[43]

When U.S. Marshal Kidd wrote the report of the activity in 1959, he made some key observations, citing leaks of internal information to newspapers as the most serious issue. Also, he thought a full study of "the location of all critical areas at or near the school" prior to the movement of special deputy U.S. marshals impacted the success of the entire endeavor. Marshal Kidd noted that radio telephones in three automobiles greatly assisted deputies. Special deputies were equipped with tear gas billy clubs, but use of this weapon was considered a final resort. With residences close by, the use of gas was not wise.[44]

Little Rock was a test for the deputies. Through formalized training and experience, the U.S. Marshals built credibility as "first responders." Their readiness changed minds in Washington, D.C. Department of Justice officials believed that the U.S. Marshals could enforce educational integration in the American South. This further pushed authority outward toward an independent headquarters. However, the shift to national oversight by the Department of Justice and a newly formed headquarters was about to usher the U.S. Marshals into modern times. By the 1960s the world had changed.

SECTION TWO—WALKING IN
FIRE: THE 1960S IN AMERICA

CHAPTER 3

CATALYSTS OF CHANGE

African-American author and poet James Baldwin published two essays in a book called *The Fire Next Time*, about America caught in the grip of racial violence and a growing consciousness of its effects on society. Baldwin's volume captured the anger and bitterness of the civil rights movement, but few saw the entirety of the Civil Rights Movement as the U.S. Marshals did. They were the instruments of change. Deputy U.S. marshals carried out the bulk of integration efforts in the late 1950s and 1960s. As desegregation catalysts, the U.S. Marshals were viewed both positively and negatively. In the Civil Rights Era, they carried out orders that most conservatives in the South resented. By the end of the 1960s, they were walking in the fire themselves—trying to prevent anarchy and destruction in society. They faced down left and right-wing elements. At times, both seemed to resent the marshals.[1]

NEW ORLEANS

New Orleans was a different city from Little Rock. It was multicultural and progressive, boasting its own literary and business centers. While a Southern city, it was buoyed by its diverse population. Creole boatmen and folks with sugar interests sat alongside African-American jazz musicians. The city's color lines were blurred in comparison to other cities in the South. The Crescent City had long been a hotbed of progressive regional movements, as evidenced by the state's embrace of populist politician Huey Long in the 1930s. Still, there was racism and segregation in the city.[2]

In the autumn of 1960, Palmer sent teams of deputies to ensure the safe integration of African-American students for the 1960-61 school year. This time, federal courts determined to carry out the full integration order.[3]

The U.S. Marshals received their orders and Special Assistant Jack Cameron was entrusted with the integration plan. His meticulous notes revealed the actions of the marshals between November 12 through 19, 1960. Cameron flew to New Orleans and met Deputy U.S. Marshals Ellis Duley and Rudolph Todd at the airport November 12. The deputies were instructed not to notify anyone about actions in the city, to remove the identification from their vehicles, and to only bring their regular gear. Specified deputies, drawn from several districts, reported to New Orleans on November 14.[4]

Deputy U.S. Marshal Billy Shoemaker rode with a fellow deputy who "owned a Buick" and they "got ten cents a mile" as reimbursement for using their own vehicles. They were told not to "bunch up," so as not to expose a massive presence of federal law enforcement. Shoemaker added, "We were asked to find a hotel."[5]

Cameron entered the Lafayette Hotel, where he met with Deputies Al Butler, Warren Emmerton, Jesse Grider, and Gilbert Bryant. They watched television editorials and observed the scope of opposition to the integration orders. Butler received official word on the order to proceed with the integration process from U.S. Marshal Victor Petitbon. Cameron coordinated the day's events, starting with the service of the papers to Louisiana Governor James Houston Davis that afternoon. Despite the delicate situation, Petitbon received a cordial welcome, and related to Cameron that the Superintendent of the Louisiana State Police, albeit "off the record," told him that the state police was not interfering with the orders. The New Orleans City Police presented no problems either. The police chief there, Joseph I. Giarusso, made available 200 policemen to help.[6]

On November 13, at 11:00 a.m., Cameron and several deputies met with Chief Giarusso to discuss a plan on how to handle potential interference with the integration orders. Giarusso expected no trouble escorting the African-American children into the schools on Monday, November 14. He felt two deputies could accompany each of the four children expected to be admitted into the two schools—William Frantz and McDonogh #19. Originally five, the number of children to be escorted was reduced when the parents of the fifth child suddenly withdrew. U.S. District Judge Skelly Wright wanted to meet with Cameron on Monday morning before any action was taken.[7]

On November 13, Cameron and Duley met with Marshal Petitbon, Chief Giarusso, and Deputy Superintendent Joseph Guillot to finalize plans for transporting the four children. The blueprint called for four motorcycle patrolmen to be posted close to each school. Four cars and men stationed themselves a few blocks around the access perimeters of the schools. Another car would be stationed as a patrol vehicle at both institutions. If violence broke out, authorities would apply an instant barricade and 300 policemen would be alerted, with about 200 posted at nearby Jackson Barracks. The deputies were to pick up the four children and deliver three to McDonogh #19 and one to Frantz. Four deputies were to stay all day at the school. Five local deputies were assigned to stay in their vehicles as back-up support.[8]

Al Butler, one of the primary riot control instructors for the deputies, remembered the events clearly: "I knew there probably would be more trouble at the school that had three children going in. That's why I went to McDonogh." The deputies wore bright orange armbands with dark lettering, and kept their pistols and credentials inside their coats. They displayed badges on the outside of their coats. Additionally, they carried a copy of the temporary restraining order from Civil Action Number 10566 issued November 10.[9]

Intelligence revealed that the lightning rods of opposition signaled minimal interference, but that mattered little. A representative of the segregationist organization, the "National States Righters" was in town to stir up trouble, and news accounts continued to be worrisome. Crowds were expected to heckle or intimidate the youngsters and their parents. The situation in New Orleans presented the deputies with scenarios that could quickly go wrong.[10]

The deputies met at the offices of the Eastern District of Louisiana at 7:15 a.m., Monday morning, November 14. U.S. Attorney Many and Judge Wright were on hand. The deputies were instructed to identify themselves to the state police or sergeant-at-arms and, in turn, receive a separate identification. Judge Wright provided the deputies with the names and addresses of the children. Additional deputies were sworn in, and three deputy U.S. marshals accompanied Bryant at the Frantz School with the lone student. Deputies Richard Smith, Butler, Herschel Garner, Wallace Dows, Warren Emmerton, Elisha Lott, and Jesse Grider were assigned the students for McDonogh #19. Butler later recalled that Dows, Lott, and Smith did not go inside the school, and likely stayed with the car.[11]

The plan further stated that the parents would be transported to the schools with the children in order to register them for class. Once the initial escort, planned for 8:40 a.m., was complete, a deputy was to call in a report to Cameron. The cars picked up their passengers at the homes and headed to the two schools. At 9:20 a.m., Dows called Cameron. A crowd of about 200 was in front of McDonogh, but the three children entered safely. An hour later, the crowd grew to 300.[12]

Cameron noted exact timing and procedure were essential to a successful plan. He planned the escort to the last detail. It was a delicate situation:

School starts at 9:00 a.m. —children will be taken in at 9:30 a.m. and will leave at 2:45 p.m. —Parents will be taken to school with children to register them. DUSMs will wear arm bands, carry sidearms, display badge on outside of coat, carry ID card in coat pocket, and carry copy of Temporary Restraining Order issued in Civil Action No. 10566 on 11/10/60. DUSMs who stay at schools will be observers. US Atty Many will explain their duties at 7:30 a.m. tomorrow when they all meet in US Marshal's office (This was arranged when Many arrived after conference). Petitbon's DUSMs & Butler, Emmerton, Grider, & Bryant were advised of the above.[13]

The television coverage grew at the Frantz School, where deputies escorted one little girl. The crowd numbered nearly 1,000—much larger than the situation at McDonogh. Giarusso's men had the crowd under control initially, but Bryant and Deputy Floyd Park took no chances. They enveloped the girl and entered Frantz, only to find her teacher missing. Park quickly moved to the principal's office, where he was told by the worried official about a break-in. The deputy called Cameron and noted that he could only see about 10 New Orleans policemen from his vantage point.[14]

Gil Bryant went to speak to a man who claimed to be a sergeant-at-arms who was asking questions about the girl who entered the school. Bryant, acting under the orders given by Judge Wright, divulged no information. About that time the judge called Cameron that he was getting reports that the crowd around McDonogh was becoming unruly and asked Cameron to go there personally. Marshal Petitbon, U.S. Attorney Many, Deputy Duley, and Cameron all went to McDonogh to review the situation.[15]

At Frantz, one little girl, Ruby Bridges, weaved among the deputies. Cameron's notes did not assign any names to the children, but the wide publicity generated by photographers of the incident revealed her identity. While there were shouts and name-calling, there was little violence. At the end of the day, most of the deputies' cars were followed by supporting vehicles to the children's homes, but the one that contained little Ruby

Bridges as a passenger was not—perhaps at the family's request. However, Marshal Petitbon checked up on the situation later in the day.[16]

There was an immediate effect in school attendance. Of the 188 children enrolled at McDonogh, 149 were removed by parents. At Frantz, the total enrollment was 576 children. Only 148 entered the school and 92 of them were pulled out by their parents by the end of the day.[17]

The next day, few children entered school grounds. However, the crowds were quite different. As the deputies waited outside the house for Ruby Bridges, a woman and child booed at them. Police cars parked at nearby intersections. At Frantz, Cameron noted it was "solid in block in front of school—nothing unruly—mostly teen agers [sic]."[18]

McDonogh only received 22 children for classes, with three more withdrawing during the school day. At Frantz, only 38 made it through the day. By November 17 and 18, only five children remained for the day. McDonogh had three students on the eighteenth.[19]

There was some indecision over operations on November 16. Chief U.S. Marshal Palmer decided to pull the deputies if no further incidents occurred, but Judge Wright disagreed and felt tensions were heightening. Assignments were made for the day. Deputies Butler, Emmerton, Garner, and Wilson Holtzman went to McDonogh; and Park, Dale Jordan, Carl Ryan, and Leon Davis went to Frantz. Two others, Deputy Joe Williams and Buford Ezell, worked in tandem with them.[20]

Judge Wright was correct. Chief Giarrusso had scattered a large crowd over the space of four blocks directly across from McDonogh. Teenagers were reportedly heading to the school, and the police took action to halt them. Then word leaked that marchers planned to take their concerns to city hall. Chief Giarrusso dispatched some of his men to seal the municipal building.[21]

Despite the pandemonium outside McDonogh, the three African-American children entered at 8:50 a.m. with no disruption. Not ten minutes later, Louisiana State Senator Willie Rainach, known as an opponent of integration, addressed a crowd at a building across the street. Chief Giarrusso, on the scene with U.S. Marshal Petitbon, Deputy U.S. Marshal Ellis Duley, and Cameron, introduced the senator to the school's principal, and the situation appeared to calm down. After 20 minutes, Cameron departed McDonogh to oversee the situation at Frantz.[22]

By the time Cameron and Petitbon reached Frantz, Ruby Bridges was already inside. The crowd was intense and angry, shouting boos and barbed comments. The principal was crying, obviously shaken by the pressure. Several officers were interspersed as observers in the crowd, one overhearing that a bomb had been thrown at Judge Wright's residence the previous night. The device missed the porch of the home. While a bomb squad searched the judge's residence for other devices, another person in the crowd attempted to incite the crowd into marching on city hall, the school board, and the Federal Building. Apparently the marchers prepared to storm the education and court buildings. U.S. Marshal Petitbon could not spare any more deputies, so he requested an additional 10 deputies from outside his district to seal off the federal building. Cameron got the clearance and asked for 14 deputies from the District of Columbia. All were in New Orleans by 3 p.m. that afternoon. The deputies were placed in the grand jury room at the courthouse to await further instructions. The marchers never showed.[23]

The deputies wrote reports about the crowds to Cameron. Deputy U.S. Marshal Charlie Burks, one of those assigned to guard Ruby Bridges, wrote that "the crowd at Frantz School on this day was moderate in size and conduct. No violent actions. Some loud talking and threats to parents whose children went into the school. Teen agers seem to be the troublemakers... In the downtown area nothing of importance seen or heard. Most of the day spent at the Post Office Bldg."[24]

There was preparation for hearings on the integration case. Local police presence increased around the schools, while deputy U.S. marshals joined them for several more days. They faced decreasing opposition and smaller crowds. On November 18, deputies largely controlled the environment around the school buildings and other areas of concern. Six deputies remained in New Orleans until the end of the month, and were replaced by nine more. The rest remained on call, and most of the deputies returned to their home districts. The integration at the New Orleans schools was under control, and the deputies had passed their first full test of the riot strategy they implemented.[25]

The photographs taken during the integration, particularly those of Ruby Bridges, were widely circulated. One of the most popular captured four deputy U.S. marshals escorting her inside Frantz. They are identified as Charlie Burks, Ray Eschment, Jim French, and Jim Davis. Since deputies switched in and out of the district, often changing posts after that first day, we can determine that this photo was likely taken during the second or third day. One influential American artist, Norman Rockwell, saw the image and decided to paint the scene. Several years later, he contacted a fellow artist friend, U.S. Marshal Robert Morey of Massachusetts.[26]

Norman Rockwell asked Morey for two badges he might pin on some models, as he painted from life rather than photographs. The badges were the first nationwide issue, known as the "eagle-top" for the bird's appearance on the top of the shield-shape underneath. They were also accountable property and could not be disseminated or borrowed. Morey quipped to Rockwell that he could not have the badges without deputies "attached to them." Instead, he sent two deputies to Rockwell's Stockbridge, Massachusetts, home studio. Deputies Fred Oczkowski and Billy Baldwin made haste on their assignment. They were received kindly by the Rockwell family, who had other models on hand.[27]

The resulting painting, called *The Problem We All Live With*, featured a little girl being escorted by four headless deputies among mob relics such as racist graffiti on the wall behind them and the remains of a thrown tomato. In the artist's depiction of the moment in history, Oczkowski walked in front of the little girl dressed in his gray coat containing a copy of the restraining order that allowed for integration. Baldwin strode behind the little girl, a local girl named Anita Gunn who served as the model for Ruby Bridges. She and her cousin Linda both served as Rockwell's models for the painting on the advice of their grandfather, a good friend of Rockwell's. Anita Gunn Tinsley later recalled that she was given a check for $25 to take violin lessons. The two other men posing as deputies were friends, too, one reportedly a city official and another who ran a local business.[28]

The painting's final irony was the presence of real deputies as models. The U.S. Marshals were both subjects of the artwork and served as models for Rockwell. Perhaps Morey's artistic sensibilities were the reason for their direct involvement in the artwork. In any case, life truly reflected art in this Rockwell painting.

McShane

The Executive Office for U.S. Marshals began with Clive W. Palmer at the helm. The transition from the Eisenhower to the Kennedy Administrations and the heightened tensions in the South brought forth a new leader. Although he served as U.S. Marshal of the District of Columbia and started a progressive training program to enhance personnel skills, Carlton Beall moved on. With extensive training and riot control preparations, James J.P. McShane became the new marshal and Beall's successor in the district office. He was tapped to lead the deputies into their next challenge, as they walked into the fire again.[29]

McShane was born in New York to Irish parents in March 1909. Having won the Golden Gloves welterweight championship in 1930 in New York, he looked like a boxer. He became a beat cop in 1936. By coincidence or providence, he was the officer on call several years later and foiled a robbery at a New York apartment. He calmed the young lady in that apartment, Ethel Skakel, fiancee of Robert Francis Kennedy. At the time he had no idea to whom the apartment belonged. According to his son Michael, McShane foiled the robbery and quickly earned the respect of her soon-to-be husband. It was the dramatic beginning of a long partnership.[30]

In the 1950s, the Kennedys became prominent in American politics. McShane retired from the New York City Police in 1957 and joined the Senate Rackets Committee that summer, where Robert Kennedy was chief counsel.[31] By the end of the decade, McShane transferred to the staff of the Senate Antitrust and Monopoly Subcommittee. Robert's brother John became the Democratic Party's candidate for U.S. president in 1960. McShane was a constant presence as a bodyguard for him during campaign appearances. His political fortunes rose with Kennedy's victory that autumn, and continued with his service with the Executive Office for the U.S. Marshals.[32]

FREEDOM RIDERS

The Executive Office for the U.S. Marshals was again called into the Civil Rights movement. The situation this time was different from New Orleans or Little Rock, however. Desegregated public transportation had grown as an extension of the seminal 1955 Rosa Parks incident in Montgomery, Alabama. Bus and other tranportation terminal restaurants and waiting areas still remained segregated in the South, however. The 1960 Supreme Court decision *Boynton v. Virginia* struck down such discrimination in interstate commerce.[33] Inspired by earlier attempts, the multi-racial "freedom rides," largely coordinated by the Congress of Racial Equality (CORE) and the Student Nonviolent Coordinating Committee (SNCC), planned a journey into the South with numerous destinations. In the spring of 1961, the Justice Department under Attorney General Robert F. Kennedy watched carefully as the mobile protest formed to travel from Washington, D.C. to New Orleans, Louisiana.[34]

For a time, the civilian riders encountered only minor opposition. However, the further south they travelled, the more violence they encountered. In Anniston, Alabama, a mob tried to burn the riders on one of the buses. It was evident that there was danger in Birmingham, and the journey could only continue with a measure of support from the state highway patrol. However, upon reaching Montgomery, the situation became critical. The highway patrol stopped escorting them and some of the riders were beaten or pelted with stones, including Justice Department official John Siegenthaler.[35]

The Department of Justice reacted immediately. They turned to McShane as their point man. He wasted no time, and left the District of Columbia district office on the afternoon of May 20 with 20 deputies for the Middle District of Alabama. They packed canisters of tear gas, armbands, and night sticks with them. Once there, U.S. Marshal Charles Prescott greeted them.[36]

When news came that the Reverend Martin Luther King, Jr. was arriving in Montgomery to speak at the First Baptist Church, there was little time for the deputies to prepare for what happened next. They had to secure federal property and ensure King's safety from the moment he arrived at the airport, as well as secure a perimeter around his speaking engagement against possible riots. McShane worked with local authorities and with agents from the Department of Treasury's Alcohol and Tax Unit (ATU). Copies of Deputy U.S. Marshal Paskal Bowser's notes indicate that some deputies arrived later in the evening of May 20, and King arrived at Donnelly Airport the following morning. Quickly dividing into teams, two cars with four people, two ATU agents, a prison guard, and a deputy, posted themselves at the airport. One car was designated as a security escort, while another remained at the airport. Dr. King arrived on Sunday and the car followed from the airport at a "decent distance" as ordered. At no time was the car to ride in front or aside King's vehicle.[37]

There was substantial danger to King. He headed for the residence of his friend, the Reverend Ralph Abernathy, but in the afternoon of May 21 signs of trouble were evident. Like other deputized members of ATU, Assistant Supervisor-in-Charge William D. Behen of Jacksonville, Florida, had to make do with limited resources and a role unfamiliar to him. He was assigned the area around the First Baptist Church on North Ripley Street. Initially Behen and his men stationed themselves several blocks away from the church, but at approximately one o'clock in the afternoon he moved with others to one block east of the church. There Behen described numerous cars of "hoodlums," who repeatedly visited the block. When a green 1957 Chevrolet with four white men circled a number of times, its tag was identified and radioed in. He spoke with the occupants, and while doing so, a 1956 convertible with a family inside pulled up alongside. The occupants of the two vehicles conversed, and it appeared the driver of the convertible was some kind of leader. He stated within Behen's earshot that he was "making the telephone calls" to others opposed to their presence.[38]

From Behen's vantage point, he could see cars stopping at a man's house near the gates of the Oakwood Cemetery, located across from the church and bordering Columbus and North Ripley Streets. This man appeared to be curious, observing the perimeter through binoculars from his porch. City and county officers, in uniforms and plain clothes, patrolled the perimeter throughout the day. Deputy U.S. Marshal Warren Emmerton felt there was a "misunderstanding as to leadership" and that federal personnel should have maintained control of the patrolling automobiles. He wanted to prevent confusion.[39]

What followed was pandemonium. Dr. King was a featured speaker at a special service at the First Baptist Church for the "Freedom Riders." Behen and his team, which included Deputy U.S. Marshal Marvin Waite, consulted with the Alabama Department of Public Safety, but stayed close to the church. Behen later reported,

> At about 6:30 PM, I was approximately 100 yards east of the church and I saw that a large crowd of young white men, with several women, were gathering near a near by [sic] liquor store at Ripley and Jefferson. This crowd continued to grow until it reached about 300 people. I received word that Reverend King had arrived at the

church at about 8:00 PM and in a short time, I saw the the [*sic*]
crowd was edging toward the church.[40]

Behen's small five-man unit, including Waite, watched from the front
line. The crowd crossed and moved toward the church, as they must have
seen automobiles arrive there. He requested that five members of the
Alabama Department of Public Safety immediately join the unit. Other
teams saw the sudden movement and converged with Behen's group,
buoying the number of federalized support to 50. Deputy U.S. Marshal
Robert Moore noted in his report the delay in the response by local
authorities. Still, some officers were not prepared for any form of riot.[41]

Behen's version of events highlighted quick-moving talks and inevitable
conflict. A representative of the Alabama Department of Public Safety
conferred with him, and ascertained extra assistance was necessary.
The mob could not be allowed to enter the church. Behen approached
the front of the mob and spoke to those in the forefront. After getting
questioned by several in the crowd, he asked them to move back. The
mob did not respond.[42] He wrote:

> We used our billies as prods and pushed the men back toward
> Jefferson Street along Ripley. Someone shouted to cross the street
> as they broke and ran to the vacant lot east of Ripley. They began
> to throw bricks and stones at the negro houses adjacent to the
> church and quite a few of the stones either fell short or were aimed
> at the officers. The mob began to pound on parked automobiles,
> break the windows of the automobiles and throw rocks at passing
> cars. I saw a car begin to burn near Ripley and Jefferson and I
> then threw a gas grenade into the crowd. I then worked along the
> street, throwing the grenades into the mob. I threw either three
> or four grenades and mob scattered and fell back.[43]

When the crowd gathered, Deputy U.S. Marshal Raymond Pope was
stationed in front of the First Baptist Church facing Patterson Park across
the street, where he had stood since about 11:00 a.m. that day. He noticed
a lot of news photographers, but little other activity until "small crowds

began to form at the Intersection of Ripley & Jefferson [Streets] & also across the Street from the Church—All these events were immediately relayed by Agent Marshburn [of the ATU] to Central Control & were acknowledged."[44] Pope went on to detail:

> At approx. 8:15 PM or so the crowd began developing into a noisy mob they made two attempts toward the Church & on the they [sic] moved toward the Church. At this time we still were not given any orders only to keep a cool head and use discretion & only to act if somebody was badly beaten. As the mob grew closer to Church they began hurling objects at passing autos. At this point there was no local law enforcement in sight and sizeing [sic] up the situation a small group of us about 50 or so headed by Agent Behen moved across the Park to Ripley & across Ripley in front of the Church where the mob was stopped. The mob soon became riotous, they began hurling rocks, stones bricks at us from across the street, at passing autos & at homes next to the Church, then gas was thrown by a few who had it. Members of the mob would pick it up and throw it back, kick it back & one even used a shovel. We suffered as well as the mob did from gas—We had side arms and night sticks only. As we began moving the mob up the street & across the Park we were soon joined by a small group of State Troopers.[45]

Young Herschel Garner, a deputy who had joined the U.S. marshals shortly before New Orleans, had been sent to Montgomery. He had arrived at Maxwell Air Force Base and moved quickly by mail truck to the scene of the riot. While en route he learned that Dr. King was inside the church. Garner reported, "We went down and kind of surrounded the church."[46] Things moved quickly. He could not remember how many deputies were present, but he recalled Jack Cameron giving orders in an urgent fashion. As their trucks arrived, Garner noticed a large angry throng headed right for the church. The deputy marshals ran in and reinforced the line, increasing the buffer zone between crowd and church. "I don't think we even had gas masks at that time. They used tear gas. The city did, they came to break up the crowd. After we'd gotten there and gotten them away from the church. The cars burning and all that was on into the night."[47]

Law enforcement stemmed the riot and maintained a protective presence throughout the service at the First Baptist Church. Exhausted, most of the deputies went to Maxwell Air Force Base. The riots against the "Freedom Riders" had ended the larger trek. Some forged on towards New Orleans, still encountering resistance. However, the federal authorities' protective stand in Montgomery brought greater public attention to the problem. Attorney General Kennedy issued a statement on the morning of May 24 that the federal government had a clear responsibility to "protect interstate travelers and maintain law and order only when local authorities are unable or unwilling to do so."[48]

Meanwhile, federal court concerns bubbled over the jurisdictional issue of arrest powers. U.S. District Judge Frank M. Johnson, Jr., called in Marshal Prescott. He in turn telephoned Jack Cameron. Judge Johnson made no bones about the danger in his conversation:

> From my past experience in conducting cases in which the Klan is interested it is my judgment that prudence requires you to have present for the hearing that is scheduled next Monday and Tuesday here in my court in this District at least 50 Deputy U.S. Marshals. A goodly number of these marshals should be stationed around in the courtroom. Others in the hallway outside the courtroom and other in the lobby of this building on the first floor.[49]

Assistant Attorney General Byron White, known as "Whizzer" for his athletic prowess in his collegiate football career, studied and analyzed the jurisdictional history of the organization and whether a federal marshal could submit to a local or state police officer's arrest, anticipating that local authorities might attempt to arrest deputies or prevent them from carrying out their duties:

> It is clear from *In re Neagle*, 135 U.S. 1 (1890) that the U.S. Marshals properly carrying out their duties are not subject to state prosecutions and may be freed by a writ of habeas corpus from the Federal

court upon the proper factual showing. On the other hand, where the Marshal violates state law he may be prosecuted by the state officials, and the only special protection which he receives from federal law is the right to have the trial removed to federal court....

The legality of the arrest, therefore, depends upon the particular facts of the case, and it is impossible to direct the U.S. Marshals in no case to submit to arrest. Since this is so, the solution to the question of whether to submit to arrest in a given situation requires a balancing of the plausibility of the grounds for the arrest, the likelihood of violence in the event of refusal to submit, and the immediate necessity for the Marshal's presence at the scene.[50]

In other words, the situation dictated the terms. Deputies balanced the imminent violence and the need for their presence before submitting to arrest by local authorities. The case, *In Re Neagle,* resulted from an August 1889 incident. Deputy U.S. Marshal David Neagle fatally shot an assailant attacking Supreme Court Justice Stephen Field. Deputy Neagle was subsequently jailed by a local jurisdiction until a decision was made regarding the special circumstances of the shooting. As it happened, the *Neagle* case was retested in the future.[51]

LEADERSHIP TRANSITION

Montgomery tested the U.S. Marshals in riot circumstances. It was also the last major crisis for Chief U.S. Marshal Clive W. Palmer. In June 1962, James Joseph Patrick McShane was the right man for the job as Chief U.S. Marshal.[52] In contrast to his tough-guy image, McShane possessed an intellectual and strategic mind. His friendship with Attorney General Kennedy ensured the U.S. Marshals' involvement in civil right enforcement actions during the turbulent decade.

It was not simply his relationship with the Kennedy family that brought him to the leadership of the U.S. Marshals. According to McShane's son Michael, the Kennedys distrusted Federal Bureau of Investigation Director J. Edgar Hoover. He recalled that the "Administration was looking for a vehicle, a tool to enforce civil rights. JFK thought Eisenhower made a mistake at Little Rock with military presence... they wanted Walter Sheridan to head the FBI—planned on firing Hoover in the second administration. They settled on the U.S. Marshals."[53]

The goals envisioned by the Kennedys required some overhauling at the Executive Office for the U.S. Marshals. Most people, as Michael McShane recounted, "didn't know the marshals still existed. The marshals had a great reputation with Wyatt Earp, and you know, Doc Holliday and all of those in the west."[54] The faded memories created an image firmly held by Americans, one parroted in countless television shows and movies. However, public image was not the only structural problem. McShane's official title was "Head, Executive Office for U.S. Marshals." However, as his predecessor Clive W. Palmer realized, the cooperation of other appointed U.S. Marshals was not certain. Michael McShane stated it simply. "Technically, they outranked him."[55]

The presidentially appointed U.S. Marshals were often reluctant to send their own deputy marshals to support activities outside their judicial districts. However, McShane's personality worked to convince individual U.S. Marshals it was in their best interest to combine resources in certain situations. That connection proved vital as the organization prepared for the challenges ahead.

PREPARING FOR CRISIS

James Howard Meredith was an unlikely catalyst for change. Tranquil and educated, Meredith was more scholar than activist. He viewed himself as a proud, multi-ethnic Mississippi man. His ancestry included a Native American leader and a Confederate general. His registration at Ole Miss was not just about civil rights. He wanted people to understand and accept his right to attend his school of choice, as an American.[56]

Meredith attended Jackson State University after an enlistment in the Air Force, but wished to transfer into the University of Mississippi in Oxford. The federal court decided in his favor. Although *Brown v. Board of Education* promised him that opportunity, he faced mountains of prejudice. Governor Ross Barnett of Mississippi exchanged harsh words with Attorney General Robert Kennedy after an evasive answer or even vague possibility of enrolling Meredith. Meredith tried to enroll at Ole Miss several times without success. Fearing Governor Barnett would further oppose the student, Attorney General Kennedy notified the President that McShane planned to leave Memphis at 3:15 p.m. on September 20, 1962. The governor reacted by telling the attorney general that he would alert local sheriffs. In another conversation with the attorney general on September 25, Governor Barnett toughened his stance and even stated, "I will never agree to putting Meredith into Ole Miss."[57]

Deputy U.S. Marshals Warren S. Emmerton and Harry Rowe, both stationed in Washington, D.C., came close to danger as they executed federal court orders in Mississippi. According to Deputy Emmerton's wife, Helen, they were to serve orders to cease and desist on Mississippi officials, including Governor Barnett. "This turned out to be a cat and mouse game. The players were never where they were reported to be."[58] The governor and other officials, including the head of the Mississippi State Police, gave the pair of deputies the slip a number of times. Undeterred, they came close to their subjects when word came that the governor was to be at the state house in Jackson the following morning. Emmerton and Rowe drove there in the early morning hours to deliver the orders. Rowe stayed by the car while Emmerton climbed the steps of the state house. Mrs. Emmerton related a near-tragic chain of events:

> Harry was beside the car (our personal car) while Warren was walking up the steps of the State House when Warren was about halfway up the steps, 25 to 30 State Troopers came out and went for their pistols. Harry left the car and came up the steps where Warren stood. Harry pulled an AR-15 from under his trench coat and held it on the troopers until they were back in the car.[59]

Things were tense for the deputies trying to carry out their orders in Mississippi. While New Orleans was uncomfortable and Montgomery was close to tragic, Oxford, Mississippi, proved violent. For a year, deputies prepared for a showdown between federal and state authorities. For example, Deputy U.S. Marshal Cecil Miller was in Oxford in late August 1962. Several deputies, after a brief training period, were secretly placed in town as students. They spoke with as many local people as possible, chatting them up in supermarkets and on campus. They were surprised that many of the college students, particularly those from Louisiana, could not have cared less about the matter. At night they went to a local motel. Miller said later in an interview, "We lived in the town in a hotel. We went to the campus every day. Made note of any activities by the state police or anyone else."[60]

Based on his reconnaissance, Miller thought it was clear the state police and Governor Barnett were not on their side. Miller noted occasionally that one or two troopers appeared around the campus police if an attempt was made to enroll Meredith, for instance. They were able to see the most vulnerable points on the campus—and determine a route of entry for opponents of the operation. Miller flew back to Washington to meet with McShane and Forsht and determine the best plan. Like other deputies, Chief Deputy U.S. Marshal Robert Courtright of Iowa was called to Washington to report to Jack Cameron after a Sunday mass. Courtright had a high opinion of Cameron: "Jack was a career man, and a damn good one. When McShane came in, he kept Cameron, because that's one thing McShane could see—the value of someone."[61]

When Courtright arrived, he met Cameron, Deputy Attorney General Joseph Dolan, and "five or six deputies," including Deputy U.S. Marshals Royal Butters of Utah, Ken Muir of North Dakota, and Leonard Hopper of Colorado. Dolan said little, except to quickly give Courtright a map. Befuddled, Courtright asked where they were meeting, to which Dolan replied they were to meet at an air base. His expression must have begged for further explanation, so Dolan drove the point home: "Don't you know? We're going on a mission this morning. We're going down to Oxford." All Chief Courtright could do was say, "You're kidding me!"[62]

On September 27, 1962, state politicians came to the campus and stood on the steps of the columned registration and administration building, known as the Lyceum and proceeded to lecture the students on Meredith. Governor Barnett and Attorney General Kennedy continued to negotiate by telephone, but nothing seemed to defuse the situation. A number of deputies were spread out about the area, and not just watching the university. As a result, Miller saw the arrival of the state officials, but did not hear their speeches.[63]

Deputy U.S. Marshal Herschel Garner recalled that personnel staged at the Naval Air Station in Millington, Tennessee—"just north of Memphis... and we had a meeting at 7:00 a.m.... had riot practice 'til 10:30. And then we left to go to Ole Miss. This was on Thursday, the 27th of September."[64] Deputy Staple's recollections revealed that most deputies, almost all young and trained, were given little information as he and his fellow deputies arrived from California:

> Arriving at Memphis Airport about 9:30 pm the three of us were met by a Marshal who drove us to Millington Naval Air Base. Our driver did not or was not able to give us answers to our curious questioning about the detail. In route he did reveal a little about the assignment. "It is big, because the Chief U.S. Marshal Jim McShane and an assistant Attorney General are at the base with us." He said as far as he knew we were the last Deputies of several hundred to arrive. In the darkness he drove us to an old, World War II, enlisted men's barracks, arriving about 11:00 pm. We were given instructions to be up for breakfast about 5 in the morning. That was fine because we had not had anything but airline snacks since breakfast that morning.[65]

At Millington, they located military surplus helmets in great supply. They spray painted each white, to distinguish them from military gear, and stenciled the words "U.S. Marshal" in black on each. Nonetheless, each deputy wore the uniform of an orange armband, vest, and the helmet, and received a gas gun. The news media quickly learned of their location and clung to the edge of the base, watching their movements. Courtright asked about them, but Dolan was unconcerned as they embarked on a helicopter to survey the roads leading south from Millington to Oxford. Shortly afterwards, the deputies were aboard other helicopters and moving right into Mississippi.[66]

From Millington, the deputies flew to a fisherman's campground located at Sardis Lake north of Oxford. None of the deputies liked the fish camp. Courtright commented it was a "terrible place... weeds higher than this and full of snakes."[67]

Courtright was sent out to the local airfield to report on activities there, and then bring back any pertinent information to the University of Mississippi campus, where the deputies were to be deployed in units. Dressed like any other local citizens, he, Hopper, Muir, and Buttars slipped into a crowd of reporters. Courtright pretended to be one of them, assigned to the *Omaha Herald*. He gathered some good intelligence, including the possibility of 10,000 non-students descending on the University of Mississippi campus that evening. However, the real goal was gathering information on retired General Edwin Walker, who had led the federal troops at Little Rock in 1957 but had since publicly aired views against desegregation. He was code-named "Big Red," and the deputies were on the lookout for his whereabouts. The trip to the airport yielded no news of Walker.[68]

Courtright's unit reported back to Dolan at the administration building that stood at the center of campus, known as the Lyceum. The Assistant Attorney General told Courtright to assign two deputies to the telephone booths in the building. Hopper was told to keep various lines open in case emergency assistance was required. Other booths directly tied them to the White House. Deputy Hopper was told by Courtright, "Don't leave there."[69]

BATTLE

In the late afternoon of September 30, 1962, U.S. Marshals personnel stationed at the University of Mississippi included 127 career deputies and more than 300 deputized federal border patrolmen and prison guards to supplement their ranks. "It was the scariest moment of my life," recalled one of the deputies years later.[70] Most of the deputies expected something like the integration of the New Orleans public school system nearly two year earlier. In Louisiana there had been sporadic resistance and even angry and unreasonable individual actions, but nothing compared to what deputy marshals witnessed at Oxford.[71]

Inside the Lyceum, Courtright sat at the communications console with several university officials and Deputy Attorney General Nicholas Katzenbach. With McShane, they listened to the instructions coming over the radio. The other party on the line, in Washington, was Attorney General Kennedy. He warned McShane to have the deputies hold their fire at all costs, unless imminent violence became evident. The leaders asked a lot of the deputies who were broken out into three sub-unit lines around the Lyceum to protect the building during registration. However, the man at the center of the issue was placed in a dormitory under heavy guard—waiting for registration to open the next morning.[72]

"We were sent there to carry out court orders," recalled Al Butler. "When you put on the badge, you do the job." On that day, it was Butler who held the line together in the front of the old columned building. A black stripe was painted down the middle of his helmet.[73]

"As long as I saw Butler's stripe, I knew we were okay," recalled fellow deputy U.S. marshal Willard "Mac" McArdle.[74]

As the crowd grew, projectiles flew out from the unruly mass. The most common weapons they used were bricks from a nearby construction site near the science building. As a throng of people moved forward, Butler advanced a group of deputies to force them back. On either side of Butler's men were two other lines of deputies led by Deputy U.S. Marshals

Don Forsht and Ellis Duley, Jr. Along with Butler, they represented the most seasoned men in riot control situations. Despite the professionalism of all the deputies, violence appeared inevitable.[75]

On the south side of the Lyceum, Deputy Bill Banta of Wisconsin took his place on the line. Beside him, Deputy Marshal Jim French, whom he jokingly called "Mr. Clean" because of his resemblance to the bald character in the television commercials, and Deputy Marshal Wilson Holtzman of Pennsylvania stood in the formation. Banta had brought in his helmet from home, unlike other deputies who received one from military surplus. After spray painting and stenciling in "Marshall," French realized there was one "L" too many. He spent the first hours scratching it off.[76]

"I had no idea what to expect," Banta recalled. Those first hours were quieter for those on that side of the Lyceum, which encountered few people at first. However, he could certainly hear them.[77]

After nightfall and the anonymity of darkness, several cars burned behind the lines of rioters, which actually helped McArdle and others to see the lines better. He later found out the cars belonged to reporters who attempted to get close. More bricks flew, along with battery acid, and buckshot, fired from an unknown person behind the crowd. On the right side of the Lyceum building, where the crowd was thinner, the shooter appeared to be concentrating fire. A shot pierced the neck of Deputy U.S. Marshal Gene Same of Indiana, nicking his carotid artery. Bleeding profusely, he gripped it as his breathing got heavy. He fell to the ground. Someone shouted up the line to get Same some help, and take him inside the building.[78]

Once Same was hit by gunfire, deputy marshals renewed the call for firing gas canisters through launchers. McShane emerged and shouted, "Masks, on the masks!! Fire!!" The deputies had pulled the gas masks from the stockpiles at Millington Naval Air Station, near Memphis, where they also obtained their vests and helmets. The first canisters did their work. The crowd edged back beyond the strip of pavement. But the wind was stiff and against the deputies, blowing the puffs of smoke right back at them. Butler used the confusion to thrust the deputies forward and establish a wider perimeter.[79]

As the mob fell back coughing, deputies apprehended some and passed the offenders back to the Lyceum for processing. Despite some early success in the greenish smoke, Butler hated the idea that the helmets were spray-painted white and could easily be seen in the dark. While many were dented by bricks, they served their purpose.[80]

The gas proved a temporary assistant. After the initial surprise, the remaining mob grew determined and angry. Also, campus authorities were unable to stop outside elements from entering the campus; many reported that state police simply allowed undesirables to enter. The introduction of these elements increased the confusion. Some screamed obscenities or warnings at the deputies. In the minds of certain state officials and citizens, the federal deputies had invaded their turf. And not since the Civil War had key elements of a state government defied the actions of the federal government. This was to many in the state, in effect, civil war.[81]

On the south side of the Lyceum, Banta heard the shotgun blasts through the trees and the peculiar whistle the buckshot made. Their vests —really the only uniform item aside from their helmet—were certainly hefty, but provided little protection. Their orange armbands with the blue lettering, and the white helmets, glowed in the dark, making them convenient targets.[82]

Deputy Marshal Gordy Coen of West Virginia felt something hit his knee. Almost jokingly, he reached down and removed a BB from his knee and looked at Banta. "Look here what I found!" The Wisconsin native was not sure what to think.[83]

After hours of this deadly chess match, the deputies began to run out of gas canisters. While they had sidearms, they were a last resort.

However, one deputy said, "we thought about using them."[84] Instead, they opted to get fresh gas supplies.

Deputy U.S. Marshal Bud Staple contacted their base for more gas containers. It was a short distance to the "fish camp," but under riot conditions this proved a dangerous commute. One of the deputies stationed there, Leonard Hopper of Colorado, was given the task of driving fresh gas containers to the Lyceum.[85]

Hopper drove a jeep from the camp with the supplies, and the Mississippi Highway Patrol watched his every move. He sped through the town, and was directed down a side road. Running the gauntlet through campus, Deputy Marshal Hopper delivered the badly needed supply of gas. In the process, one of the containers leaked and Hopper accidently inhaled a potent whiff of it, and momentarily went out of breath.[86]

The crowd again grew more aggressive. The rioters commandeered a large bulldozer and ambulance. The deputies waited until a rioter drove the piece of construction equipment close. Once the bulldozer blocked the view of the crowd, Deputy Marshal Carl Ryan broke out of the line, as another deputy pulled the operator from the machine and sent him back to the Lyceum for processing. Ryan now controlled the bulldozer, shifted the gears and turned it back toward the rioters themselves. Then he shut the vehicle down and took the keys, creating a new barrier between the angry onslaught and the deputies. The deputies repeated the tactics and rendered the ambulance useless to the crowd.[87]

About that time, nearly 50 federal Mississippi National Guardsmen under the command of Captain Murry Falkner, the nephew of author William Faulkner, entered the university grounds to aid the marshals. Falkner had little success getting through the enraged crowd and was seriously wounded by a brickbat, but his men reached the deputies. Falkner's men completed their appointed task and stood within the line of deputies.[88]

However, once McShane and Katzenbach realized the crowd numbered in the thousands, emergency military aid came from the U.S. Army 101st Division. After a long day, the massive presence arrived around 1 a.m. on October 1 and warded off the rioters. By the time they arrived, 79 full-time deputies had been injured, and one had almost died. Eighty-one more injuries were added from the deputized border patrol, prison guards, and National Guard. Gene Same had been saved by an alert border patrolman named William Dunn, who administered first aid repeatedly until the deputy's condition stabilized.[89]

The marshals' line held and never broke. Despite serious injuries, the U.S. Marshals stood their ground for hours without injuring any rioters or sustaining a fatality among their own ranks. Sadly, an unknown sniper killed several reporters at different locations on campus.[90]

McShane and his deputy marshals had faced the worst case scenario, and proved themselves as battle-tested for the remaining operations of the 1960s. James Meredith attended classes at the University of Mississippi, and graduated from there in the summer of 1963. He never forgot his protectors, and thanked many of them for the first time since his graduation in a private meeting during the 40th anniversary observances in Oxford.[91]

AFTERMATH

Courtright was pressured to find "Big Red," which he finally did. Walker was on campus in a fraternity building. The old military man, according to Courtright, who was watching from an outside window, actually instructed students on how to make firebombs. He was detained, and news spread that Walker was under arrest. After the riots ended, Al Butler watched as an unknown woman walked up to the old soldier, slapped him, and charged off in a huff. It was General Walker's sister, enraged at how the family honor was diminished by his actions.[92]

The reaction to Oxford in the aftermath of the effort to enroll James Meredith was only slightly less dangerous. Posters, songs, and pamphlets appeared, usually accusing deputy U.S. marshals of invasion or worse. A newsletter called "Rebel Underground," seized by a professor and turned over to the deputies, made it clear the confrontation was personal:

> As to the yelling "FIRE," the only occasion that we can recall in which this was done in our local situation was the Indicted Felon, McShane, who was sent to us after being fired from the NYC Police Force for being involved in "Fixed" Prize Fights and Illegal Promotions. McShane, with his criminal background was the logical choice of the Marxist Masters in the White House to provoke violence and disorder.[93]

The publication was crudely written, but interesting in that it took pieces of the Chief U.S. Marshal's background and twisted them into false banter. The claims were ridiculous but personal and meant to incite or intimidate. During a visit in November, while checking on the Meredith detail, McShane was arrested by state troopers in Oxford. Knowing full well a federal judge would invalidate the arrest, the local sheriff did not bother to fingerprint McShane and just sat in the office with him. Sure enough, a federal judge followed U.S. Supreme Court precedent of *Neagle*. McShane was released in three hours.[94]

Similar intimidation was also directed at the deputies—sometimes not in Mississippi. Deputy U.S. Marshal Duane Caldwell found out upon his return to St. Louis, Missouri, that his wife had been threatened by a number of phone calls. The same was said of other deputies who resided primarily in the South. Somehow their personal information had been divulged.[95]

Even civic groups like the Mississippi State Junior Chamber of Commerce in Jackson issued a brazen propaganda pamphlet raging against the Kennedys and the U.S. Marshals. In "Oxford—A Warning for Americans," the group devoted two full pages to the "conduct" of the deputies, citing references to blood on the clothes of the youthful attackers. They complained that deputy U.S. marshals went on a rampage, even firing gas canisters at the back of the head of a Mississippi Highway Trooper. A notation that the deputies were inexperienced with gas projectiles was generally true, but they did receive some basic training.[96]

The lessons and feelings from participants at Oxford were numerous. Retired Deputy U.S. Marshal Bennie Brake of Georgia recalled, "Mississippi... I don't know what that thing was. I remember the people in my face... We had to hold [the Lyceum]."[97]

Frank Vandegrift's recollections were even more vivid. "Well, you're in the middle of a riot, it's hard to, to be objective about its intensity... you got bricks being thrown at you and cars overturned and there's fires burning around you, and you know, tear gas is all over hell and creation..."[98]

In recollecting the events, James Meredith suggested a solution: "How can we unite? We can unite under the Constitution of the United States."[99]

TUSCALOOSA

In a memorandum to the districts dated July 24, 1963, Chief U.S. Marshal McShane sent a number of requests to different U.S. Marshals around the country, specifying a special assignment and the type of deputy he sought. It stated in part:

> We would like to use subject deputy on the guard detail at the University of Alabama for about two weeks. Please have him report to the deputy U.S. marshal in charge, Room 200, Town House Hotel, 24th Avenue and 10th Street, Tuscaloosa, Alabama.... Subject deputy should take sport clothes, his badge and ID card, handcuffs, and a snub-nosed revolver with him on this assignment.[100]

Ominous words, but justified given the preparations needed to integrate the University of Alabama at Tuscaloosa. From Oxford, McShane knew more groundwork was needed to avoid a repeat of the riots there. Deputy

U.S. Marshals Paskal Bowser and "Mac" McArdle met with McShane as early as December 12, 1962, to discuss expectations. After conveying their observations, they described to McShane the layout of the University of Alabama's campus, number of students, and local officials, such as police and fire departments. On the back of a mimeographed page, Jack Cameron wrote that additional personnel were needed for continuing the Meredith detail at Oxford, sketched out some rough plans for FBI assistance, the presence of Justice Department official Joe Dolan, and to request a reserve camp for training purposes.[101]

Serious work on the Tuscaloosa project began in June 1963. On the eighth, Cameron noted an important meeting in Deputy Attorney General Katzenbach's office in Washington. Also in attendance were Dolan, Assistant Deputy Attorney General William A. Geoghegan, Justice Attorney John Doar and McShane. By this time, the words and actions of Alabama Governor George Wallace suggested that the Tuscaloosa integration would not go well. The two African-American students to be registered at Tuscaloosa were Vivian Malone and Roderick Hood. The date of the operation was initially set for June 10, 1963, at 10:30 a.m., but it was delayed by a day. The committee compiled a list of personnel and equipment needed for the operation. They decided on a transfer of six U.S. Border Patrol cars with ten personnel to man the vehicles, an airplane, 20 deputy U.S. marshals, and an Army motor boat. The deputies were to report to the Army Reserve Training Center on Tenth Avenue in Tuscaloosa by noon on the ninth.[102]

For the registration, Vivian Malone would travel in Border Patrol Car #1 with Katzenbach and U.S. Marshal Peyton Norville, Jr. among others. Car #2 would carry Hood, U.S. Attorney Macon L. Weaver, Doar, and an unnamed deputy U.S. marshal. The remainder of the cars contained either Department of Justice officials or U.S. Marshals personnel. The Special Assistant for Information to the Attorney General, Edwin O. Guthman, handled the reporters at the campus law building. Cars #5 and #6 were used for protective cover and were stationed near the campus'

Foster Auditorium. A press conference was planned to announce the enrollments, followed by the arrival of cars #1 and #2, for registration. They planned to take Hood to his dorm at Palmer Hall. The airplane would be used to look for potential crowds that could be missed on the ground. The boat was to dock and wait on the Black Warrior River as a possible escape route. Cameron concluded the planning memo with a humorous quip: "If the boat is full—Swim for it!!!"[103]

Despite careful planning, there were indications of trouble. Violent rhetoric, a familiar tactic aimed at the deputies and Washington, hinted that a full-scale protective detail might become necessary. By the summer of 1963, James Meredith's protective detail was ramping down with his impending graduation from the University of Mississippi. Some of those deputies rotated duty to Alabama. Deputy U.S. Marshals Al Butler, Cecil Miller, Ancil Gordon, and Don Forsht were all selected for duties in Cars #5 and #6. Cameron mapped out instructions for the operation. If Malone and Hood entered the auditorium to register, two deputies would join them at a press conference announcing the fact. Then Al Butler, with Deputy U.S. Marshal Gordon escorting Malone, would proceed to her dormitory. The building was to be fully monitored. Five deputies were assigned to the elevator bank, while two more guarded a stairway access. Three deputies would escort her whenever she left the dormitory, while several stayed behind there. A similar strategy was planned for Hood's escort. If they were not allowed in the auditorium, the same residential detail would be used without a press conference.[104]

On June 11, Governor Wallace was "standing in the schoolhouse door." He believed he would face derision from his own constituents if he did not show official resistance. However, Wallace relented and eventually both students registered. The deputies remained in the background.[105]

The days that followed were just as complicated for the deputies. Cameron noted that a former Klan member informed the deputies that segregationists asked questions about the detail—including the length of time of the operation. Oddly, even the barber who cut Hood's hair was threatened by telephone. A fire alarm, most likely a scare tactic, was set off in Vivian Malone's dorm. A local man planned to lead demonstrations on campus.[106]

Deputy U.S. Marshal Oscar L. Davis of the Northern District of Georgia reported to Tuscaloosa on June 21. On the twenty-seventh, he notified Headquarters that Vivian Malone preferred residence on campus because she feared using public transportation.[107] By June 28, he telephoned Cameron with some astonishing news. There were 150 local demonstrators on campus, but their leader was on probation, which constituted a violation. After some exchange with U.S. Marshal Norville, Davis learned that "someone in L.A. has offered contracts as follows: $25,000 on President Kennedy, $10,000 on Martin Luther King, and $5,000 on Hood."[108]

Hood's personal actions brought about some controversy for his protective detail. He talked to the press and upset others working for civil rights. According to Homer Henry at Headquarters on July 1, Dr. Martin Luther King called Hood and told him that he (Hood) got into the University of Alabama because of the sit-ins and other actions taken by his (King's) followers. There was pressure to bring an end to his scholarship. While Hood was not scared about the death threats, the resulting controversy convinced him to withdraw to a hotel without a protection detail. Cameron overruled a request to remove protection until further notice, but Hood spent the weekend undisturbed at the hotel.[109]

Malone was casually pursued by European journalists for interviews, including one from Moscow and two others from Radio Free Europe. Both Hood and Malone spent weekends with their families during the summer. Both received invitations for speaking engagements. Other newsworthy events occurred at the time—including plans for the admittance of another student. A Nigerian man planned to start at the University that fall.[110]

Still, Hood seemed to be the focal point of anger for most of the objecting parties. Governor Wallace was angry about deputies accompanying Hood off campus, especially when getting haircuts. The deputies were told to back off Hood when he left campus, which gave segregationists opportunities for harassment. They burned crosses on a golf course where Hood regularly played. Negative newspaper articles continued, personally attacking him. By mid-August, Hood withdrew from the university following news that his public statements prompted expulsion from the university. Hood's decision was a sudden one, as one of the detail deputies found out from a radio report. A newspaper man then telephoned Malone to ask her if this changed her plans. She said Hood's plans did not coincide with hers.[111]

Vivian Malone continued her education at the University of Alabama. She returned in September, just after the Meredith detail in Mississippi ended. Although plans were drawn to reflect increased intensity from the opposition, it was not as difficult as the initial registration process. However, several bomb scares occurred during the fall and Klan activity in the area was more visible. The local police apprehended several Klan members on September 22, when several were firing guns at local African-Americans. Deputies planned extensive protection for Malone during her attendance at an Alabama football game.[112]

There were many changes taking place in the protective details. By mid-October, the University hinted that deputies should leave in June 1964. John Doar revisited campus to get an idea of the situation, and the National Guard planned on cutting its detail significantly. Deputies found that the Klan was watching Doar throughout his visit. Deputy U.S. Marshal Davis, who had the most difficult spans of duty, developed an ulcer and other medical problems and had to be taken off the detail. Doar moved the withdrawal date to February.[113]

The decision to draw down turned out to be somewhat premature. In the early morning hours of November 16, 1963, an explosive device detonated near Vivian Malone's dormitory. It was about 20 yards from the building and 130 yards from her room. The resulting hole was 14 inches long, 4 inches wide, and 3 inches deep in a concrete road. The local authorities notified Deputy U.S. Marshal Don Weaver, who replaced Davis on the detail. Security immediately tightened, and the police chief and university officials received threatening calls about another bomb if Malone did not leave. In a bold move to stem the latest violence, Dr. J. Jefferson Bennett of the university visited Governor Wallace, and apparently told him that the bombings in Tuscaloosa must end. On November 21, Bennett asked Weaver what the deputies might do if four or five carloads of Alabama Highway Patrolmen attempted to have Malone removed. Weaver responded that the deputies would do all in their power to resist them, and were authorized by a federal court order to do so.[114]

Deputy U.S. Marshal Herschel Garner took over for Weaver shortly after the warning from Dr. Bennett. Sentiments had cooled by this time, as Weaver reported only sporadic verbal comments and suggested adjustments to Malone's detail. He found a copy of an underground newsletter published off campus, causing continued concern for Malone's safety. However, although it contained charged rhetoric, no further intelligence surfaced. After the Christmas break, Deputy U.S. Marshal Dick Smith replaced Garner. After a long lull in activity, university officials advised that the deputies should depart in January. The number of deputies dwindled until the final class of the semester for Malone on January 24, 1964. Homer Henry noted, "DUSM Dick Smith called— Says it is all over. He talked with just about everybody and they are well satisfied."[115]

CHAPTER 4

FOCAL POINTS

A PROTECTIVE PHASE

By late 1963, the Executive Office for U.S. Marshals was a highly visible presence in the South. The often-dangerous job of integrating schools overshadowed many other notable duties. For instance, the number of high-profile protective details of witnesses against organized crime grew, as did the publicized trials. Chief U.S. Marshal James J.P. McShane led the deputies through a tumultuous period that thrust them further into the national spotlight. There was much to learn and little time to digest it.

One of the most crucial learning curves involved a growing understanding of the mob. The so-called Apalachin Conference, held at a residence in rural New York in November 1957, was supposed to be a meeting among representatives of various mob families, although at the time, the government officially denied there was an organized hierarchy. That year a number of related murders snagged headlines, notably the assassination of Murder Inc. founder Albert Anastasia in a New York barber's chair.[1] Local police became suspicious of the gathering in the little hamlet of Apalachin, and a raid netted a number of the mob figures. While U.S. Marshals had little involvement in the actual arrests, they increased protection details on witnesses. The exposure of the mob through the Apalachin event was a factor in the establishment of a formal Witness Security Program.[2] As organized crime became a focal point for law enforcement during the 1960s, deputy U.S. marshals played a role in high threat trials of note.

For instance, Deputy U.S. Marshal Ronald Messa had regular run-ins with Carlos Marcello, who was the crime boss in New Orleans. In March 1961, Attorney General Robert Kennedy attempted to get Marcello deported to Guatemala. With his partner, Deputy U.S. Marshal Thomas Grace, Messa obtained court orders that Marcello was in alien status and could be deported upon arrest. "We drove over to his hotel, which we knew about," said Messa. The Town and Country was the boss's hotel of choice. After meeting with officials, the deputies re-arrested Marcello. He was taken to the airport by the two deputies, and escorted to a plane bound for Guatemala. However, Marcello returned to New Orleans within weeks.[3]

In spring 1965, U.S. Marshal Victor Wogan, Jr. prepared for the witness-tampering trial of Marcello in New Orleans. On April 8, he sent a letter to Chief Marshal McShane with proposals for safety measures. The Judge and U.S. Attorney asked the jury to be locked down, and they requested six additional deputies to work eight-hour shifts, attending to the jury. McShane, in typical style, penned a two-line response in a memo to Special Assistant Jack Cameron.

1- Prepare Reply

2- Give him what he wants[4]

The trial was assigned to U.S. District Judge Herbert W. Christenberry on August 2, 1965. Although there was the possibility of a delay in the trial, McShane took no chances. He started pre-planning in July and added eight deputies to the detail. On July 30, there was a briefing for the assigned deputies and local police to cover all the procedural details. Some of those details became a source of internal arguments.

U.S. Marshal Wogan wanted one of his own deputies to lead the detail, but McShane sharply disagreed. It was likely that his memories of Montgomery, Alabama, and the possibility of untrained deputies in riot control maneuvers caused the reaction.[5]

By July 23, 1965, eight deputies were picked for the Marcello trial. Deputy U.S. Marshals Bill Shoemaker, Wallace Camp, Bill Humber, Simpson Otwell, Carl Gardner, Glenn Thompson, William Evins, and George Saegert were drawn from states in the South. U.S. Marshal Wogan was pleased with McShane's arrangements, stating in a memorandum that "I appreciate your splendid cooperation in making these out-of-district deputies available for this all-important trial."[6]

Plans for the trial quickly unfolded. Deputy U.S. Marshal Joseph Williams of New Orleans was assigned as supervisor. Most of the visiting deputies lodged in the John Mitchell Hotel four blocks away. At the Royal Orleans Hotel, where the jury was to be sequestered, a deputy's duty station was set up near the block of rooms. The jurors had their own wing, but very few of them had rooms that faced the U.S. Courthouse across the street. They were not to communicate with anyone except other jurors or the duty deputy. A special room was set up for television viewing, but as word of the trial could leak through news coverage, programming was subject to censorship. Female deputies were made available to attend to the needs of women of the jury. When traveling, the jurors moved as a group. The deputies contacted the families of the jurors and asked them for changes of clothing and other necessities.[7]

The Marcello trial proceeded without much incident, aside from several rotations of out-of-district deputies. Camp and Humber left on August 7 while Deputy U.S. Marshal Joe Allen finished out the last ten days. McShane was pleased with the way Deputy U.S. Marshal Williams handled his tasks, and complimented him in a letter to U.S. Attorney Louis C. LaCour. The high threat trial was over, but it was one of many.[8]

In retrospect, the Marcello trial proved easy compared to witness protection in labor cases during this period. The federal government faced a complex situation when it came to dissecting crime rooted in non-criminal organizations, like labor unions.

Dave Beck and his successor James Hoffa headed the International Brotherhood of Teamsters. Beck preferred a quiet and clean-living image. For instance, several deputy marshals noted his obsession with weightlifting. Eventually, he was found guilty of tax evasion and convicted for racketeering. Although his appeals lasted awhile, Beck eventually went to prison. The trials of Hoffa proved more complicated for the U.S. Marshals.[9]

EDWARD GRADY PARTIN AND JIMMY HOFFA

Many Teamsters were indicted by grand jury and prosecuted by a Justice Department team under Special Assistant Walter Sheridan. The Justice Department successfully prosecuted a Teamster named Edward Grady Partin on 26 charges of embezzlement involving union funds from Baton Rouge Teamsters' Local 5. Partin, formerly convicted of burglary, was given to violent behavior. In 1950, he had emerged as secretary-treasurer and business manager of the Local 5. When the curtain came down on Partin's activities, he claimed that Attorney General Kennedy was in danger from various Teamsters, particularly International Teamster President James R. Hoffa. He even claimed he was approached to provide plastic explosives to blow up the Kennedy home in McLean, Virginia.[10]

Although skeptical of the details, attorneys in the Justice Department took no chances. Beginning in late 1962, Partin turned informant on Hoffa, revealing the possibility of witness tampering. According to reporter Clark R. Mollenhoff, Partin heard Hoffa say he had a juror "in my [Hoffa's] hip pocket" and six off-duty policemen to personally protect him.[11]

In October 1962, the first of many trials involving Hoffa began in Nashville, Tennessee—this one on labor violations. All U.S. marshals in the region were requested to spare deputies for shifts in the detail.

The proceedings took an ominous turn on December 5 when a disturbed young man entered the courtroom and fired a pellet gun at Hoffa while the jury was out. Although no injury occurred, security was beefed up and the jury sequestered. The trial continued until nearly Christmas, with the deputies transporting witnesses and evidence. The jury deadlocked on the violations in question.[12]

With Partin as a protected witness in later legal actions, the U.S. marshals were involved in Hoffa trials for several more years. One grand jury convened in Nashville on the matter of witness tampering. Partin took advantage of his Fifth Amendment to avoid self-incrimination while testifying in April 1963. However, the following month Hoffa was indicted for witness tampering. The trial proceedings moved to Chattanooga, creating logistical problems for the marshals. Deputy U.S. Marshal John Hines of North Carolina was one of the deputies tasked with providing protective custody to a Tennessee attorney testifying about jury tampering for Hoffa. Interestingly, Hines later saw Hoffa himself at the Lewisburg federal prison while taking prisoners there.[13]

The Hoffa trials concluded successfully. Special Assistant Sheridan had enough evidence to get a conviction of Hoffa and three others for obstructing justice. U.S. District Judge Frank W. Wilson sentenced Hoffa to eight years. He appealed.[14]

During the period Hoffa sought appeal, Sheridan extended protective details of Partin's family in Baton Rouge. Special Assistant Homer Henry noted that an official at the Department of Justice called Sheridan on February 4, 1964, looking for McShane. As the Chief Marshal was unavailable, the official told Henry he "had a very important witness and wanted a deputy U.S. marshal to escort this witness's children to and from school, starting tomorrow. He gave the name of Mrs. Edward G. Partin...."[15] Deputy U.S. Marshal Joseph Williams was dispatched to transport the children as requested. Williams and Deputy U.S. Marshal Tom Grace took turns taking the children to and from their Baton Rouge school.[16]

Jack Cameron filed numerous memos on several areas of concern during the detail. It was reported that shots were fired at a Teamster's house in February—about the time of the sentencing. Chief Deputy W. Buford Ezell advised that Partin appeared on television bragging about his testimony—and stated further that his family was "under guard." They quickly moved Partin to a local hotel. His actions drove the deputies to distraction.[17]

In the spring of 1964, media interest in the high-profile Hoffa trials required the U.S. marshals to enact a special assignment during jury selection. There were renewed fears of jury tampering or intimidation. Chief U.S. Marshal McShane entrusted this assignment to Paskal "Dusty" Bowser, a veteran of earlier school integration assignments with a knack for organization. The new trial took place in Chicago, and Bowser contacted U.S. Marshal Joseph N. Tierney to coordinate agency procedures for the forthcoming jury selection.[18]

On April 1, Bowser flew to Chicago and checked into the Palmer House Hotel. Chief Deputy Edward Sullivan drove him to the district office, and he visited U.S. District Judge Richard B. Austin. The U.S. Attorney's Office provided details on assignments, but concerns over possible visits by Hoffa's attorney to individual jurors prompted the decision to utilize the U.S. Marshals. The situation was so tense that Bowser was not given free access to the witness list, which was completely under lock and key by the chief clerk of the court. As instructed, Bowser attended a pre-announced public drawing of a hundred prospective jurors. Although the names were not released, Hoffa's chief defense counsel, Maurice J. Walsh, came in tow with a number of reporters.[19]

The trial moved at a grinding pace. Hoffa and his co-defendant Zachary Strate, Jr., faced jail time and fines on witness tampering charges. However, his attorneys and friends worked hard for him. A Teamster-sponsored resolution to investigate the Justice Department was bandied about, but it was too late to personally target Attorney General Robert Kennedy. He had already left office.[20]

Deputies Robert L. Carpenter of the Middle District of North Carolina, and H.M. Henderson, of the Eastern District of Texas, were tasked with protecting Partin in September 1964. An ominous warning came on the way to Childersburg, Alabama, where Partin was participating in his hobby of racing cars. Carpenter received a tip that "two men from Alabama were in town to do a job, to get Ed Partin."[21] The deputies were given descriptions of the men and their vehicle. When they arrived in Childersburg on September 4, the deputies, along with local police, found the two men at a local drive-in restaurant. They found two guns in their car. Under questioning, the two men stated they were angry for being forced to give depositions in the Hoffa case.[22]

Deputy Ronnie Messa joined the Partin detail later that month. With a good ear for intelligence, he caught wind that a Hoffa operative was looking around Baton Rouge for the witness. Cameron told Messa to keep his eyes open. When Partin departed for Montgomery, Messa took the extra step of contacting that city's chief of police. Security was beefed up at the track. Ironically, Partin was unable to race his car due to a broken tie rod.[23]

The seemingly endless Partin detail continued into 1965. In late October 1964, the Department of Justice tasked McShane to continue the detail "until next May or June before the Supreme Court hands down the final decision in the case involving Partin." The perception of danger had increased during this phase.[24]

Although the detail continued, problems of Partin's own making did not help. On December 2, 1964, Deputy U.S. Marshals Jesse Grider and Charlie Burks were eating at a local pancake house when someone threw a tear gas grenade into the restaurant. Grider gave chase, but found no one. Later he told Jack Cameron that he believed the situation was arranged by Partin. The protected witness had asked the owner of the restaurant to fire two employees, as both were supposedly associates to Hoffa. The owner did not fire the employees. However, any connection between the two and Hoffa was non-existent. Grider believed the target of the attack was the restaurant owner.[25]

The restaurant incident only highlighted the logistical problems of a long witness detail. Uncertain of the length of court proceedings in the trial, the marshals asked Partin about his plans for Christmas. Partin stalled on an answer, eventually sending Deputy U.S. Marshal Dick Smith a handwritten note from a yellow legal pad. It said in part, "Dick I am going to New Orleans for about a week... Please stand by at your house until I get in touch with you because I don't know where I will stay or when I will need you. I will call Mr. [Deputy U.S. Marshal Rufus] Campbell the same way."[26]

The Baton Rouge detail extended beyond Christmas, but Partin pressed his luck. He attempted to have the government purchase his travel to Birmingham in January, but failed. He made at least one other attempt.[27]

By late March 1965, Cameron reported that "the detail is running smoothly—now."[28] That proved temporary. In July, Deputy U.S. Marshal Bill Whitworth was on the detail when he reported to Cameron that their witness planned a trip with his children to Yellowstone National Park later that month.[29]

All became impatient with the Partin detail during 1965 and 1966. More unpleasant incidents occurred while Hoffa's appeals went through the courts. A lawsuit was filed against Partin, followed by a Congressional opinion that the deputies were being misused. Representative Robert F. Ellsworth of Kansas remarked on the record:

> It appears that the Justice Department, in its passion to pursue Jimmy Hoffa, is sacrificing the public interest by supporting and defending its anti-Hoffa witness, Edward Partin... Further, I am reliably informed that U.S. Marshals are in constant attendance upon Mr. Partin as he pursues his private activities, marching in picket lines, driving in automobile races in Alabama, and so forth...[30]

The logistics of moving protectees from one place to another during the hearings were a nightmare. Additionally, in April 1967, Deputy U.S. Marshal Cecil Miller was assigned to protect Assistant U.S. Attorney William Bittman, one of the prosecutors of the Hoffa case in Chattanooga.[31]

News organizations followed every move of the appeal. The defendant Hoffa appeared on May 5. U.S. Marshal Harry Mansfield of the Eastern District of Tennessee issued instructions to his deputies. They were to secure the courts, ensure all spectators stayed in their seats, and screen entry through the main hallway.[32]

U.S. District Judge Richard Austin sentenced Hoffa in September 1967. The U.S. Marshals arranged for his transfer from Lewisburg Penitentiary in Pennsylvania to the U.S. Attorney's Office in Chicago to be present for sentencing. Bureau of Prisons (BOP) Director Myrl Alexander wrote Deputy Attorney General Warren Christopher that the U.S. Marshal and a deputy from Scranton would provide transportation. Hoffa received a sentence of five years and a fine of $10,000.[33]

Hoffa remained a problem for marshals until finally imprisoned by BOP. Bowser, Chief of Special Assignments by June 1969, was told that news reporters followed the transport of Hoffa, and noted that he dined on a steak at one of his favorite Detroit-area restaurants with the full permission of a deputy. The account, though erroneous, created an image problem. Bowser found out that the deputy and another guard had three prisoners in custody, including Hoffa. Traveling as far as they could, the band of lawmen and prisoners stopped at a restaurant near Detroit located a mile from the jail. The actual meal was sandwiches and soup, not steak. Hoffa was immediately recognizable anywhere in the Detroit area; a waitress at the restaurant had actually worked for him. After turning in his prisoners, the deputy faced a large throng of reporters, which he avoided. One subsequent editorial stated that the deputy's job was endangered by "his perfectly humane act."[34]

The Marcello and Hoffa trial protective details were two of the most intense involving organized crime. However, there were other seminal moments in the history of organized crime that involved the U.S. marshals. An imprisoned mob official, John Valachi, sat and spilled out the secrets of the Mafia to Congress. McShane sat beside him. Prior to Valachi's admission that there was a Mafia, the mob was not publicly revealed as an organized criminal enterprise. Necessary measures of protection increased with the details involving Marcello and Hoffa. Ultimately, the measures and details became an organized program.[35]

THE JACKSON MARCH: SUMMER 1966

One of the most memorable photographs of the 1960s, taken by Associated Press photographer Jack Thornell, is the image of a wounded James Meredith, felled by a shot at the beginning of his "March against Fear." The solitary walk from Memphis, Tennessee, to Jackson, Mississippi, was an individual effort planned by the former University of Mississippi student to protest racism, but just one day into it, on June 6, 1966, he was shot. In the photograph, Meredith's face is contorted in pain. A group of supporters continued the planned march, amid evident danger. However, the walk would include the protection of 12 deputy marshals, requested by the Department of Justice.[36]

An assistant to Attorney General Nicholas Katzenbach called Jack Cameron to discuss the event. Cameron was informed that 12 deputies were needed on a conditional basis and would use rental cars and walkie-talkies. Cameron found the equipment inadequate and requested in-car radios instead. The department granted his request.[37]

Preparations were quickly organized, and a group of 12 deputies, led by Al Butler, were placed on a two-hour standby list. The needed equipment was provided: ammunition, vests, helmets, gas masks, night sticks, arm bands, and copies of the oath of office for those specially deputized. Each man carried his own credentials, badge, handcuffs, and sidearm.[38]

Meredith's shooting mobilized civil rights organizations and leaders, who quickly converged on Mississippi. Dr. Martin Luther King, Jr. rallied thousands of people, including members of the Congress of Racial Equality (CORE), the Student National Coordinating Committee (SNCC), and the Black Panthers. The throng moved through Mississippi and marched on roads toward the state capital of Mississippi. This intense reaction alarmed the Justice Department, who immediately turned to the U.S. Marshals.[39]

Deputy Attorney General Ramsey Clark approved air transport for 18 deputies, including Paskal Bowser, to Meridian, Mississippi. Most of the deputies worked out of the District of Columbia office and had served during the Meredith detail in 1962-63, including Butler, Wade Beall, Warren Emmerton, Jim Howard, and Ray Pope. They arrived in time to assist the U.S. Marshal for the Southern District of Mississippi in planning protection for the final portion of the march into Jackson. At Meridian, Butler, Emmerton, and Bowser each rented vehicles and drove the nearly 300 miles to Jackson.[40]

The number of marchers was confirmed to be 12,000 strong as they approached Jackson. Early on June 26, the deputy marshals found a contingent of state highway patrol, city police, county sheriffs, and state game and fish officers waiting for the crowds. Meredith and King led the singing crowd through a poorer district of the city. Although most white citizens watched quietly, angry hecklers followed the marchers and hinted at violence. The deputies took positions on the perimeter of the peaceful band to prevent any violent actions by the crowd. In addition, the presence of church leaders of all faiths bolstered the protective shield.[41]

The opposing groups faced off at the state capitol, where helicopters flew overhead. Through the tension that afternoon, the marchers heard speeches from Meredith, King, and Stokely Carmichael. The marchers kept good order, but the U.S. Marshals provided vital support.[42]

From their protective work throughout the Civil Rights period, Congress' awareness of the U.S. Marshals increased. In February 1966, Chief U.S. Marshal McShane wrote Representative Silvio Conte,

This is in reply to your letter of January 26 to Mr. John Doar requesting information with regard to when, where, why, and for how long deputy U.S. Marshals have been used in the South during recent civil rights moments... Deputy U.S. Marshals have been involved in the enforcement of federal court and Presidential orders, and the incident protection of the civil rights of individuals...[43]

PRESIDENT JOHNSON AND THE MARSHALS

Under the leadership of James McShane, a second U.S. Marshals general conference was held in September 1966, and personally attended by President Lyndon B. Johnson. As a Texan, the President witnessed the fading "Old West" days of the U.S. marshals of his youth. He also knew there were serious issues facing law enforcement and he wanted a national strategy against crime. In his remarks to the appointed U.S. marshals assembled at the White House, President Johnson noted that major crimes were committed at "nearly five a minute." He continued that "as Federal law enforcement officers, you have a stake in helping to formulate" the proposed strategy:[44]

The United States Marshals have a proud record. From early frontier days, you have accepted the challenge of change. Often you were the first to carry the Federal writ into lawless communities. Today, you are discharging your increasingly difficult duties with devotion and dispatch. And you are doing it, I might add, with a record of economy and efficiency unequaled by any branch of the Federal service. The Marshals Service has had less than a 2 percent increase in personnel over a period of 30 years. I consider that truly remarkable.

I am also pleased that, in my Administration, legislation has finally been introduced to place U.S. Marshals under the Civil Service system. Enactment of this bill will complete the task of making the Marshals Service a merit service and a career service. It will protect the rights of the individual Marshal, and it will benefit both your Service and the country you serve.

But no matter how capable, no matter how dedicated, Federal law enforcement officers cannot win this fight alone. That is why I have asked the Attorney General to work with the governors of the 50 States to establish state-wide committees on law enforcement and criminal justice.[45]

The President's words buoyed the spirit of the deputies, but the reality remained that the task at hand was larger than the available resources. McShane requested more assistance from the Justice Department. He was already pushing himself very hard, with only Delores Klajbor and Jack Cameron as major assistants since Homer Henry retired in late 1965. Two key vacancies went begging and renewed training was badly needed. McShane's colorful request to Acting Attorney General Ramsey Clark in October 1966 stated in part, "Miss Klajbor and Jack Cameron who have been in the office since it was established in 1956, say, 'This is the worst mess we have been in since we have been here'... As for me, all I can say is, 'HELP—HELP—HELP'!!"[46]

1967: NEO-NAZIS AND ANTI-WAR DEMONSTRATIONS

If Chief U.S. Marshal James McShane had expected things to calm down after the first half of the decade, 1967 would prove a discouraging year. The country was changing in many ways, and the U.S. marshals increasingly faced extremists and everyday citizens in tense circumstances.

In August 1967, neo-Nazi leader George Lincoln Rockwell was shot by a disgruntled follower outside an Arlington, Virginia, laundromat. The Neo-Nazi leader had cultivated followers for years, advocating an atmosphere of violence. To complicate matters, Rockwell was a World War II veteran, and officially entitled to burial in a national cemetery. His followers wanted to display their symbols at the gravesite and bury

Rockwell in his Nazi uniform. Those requests were disallowed by the military.[47]

On August 28, Frank Lockwood of the Army's Office of Support Services called the U.S. Marshal's office in the Eastern District of Virginia. The burial ceremony was scheduled at the national cemetery in Culpeper, Virginia, on August 29. Lockwood desired the presence of law enforcement at the services. He grew concerned about a possible riot situation, so he contacted Paskal Bowser.[48]

Bowser spoke with both McShane and Klajbor. Both preferred not to involve the U.S. marshals in an explosive situation like the Rockwell funeral. It was left to Bowser to call the Department of Justice and explain the situation to them. The Criminal Division thought that Lockwood's initial call should be returned as a courtesy. Unfortunately, Lockwood was not reached until the following morning, leaving little time for a strategy. The Deputy General Counsel for the Army had been in touch with the Department of Justice, and formally asked for deputies to be made available for the Rockwell funeral that morning. The Army had intelligence that Rockwell's "storm troopers" planned to appear in full Nazi regalia on federal property. They were not to enter Culpeper National Cemetery attired in this manner.[49]

Despite his initial position on marshals' involvement in the matter, McShane instructed Bowser to contact the District of Columbia office and "have 24 deputy marshals on half-hour standby. He said we were to go to the Pentagon, board helicopters, and fly to Culpepper [sic], Virginia."[50]

A frantic series of calls ensued. Bowser called U.S. Marshal Luke Moore of the District of Columbia, who lined up the personnel. As the airlift was arranged, U.S. Marshal Moore sent nine deputies to the Pentagon.[51]

It was at the helicopter pad that morning that Bowser first saw General Carl Turner, the Army's Provost Marshal. He arrived at the same time as the deputies from the district. Bowser called Deputy Attorney General Warren Christopher and asked for any remaining instructions. The deputies were present to provide civilian arrest authority, while the military police maintained primary response should the mourners become violent. The deputies had a limited role and were to interfere as little as possible. Along with General Turner, Bowser and his contingent departed the Pentagon.[52]

Discussing tactics aboard the helicopter, General Turner outlined his strategy to Bowser. Any funeral attendee was expected to remove symbols of the American Nazi party before entering the grounds, including armbands and lapel pins. As a contingency, Bowser agreed to act for the military police should it become necessary. After the short flight to the Culpeper airport, the group was greeted by an escort of Virginia state troopers. The multi-jurisdictional operation moved quickly to the cemetery in Culpeper.[53]

The superintendent of the Culpeper National Cemetery tried to stop the procession at the memorial gates because of American Nazi Party adherents dressed in full regalia. The *Washington Post* reported that most of the attendees were sympathizers and family members. A separate contingent of Virginia state troopers stopped the hearse carrying Rockwell's body in the cemetery. The former ideologue's body lay in a polished wooden coffin draped with silver cloth. General Turner and Bowser arrived just prior to the military police. It was a tense few minutes, with Turner attempting to deal with the procession leaders, including Matthias Koehl and Douglas Niles.[54]

Bowser and the deputies watched as General Turner faced down Niles and the rest of the procession at the cemetery gates. The arriving military police took up positions behind him. The general reminded the group of the conditions to attend the burial. Niles remarked that the floral arrangement had the American Nazi Party symbols on it and they would not remove them. As he moved toward the gravesite, MPs apprehended him. They passed him to the deputies, who formally placed him under arrest at the superintendent's cottage. This law enforcement action incited the mourners and a fully uniformed "storm trooper" climbed on the roof of the hearse. He began delivering a speech urging the crowd to rush the line of police, then leapt forward himself. MPs immediately apprehended him and took him to two deputies standing nearby. A youthful follower attempted to rush the line and was likewise arrested.[55]

The situation became a standoff as the two lines faced down each other. The growing media presence was impressed with General Turner's cool demeanor under the strain. One reporter asked him what he was waiting for, and he calmly replied, "just waiting for a cigar." When Niles' wife shouted that if she were driving the hearse, the General would have been flattened, Turner puffed on a cigar and said nothing. At approximately 4 p.m. that day, the general gave Koehl a choice: remove the Nazi ornamentation or depart within 15 minutes. The time ran out, and the choice was made for them. The mourners departed, taking the hearse with them. Rockwell's body was later cremated.[56]

The tense standoff at Culpeper National Cemetery served as a precursor to demonstrations to follow. By October 1967, many U.S. citizens opposed American involvement in the Vietnam conflict.

In mid-October, McShane and Jack Cameron briefed deputies to expect a large-scale demonstration at the Pentagon. Warning signs for such an event had become evident earlier that month. On October 18, Jack Cameron had prepared the detail. Three deputies from Boston assisted the detail, and a site communications system was initiated under Deputy U.S. Marshal Walter Allen. Although deputies rotated in, no potential riot or crowd gathered at first. Allen was ordered to close down his communications system, and the entire operation was about to shut down when four unauthorized persons appeared at the Pentagon's river entrance. Later that day, the number doubled. It appeared they did not intend to leave the property. As the official business day at the Pentagon was over, Deputies Al Butler, Frank Vandegrift, Paskal Bowser, and Allen approached the group. They instructed the small group to leave. While one of them became angry, he was quieted by his companions. They stated they were not demonstrators and left.[57]

It appeared the small contingent was a leading element, and the U.S. Marshals prepared for a larger group. They increased the number of supplemental deputies, including deputized female guards to process any females on hand. The units were then placed under "area commanders" until Vandegrift, Jesse Grider, and Don Forsht reorganized them into smaller groups of five. A separate unit, formed for processing, was headed by Deputy U.S. Marshals Joseph Wasielewski and Ellis Duley. Personnel guarded the Pentagon's water and power plants, as well as its transport and processing centers. A total of 242 deputies were included in the operation. Some estimates place the number at 263.[58]

On October 21, the protest at the Pentagon materialized. Protestors left the Lincoln Memorial and marched to the Pentagon, which they viewed as symbolic of military power. Among the protestors that day was author Norman Mailer, who later wrote an unflattering portrait of the deputies in *The Armies of the Night*. As described in other accounts, some protestors were violent and others friendly. When a small number of the crowd physically charged the building, the deputies used night sticks to repel the aggressors. They had no other less-than-lethal tools to maintain order and control. Of the protestors, 683 people were arrested, and 580 convicted of federal violations.[59]

One interesting side story of the event was a letter from Congressman George Bush, asking about the status of Reverend John Boyles, the assistant chaplain of Yale University. Chief U.S. Marshal McShane wrote to Bush and explained that Boyles was arrested and charged after "breaking through the restraining line of soldiers and United States Marshals and refused to move back when ordered."[60]

The cost of the detail was nearly $100,000, a considerable amount in 1967. In addition, 13 deputies were injured, one with broken fingers. Several had their clothing torn and ruined from the experience.[61]

Historically, the U.S. marshals had protected federal court buildings and other vital structures and the U.S. mail during the Pullman Strike of 1894. However, the Pentagon protest expanded this duty to a new level.[62]

There was much irony from the Pentagon operation in Norman Mailer's account of that event. Mailer's *The Armies of the Night*, completed in 1968, depicted the deputies who guarded the Pentagon as militaristic and unsmiling—almost inhuman. He even included details about their individual backgrounds. Only six years earlier, the deputies were popular and heroic agents of change. To Mailer and the protestors they faced at the Pentagon, they had "ice cube" eyes and "stone larynxes." The author brazenly compared them to Nazis. Many of the same deputies who played an important role in desegregating the South were present at the Pentagon. As they did then, the deputies accomplished their job professionally despite the anger directed at them:[63]

Given Mailer's incendiary style in previous works, it was a literary device incorrectly used in this case. The anger of the times, and the anti-war feeling for Vietnam, colored Mailer's portrait of deputies. He captured the feeling of the movement, but in the process misunderstood the public image of deputies doing their duty.[64]

In just half a decade, public perception of the deputy U.S. marshal swung from heroic heights as agents of change to being viewed as oppressors by some. However, the views of the marshals themselves were consistent—carry out the law. It was society's view that changed. As the mood of the 1960s darkened, the Executive Office for U.S. Marshals fought through the changes.

CHAPTER 5

END OF AN ERA

The year 1968 was full of conflict and change. The same was true of the United States Marshals Service. The simmering social conflict of the previous year gave way to a violent footnote in the deaths of Martin Luther King, Jr. and Robert F. Kennedy, McShane's good friend. The positive images of marshals and their deputies, born of their response at the mob trials of Hoffa and integration in the South, were replaced by the negative media accounts from anti-war protests and trials. One of the most conflicted moments in U.S. Marshal's history was serving Dr. King with a restraining order to march just a day before his assassination.

DEATH OF AN ICON

On occasion, the U.S. Marshals protected Dr. King from danger. Deputies encountered the civil rights icon on at least four other occasions: the March on Washington, his speech for the Freedom Riders, the protest march at Jackson, and again at Selma, Alabama. In all these encounters, deputies protected Dr. King from possible harm.

By 1968, events reversed themselves. Jack Cameron received word of a pending strike by the sanitation workers against the City of Memphis by March 26. Cameron asked Bowser to get four men to report to the Memphis office, because of his concern for the safety of those at the federal courthouse. Four deputies from Little Rock, Arkansas, and Oxford, Mississippi reported to Memphis. U.S. Marshal Cato Ellis confirmed their arrival to Chief U.S. Marshal McShane on April 1.[1]

The sanitation workers' strike attracted Dr. King with new plans to march in protest, but his group lacked the proper permit. Because King and his followers planned to march regardless of license, opposition forces sought a restraining order in federal court. U.S. District Judge Bailey Brown issued the order, and dispatched the U.S. Marshals with the rather awkward duty of presenting the papers. U.S. Marshal Ellis did this himself on April 3, 1968, outside of the Lorraine Motel, while unexpectedly running into newspaper photographers who captured the moment for posterity. Ellis was surprised and saddened by the moment, not wishing to be a focal point. Dr. King and three other high-ranking civil rights figures smiled and laughed, taking in the moment. Despite the publicity around the delivery of the restraining order, Dr. King did not march that day. However, the wait was tragic. The next day, while Dr. King was on the balcony of the hotel, a sniper killed him. The man who along with the marshals personified the Civil Rights movement was dead. For U.S. Marshal Ellis, it was a strange irony to serve Dr. King court orders to stay the march, but be unable to prevent the tragedy that followed.[2]

The hearing on the Memphis march began the day of Dr. King's assassination and made significant progress to resolving any outstanding concerns. On April 5, the court reconvened and approved conditions for the march. The plan for the march called for the involvement of the U.S. Marshals. One specific portion of the plan specifically stated that "adequate police forces will be present to accompany the march and to maintain moving and stationary positions between marchers and the sidewalks."[3]

Cameron was asked to accompany 30 deputies to Memphis on April 6. The Border Patrol set up a communications center, while the deputies looked after the marchers, the local police, and National Guard units as well. After swearing in all deputies and border patrolmen, Cameron split the men into nine teams, supplying each with a walkie-talkie and copies of the court papers. One team manned Memphis police headquarters, while others were positioned at various stations along the march route. Given the potential for riots, tear gas was readied. A team under Al Butler drew the job of guarding the federal building. Charlie Burks scanned for possible snipers.[4]

On April 8, the march started on schedule at 11:00 a.m. at Clayborn Temple AME Church at the corner of Hernando and Pontotoc Streets. Cameron reported the number of marchers at approximately 40,000 people.[5] The flyer given to marchers billed the occasion as "Community on the Move for Equality" and gave the full route and instructions. It read in part:

> Dr. King came to Memphis to help all of us and especially to help the Sanitation Workers win economic justice. We asked him to come because we wanted to win this strike as human beings and as men—not as animals who use violence.
>
> Dr. King died in Memphis, trying to help us. Today we honor Dr. King for the great work he did for all people and particularly for his great love and sacrifice for us. How best can we honor him now? The answer is simple: we honor him by making sure that the Sanitation Workers win their rights non-violently.
>
> This can be done if we do not lose our heads. This can be done if we stand united. This can be done if we let no man, black or white, trick us into violence for its own ugly purposes.[6]

Reverend James Lawson further asked that the marchers "follow the orders the marshalls [sic] give you. They are there to help you. They know where drinking water, doctors, nurses and toilets are located...

March silently, in honor of the memory of Dr. King. Sometimes silence speaks louder than words."[7]

Largely thanks to the march's organizers like Reverend Lawson, no major disruption occurred in Memphis. The crowd gathered at City Hall Plaza and heard speeches by Dr. King's widow Coretta, Rev. Ralph Abernathy, and labor leader Walter Reuther. Although Cameron reported that most of the crowd departed during the long afternoon of speeches, those remaining completed the march back in peace. Cameron noted "this was the most orderly march of this type I have ever witnessed."[8]

Unlike Memphis, people in other cities reacted to Dr. King's death with violence. The U.S. marshals braced themselves in Washington, D.C. once they heard the news. U.S. Marshal Luke Moore, an African-American, posted deputies at federal court facilities. Widespread looting and fires enveloped the Shaw neighborhood, destroying jazz music halls and numerous businesses. Despite these horrible losses, Moore was lucky. With the assistance of the Metropolitan police and other units, the deputies successfully prevented any major catastrophe to many federal buildings.[9]

While the events were awkward for U.S. Marshals Ellis and Moore, the summer months were tragic for McShane. On June 5, Robert Kennedy was making a run for the Democratic nomination, as President Lyndon Johnson was not running for re-election. He enjoyed a popular run against fellow Democrat and Vice-President Hubert Humphrey, and finished a rousing campaign speech at the Ambassador Hotel in Los Angeles. As Kennedy was being escorted through the kitchen entrance afterwards, a man named Sirhan Sirhan shot him at point blank range. McShane could do nothing for Kennedy, but immediately thought of his family.[10]

McShane called Al Butler, ordering him to take deputies to Hickory Hill, the Kennedy home in McLean, Virginia. The White House was concerned an attempt would be made on the family. As he did following President John Kennedy's assassination, Butler started making the arrangements for the family's protective detail. The deputies immediately covered any possible entrance to the estate and stayed on the detail until it was considered safe.[11]

THE CATONSVILLE NINE AND OTHER PROTEST ACTIONS

In May 1968, a group of citizens broke into the second floor of the Knights of Columbus Hall in Catonsville, a suburb of Baltimore, Maryland. The facility stored files that belonged to the Selective Service System. The group removed approximately 300 files, carried them to the parking lot outside, dumped them into numerous metal wastebaskets, and set the papers on fire. As the files burned, the nine responsible persons paid little attention to the media cameras that captured their images. The nine, mostly clean-cut and well-dressed, prayed while they destroyed federal property in protest.[12]

The nine were quickly identified: Jesuit priest Philip Berrigan and his brother Daniel; peace protest organizer George Mische; former nun Mary Moylan; Thomas Melville, a former priest, and his wife Mary, both missionaries; compatriot John Hogan; protester and artist Tom Lewis; and a young, religious mid-westerner named David Darst. Most had experience in protest activity. Lewis and Philip Berrigan participated in a file raid at the Baltimore Customs House in 1967. The group on that occasion was known as "The Baltimore Four." They poured blood over draft cards to render them unusable. The basis of their protest was antipathy for war. In particular, Daniel Berrigan had an unpleasant experience with government officials in Hanoi in January1968.[13]

After the files burned, the nine were quickly captured. The trial was held at the U.S. District Court Building beginning October 8, 1968. Lawyer William Kunstler represented the defendants at trial. Like many trials of this type, deputies found themselves in a protective role and far from appreciated. However, they were featured in the written words of an author. Daniel Berrigan wrote *Trial Poems* while awaiting trial. Lewis, a noted artist, began a series of illustrations. Later, Berrigan wrote a play,

The Trial of Catonsville Nine, as a living transcript. Deputies were not portrayed as Mailer had viewed them, but as the voiceless instruments of the district judge. In the end, the Catonsville Nine were found guilty and sentenced. However, some of them appealed all the way to the U.S. Supreme Court. Moylan and the Melvilles decided to serve their time. Darst was killed in an automobile accident. The Berrigan brothers went underground to escape, and they remained fugitives for several years.[14]

The Berrigans were not the only activists the U.S. marshals had to face in high profile trials. The "Chicago Seven" trial was also controversial. The criminal activity that led to the trial occurred during later 1968, and the trial began in September 1969. The "Boston Five" trial of Dr. Benjamin Spock and four others took place in June 1968, with a protective plan devised by deputy marshals. This latter proceeding grew out of a major Pentagon demonstration and preceded the actions of the Catonsville Nine. Eventually, the charges against the "Boston Five" were dropped, reversed, or dismissed.[15]

Prior to Kennedy's assassination, the National Park Service accommodated plans by the Southern Christian Leadership Conference to set up tents and build "temporary structures" designated as "Resurrection City, U.S.A." on the National Mall in Washington, D.C. Rev. Bernard LaFayette, Jr., the national coordinator of the Washington Poor People's Campaign, hosted the gathering of approximately 3,000 people. The plan seemed harmless enough. A blueprint revealed that a shop, clinic, city hall, and art gallery were among the residential and facility units. A large dining tent was at the center. Resurrection City was only to last from May 11 to June 16, 1968. Although the agreement provided that there would be "marshals, appropriately identified, in sufficient numbers to maintain good order, but this shall not limit, impair, or otherwise interfere with the authority of law enforcement agencies in the exercise of their responsibilities," it did not go as planned.[16]

Due to a manpower shortage brought on by riot alerts, the U.S. Marshals turned to other federal law enforcement agencies to lead protection of the makeshift city. Jack Cameron deputized 37 Border Patrolmen, who worked with Al Butler and Paskal Bowser. Things started well enough. Most efforts were peaceful.[17]

A notable exception was sparked by a letter circulated among the attendees and visitors, entitled *American People Should Know the Facts about the Treaty of Guadalupe Hidalgo.* The letter referred to the treaty that ended hostilities between Mexico and the United States on February 2, 1848. The typed flyer exemplified the darkening mood of the inhabitants. They called the Treaty of Guadalupe Hidalgo an "organized criminal conspiracy" against the people of the Southwest.[18]

The deadline to close Resurrection City passed, but its occupants refused to disperse as agreed. Trash lined the residential areas, and the relationship with patrolmen worsened. By June 19, the use of tear gas became necessary. Despite good intentions, the gathering morphed into angry protest far beyond the original scope. The camp was cleared.[19]

After the death of Robert Kennedy, the Marshals Service staff at headquarters began to slowly change. William J. Neptune arrived in late 1968 as first assistant to McShane, closing a gap in the leadership ranks. In August 1968, Klajbor transferred to another position in the Justice Department. All of these changes affected the Chief U.S. Marshal, who faced shifting political winds.[20]

The death of Robert Kennedy also affected McShane deeply. He continued to devote himself to Marshals Service business, such as overseeing the creation and approval of a national seal for the U.S. Marshals. However, his son Michael noted his intense sadness and his increase in drinking alcohol as the Chief Marshal dealt with the loss of his friend. McShane developed a case of pneumonia in mid-December 1968 and took an uncustomary amount of time off. His condition worsened. Still, people were shocked when James J.P. McShane died on December 26, 1968. He was only 59 years old.[21]

THE GENERAL

The U.S. Marshals reeled after the death of James McShane. He was a friend to most, and a guiding hand who represented the civil rights era for the agency. He died in office and on the job. News of McShane's death was a surprise to employees. However, winds of political change were apparent even before his last illness.[22] The nation had elected Richard Nixon as president. McShane, a Democrat closely aligned to the Kennedys, faced certain challenge to his leadership in the new Republican administration. The structure of the Executive Office for U.S. Marshals remained uncertain. Key staff had departed. Delores Klajbor's departure opened a key legal position within the Executive Office for U.S. Marshals to be filled by Nixon's new Attorney General, John Mitchell.[23]

On March 24, 1969, Attorney General Mitchell appointed Carl Turner as Chief U.S. Marshal of the Executive Office for United States Marshals. A native Oklahoman who earned a bachelor's degree from Southwestern Teachers' College in 1939, he had extensive Army experience. By 1950, he had worked for the military police and advanced to the post of Provost Marshal General of the U.S. Army in 1964. Turner had received mass television media coverage during the Pentagon riots and at the George Rockwell funeral in 1967.[24]

Turner, who was called "The General" by employees, was an effective organizer in the Army, and joined the U.S. marshals with the same mindset. He hand carried a request to Deputy Attorney General Richard G. Kleindienst to ask for a deputy chief United States marshal. He received his wish.[25]

The Department of Justice turned to a Kentucky native named Bill Hall to fill the position of general counsel. Hall had spent time as an FBI investigator and a lawyer in a private legal practice; he possessed administrative and operational experience. Hall reflected on his thoughts during the interview process.[26]

The interview was very perfunctory. It lasted just a few minutes. Sen. [Strom] Thurmond actually went with me to this interview and sat in on it. It might have lasted 15 minutes, tops. I was told that the position was mine if I wanted it. So I thought about it, and I was very disappointed in the accommodations of the headquarters... This was a Federal Triangle building. It was on the ground floor next to a bank, between a bar and the bank. It was very narrow. A corridor with offices on each side. Only the two front offices had windows. I guess there were probably three offices, maybe four, on each side of the corridor, so a total of maybe seven or eight offices. Very spartan, poorly furnished, and not impressive.[27]

When he arrived at the Executive Office for U.S. Marshals in April 1969, Hall was one of only 15 employees located at headquarters. The primary duties for Hall included the examination of federal tort claims and providing legal advice when needed from "in-house" counsel. He saw little of Turner.[28]

Hall reported to Jack Cameron, who was on his way out. Cameron did not get the top position, even though he had served as acting Chief U.S. Marshal following McShane's death. The two got along well during the transition. Years later, when Cameron wished to return to the organization, Hall happily took him back.[29]

On May 21, 1969, Attorney General Order 415-69 stated that the "Office of the Director, United States Marshals Service, shall be under the supervision of the Deputy Attorney General and shall direct and supervise the United States Marshals...."[30] With this order, Turner became the first Director of the USMS.[31]

The process to officially change the office took a longer course, fully realized a year later. With these initial victories under his belt, Turner desired to bring military polish to the U.S. Marshals. However, deputies considered themselves civilian law enforcement officers. Pressed into the image of military members, it rubbed them the wrong way.

On June 12, 1969, Turner released one of the most controversial documents of any director. The U.S. Marshals Circular titled "The Road Ahead," and numbered USMC 69-2, struck deputies and administrative employees as some kind of manifesto. In fairness to Turner, the four-page circular was probably a brusquely worded document intended to guide rather than lecture. However, that mattered little. Deputies felt punished for doing a good job.[32]

"The Road Ahead" essentially was a bulleted memorandum with 18 points. He wrote, in part, "In the course of my inquiry I have made certain observations which, when viewed in the light of my previous experience, have precipitated the conclusions I will discuss with you quite candidly."[33]

First, Turner indicated that he was looking for difficulties. He went on to stress professional posture, spirit, honesty, reliability, and high standards of appearance. In the sixth point, Turner noted that supervisors were accountable for all actions by subordinates, and that each needed to create a command chain for their operations. However, several points were phrased more controversially. The tenth point stated employees could "shape up or ship out," while in the thirteenth he described that "Protuberant waistlines and flabby backsides and jowls cannot be reconciled with good physical condition."[34]

The organization of the circular lacked the order Turner was known for. The points more favorable to the workforce were buried in the back of the memorandum. He intended to improve the pay grade structure, and also clarified reimbursement for mileage. However, the negative tone in the first points of the "Road Ahead" seemed to emphasize a need to conform. The words of the message seemed overly harsh. In short, it shocked the deputies instead of inspiring them.[35]

The main reason behind the memorandum was a growing headquarters. Turner confided his plans to Hall. He decided to modernize the marshals. Hall recalled, "His charter from then-Attorney General [John] Mitchell had been to reshape the Marshals Service and bring it into the 20th century [sic]."[36]

After U.S. Marshal Luke Moore departed after the 1968 election, Al Butler served as Acting U.S. Marshal of the District of Columbia during the Turner era. Since the 1950s, the appointment in D.C. was considered a senior leadership position, and Turner wanted the post for a former military associate. Turner knew he couldn't remove Butler without raising the ire of the federal judges, who supported him. He called Butler into headquarters, and told him, "Son, you know you can't always win. Sometimes you have to be a good loser." Butler retorted, "Sir, I never try to lose." Turner kept Butler's position in his sights throughout much of 1969, but no change occurred.[37]

Turner brought leadership into headquarters who reflected his philosophy. Reis Kash had worked with Turner previously, and made the transition from the military to the civilian organization. Donald A. Synnott, a fellow soldier from the military police corps, joined and served as deputy chief. Holdover officials from the Department of Justice such as Bill Neptune stayed on, but largely stayed in the background.[38]

Turner made no secret that he wanted the U.S. Marshals to be a uniformed service. The roots of new programs in Internal Inspections and Air Piracy began in earnest also.[39]

By early August 1969, Neptune began implementing an approved staffing plan. There were 38 positions in the Office of the Director. The target was to completely fill all positions in three months. He wrote to the chief in Administrative Services, William H. O'Donoghue, that corresponding space needs were urgent and that he needed to provide space for 40 people. Turner, signing as "Director" in an internal memorandum to O'Donoghue dated August 22, requested space on the twelfth floor of a building on Indiana Avenue. The remainder of the staff space was to be located on the third floor.[40]

Ironically, Turner failed to make the transition himself. The General coveted the title of "Director" and made significant progress toward the name and organizational changes. However, his ambitions created detractors. He also had his personal issues. Rumors abounded that Turner, since the time he was provost marshal general in the Army, fancied guns so much that he collected or sold them. On its face, that was not a problem. There was further talk, however, that he sold some guns that were not his to sell. In fact, the Senate Permanent Subcommittee on Investigations looked into the matter and called for his testimony. Many in the leadership levels of the Justice Department and Executive Office of the U.S. Marshals believed Turner overreached, and the Subcommittee moved to investigate him. In a June 1973 interview in *The Nation*, then-Attorney General Ramsey Clark stated that "General Turner appropriated the guns for good people, his personal collection and his bank account..."[41]

By early September 1969 the situation was no longer tenable for Turner. Hall recalled that on September 2, "I heard the phone ring in his [Turner's] office, then I heard a door close. He was gone."[42] Indeed, Turner resigned. He later pleaded guilty to charges of illegal gun sales. Don Synnott took over in an acting capacity, and reported to employees in a circular that Turner had resigned. Bill Hall was promoted to Acting Deputy Director. Synnott finished the circular by lauding the "admirable example of General Turner's aggressive and imaginative leadership [that] will serve as a continuing source of inspiration as we implement and extend his progressive policies and programs."[43]

Almost six months of the Turner administration left some important hallmarks in the history of the U.S. Marshals. The official title of Director, U.S. Marshals Service, was attained but never fully executed until after his departure. Ironically, the manner of his departure deprived him of achieving permanent recognition as a director. His desire to make the USMS more like a military organization bore some fruit with the formation of the Special Operations Group several years later.

Turner's intent may have been noble, but his delivery was lacking. The rapid changes he instituted in the name of professionalism went too far, too fast. He underestimated the level of employee resistance to his aggressive ideas and lost allies within the Department. Deputies were not military police. Lastly, his emphasis on personal integrity and honesty backfired when he failed to set a personal example with the gun charges and conviction against him. After a brief term in prison, Carl Turner worked for his son's contracting firm. One former employee remembered him working on some plumbing at his home many years later. Carl Turner died in December 1996.[44]

SECTION THREE—THE SEVENTIES:
MOVING BEYOND CIVIL DISTURBANCE

Chapter 6

The New Director

The 1960s ended abruptly for the United States Marshals Service with the sudden death of Chief Marshal James McShane and the resignation of Carl Turner. A leadership vacuum remained to be filled. Most of the experienced deputies needed a director to draw everything together. The Justice Department, in May 1969, had allowed Turner to use the title of Director, but he never fully utilized the new office. His untimely departure because of illegal activities erased most of his official recognition as Director. A more permanent legacy was the change of the agency name. The Executive Office for U.S. Marshals officially changed with Department of Justice Order 415-69 in May 1969, to the U.S. Marshals Service.[1]

Don Synnott acted as director from September 1969 until March 1970. Few initiatives took place during his short tenure, although internal memoranda indicated he was unsure of the future. He still had the dependable assistance of both Bill Neptune and Bill Hall, but most other leaders from the 1960s were gone.[2]

Out of this uncertainty emerged a director who changed the course of the Marshals yet again. On January 16, 1970, Attorney General John

Mitchell officially appointed Wayne B. Colburn as Director of the U.S. Marshals Service.[3]

Colburn had served as the U.S. Marshal in San Diego. On September 19, 1966, he became the first U.S. Marshal for the Southern District of California after Congress renewed the federal judicial district. Four district offices in California replaced the two that were divided near Los Angeles. Colburn proved adept at the task of managing an office with a distinct culture.[4]

Wayne Colburn had grown up in Oklahoma, but joined the U.S. Marine Corps in the 1930s and served in China. Following a short stint as a milkman, he joined the San Diego Police Department on March 22, 1942. He left the police force briefly to serve on active duty during World War II, but quickly rejoined the department following his war service.[5]

Colburn made sergeant in 1950 and lieutenant in 1953. He took on the "problem shift," working 8:00 p.m. to 4:00 a.m., hours that saw the largest number of crimes. San Diego Police Chief Elmer Jensen took a shining to the lieutenant and ensured he received extensive training. By 1957, Colburn was a captain and addressing community problems.[6]

The turmoil of the 1960s in Southern California tested him. Colburn was promoted to inspector for the San Diego police in 1962. On March 8, 1965, San Diego Police Chief Wes Sharp selected the inspector to run a special operation to arrest an unstable man who was holed up with a gun at a pawn shop. Colburn ran no special response teams, but possessed gut instinct and planning ability. The gunman had held off police for four hours and shot one pawn shop employee to death. Being possessed of a cool head, Colburn managed to end the standoff without losing more innocent lives. He and his men found a way to enter the store from above. They stormed the store and surprised the gunman.[7]

Unrest in the summer of 1965 persuaded him to establish a police command post in one of San Diego's vacant lots; he had a knack for community policing during his career. The media attention from the pawn shop arrest and his general policing tactics caught the eye of individuals at the federal government level, and contributed to Wayne Colburn's promotion to federal law enforcement.[8]

In January 1970, Wayne Colburn brought his experience and planning skills to the directorship of the Marshals Service. Past leaders had relied more on the unilateral decisions of each district U.S. Marshal or fiscal ties created by the Justice Department to enact larger domestic agendas. McShane had moved toward centralization of control and agency-wide decision making. Juggling personnel from across the country for key operations became increasingly difficult as U.S. Marshals pushed back in the districts. For Colburn, centralization meant organization and efficiency. He wanted to transform the U.S. Marshals Service into a separate bureau comprised of all the districts and headquarters, but this was made difficult because every U.S. Marshal was appointed by the President, generally outside the control of the Director.[9]

One practical order of business for Colburn was acquiring more office space. The main Department of Justice building simply ran out of room. The number of headquarters employees had increased to 30 by 1970. An article in the October 1971 issue of the *United States Marshals Service Newsletter* reported the headquarters move to 521 12th Street Northwest in Washington, D.C. The employees occupied the second and third floors of the "Safeway Building," the unofficial name given the central headquarters because of the grocery chain operating on the ground level. The full move was completed in the fall of 1971. With facilities not completely functional with the separation, the Service shared resources with other agencies.[10]

More changes ensued. Attorney General Mitchell's Justice Department altered priorities. During the transition, Colburn set out to change the central command structure of the Service. The physical move out of the main Justice building space created literal and figurative separation. In *Lawmen*, Ted Calhoun explained how Colburn simultaneously began reconstruction and aggressive expansion. He wanted to speed up training in modern policing methods, while launching into new, relevant duty areas in development. This was evident in the formation of both a formalized witness security program and the Special Operations Group.[11] In one newsletter entry, Colburn thanked Federal Bureau of Investigation Director J. Edgar Hoover for making the agency's firing range available to U.S. Marshals personnel. At the same time, Colburn announced the formation of the U.S. Marshals Training Academy. It would "accommodate continuous basic training, as well as advanced specialized training seminars."[12]

People either strongly liked or disliked Colburn. He was gruff and believed in tight order, but valued good relations with the local police forces. Elizabeth Howard, who worked as a clerk-typist while taking classes at American University, added that Director Colburn "was one of those friendly types ... he loved to engage you in conversation no matter what your rank and title was—which I found soothing to some degree."[13]

Director Colburn found support among the USMS leadership as well. Bill Hall, the general counsel under Turner, was a natural counterpart. The soft-spoken Hall understood Colburn's grand plans. Synnott initially remained on-board as Deputy Director. Donald Hill, an old police department companion from San Diego, came on board to manage facilities. Reis Kash also saw increased duties.[14]

Colburn fired off a series of directives by late 1970 that seemed ambitious and certain to draw fire from the field. In "United States Marshals Service Directive 70-8," issued September 2, 1970, he notified all U.S. Marshals and their deputies of the requirement to file incident reports with the Director "prior to any notification of Federal, state, or local authorities."[15] xception was made for incidents requiring the attention of the FBI. The message was clear: no U.S. Marshal was to bypass Colburn.[16]

In January 1971, the Department of Justice ceded hiring and separation authority to the Director for employees up to Grade 13 in the General Series, with the exception of appointed offices and attorneys. This directive became the genesis of the human resources function of the

Marshals Service, and the creation of a personnel office. An outline revealed the responsibilities of this office that included examinations, recruitment literature, a summer "Youth Opportunity Program," merit promotion, and a fully developed training program.[17]

Bill Hall was promoted to Associate Director. He noted that Colburn quickly set up a training center of sorts. Al Butler and Don Forsht set up a two-week training program that shifted the emphasis of the Service from riot control to court security and protective operations. They brought the course to the field, with the first site in Brownsville, Texas. However, Hall claimed Colburn's real interest was in prisoner transportation.[18]

With the addition of a new core of leadership and an operational plan, Director Colburn moved the U.S. Marshals in a different direction. While the 1960s dealt more with external events, the 1970s was about internal focuses. As the deputies adjusted to the changes, individual duty programs formalized.

CHAPTER 7

THE RESURGENCE OF
PROTECTIVE OPERATIONS

Director Colburn established priorities in many directions at once. He was trying to establish a centralized and efficient bureau. The Marshals Service needed to change and adapt to the new missions ahead of it.

The Marshals Service initiated new programs to address protection of the judiciary, in-air piracy, and witness protection. Partnerships with the Department of Transportation and other Justice agencies grew. The partnership with the former began after a series of high-profile hijackings of airplanes that plagued the country in the late 1960s. However, the connection to the U.S. Marshals intensified after a transported federal prisoner tried to commandeer a flight.[1]

On July 5, 1968, U.S. Marshal Beverly W. Perkins of the District of Nevada sent the front page of the *Las Vegas Sun* to Washington. In bold letters, the headline read *"Dynamite" Ruse Backfires.* Trans World Airlines Flight 329, en route from Kansas to San Francisco, created the key ripple in the formation of a new program. On that flight, federal prisoner John Hamilton Morris had attempted to escape and to redirect the plane to Hermosillo, Mexico. He was on his way to trial in San Francisco to face robbery charges. Airline regulations prevented Morris from being handcuffed. Although escorted by two deputies, Morris told the flight attendant that he had dynamite in a container under his seat, and mentioned the man next to him was armed. She panicked, not realizing he was an escorted prisoner. Morris' trick worked long enough to cause embarrassment, because a second stewardess overheard the conversation and alerted authorities. The deputies forced the prisoner back into his seat, and the plane made an emergency landing in Las Vegas, where police surrounded it on the ground. After some time, officials sorted out the mischief. Morris' "container" was packed with nothing but his clothes and a toothbrush.[2]

Still, McShane was not amused. He wrote in large scrawl on a blue-colored memo to his assistants, "What is Status of this?"[3]

While air piracy was first addressed in the Federal Aviation Act of 1958, news of a rash of aircraft-related crimes reached the Office of the Deputy Attorney General. In turn, the U.S. Marshals were tasked with developing an integral program. As acting director, Don Synnott signed off on the measure, creating the Air Piracy Initiative, the precursor of today's federal air marshals that are part of the Transportation Security Administration, Department of Homeland Security.[4]

United States Marshals Service Directive 69-9, dated October 24, 1969, was entitled *Anti-Hijacking Support to Federal Aviation Administration*. Deputies were assigned to "provide police protection aboard air carrier aircraft and, specifically, to prevent crimes of a nature specified" as aircraft piracy, interference with crew members, crimes or carrying weapons onboard, and false information contingent to these matters.[5]

Deputy U.S. Marshal John T. Brophy, stationed in the Southern District of New York, assembled a unit with the daunting job of fully developing the Air Piracy Program. They set standards for response to various forms of threats or disruptions. By the middle of 1970, the "sky marshals" became a special hybrid deputy trained for such duties. In the event of a "disruption," authorities would contact the district office, which in turn would provide personnel. Some of the monitoring procedures common today were enacted in 1970, such as paying attention to cash purchases of tickets or one-way travel. In addition, guidelines of passenger behavioral patterns were proposed for the deputies to consider as potential threats.[6]

The plan was easier to draft than to implement. Brophy depended on the assistance of each U.S. Marshal, who often viewed centralized authority with suspicion. Deputies in the Air Piracy Program complained to Brophy about limited jurisdiction. *Police Chief,* the official magazine of the International Association of Chiefs of Police, covered the regulations in its May 1971 issue. The original "Sky Marshals" had "specific jurisdiction under the offense of air piracy from the time power is applied to an aircraft prior to take off until the time the power is removed at landing."[7]

The program adopted additional guidelines, and Director Colburn called for new hiring in January 1971. The training period was brief—at first in one intensive session under the jurisdiction of the Federal Aviation Administration. The first "Sky Marshals" were considered temporary hires with an eye toward converting them to full career-conditional status later. The following month Brophy apportioned manpower to 33 initial airports with emphasis given to major cities like New York and Los Angeles, and locations like Honolulu. Even with added personnel, the new mission taxed some districts heavily and stretched resources. Director Colburn often had to remind these jurisdictions of the importance of the program.[8]

The Air Piracy Program received extensive coverage in the news media. In August 1971, *U.S. News & World Report* followed up with news articles on its effectiveness. By then 229 arrests had been executed on the ground, and about 110 pistols, knives, and other weapons seized. Passengers could voluntarily register weapons with the deputies prior to boarding. It did not hurt that the administrative leader of the Sky Marshals was retired Lt. Gen. Benjamin O. Davis, the famous leader of the Tuskegee

Airmen in World War II. He attained the position of Assistant Secretary of Transportation for Environment, Safety, and Consumer Affairs.[9]

Assistant Secretary Davis knew he was fighting a different kind of war—one of persuasion and politics. In his interview for the *U.S. News & World Report* story, Davis was upbeat. He noted a "distinct turnabout in the hijacking situation. We have stopped being 'patsies.' The Government and the airlines have adopted an attitude of resistance—not recklessness, but a willingness to act when the opportunity arises."[10] Colburn advised Davis periodically, writing in September 1971 that in light of a recent court decision, both the FAA and U.S. Marshals had to "effectively police their actions." He gave General Davis an example of significance "in eleven of the last fourteen hijackings the hijacker met the profile but was either not designated a selectee or cleared for boarding by airline personnel."[11]

Regular accounts of the Air Piracy Program appeared in the *United States Marshals Service Newsletter.* In October 1971, Deputy U.S. Marshal Budd Johnson of the Southern District of California ran down a suspect trying to run past a magnetometer at Lindburgh Field. Johnson needed most of his vigor to catch the man, but then he realized why. In the suspect's suitcase were 35 ounces of heroin! The *Newsletter* humorously noted, "Deputy Johnson is our unanimous candidate for the 1972 Olympics."[12] On September 4, 1971, Deputy U.S. Marshal Gerald Perman wrestled with a female suspect in the Detroit Metropolitan Airport. She was carrying two sticks of primer powder, a loaded pistol, and a letter demanding the release of two African American militants from prison. In subduing the suspect, Deputy U.S. Marshal Perman foiled a hijacking plot. There were many more foiled attempts, too many to recount.[13]

REVITALIZATION OF COURT SECURITY

Court security enhancements changed with the times. Twenty-seven-year-old Dave Neff joined the U.S. Marshals as a deputy in April 1971.

Trainers Ed Scheu and Dick Reynolds taught him a basic class over a two-week period in the "Safeway Building." Neff noted that very little was taught in court security training—"not much at all, other than the deputies attended court on request of the judiciary, or whenever the marshal told you to go to court... You learned in the district where you worked about court security..."[14]

Former U.S. Marshal Jesse Grider of Kentucky recounted that during the integration of the schools in the 1960s in Alabama, Judge Frank M. Johnson in Montgomery presided over a case involving the Ku Klux Klan. A burning cross was placed in the front yard of the house of the judge's parents. A long protective detail of the judge ensued. Soon after, Grider attended several schools to learn more about investigative techniques focusing on court security. Reis Kash and others believed Grider was their man in that arena. "They felt that since I was familiar with operations of federal courts and so forth that I might be the guy who could be of some help to security... because I did know the functions from the field," recalled Grider in 1991.[15]

In fact, Reis Kash had started surveying federal courthouses in 1970. During a breakout of a cellblock at a local court in California, a state judge named Haley was killed. The potential of a federal courthouse being stormed from the inside was not lost on Colburn or Kash. Knowing that multiple agencies resided in federal courthouses, Grider pointed out the need for a memorandum of agreement with those agencies, primarily the Postal Service and the Administrative Office of the United States Courts. Grider noted that the Secret Service had been considered for the role of providing security at the courts by members of the judiciary.[16]

Grider traveled to California to witness the security arrangements for the state trial of Charles Manson, the leader of a cult that savagely murdered actress Sharon Tate, coffee heiress Abigail Folger, and others in the summer of 1969. He had a wide circle of followers, so court security was a priority for the sheriff's office. Based on his observations of the security in place at that trial and his other experiences, he built a conceptual framework. Grider related, "We started doing surveys of all the buildings and make [sic] recommendations."[17]

BIRTH OF THE WITNESS SECURITY PROGRAM

In a U.S. Marshals newsletter dated November 1970, Director Colburn noted "sensitive witness security" as a new mission—alongside increased judicial security and air piracy functions. An act of Congress tasked the Attorney General, who in turn utilized the U.S. Marshal with the protection of witnesses with knowledge of matters pertaining to organized crime or "major criminal activity."[18]

The mystery surrounding witness protection—properly called the Witness Security Program, or WitSec by most people familiar with the mission—has produced much media interest over the course of its existence. The program has been portrayed in movies like *Eraser*, which depicted a fictitious futuristic program, and in cable television series like *The Sopranos*, where the boss of a crime family acidly speaks about the number of "squealers" in the program. Truth is stranger than fiction, and in this case, most people only had vague ideas about the early program.[19]

The federal government created WitSec out of necessity because of the large numbers of organized crime victims killed or assaulted prior to testifying in court and to protect them after they did. In 1941, mobster Abe Reles, who intended to testify against the mob, fell from his hotel room window while under guard. Witnesses to murders and other criminal activity by the growing Italian-American-based criminal syndicates frequently wound up dead. It became apparent to law enforcement and lawmakers that La Cosa Nostra, or "the American Mafia," existed and thrived in the United States.[20]

After the infamous 1957 Apalachin Conference, when police in New York caught a number of mob chieftains in a raid, and other reversals of fortune by mafia figures, opportunities opened up for informants to work with law enforcement. Joseph Valachi, a member of the Genovese

Family in New York, turned informant and testified before Senator John McClellan's Subcommittee on Investigations in October 1963. He revealed key secrets of the La Cosa Nostra organization. He did so at the prompting of federal officials and at great risk to his life, but also to save himself. He had killed a man while in custody and was out of options. Photographs of the hearing show James McShane sitting right next to him during his testimony. Al Butler transported Valachi to and from his D.C. jail holding cell during the hearing.[21]

Butler recalled the inmate's fate thereafter. "I was one of the deputies who transported him to Michigan, to an institution and they had a suite for him... because he could not be around any inmates, and subsequently a few years later, the BOP transferred him down to Texas to get him out of the cold weather, and that's where he died. He died a natural death down there."[22]

Title V of the Organized Crime Control Act of 1970 (Public Law 91-452), created the original program, while the Comprehensive Crime Control Act of 1984, or Witness Security Reform Act, revised its parameters, keeping the general tenets of U.S. Marshals participation largely intact. The Department of Justice Criminal Division, through its Office of Enforcement Operations, along with U.S. Attorney's Offices as the requesting agency, primarily determines who enters or leaves the program. The Marshals Service does the yeoman's work that includes protecting, transporting, and securing new identities for the protected witnesses and their dependents. No participant following the guidelines of the Marshals has ever been harmed or killed while in the program. That success rate allows WitSec to remain a vital tool in the prosecution of criminal organizations and terrorists.[23]

Still, when the program was in its infancy, gangsters made imaginative attempts to quiet protected witnesses. Deputy U.S. Marshal John J. Partington worked with the primary departmental architect of the formalized program, Gerald Shur, on the case of one Joseph "the Animal" Barboza, a member of the New England-based Patriarca mob family. After

Barboza's 1966 arrest, Ray Patriarca murdered Barboza's allies and tried to kill him. Stuck in prison, the "Animal" decided to testify. Partington, who had grown up in Providence, knew a great deal about Patriarca. He was assigned to protect Barboza during the trial. The two men, protector and the protected, argued frequently. However, the protective operation worked because of a masterful job by the deputy in fooling potential assassins with misdirection. The Patriarcas sent disguised assassins and planted bombs to kill Barboza. However, all their attempts failed, and Barboza's testimony helped convict nearly a dozen members of the crime family. As Shur detailed in his book *WitSec*, co-authored by Pete Earley, Partington's ingenuity earned him the title "father of the Witness Security Program."[24]

The frequency of witness relocations increased, as did public and journalistic interest in the new USMS mission. By 1975, when Jack Cameron supervised the program, the *Washington Star* reported that the witness relocation program was "a growing $11 million dollar a year operation that will move some 700 witnesses and their families to new homes this year."[25] Today, more than 8,500 witnesses and 9,900 authorized family members have entered the program since its inception in 1970.[26]

SPECIAL OPERATIONS GROUP

The *Wall Street Journal* reported unrest in Puerto Rico on June 10, 1970. The reports caught the attention of Congress and the U.S. Navy, who conducted munitions exercises in the vicinity. The U.S. Marshals were sent in. After becoming involved, Marshals Service leadership realized the need for a specially trained cadre of deputy marshals to be called up in a moment's notice to serve lawful actions in potentially hostile environments and sensitive situations. On the flight back to the mainland, while debriefing about the recent sensitive mission that could have turned out poorly, Director Colburn and Associate Director Hall borrowed parts of an idea first planted by former Chief U.S. Marshal Turner to form the Special Operations Group, or SOG.[27]

The two executives, along with U.S. Marshal Jose Lopez, Inspector Jim Gardner, and two deputies, had just executed federal arrest warrants on Puerto Rico's Culebra Island. For many years, U.S. armed services performed military exercises with live munitions, like missiles and bombs. The local residents of the island grew tired of the noise, dangers, and intrusions of the exercises and staged protests on the beaches to prevent use by the military. Attorney General Mitchell tasked the Marshals Service with ensuring order and safety during the exercises, and to remove unlawful agitators. Director Colburn had a difficult time relying on the older riot control protocols used during the Civil Rights days.[28]

The Puerto Rican Independence Party (P.I.P.) occupied a part of the United States Naval Station used for military exercises, and used the tactic to stop them. Intelligence revealed at least some of the occupants were armed. Bench warrants were issued for six of the protestors. The warrants required a great deal of legal work before Colburn could fly in deputies for the operation. Therefore, he personally led an arrest team with Hall, Lopez, Gardner, and the other deputies. Hall reported that the "weather was extremely foul with high winds and driving rains" in the middle of the night when the helicopter deployed the arrest team in an area occupied by P.I.P. The helicopter landing shocked the occupants, who gave little resistance. The team brought the arrested members back to San Juan. When the situation at Culebra Island ended, the need for a permanent team was evident. [29]

In 1971, Director Colburn created the Special Operations Group, or SOG, by the authorization of Attorney General Mitchell. SOG represented the first official, uniformed deputy marshals. The use of uniforms by deputies was originally Carl Turner's idea when he briefly led the U.S. marshals. Colburn considered uniforms on a smaller scale, for this express purpose.[30]

SOG participants were trained in tactics for sensitive missions, such as riot control and rescue operations. They were drawn from deputy ranks within the districts and created a nationwide unit to respond to any situation calling for their services.[31] SOG could be called upon quickly by the Attorney General or Director, without the political obligations making a formal request through individual U.S. Marshals. However, calling upon the deputies required coordination with the districts.[32]

Hall explained, "Wayne Colburn and I were talking over about the need for a special disciplined unit to handle these situations. We began looking around, and found our men in Bill Whitworth, Al Butler, and Jim Gardner. These men knew how to put it together."[33]

SOG members originally wore bright blue "flight suits," designed to make the unit easily recognizable. However, the uniform brought ridicule, and Hall even noted that the bright color made ideal targets. Modifications in color mitigated any need for worry. However, the uniform was notable as the first in the organization.[34]

The first SOG team trained in April 1971. The *United States Marshals Service Newsletter* in October 1971 announced that SOG provided a force for ready and rapid response. On an early mission, SOG provided security support for a trial in Birmingham at the request of the U.S. marshal. A woman attempted to bring in a .38 caliber pistol into the court, but members of the SOG reacted quickly to avert possible tragedy. With the announcement came widespread interest in joining and an informal competition ensued. However, there were restrictions on which deputies could apply for SOG positions.[35]

Hall wrote in the newsletter on this very issue:

> There is a misconception in some offices that only one deputy per district will be allowed to apply for the Special Operations Group. This is incorrect and contrary to the Director's policy. All deputies who feel that they meet the requisite standards of physical condition, attitude, and willingness to accept dangerous assignments under adverse conditions, are encouraged to apply.[36]

In a memorandum dated September 4, 1973, General Counsel John Lockie, Hall's successor in that position, solidified the legal authority for

SOG's use. In the memo, Lockie justified SOG's formation by highlighting the historical duties of the United States Marshal, including the similarity to those of a sheriff "at common law." This included the execution of lawful process of the federal courts and "general enforcement, maintenance, and administration of Federal authority. *United States v. Krapf*, 285 F2d 647, 649 (3rd Cir., 1961)."[37] Lockie emphasized that the Attorney General had the authority to task any employee or officer of the Department of Justice to perform duties within its purview, and that SOG followed properly issued orders. While this legal opinion covered SOG's past activities, Lockie warned Colburn about the requests to assist other executive departments—hinting that use of SOG must be carefully considered.[38]

One peculiar SOG activation entailed security for the International Transportation Exhibit at Dulles Airport, a short distance from Washington, D.C., in northern Virginia, in late May and early June 1972. The request came from the Department of Transportation, implying an extension of its air piracy efforts. Through foul weather, 15 SOG deputies assisted in the screening of more than two million visitors to the expo and provided general enforcement. Additionally, some of the enforcement personnel wore suits or dresses to freely mix with the crowd.[39]

Today, SOG is comprised of volunteer deputy U.S. marshals who complete rigorous training in specialties such as high-risk entry, explosive breaching, sniper/observer, rural operations, evasive driving, less-lethal weapons, waterborne operations, and tactical medical support. Members also act as the agency's primary response force for any critical incident nationally and worldwide as ordered by the Attorney General or the Marshals Service director.

GUARDING PRECIOUS THINGS

On October 12, 1970, U.S. Marshal Raymond J. Howard of the Eastern District of Wisconsin sent Reis Kash a memo with the subject line—"Moon Rock Security." The moon rock was brought back by astronauts at a time when space travel was new and exciting. Wisconsin Representive William Steiger brought the sample for viewing at museums in Ripon and Fond du Lac and entrusted it to Howard. Howard received it, and then arranged for overnight storage in a bank vault. While not the first time deputies were entrusted with guarding items of high historic or monetary value, it was certainly the most odd.[40]

The *Milwaukee Sentinel* reported that fellow law enforcement officers played a joke on the Marshal by leaving an old bone in a paper bag that contained the tag, "Left Here by Congressman Steiger to Be Turned Over to Marshal Howard." Marshal Howard's stewardship of the moon rock ended on September 5, when he delivered it to a colonel of the Minnesota Air National Guard outside Oshkosh.[41]

Deputy U.S. marshals also guarded precious objects obtained through federal court seizures. The government seized a large number of valuable commodities during the 1970s. In 1978, three deputies from the Central District of California confiscated a collection of gems and jewelry that would have given pause to anyone. Deputy U.S. Marshals Bill Keith, John Diluberto, and Michael Southern attempted to locate and seize the collection of a San Diego financier who had lost a major federal court case. In a panic, the financier rushed to "sell" them to a phony buyer. While being inspected in a bank lobby, the jewels remained under the watchful eyes of the three deputies who waited for the opportunity to seize them. The collection valued at about $21 million dollars, at the time, included an eight-pound ruby and two slightly smaller sapphires. Diluberto remarked that potential buyers never suspected an undercover operation foiled the "sale."[42]

OTHER ADVENTURES IN EARLY PUBLICITY

Over the years, deputy marshals secured the Watergate tapes, an Edsel automobile, and even the North Carolina copy of the Bill of Rights.

Deputies appeared to be temporary caretakers of such objects, but they managed the items with pride and trust. The duties generated publicity.

Movies about the Old West deputy U.S. marshals, often featured in action sequences, appealed to mass audiences. In the past, people connected with the Old West image of deputies as portrayed by Clint Eastwood, John Wayne, and Randolph Scott. Over time, some felt the U.S. Marshals needed to remake their own image. In late 1971, U.S. Marshal Gaylord Campbell for the Central District of California even asked Director Colburn about the possibility of a television series. Partially to coordinate responses to an increasingly interested public, Headquarters found a specialist to handle such special projects and to focus the message of the Marshals Service regarding important cases and organizational changes.[43]

Director Colburn hired Public Information Officer Christian Rice to address the numerous media requests, as well as film and book proposals during the early 1970s. He was the first head of public affairs within the organization, and immediately saw Hollywood's interest.[44] Rice notified a prominent producer that "there are two other independent producers who have expressed an interest in an arrangement with the Marshals Service."[45] In the end, government bureaucracy made it difficult to bring any such large-scale public affairs projects to fruition.

Several U.S. Marshals appointed during this period brought their own publicity to the agency. Two Texans, T. Parnell McNamara and Clint Peoples, recalled an image of the Old West. U.S. Marshal William "Big Six" Henderson from Kentucky had been a famous revenue agent. When asked if he earned the moniker for handling a weapon, "Big Six" explained that he had been a semi-professional baseball pitcher. U.S. Marshal Peoples spent a career as a Texas Ranger, and wore his old guns until the day of his swearing-in. The ceremony took place at the federal courthouse in Dallas on May 15, 1974, and Peoples wore his black alligator boots and a blue suit.[46]

U.S. Marshal Campbell never shied away from the spotlight in Los Angeles. A lengthy article entitled "The Growing Role of the U.S. Marshall [sic]" appeared in the *Los Angeles Herald-Examiner* on September 24, 1971, the agency's 182nd birthday. Campbell noted that the district had grown from 16 deputies in 1969 to 89 when he was marshal. He told *Examiner* reporter Richard Cox, "Ask 75 per cent of the people what a marshal does and they won't be able to tell you... television is killing us."[47]

In reality, television programs up to that point had only highlighted the historical image. As television portrayed the Marshals' Old West image, accuracy often took a back seat. Over the course of the next decade, current events and the media would refurbish that inaccurate and nostalgic image.

Director Colburn came up with a splashy magazine called *The Marshal Today* in autumn 1973. Although the hiring of Rice gave it emphasis, the idea of an internal agency publication was not new. The *U.S. Marshals Bulletin* had been in existence since 1946. However, the content was limited to the bare essentials. There were few pictures, stilted text, and a plain blue or yellow paper cover. Each cover of the new publication featured deputy U.S. marshals in action. Notable accounts appeared on key operations, along with accomplishments and helpful information for employees. It kept employees informed with a more interesting format. In 1978, *Marshal Today* transitioned into *The Pentacle*. Initially simple in style, the publication dropped the cover photo and utilized a newsletter format with more pictures and broader news stories.[48]

Although Director Colburn had left the agency by the time *The Pentacle* appeared, an agency publication continued to prosper for decades. Employee Susan Olson served as editor of the *Pentacle* in the early days, and later Beverly Dodd took over as managing editor. While the look continued to change, the *Pentacle* lasted into the early 1990s.[49]

CHAPTER 8

FACING PROTEST AND PERIL

ENTER AIM

Native Americans interacted with and sometimes became deputy U.S. marshals in the "rough-and-tumble" territories of the nation's early history. In the early period of territorial settlement of the current state of Oklahoma, for instance, a number of Cherokee, Choctaw, and Creek tribesmen joined up to enforce the law as members of the mounted tribal police, known as the "lighthorse." When federal territorial lines expanded into Indian Territory, some became deputies themselves. Historian Art Burton, in his book *Black, Red, and Deadly*, explained that the sheer size and diversity of the Indian Territory made for rapid law enforcement integration. Names such as Sam Sixkiller, who died in the line of duty, proved that federal reputation transcended race. However, in the 1970s, some tribal interactions with U.S. marshals were not always peaceful.[1]

In 1968, about 1,400 Native Americans of various tribes formed the American Indian Movement, or AIM, in Minnesota to pursue new policies. In the socially conscious 1960s, AIM was an expressive organization, patterned after other activist movements. They sought to demonstrate at symbolic locations and speak out on the plight of Native Americans.

In November 1969, they seized Alcatraz Island in San Francisco Bay. A large number of families, including women and children, formed encampments. The federal prison, once considered the most inescapable prison in America, had closed in 1964, leaving unattended fields and a hulking shell. The prison and land were entrusted to the stewardship of the General Services Administration (GSA), which had converted the defunct structure into a tourist attraction. However, there were tribal claims on the property. Adam Fortunate Eagle wrote in his book *Alcatraz! Alcatraz!* that several members of the Sioux staked claims on the island in 1964; he also noted that an attempted occupation by AIM was abandoned shortly before the arrival of several deputy U.S. marshals. An 1868 treaty suggested Native Americans could claim territory of the Federal Government "not used for specific purpose." AIM offered $5.64, the same amount proposed to the previous California tribe for the acreage. GSA valued the federal property at more than $2 million in 1964.[2]

On Thanksgiving 1969, approximately 100 AIM members occupied Alcatraz to enforce the claim. GSA initially felt the action was symbolic and temporary, and made no attempt to remove them. There appeared to be order in the occupying party, according to Adam Fortunate Eagle. In early 1970, AIM official and Mohawk tribesman Richard Oakes emerged as a spokesman. However, stability faltered when he was removed from the leadership role later that year. The island's lighthouse was utilized by activists. Although the Coast Guard extinguished the signal in May, the tribal occupants used generators to relight it. In June a fire broke out in an oil shed and destroyed several properties on the island. However, despite the conditions, the AIM members carried on.[3]

For about 18 months, the Federal Bureau of Investigation and U.S. Marshals watched. Over the long occupation, the AIM numbers on the island dwindled and they reported crimes among themselves. As a result of the living conditions, some became sick and others disillusioned. Some left Alcatraz and the remainder failed to come together as a cohesive group. When the number of occupants diminished to 50, the U.S. Marshals made their move.[4]

While Director Colburn and Associate Director Hall visited San Francisco in June 1971, an advance team from Headquarters under Bill Whitworth, James Corrales, and James Upper reported their findings. The group decided to try a landing on June 16 using SOG deputies. However, the date moved up when all but 17 occupants departed the island to sell copper fixtures removed from the facility for cash. On June 11, the SOG team, 20 deputies from San Francisco, and the leadership gathered in preparation for the initiative. After Colburn explained the plan, the team boarded two Coast Guard cutters.[5]

The landing was unopposed. The *United States Marshals Service Newsletter* relating the account noted that "anxious moments shared by all since it was deathly quiet, and the scene was perfect for an ambush."[6] The remaining 17 occupants included men, women, and children; the Marshals team removed them without incident or arrests. Instead, the activists were temporarily housed in hotels. An FBI team secured the island before any of the men who went ashore could return. This event marked the first of several skirmishes between AIM and the U.S. Marshals.[7]

DEADLY DUTIES AND TRAINING

The 1970s had its share of key moments of deadly consequence and brushes with ideological or political organizations. While AIM was an example of the latter, Director Wayne Colburn saw the extremes of both during his term. In simply doing the job, such as serving process or securing federal facilities, hardships arose in resolving crises.

In the districts, activity continued as before. U.S. Marshal W.B. "Big Six" Henderson—known for many years as a revenue agent, busting moonshine stills in his native Kentucky—traveled to serve process as a U.S. Marshal. In late 1971, he served a man he had arrested almost two decades earlier. The man had never paid his legal fines from the old incident and "Big Six" went to collect. His target asked, "Didn't you arrest my son for bootlegging while I was gone?" Henderson answered, "Yes, sir, and I got your daddy for making liquor too. I guess you could call that a family affair."[8]

Closer to headquarters, four deputy U.S. marshals observed orders to escort a federal prisoner to his father's funeral in Washington, D.C., on September 24, 1971. The deputies waited on guard in the church as the prisoner's family and friends filed past the casket. One mourner returned with a weapon. He held the deputies at gunpoint, and took their firearms and prisoner. The man warned the deputies not to follow them into the street unless they wanted to die. The prisoner and his rescuer fled. A few blocks away, Deputy U.S. Marshal Norman Sherriff came across them. The five-year veteran was well-liked and considered one of the most professional deputies in the office. He engaged the two criminals in gunfire and was shot. A squad of officers caught the men minutes later, but Sherriff was dead.[9]

Director Colburn memorialized his lost deputy with a solemn internal ceremony, saying a few words, followed by a moment of silence and a prayer. The rare, tragic death reminded all in the Marshals Service how dangerous their job was.[10]

The organization renewed its focus on training personnel. Employee Carleton Parish credited Frank Sidella, a specialist with a military background, with setting up a brand-new training academy at the Safeway Building. Parish assisted Sidella's assistant, Frank Cefalu, to develop audiovisuals for the initial training programs.[11]

Sidella had a daunting job developing the training academy to handle waves of new trainees. Sidella possessed a good organizational background, and worked closely with Cameron to establish the academy. One memorandum from Cameron to Sidella, dated October 19, 1971, stated, "Mr. Colburn mentioned today that he would like your ideas on a CDUSM [Chief Deputy U.S. Marshal] training program which would begin as a correspondence course and terminate in a 2 week class in our

Academy. This would give us a chance to observe the CDUSMs & know who to transfer or promote, etc."[12]

BIA TAKEOVER

It was no secret AIM detested the Bureau of Indian Affairs. In the autumn of 1972, members of AIM arrived in Washington. They wanted to set up camp at a visible landmark in the capital city to protest, conduct workshops, and plan educational events. Their plan recalled the "Resurrection City" concept on the National Mall of just a few years before. However, the camp featured programming on broken treaties between tribal nations and the United States over history. The theme made encampment suggestions by the BIA difficult. Officials suggested several alternative locations, but AIM leadership refused. Instead they took over the BIA building on November 3, 1972.[13]

The AIM members entered the building at the end of the day and reportedly numbered around 500, representing 250 different tribes. They blocked all entrances and renamed the building "The Native American Embassy." Although a few employees remained, they escaped and were never in danger. A scuffle ensued with the building's security team, but AIM maintained control of the building. Russell Means emerged as the group's spokesman, and he notified reporters that they reached a deal with the White House and BIA to stay overnight. The four-story building was secured by the occupants. They removed chairs, photocopiers, and desks to make barricades.[14]

The takeover happened in the midst of the election contest between incumbent President Richard Nixon and Democratic challenger Senator George McGovern. While the *Washington Post* initially gave the AIM takeover adequate ink, it quickly faded from the headlines. The election overshadowed almost all other news.[15]

Two days later, the occupants remained in the building. Means and the AIM national field director, Dennis Banks, focused on a manifesto that the *Washington Post* called "a list of demands." A federal district judge upheld the Army's refusal to allow AIM to conduct a religious service in Arlington National Cemetery. Another ruling ordered the occupants to vacate the BIA building. A U.S. Marshal handed the eviction notice to AIM leadership, and Means told reporters he expected the police would assault the building. The U.S. Marshals remained vigilant.[16]

The occupation of BIA lasted for five days. Associate Director of Operations Reis Kash assessed whether or not to assault the building. At great risk to himself, he slipped into the building dressed as a janitor. When discovered, Kash convinced the AIM members he was there to clean up. He took detailed notes and created a report to convince others not to breach the building. He stated an assault would likely lead to hand-to-hand combat situations and casualties.[17]

Bill Hall later indicated that the nation's tragic experience at Kent State University in 1970 was a factor in the decision not to engage the occupants in the BIA building. Officials at the Justice and Interior Departments decided against any plan to force removal. Instead, they offered the AIM occupants travel money and a ceremonial entry to Arlington Cemetery if they departed peacefully. The demonstrators accepted the money and headed west—to Wounded Knee, South Dakota.[18]

WOUNDED KNEE

The culmination of events between the Marshals Service and AIM took place in South Dakota, not in Washington, D.C. The incidents at BIA and Alcatraz created an inevitable boiling point between the two organizations. Colburn did not seek the confrontation at Wounded Knee, but the relatively new Special Operations Group was fully tested there. Much has been written and disputed about the events and general tactics conducted at Pine Ridge in 1973. However, 40 years later, both sides involved in this confrontation had learned much about the other from the conflict.

AIM sought another symbolic place to unite their cause. The Pine Ridge Reservation in South Dakota was the scene of the famous 1890 altercation that ended the life of Lakota Sioux Chief Sitting Bull and later left many dead. In that historic incident, a pitched battle against the military resulted in many deaths. AIM leaders Dennis Banks and Russell Means chose Pine Ridge strategically and symbolically for their next action.[19]

The president of the Sioux Tribe at the reservation, Richard Wilson, did not welcome AIM and set up roadblocks to hamper their movement. A small BIA police force sat in close proximity, and other federal agencies assisted, but AIM overmatched any potential opposition. A small group of AIM members took over several government buildings within the reservation, but the most visible structure they held was a white framed church located on top of a hill. They flew the AIM flag over the church in plain view.[20]

The Interior Department requested assistance, and the Justice Department sent SOG to South Dakota through departmental channels. They utilized military gear and wore military fatigues. Military surplus vehicles, including tanks and jeeps, were present. Federal responders were concerned about snipers. However, when the SOG members arrived in February 1973, nothing indicated a lengthy operation. Negotiations between the federal government and AIM began as deputies and FBI agents dug in around the perimeter. In the bitter cold of February and March, SOG deputies coordinated with Headquarters. Snowstorms produced blizzard-like conditions. Deputy U.S. Marshal Ernest C. Tautimes recalled that Hall came out the morning after a particularly vicious storm to thank him for standing a 24-hour shift without any relief.[21]

Only periodically, violence arose. At night, AIM members crossed the plain close to the federal encampments. The only serious fighting took place in late March, when members attacked all of the six roadblocks. U.S. Marshal Lloyd Grimm of the District of Nebraska stood up in the open to observe AIM movements. A bullet seriously wounded him in the back and chest, permanently injuring his spine and committing him to a wheelchair for the rest of his life. Hall observed the horror from only 30 feet away. An anti-AIM Oglala Sioux Council Member, Leo Wilcox, received threats for his stance. He was found dead in his burned car just outside the reservation. Inspector Wayne McMurtray, one of two SOG deputy commanders, sustained wounds from shell fragments as he drew fire to determine the position of gunfire.[22]

Director Colburn knew the Wounded Knee operation was risky. Negotiations continued for 10 weeks, while patience prevailed and a direct assault was avoided. The long stand-off finally ended on May 8, 1973. The occupying AIM members were arrested and left their arms behind.[23]

HEADQUARTERS REORGANIZATION, BUREAU STATUS, AND POLITICS

After the events at Wounded Knee, changes came quickly. Shortly afterwards, the U.S. Marshals Service received bureau status with approval by Attorney General Richard Kleindienst. Director Colburn reorganized the agency to meet increased responsibilities. The Internal Services Office formed, which combined the Management, Training, Personnel, and Internal Inspections Divisions. Jack Cameron rejoined the U.S. Marshals Service as Associate Director for Internal Services. He forwarded a statement to Director Colburn about an upcoming budget hearing. He believed that Colburn faced a "growing interest in employee unions," as well as requirements for new programs, challenges about duplications of effort, and dramatic increases in training due to the growth in personnel.[24]

On May 17, 1973, DOJ Order 516-73 listed the U.S. Marshals Service as a bureau. Colburn now had the ability to finance operations without the extra departmental oversight. The Department of Justice no longer needed to monitor the day-to-day financial activity of the 94 district offices.[25]

An organizational chart in 1973 showed an increase in agency strength. Colburn retained John W. Lockie as general counsel and three associate directors. Don Hill was the Associate Director for Administration. The two others were Jack Cameron, who led Internal Services; and Bill Hall, who oversaw Operations. Hall became Deputy Director on August 5, 1973; he had served a dual role for three years.[26]

Effective August 13, 1973, the new realignment rapidly changed the middle leadership ranks. Anthony J. Furka took over as Chief of Prisoner Coordination, replacing Joe Wasielewski. Bart Schmitt was promoted to Assistant to the Associate Director for Administration Don Hill. Frank Vandegrift, formerly Chief Deputy U.S. Marshal in the District of Columbia, headed to Headquarters as Chief of Court Security and Safety. These moves represented a changing of the guard. Ken Holecko was promoted to Chief of Labor Relations with the realignment. Sylvia Forst, the front office assistant who was one of the last administrative links to the Palmer and McShane eras, retired in March 1973.[27]

Temporarily rescinded in October 1973, DOJ Order 565-74 again listed the U.S. Marshals Service as a bureau on May 11, 1974, followed by another order nine days later that removed some of the organization's independent fiscal controls. The reason appeared to be that Attorney General Richardson disagreed with his predecessor.[28]

An unprecedented political experience coincided with their fluctuating bureau status. As part of the Executive Branch within the U.S. Department of Justice, the U.S. Marshals answered to the President, typically through the attorney general. Additionally, they carried out the orders of the Judicial Branch issued by federal judges and magistrates. That meant U.S. marshals served papers on the powerful as well.

In 1973 as part of an awkward and legal twist of jurisdiction, marshals served subpoenas on the sitting President of the United States, Richard Nixon, and his aides. Allegations of misconduct by the commander-in-chief relating to the break-in at the Watergate complex created a national crisis, and set the Marshals Service on a peculiar course in U.S. history.

Deputy U.S. Marshal Melvin McDowell was in Washington, D.C., on
the night of October 20, 1973. One of many deputies on detail from out of
district, he glanced at the television and heard that the Watergate Special
Prosecutor, Archibald Cox, wanted certain White House tapes turned
over. In response, the White House ordered Attorney General Elliott
Richardson, who had replaced Kleindienst, to fire Cox. Instead, Richardson
resigned, as did his deputy, William Ruckelshaus, when given the same
orders. The Solicitor General then fired Cox. This series of events, known
as the Saturday Night Massacre, drew in the U.S. Marshals.[29]

Officials at USMS Headquarters ordered McDowell to report to the
Watergate prosecutor's office and secure the facility once Cox left. Several
deputies were posted at office doors on several floors. All persons entering
and exiting showed identification and signed in and out. Utilizing the
building's security force, the deputies controlled the office until relieved
the next morning. This action would not be the last service deputies
performed relating to Watergate.[30]

Tocks Island

Wounded Knee did not represent the U.S. Marshals' last controversy
with protestors. In the early 1970s a small sliver of an island in the
middle of the Delaware River near Stroudsburg, Pennsylvania, became
the epicenter for hippie living and the beatnik lifestyle. The Army Corps
of Engineers wanted to construct a dam to generate a fresh water supply
for New York City and Philadelphia, while creating a vast lake and
recreational area between Pennsylvania and New Jersey. In the later 1960s,
Congress appropriated the necessary funds for the federal government
to purchase the privately owned land of Tocks Island in the Delaware
River, but delays by the Delaware River Basin Commission and other
parties lasted several years. The Corps of Engineers slowly began the
process to remove or demolish the empty buildings on the property.[31]

In August 1970, a court order halted a proposed rock music festival on the island. The vacant buildings filled with squatters, who passed the word to others that empty residences were free. The numbers swelled to 120 men, women, and children, and brought development plans to a crawl. By the summer of 1971, the Corps of Engineers began destruction of residential structures after ensuring they were empty. However, the squatters armed themselves and threatened the Corps of Engineers.[32]

The Corps took their case to the Department of Justice, and on September 2, 1971, U.S. District Court Judge William J. Nealon issued a Writ of Assistance to U.S. Marshals to "remove River people or Squatters from three tracts of land in Monroe and Pike Counties."[33]

By this time, the Supervisor of the USMS Civil Disturbance Unit, William C. Whitworth, reported that 20-50 squatters occupied the restricted area. Further, the Writ of Assistance was limited to four structures linked to criminal activity. With the concurrence of the Deputy Attorney General, Whitworth and Bill Hall concentrated on specific housing tracts to execute the court order. U.S. marshals found illegal drugs in one of the structures and state police removed the occupants. Whitworth mapped the area and noted that the number of squatters in the surrounding building increased to about 25 people.[34]

For several years, the occupants proved to be troublesome. Law enforcement tallied 360 individual criminal acts, including arson, narcotic trafficking, and assault, since they arrived in 1970. They transformed the cluster of buildings and fields into an odd type of community, a self-contained group of collapsing buildings and fields replete with livestock. In the courts, the squatters appealed their eviction to no avail.[35]

On February 27, 1974, a SOG team of about 90 deputy marshals executed the court-ordered eviction. The approximately 66 squatters presented no problems, but many weapons were recovered. Concerned about procedure, Whitworth planned carefully. The occupants were given time to depart and a letter of information outlining procedures. Public Information Officer Rice, through the Department of Justice, issued a press release that explained the background and intent to reporters. Although intended to be as low profile as possible, Rice wrote several responses to bad press on the removal. With lessons learned from Wounded Knee, the deputies did their work quietly, serving eviction notices and only using handcuffs when necessary.[36]

SOG, working with the New Jersey and Pennsylvania State Police, started evictions along the five-mile increment of land. They allowed the squatters to remove belongings prior to escorting them off the property. Although loud, the crowd moved to the main road when ordered. Deputies collected 27 rifles, two crossbows, a sawed-off shotgun, six pistols, three pounds of marijuana, and two bags of heroin. They only needed to deploy tear gas once when one man refused to leave his shanty.[37]

Widespread praise countered the limited negative press on the court-ordered evictions at Tocks Island. Because of the sensitivity with which this operation was conducted, there was little criticism leveled against the Marshals Service, in contrast with the scalding press accounts generated by the Wounded Knee operation. Attorney General William Saxbe complimented the agency for "handling the Tocks Island eviction matter in an excellent manner."[38]

WATERGATE: TAPE AND SUBPOENA

In 1974, duties relating to Watergate continued. Deputy U.S. marshals carried the secret White House telephonic tapes, with their infamous gaps in the message that had been erased, in a steel box. They meticulously filled out multiple hand receipts, as experts in New York and Boston examined the content of the tapes. Maintaining the chain of custody, deputy marshals dutifully handled the evidence of national importance. Deputy U.S. Marshal Donald Waite made numerous trips north with the steel box. Waite remarked, "We would pick the box up from the clerk, and he would repeatedly warn us [of its importance]."[39]

On March 7, 1974, the court tasked Waite with delivery of the "Rose Mary Woods tapes," named after President Nixon's secretary, in the familiar steel box. Deputy Clerk James P. Capitanio of the U.S. District Court typed out a receipt for Waite to sign. Titled "IN RE—SUBPOENA DUCES TECUM ISSUED TO RICHARD M. NIXON FOR PRODUCTION OF TAPES, ETC,"[40] the complete text of the receipt read:

> Receipt is acknowledged, this date, from James P. Capitanio, U.S. District Court for the District of Columbia, of the items listed below, said items having been turned over me for the purpose of delivering same to the Court approved panel of experts:
>
> {a} Uher tape recorder, Universal #5000 Model, Serial No. 2321-33929 (Exhibit #60).
>
> {b} Ear phone for use on Uher tape recorder. (Exhibit #60-A).
>
> {c} Foot pedal for use on Uher tape recorder. (Exhibit #60-B).
>
> {d} Sealed envelope containing defective rectifier which panel of experts removed from Uher tape recorder set forth in {a}above. (See Exhibit A to receipt of Donald Waite filed 2-26-74–photograph of pen and ink notation on fron [sic] and back of envelope).
>
> {e} Original copy of June 20, 1972, EOB, tape, identified with markings on box "Start 6-12-72 (8AM) - End 6-20-72 (3:45 p.m.) run out."[41]

Deputy U.S. Marshal Gary Smith guarded the tapes on occasion, too. Like Waite, he understood the importance of working closely with U.S. District Court Judge John J. Sirica about duties related to the Watergate investigation. According to his hometown newspaper, one of Smith's prouder moments came from a letter from Judge Sirica extending his thanks. It read in part, "By your fine service you are a credit to yourself, as a citizen, and to the office of the United States Marshal."[42]

Protecting the Woods tapes comprised just one of several duties handled by deputy marshals during the Watergate investigation. The duty of serving subpoenas by the court to all those involved in Watergate was intense for the deputies.

In April 1974, Watergate prosecutor Leon Jaworski asked for additional tapes and papers of some 64 conversations. He invoked his power to issue a formal court-ordered subpoena. U.S. Marshal for the District of Columbia George K. McKinney, along with Deputy U.S. Marshal Kenneth Small, brought the subpoena to the President's defense counsel, James St. Clair. Judge Sirica gave the counsel until May 2 to comply with the order. The *New York Times* noted the only other subpoena previously issued had caused the dismissal of former Watergate Prosecutor Archibald Cox and the "Saturday Night Massacre," and cost Attorney General Elliot Richardson his job.[43]

Marshal McKinney later told the press that St. Clair told him to forget serving the paper. The lawyer challenged him on constitutional grounds before hanging up the phone. Calling again, McKinney informed St. Clair that he would "deputize every Secret Service agent in the White House" to serve the subpoena. The counsel again hung up the phone, but quickly relented and invited the Marshal to the Executive Office Building for a personal meeting with President Nixon.[44]

The marshal served at the pleasure of the President. Understandably, the duty made McKinney feel uneasy. "Anytime you're dealing with the chief executive in an adversarial role—that's different.... But I was worried. When backed into a corner, there was no telling what Nixon might do."[45]

The meeting between President Nixon and U.S. Marshal McKinney, which took place on April 18, 1974, turned out harmless. As he and Deputy U.S. Marshal Small entered an outer office, they saw President Nixon in the next room. Although Nixon and McKinney stared at each other, St. Clair took the subpoena and asked some questions. McKinney and Small left without any further contact with Nixon. The President resigned in August 1974.[46]

THE CELL BLOCK INCIDENT

On the heels of jail riots at Attica State Prison in New York and other facilities, a dangerous hostage situation and attempted prison break at a federal facility occurred in July 1974. Associate Director for Operations Reis Kash wrote the narrative:

> On the afternoon of July 11, 1974, two self-styled "professional criminals" with a long history of crimes of violence including escape and kidnapping were brought from the District of Columbia Jail to the cell block operated by the U.S. Marshals Service in the basement of the U.S. District Courthouse. The prisoners were to confer with counsel in connection with new and serious crimes. Though both were escape risks with an established propensity for violent crimes, it appears that no special precautions were taken in handling the two.
>
> At about 2:30 p.m., as the two criminals were being prepared for return to the District Jail, one suddenly produced a caliber .22 semi-automatic pistol, which he had apparently concealed in the small of his back, and forced unarmed deputies away from the main exit from the cell block. The two criminals attempted to flee from the cell block, but were frustrated in their dash for freedom by a third deputy who slammed the steel door in their faces, effectively preventing their immediate escape.
>
> At gunpoint, the two gangsters compelled the deputies to unlock the control room weapons cabinet from which the convicts took seven loaded handguns, including a 357 magnum revolver and a 9mm semi-automatic pistol. ... The convicts were then in effective control of the 10,000 square foot cell block and held four deputy U.S. marshals, two Department of Justice employees, one lawyer and 16 prisoners in their custody.[47]

Things looked bleak, and the news media quickly jumped into the fray. They kept track of every move made by the two inmates, Frank Gorham, Jr. and Robert Nathan Jones (also revealed to the press by authorities as Otis D. Wilkerson). The Metropolitan D.C. Police barricaded the area.

SOG studied the situation and conditions, and their leadership felt they could breach the cell block in just under a minute. The deputies were supported by personnel from the FBI, the Bureau of Prisons, and the Federal Protective Service. The D.C. Fire Department provided paramedics and ambulances on stand-by. A leadership contingent gathered in a courthouse office. They included U.S. Marshal George K. McKinney, U.S. Attorney Earl Silbert, Deputy Attorney General Lawrence Silberman, FBI agent-in-charge Donald Moore, Director of the Bureau of Prisons Norman Carlson, Division Chief Reis Kash, and Deputy Director Hall.[48]

Gorham threatened to kill the hostages if their freedom was not granted. Faced with the possibility of spending 73 years in prison for another escape, he had little to lose. Kash wanted to distract and exhaust the captors. Carlson provided prison psychiatrists to assist in the negotiation process. The group of leaders reviewed the records of the two prisoners. They decided to leave the cell block telephones in operation and allow the captors access to the press. The press, covering the Watergate grand jury at the time, limited some options to resolve the situation. While they considered explosives to access the block, the leadership contingent realized the presence of news cameras and crew ensured a larger than normal viewership of the attempted jail break.[49]

In a surprise move, the prisoners released Deputy U.S. Marshal Raymond Miller at 1:30 a.m. on July 12. Deputy U.S. Marshals Joseph Driskell, Calvin Mouton, and William Colquit, along with the other civilians, remained captive in the cell block. Miller was debriefed, and he confided to his wife that he felt like he "lived 10 years in a few hours."[50]

Gorham's father, an inmate at St. Elizabeth's Hospital, was brought to speak with his son. However, officials decided not to allow contact between father and son. By July 14, a group of people was gathered in the streets around the courthouse. The constant barrage of news media brought strong media opinions on the decision to keep the inmates inside the courthouse.[51]

That same morning, Gorham and Jones held a meeting with the hostages and notified them that "things would get serious" the next day. One of them brandished a fire axe. They wanted a plane to take them to Africa. Gorham and Jones emptied the cell block, and allowed the hostages access to the telephones and the open cell block. Mouton called Bill Hall and they quietly collaborated on an escape plan for the hostages. Mouton had found two brass keys left in the restroom. The keys, placed by deputies in the cell block office and lavatory, opened a door to a corridor with an elevator. That enabled hostage access to the elevator, but another key was needed to operate it.[52]

Hall came up with the solution. He would slip the elevator key into a box of sanitary napkins requested by a female hostage. Mouton knew the layout of the building and which elevator to use. Hall reached him and notified him where the key was. The box top was re-glued to look like new and mingled with other supplies for the hostages. The ploy worked. Mouton waited to launch the escape plan. All the hostages, except the lone prisoner, were notified. Later, as Gorham fell asleep and Jones was distracted on the telephone, all seven quickly moved to the elevator. There was a momentary scare when a door did not open to the first floor, but they were able to exit from the second floor. Once Gorham and Jones realized they had no hostages, they surrendered.[53]

Despite the heroic efforts of all involved, a wave of negative news about the U.S. Marshals Service followed. The *Washington Star-News* noted the cost of the operation exceeded $300,000. News stories surfaced about the available weapons in the block and how the inmates overpowered the deputies.[54]

Senator Edward M. Kennedy released a statement praising all in the settlement of the disturbance. In sending it, he sent a signed note to Chris Rice, "Rarely have I been prouder of the city than in these difficult hours, and I commend you for the role you played in avoiding a serious tragedy."[55]

Last Phase of Watergate

John D. Ehrlichman, a principal aide of Nixon's, was indicted for various criminal acts relating to the Watergate break-in and the trial date was set for early September 1974. The former president, at his San Clemente, California, home, was called as a defense witness at trial. The court issued another subpoena for Nixon. This time U.S. Marshal Gaylord Campbell in Los Angeles received the service order. Delivery of the mail containing the subpoena was delayed, and this caused the service of the order to Nixon to take longer than usual. Chris Rice, spokesman at Marshals Service Headquarters, announced the reason for the delay to dispel any fears of a conspiracy.[56]

When the subpoena arrived in Los Angeles, Campbell planned the arrangements for its delivery with officials in Washington, D.C., causing further delay. The *Los Angeles Times* reported Campbell's statement:

> Due to the unique nature of the case I am negotiating with Mr. Nixon's representative on a mutual agreement of time and place for service.[57]

On August 28, 1974, 11 days after Rice's announcement to the press, Director Colburn reported there was no rush in serving Nixon, as long as it was accomplished prior to Ehrlichman's September 9 trial. However, behind the scenes, Colburn and officials approached the issue with sensitivity. Rice instructed all Marshals Service parties not to notify the news media until after service of the subpoena. U.S. Marshal Campbell carried out his instructions.[58]

The Aftermath of Wounded Knee

Even as the political drama of Watergate was playing out that year, the ripple effect from Wounded Knee was felt into the following year. The trial of the two AIM leaders, Banks and Means, began on January 7, 1974, in St. Paul, Minnesota. Each faced 10 felony counts. There were six attorneys between the two defendants. One of the defense attorneys was William M. Kunstler, known for his work with antiwar defendants.[59] On the very eve of the beginning of the trial, they and several of the lawyers addressed a rally of a few thousand at the University of Minnesota. Banks told the crowd, "Let the public determine who is guilty at Wounded Knee... I am positive that when the public sees the evidence, they will have no choice but to declare that the U.S. Government is guilty."[60]

U.S. Marshal Harry D. Berglund kept careful watch on the conduct of the trial. The normal protective protocols were adjusted for the media, and the presence of actor Marlon Brando during the trial's first weeks heightened requirements. U.S. Marshal Berglund sent Hall a local newspaper editorial on the trial from January 30, which focused on security at the federal courthouse during the trial. It was apparent this may have been the writer's first encounter with a magnetometer:

> Federal marshals are trained to watch the blinking metal detectors as a security measure. Anyone entering the courthouse must pass through the detector. The light blinks the same for jewelry as it would for a gun. If the light blinks, the visitor, who may feel his privacy has been violated, must explain the metal that turned the light on.[61]

The editorial went on to comment on personal searches that AIM conducted,

> Two years ago at AIM's national convention at Cass Lake, armed security guards searched individuals and vehicles for weapons and alcoholic beverages. A physical search was more objectionable than metal detectors... At a meeting on the Pine Ridge Reservation the day before the occupation of Wounded Knee, supporters of AIM detained over two hundred people, including reporters, for more than two hours to prevent security leaks during critical deliberations with hereditary tribal leaders.[62]

Despite the pyrotechnics at the trial, several deputy U.S. marshals testified on the conditions of the property after the siege ended at

Wounded Knee. Deputy U.S. Marshal Jim Propotnick stated that he and three others were the first to enter the occupied area. While the team found no rifles or pistols, they located empty ammunition casings and grenades. A booby-trap bomb, activated by a trip wire, was disarmed. Propotnick found the device near a bunker dug by AIM members.[63]

Kunstler, one of the defense attorneys, sought to limit the ability of deputies providing security at the trial to speak to jurors, citing several high profile trials in which he claimed they had unduly influenced the members of the jury. He also asserted that the wounding of U.S. Marshal Grimm affected the jurors' objectivity.[64] The defense rested in August, after Russell Means declared the 1868 treaty rights superseded "all federal, state and local laws."[65] In the days afterward, spectators disrupted testimony, and amid the objections for the removal of the trouble-makers, a fistfight broke out between the deputies and the group. One of the deputies sprayed mace at a particularly aggressive protestor.[66]

In September 1974, the proceedings ended with charges dismissed against both Banks and Means. U.S. District Judge Fred J. Nicol had almost ended the trial in April when several key documents were reported to be altered. Although the U.S. Marshals were not involved, it affected witness testimony. When a juror became incapacitated with a stroke, prosecutors balked at allowing the remaining eleven jurors to render verdict. Judge Nicol then dismissed the charges. In December, the Justice Department appealed to no avail.[67]

The St. Paul trial did not end AIM's activism, but it blunted the intensity of their future activities for a time. When members occupied a New Mexico electronics plant, they accepted an offer of amnesty after a week. There was renewed violence at Pine Ridge in early 1975, but the Justice Department developed a new Indian Resources Section to deal with the conflict. This new section, separated from the General Litigation Section of the Land and Natural Resources Division, focused exclusively on natural resource rights for Native Americans. In retrospect, the events between AIM and the U.S. Marshals required a legal ending.[68]

AIM, Tocks Island, the Cell Block Incident, and Watergate represented critical issues of national significance. While some crossed over from the 1960s, the potential violence or fallout was clear. Although all of these challenges lasted well into 1974, they moved the U.S. Marshals Service into uncharted territory.

CHAPTER 9

REGIONALIZATION, PATTY HEARST AND GUAM

REGIONALIZATION AND OTHER REFORMS

Director Colburn developed a powerful management and oversight structure at Headquarters. However, few reforms provoked more controversy than Regionalization. This one initiative subdivided the director's own power into five distinct regions, each with a Regional Director. This concept seemed to portend an eventual end to a centralized Headquarters with one director. Why was Colburn making such a drastic shift in leadership policy? In fact, he wanted five directors to promote closer harmony with the district offices. Each U.S. Marshal remained a presidential appointee, and that created awkward interactions at times between Headquarters and the districts. Initiated in the late 1960s, Colburn looked to this reform to the USMS structure to solve the relational challenge.[1]

Even prior to its formal proposal, not everyone agreed with the Regionalization concept. In a memorandum to Don Hill, dated June 17, 1974, Jack Cameron voiced his reservations about the structure. He received a preliminary task force study on the organizational structure, and stated:

> Their recommendations for regionalization appear to be based on regionalization for regionalization's sake. Nowhere in their report did I find any substantive reason for regionalization other than that 94 present districts present too broad a span of control. The only other reason for regionalization is to conform to OMB guidelines. They arbitrarily suggest regionalization of the Witness Security Division, for example, without any apparent knowledge of the work to be accomplished or the most effective organization thereof. They would merely throw it in with Court Security with no apparent realization that the programs are not related or comparable.[2]

In September 1974, an integrated team of personnel from the Department of Justice and the USMS, the Office of Management and Finance task force, reported to the Deputy Attorney General. Among the key recommendations were the creation of regional desk officers to coordinate district operations and the exploration of automating prisoner movement systems. In February 1975, Colburn met with Assistant Attorney General for Administration Glen E. Pommerening and proposed the formation of Regional Directors, instead of the desk officers. The proposed plan established five regional directors who report to the Deputy Director at Headquarters.[3]

Colburn wanted to abolish the position of Deputy Associate Director for Administration (Controller) and make it an assistant director position. He also proposed a new position, Assistant Director for Field Activity Support, a merger of the Associate Director of Operations and Witness Security positions. Colburn reasoned that witness security staff could be temporarily placed with the Assistant Director for Field Activity Support, or directly under the Regional Directors. The regional office space already existed in the pertinent districts. The Assistant Attorney General concurred with the general concept. The action plan further explained Regionalization in greater detail. The Regional Directors would sit in Washington, D.C., not in the regions they planned. Witness Security was scheduled to move to new space in September 1975.[4]

Regionalization forged ahead despite internal reservations. The five regions were: Northeast (I), Southeast (II), North-Central (III), South-Central (IV), and West (V). Few physical moves to regional offices actually took place. However, challenges to Colburn's concept stalled these movements over time. Cameron's concerns focused on the concentration of administration over operations. He felt this was simply raising the number of high salaried managers rather than encouraging effective control.[5]

Even as Regionalization slowly moved forward, Colburn achieved greater triumphs in his functional reforms. By 1975, the Prisoner Coordination Section, or P.C., grew phenomenally. In fiscal year 1968, U.S. marshals moved 23,000 prisoners. In 1971, they transported 33,000. In fiscal year 1974, P.C. transferred 50,000 prisoners. Deputies worked through three coordinators and documented every movement. Once accomplished on horseback in the Old West, prisoner movements transitioned to automobiles or buses.[6]

The increasing number of prisoners required an efficient and reliable transportation system. On September 1, 1974, the Bureau of Prisons and the U.S. Marshals combined forces to form a bus transit program for prisoners. The system allowed prisoners to transport en masse, thus easing the work burden on the district offices. Coordinators scheduled and cleared each move with the receiving district to ensure each prisoner's smooth arrival.[7]

Female prisoners required a change in the personnel structure of P.C. The Marshals Service needed more female deputies. For a time, the U.S. Marshals worked around the challenge by temporarily deputizing women as guards. Some deputized their spouses. Deputy U.S. Marshal Ernie Mike's wife, Ruth, participated in female prisoner movements with her husband. The need to hire more professional female deputies took on new urgency. In late 1974, the employment of women increased to 16.6 percent.[8]

In 1975, the structure of P.C. consisted of a chief, a senior coordinator, two assistant coordinators, a secretary, deputy liaison, and clerk-typist. Four years later, it outgrew its office space, necessitating a move. Prisoner Coordination became the first separate divisional office in Headquarters. Division Chief Reis Kash took over P.C., and organized the move to Kansas City. The staff grew to 11, and the new location saved money and personnel costs. The new prisoner airlift program started in March 1979 and transported 300 prisoners from coast to coast, making 20 stops. The entire division finished the relocation by June 1979, complete with the installation of new computers. The future of the USMS prisoner airline had been established.[9]

U.S. Marshals Service management also studied the hospitalization of prisoners in federal facilities. In February 1974, Colburn began addressing the issue of formalizing a standard for security when federal prisoners needed medical care. The appropriation for support of prisoners included transferring inmates to medical facilities. Colburn also highlighted the need to utilize local facilities when necessary. He worked closely with Bureau of Prisons Director Norman Carlson in coordinating this across the country.[10]

Other functions of the Service exceeded performance expectations because of reforms. By 1975, the Witness Relocation Program represented an "$11 million a year operation" that moved over 700 families. Jack Cameron ran WitSec at this time. In a rare early interview with the *Washington Star* in April 1975, Cameron emphasized the need for those in the Program to follow the advice of inspectors. Department of Justice official Gerald Shur illustrated a worse-case scenario. A protected witness experienced a death in the family, and the deputies took him to the funeral. However, deputies admonished him not return to his old home. He did. When he turned the doorknob of the home, he triggered a bomb that killed him. The refusal of witnesses to enter the Program was equally dangerous. Shortly after a Las Vegas man refused protection, an assailant killed him with a shotgun blast while the victim was entering a hotel room.[11]

Finding new identities for witnesses proved a challenge too. Cameron stated, "We had a fellow who claimed he was a civil engineer... and he asked that we get him a new license... we found he didn't even have a college degree... He was upset when he found we weren't going to perpetrate his fraud..."[12]

That same year, Cameron set a window of 90 days, from beginning to end and including testimony against criminals, for witnesses to complete their tenure in the Program. He stated, "I mentioned our 90-day goal... If we don't realize this, instead of maybe 250 or 300 on the rolls, we're going to have 500 or 600. We've got more and more coming into the program. It could get out of hand if we're not efficient."[13]

The public's fascination with WitSec grew, but a new life under protection for witnesses meant trimming down and breaking old habits. Many experienced radical lifestyle changes. The mid-1970s brought complex issues to the Program, like caring for families, finding new jobs, and juggling multiple witnesses. *Argosy*, a popular pulp magazine specializing in fictional stories, featured an article on the program in its May 1975 issue. The agency claimed to have given new identities to 1,007 witnesses and 2,500 family members.[14]

Guam

The Department of Justice issued a release on July 9, 1975, which stated, in part:

> United States Marshals have been assigned to provide security on Guam for Vietnamese refugees waiting to be repatriated to Vietnam, Attorney General Edward H. Levi announced today.

About two dozen Marshals were assigned to the project at the request of the [Department of State's] Inter-Agency Task Force for Indochina Refugees.

Wayne B. Colburn, director of the Marshals Service, said Marshals escorted the refugees on flights from California to Guam last week.

Refugees on Guam waiting to return to Vietnam are being housed in civilian rather than military areas and thus civilian security forces are required, Mr.Colburn said. The force of Marshals, including both women and men, will remain on Guam as long as needed, he added.[15]

At the conclusion of the Vietnam War, a number of refugees sought repatriation to their native country. The island of Guam provided a shelter for some 2,200 possible repatriates. The United Nations High Commissioner for Refugees had jurisdiction over negotiations, interviews, screening, and processing. The Attorney General wished to avoid the demonstrations and threats from delays to repatriate those encamped elsewhere in the United States, such as Camp Pendleton, California. From there, Vietnamese citizens departed on Air Force planes for Guam. Despite the horrors of war and the offer of employment in the United States, some wanted to return to family they had left behind. From Guam, all awaited entry papers to return to Vietnam.[16]

The lead deputy for the Guam mission was Special Operations Group Commander Bill Whitworth, the tough South Carolinian. Whitworth brought about 25 deputies, mostly from SOG, to the island territory. Deputies from the West Coast accompanied the refugees from Camp Pendleton. Public Affairs Chief Chris Rice noted that deputies rotated duty, changing every three weeks.[17]

The restless refugees failed to understand bureaucratic delays. In July, refugees participated in generally non-violent demonstrations. They marched out of the housing units at the end of the month and demanded an immediate return, making local officials nervous. Tempers grew short with each passing week. A group of Congressmen visited the repatriates in early August, but their visit failed to quell their anxieties.[18]

Instead, some refugees eventually resorted to violence. They threw rocks, and injured four deputies at Camp Asan, which they called "Devil's Island." In California, 20 refugees threatened to burn themselves to death if not returned to Vietnam immediately.[19]

Deputy U.S. Marshal Willard "Mac" McArdle witnessed some of the rioting in Guam. He recalled, "[They] burned down the fence, and when they did, there were only fifteen of us there... no firearms, no nothing."[20] The rioters destroyed the food supplies and disappeared into the jungle, but not before they had stolen knives from the kitchen and obtained crossbows. The deputies rounded up the group, but not before a number of both parties ended up in the hospital.[21]

President Gerald Ford permitted about 1,600 refugees to sail from Guam to Vietnam on October 16, 1975. By the end of that month, Saigon accepted the refugees back.[22] Deputy Director Hall sent the General Counsel on the Interagency Task Force on Indochina a bill on November 26, 1975, seeking $973,875 for overtime and guard pay. Hall wrote, "The marshals were assigned to provide security and to prevent demonstrations or violence by the refugees while waiting return to Vietnam... a total of 176 deputy U.S. marshals provided services during this tour of duty. The manpower count of deputies on Guam per day ranged from 30 to 80 men..."[23]

BUSING

The last vestiges of the Civil Rights era case *Brown v. Board of Education* were addressed by Supreme Court cases in 1971 and 1974. The desegregation of public schools required transporting minority students from one geographic area to specified institutions in another area, in a strategy commonly called "busing." Across the country, demonstrations and violent protects, including attacks on other citizens, marred these efforts. Some considered the unrest in Boston as the worst case. District of Massachusetts U.S. District Judge Wendell Arthur Garrity ordered the establishment of a full protective plan for busing in Boston, including federal support. Deputies handled the task of keeping order, alongside an entire task force of federal units. Assistant Attorney General for Civil Rights J. Stanley Pottinger oversaw the operation when schools opened on September 8, 1975.[24]

To assist with the Boston busing plan, the Marshals Service deployed 37 SOG members to work with out-of-district and Boston deputies. They wore their uniforms with blue armbands and a helmet with a faceguard. Seven pairs of deputies manned vehicles, providing general support to the Boston Police Department. U.S. Marshal John A. Birknes, Jr. and North Central Regional Director Reis Kash implemented an operations order that spelled out the plan of action. Northeast Regional Director Jack Cameron joined Kash. SOG Commander Whitworth mapped out the actual movements.[25]

Some called the tense situation the "Boston busing crisis." During the first weeks of the school year, parents demonstrated daily. The possibility of mass riots created another concern. Deputies provided vital support in school zones and to the Boston police. A youngster who assaulted a deputy with a brick represented the only attack against Marshals Service personnel.[26]

A more concerted effort to block court-ordered busing occurred in Louisville, Kentucky, in 1975. Chief U.S. District Court Judge James F. Gordon of the Western District of Kentucky issued a desegregation order for a number of schools, which led to the busing of 22,600 children. Federal marshals oversaw the transition with local police. The Ku Klux Klan and a group called "Concerned Parents, Inc." worked to defy the orders. Gordon's plan called for 12 percent enrollment of African-American students at each school.[27]

Judge Gordon implemented the desegregation plan at the end of summer. Jefferson County Public Schools officials sent out a news release dated August 5, 1975, to announce the appointment of a special subcommittee that included law enforcement personnel. "Big Six" Henderson retired, leaving Jesse Grider as the acting U.S. marshal for the district. The soft-spoken Southerner, experienced in dangerous work, turned out to be a positive presence during the crisis. Grider gave an interview to the *Louisville Courier Journal* on August 25. He said, "I want to stress the safety of the children... I don't think the people in Kentucky would disagree with that."[28] Grider mentioned that his own 12-year-old daughter was bussed, and also used the opportunity to educate the public about the historic importance of the U.S. Marshals.[29]

Despite Grider's efforts, opposition to Judge Gordon's busing order intensified. The U.S. Supreme Court denied the efforts of the anti-busing forces to overturn the decision in the courts. In early September, three people were hospitalized after a skirmish with police. A crowd of 700 people gathered in front of the federal building. When they moved toward the building, Deputy U.S. Marshal Tom Draeger, at six-foot five-inches, blocked the way. The standoff lasted several minutes, but Draeger did not budge. The leaders of the protest regained control, and urged their supporters back to the perimeters of the property. When later asked if he wondered for his safety, Draeger answered, "Of course I had doubts... You'd be a damn fool if you didn't."[30]

Law enforcement authorities arrested 300 people, and protestors set ablaze two buses in Louisville. Because of the escalation in violence and arrests, the state government assigned National Guardsmen to buses. This action reduced options for opponents to busing. In reaction, those foes focused on voicing their opposition in the press. By late September, the crisis had abated enough to end the service of the National Guard.[31]

On September 23, 1975, Judge Gordon wrote Director Colburn and commended the conduct of the deputies. Attorney General Edward H. Levi received a copy of the letter, and wrote Colburn his own approval note.[32]

The anti-busing groups remained formidable. Sentiment on the issue of busing was divided, and articles on the subject spilled into the following year. However, it was deputy U.S. marshals who made the difference when things were at their most tense. Once again, despite taking unpopular risks to some, they carried out their duties with aplomb.

PATTY HEARST

In February 1974, members of a revolutionary group called the Symbionese Liberation Army (SLA), kidnapped Patricia Hearst, the granddaughter of newspaper magnate William Randolph Hearst. Like many radical organizations of the late sixties and early seventies, the ideology of the SLA hinged on class warfare and violent acts. Hearst later appeared with her captors in criminal acts, such as the Hibernia Bank robbery in April 1974. Over the course of the following year, most members of the SLA were either arrested or killed. The remainder of the group, which included Patty Hearst, faced trial after apprehension.[33]

Female deputy marshals transported Hearst to and from prison, and during trial as needed, for hearings between late 1975 and 1976. Throughout the proceedings, numerous pictures emerged of Hearst with a female deputy at her side. Deputy U.S. Marshal Janey Jimenez accompanied the prisoner to locations of her captivity, also called "safe houses" of the SLA.[34]

Jimenez submitted to several interviews regarding her assignment to guard Hearst. However, the deputy became sympathetic to, and formed a friendship with, her prisoner. This displeased some of her colleagues in the Northern District of California, who monitored the news media closely. In the summer of 1976, Assistant Director of Administration and Finance Bill Russell learned of a book deal for Jimenez to describe her duties and time with Hearst and expressed disappointment.[35]

News of the book deal created ethical consternation at the Marshals Service. Russell told a reporter with the gossip newspaper *The Star* in September, "Patty and Janey grew up in the same era and although their financial back around [background] was vastly different, there were many things common in that era."[36] Russell also hinted that the friendship hurt the deputy's objectivity, and that the bad press negatively impacted the U.S. Marshals. Ultimately, Jimenez quit the Marshals Service and published her book, entitled *My Prisoner*, in 1977.[37]

The Hearst trial was not over in the federal court in San Francisco, and the deputies handled the needs of the jury after they were sequestered in February 1976. The jury for the trial consisted of seven women and five men. Deputies maintained a 24-hour detail at their hotel and arranged for transportation to and from the trial. The agency's bus broke down, but the Coast Guard lent their vehicle. During the first month, each juror on the Hearst trial earned $20 a day. After that, the court paid them $25 a day. By mid-March, the bill totaled over $40,000.[38]

The 22-year-old heiress made a sympathetic subject for news headlines. She felt manipulated by her captors, but wound up charged with 11 felonies, including six counts of assault with a deadly weapon.[39]

U.S. District Judge Oliver J. Carter presided over the trial in San Francisco. Jury deliberations began on March 19, 1976. The jury found Hearst guilty on firearms charges on March 20. Initially, Judge Carter sentenced her to 35 years in federal prison, contingent on a psychiatric evaluation. In June, before the results of that evaluation, Judge Carter suffered a fatal heart attack. A subsequent review reduced the sentence to 7 years.[40]

Marshals made further preparations to handle the prisoner when transporting her to face charges in Superior Court in Los Angeles in March 1976. Deputies avoided publicity and refrained from personal attachment to Hearst. A Coast Guard airplane carried Hearst and the deputies to a nearby airport. From there, a helicopter carried them to the district office, where they dashed to an unmarked car driven by the U.S. Marshal himself. A sheriff's vehicle drove ahead, and another car tailed behind.[41]

The long trial and special procedures put a strain on U.S. Marshal Francis X. Klein and his deputies. When transported from the hospital, where she was undergoing her psychiatric evaluation, to federal prison in San Diego in late April, one of her lawyers claimed she was "kidnapped" a second time—by deputy marshals. Once it was determined that she was to be evaluated in San Diego, her lawyer claimed deputies told her to get dressed in three minutes or they would blanket her themselves. Marshal Klein angrily denied the charges—and wrote it off as grandstanding.[42]

Although the jury found Patty Hearst guilty, the final decision came from the White House. Her lawyers appealed in November 1976. President Jimmy Carter commuted her sentence in February 1979. President William Jefferson Clinton granted her a full pardon in 2001.[43]

Coincidentally, the Patty Hearst trial served to publicize the second official badge issued by the U.S. Marshals. Director Colburn instituted the new design in 1970 to replace the old "eagle top" badges made famous during the Civil Rights era. The director wanted to exert the changes in the agency with a more modern design. Daily coverage of the Hearst trial exposed the new badge, which fit in a case or on a belt, and earned it the moniker the "Patty Hearst Badge."[44]

CHAPTER 10

AN EVOLUTION OF LEADERSHIP

TRANSITION

Constant change marked the mid-1970s transition of the Marshals Service, attaining the status of bureau, rearranging leaders, and taking on new missions. The agency's internal structure shifted gears along with its growth. Traditional duties expanded, and staffing increased.[1]

There was a staff increase in a young, college-educated administrative staff. In 1974, Elizabeth Howard joined the U.S. Marshals as a clerk-typist while taking classes at American University. Initially working in procurement, she moved to the budding communications center, which served as a conduit to the districts. "That was back when they had the old Model 33 teletype machines that went 'clickity-clack, clickity, clack.'"[2]

There was minimal legal staff then. Gerald Auerbach, fresh out of law school, joined as the new law clerk in 1974. "When I got there, it was a very small headquarters... the legal office maybe had five people at the time."[3] Auerbach currently holds the position of general counsel for the Marshals Service and advises the executive staff and other employees on all legal matters.

Chris Rice's tenure as public information officer ended abruptly. While serving in a military reserve unit in Massachusetts, he received a call from Washington, D.C., to draft a speech for Director Colburn. Apparently annoyed by the demand, Rice drove back to Washington and hurriedly prepared the speech. Late at night and anxious to get back to his unit, he drove his car to Colburn's residence with the prepared remarks. Instead of stopping his car and slipping the speech between the storm and main doors of the home, he wrapped it around a small rock and launched it at the front door, never fully stopping his vehicle. The missive found its mark. It thudded against the storm door, breaking the glass and waking the family. Rice continued on his way, and was unaware of the damage until he received a call from Washington asking him to return. Rice left shortly thereafter, but otherwise continued a successful career elsewhere in the federal government.[4]

By May 1976, Director Wayne Colburn had grown tired of the demands and challenges of leading the bureau. Deputy Director Bill Hall noted that "the Director was exhausted by the years of difficult work."[5] The battles with individual marshals over centralization, the growth of Headquarters and agency status, the efforts to establish regionalization, Watergate, a lawsuit alleging racism, and multiple conflicts with the AIM had taken a hefty toll on the director. His constitution taxed, Colburn formally retired to his home in California, having served for almost six years. He had overseen more rapid change than any agency leader before him.[6]

On May 19, 1976, Attorney General Edward H. Levi announced the formal transfer of the reins of power from Wayne Colburn to Bill Hall. The young lawyer, whom Colburn implicitly trusted, had completed a rise from general counsel to deputy director. Hall's administrative, legal mind had perfectly complemented Colburn's.[7]

The new Director took a balanced view towards power, and handled it gingerly and sparingly. He brought John J. Twomey, a former prison warden and U.S. marshal in Chicago, to Headquarters as the new deputy director. A man who understood both administrative and operational arenas, Twomey became an important power broker in the Service. Hall also depended on the administrative mind of a young graduate from the University of Pennsylvania in Erie, Gary Mead. In 1974, he had joined the Marshals Service to head interagency training. Former DEA agent Howard Safir developed operational planning—first with Witness Security, then overall operations. These three major figures would represent a sustained support core of Marshals Service leadership until the early 1990s.[8]

As new leadership arrived, another famous name retired. A legend in Texas, T.P. McNamara had served as a deputy marshal for more than 35 years before retiring December 31, 1977. Appointed by his uncle Guy McNamara in 1942 to operate the Waco sub-office, McNamara gained a reputation so respected that President John F. Kennedy offered him the job of U.S. marshal for the Western District of Texas. He turned it down, and stated he never intended to leave Waco. After his retirement, his two sons, Mike and Parnell, became the standard-bearers of the Waco office. The brothers kept law and order in Waco for decades.[9]

U.S. Marshals Service Headquarters spread out between five different sites in the D.C. area. In March 1978, Director Hall announced that most functions would be consolidated at one location and moved the headquarters to a more spacious, but remote, location. The developers of the Tyson's Corner Center in McLean, Virginia, constructed a mixed-use property. Located 15 miles west of Washington, the building rested just off the Capital Beltway and a short drive from Washington Dulles International Airport.[10]

Administration Services Chief Tom Milburn and several others designed the blueprints for the new Headquarters, situating it above the stores of the mall. The agency's warehouse would operate at the garage level. In June, employees who would occupy the "Star Building," so named for the defunct *Washington Star* newspaper in which they worked, moved to Tyson's Corner. Those in the Safeway and Todd Buildings relocated a month later.[11]

Director Hall held true to Colburn's programs. He intended to carry out Colburn's plans for Regionalization. However, the election of 1976 changed everything. New Attorney General Griffin Bell disliked the idea of Regionalization and halted the process. Director Hall objected, but ultimately conceded. There was little he could do. He turned his attentions to smaller-scale reorganization and expanding existing programs.[12]

In 1976, he moved basic training for deputy marshals to the Federal Law Enforcement Training Center (FLETC), a former naval air station near Brunswick, Georgia. The idea for a consolidated law enforcement training originated back in 1968, but the desired location in Beltsville, Maryland, was mired in legal issues. Georgia offered better needed space to conduct multi-jurisdictional training than similar facilities in Washington, D.C. The agency consolidated coursework into two parts: an eight-week school in criminal investigation and a three-week basic training course. Gary Mead, who was instrumental in the reprogramming, wrote about the advantages in the magazine *Marshal Today*. Housing and food were provided at no cost to the agency, which considerably trimmed the budget.[13]

By mid-1978, the specialty programs thrived despite obstacles. The Special Operations Group held an advanced training course on terrorist tactics in Jackson, Mississippi. Agency leadership presented awards to students at the end of the course. In addition to SOG, the Witness Security Program moved beyond the development stage. However, criticism continued.[14]

In April 1978, Director Hall defended the Witness Security Program before the Senate Judiciary Subcommittee on Administrative Practice and Procedure. Complaints from witnesses prompted the hearing. Hall explained the challenges of working with numerous agencies and balancing the satisfaction of the witnesses. Hall resolved the criticism, in part, by requiring a memorandum of understanding with witnesses along with pre-entry briefings, and instituting a training program for WitSec inspectors.[15]

Ben Butler of New York became chief of the Court Security Division. An African-American, Butler increased the agency's visibility and showed needed diversity. Although not highlighted at the time, he was the first African-American to rise to the upper managerial levels in Headquarters. Given the organizational diversity in the early 1970s, Butler's promotion was a positive start.[16]

By 1978, a most unusual mission was fully operational. In June 1975, the Marshals Service acquired the mission of escorting U.S. Air Force missile systems containing nuclear warheads from military facilities. The origins of this duty dated from December 1973, when the Air Force wrote the Office of the Director for assistance in transporting the missiles. Discussions continued into the following year, and representatives visited two missile bases. An official memorandum of agreement was reached, and the Air Force was to reimburse costs incurred in providing missile escort deputies. The original cadre of 12 deputies protected Air Force personnel and assets being moved from six, isolated bases from the air and by roadways. By 1978, deputy marshals had escorted nearly 1,000 Minuteman II and III systems. One of those deputies was Eugene Coon, who later served as the longtime chief of WitSec and acting deputy director.[17]

The changes implemented by the agency between 1975 and 1978 ranged from internal adjustments and reorganization, the results of trial and error, to larger external duties. By the close of the decade, more changes were in store.

CHALLENGES: TONGSUN PARK'S DETAIL AND CUBAN FREEDOM BOATLIFT

In the *Federal Times* dated October 23, 1978, an editorial written by Inderjit Badhwar entitled "Let Them Eat Cake" spoke of the "hard times" the U.S. Marshals Service went through during the decade. Supposedly an experienced deputy had related that morale was low, and that the

"senior marshals get the gravy."[18] Badhawar related everything from
the rumored cost of a deputy's badge ($30) to its policy on firearms.
According to him, the move of U.S. Marshals Headquarters from D.C.
to Tyson's Corner seemed suspicious and overly costly. He used the
example of the security detail for Korean businessman Tongsun Park as
proof of fiscal irreverence. Badhawar's source had obviously expressed
displeasure with Headquarters.[19]

Conversely, many U.S. Marshals personnel reacted strongly to the
article. Deputy U.S. Marshal Stanley Olivers of the District of Minnesota
wrote that the move to Tyson's was "a great move," and that morale
remained high. Chief Deputy Thomas C. Kupferer Jr., stationed in New
Orleans, shot back at Badhawar in the *Federal Times* of December 4,
1978, stating that Badhwar's article "indicates a complete lack of truth...
he reports the Marshals Service is broke. If he had taken the time to
contact the service director or the Department of Justice, he would have
discovered his source to be completely mistaken."[20]

Badhawar's editorial clearly stirred up passions that were a by-product
of the controversial witness detail of Park, an amiable Korean businessman
who had founded the popular George Town Club in the mid-1960s.
Park's influence peaked during the 1970s. By 1976, Park had become
the central suspect in "Koreagate," the suspected influence-peddling by
South Koreans with members of Congress who lobbied to keep American
troops in South Korea. A federal court convicted Park on bribery charges
in 1977. Due to the sensitivity of international relations, the government
felt Park was more valuable testifying to Congress than sitting in jail.
There was only one problem: Park resided in Korea.[21]

On February 24, 1978, representatives of the Witness Security Program
met with officials of the Department of Justice. U.S. Deputy Attorney
General Benjamin Civiletti had met with Park and South Korean officials.
He authorized funding above and beyond normal levels as part of a
deal to return Park to the United States to testify before Congress. The
security detail of Park required 22 deputy marshals. Upon Park's arrival

in the United States, the team picked him up from Washington Dulles International Airport and took a circuitous route to a hotel in northern Virginia. The periods of testimony before Congress were February to mid-April, then mid-May to late June 1978. Reporters wanted more information on the case and Park's situation, but the detail required secrecy uncommon in most details. The necessary lack of transparency likely frustrated Badhwar and others.[22]

Reporters queried Public Affairs Officer Bill Dempsey for details about the Marshals Service arrangements for Park. A breakdown of costs for the security detail revealed a total of $61,696. Adding other related costs, the Department released a more general figure of $70,000. The public release of information sparked articles about excessive spending. In reality, overtime represented the largest cost. However, Badhwar concentrated on meals and wine for Park, and misrepresented expenses at more than $1 million dollars to the agency. In fact, subsistence paid by the agency totaled just $4,372. If there were further expenses in these categories, someone else paid them. Bill Dempsey fended off the criticism with an official release, while the Internal Revenue Service seized Park's belongings from his Georgetown home. Not surprisingly, more negative articles followed for a few months. With Dempsey's press release and the passage of time, the story lost intensity.[23]

THE MURDER OF A FEDERAL JUDGE

A tragic incident in late May 1979 sparked significant change for the Marshals. U.S. District Judge John Howland Wood, Jr., of the Western District of Texas, had faced his share of hard cases as an experienced and respected federal jurist. President Richard Nixon had nominated him to the federal bench in October 1970. He acquired the nickname "Maximum John" for his sentencing of drug violators.[24]

Organized crime became a problem, particularly in El Paso. A man named Jamiel "Jimmy" Chagra ran his operations there. Wood presided over the prosecution of Chagra by U.S. Attorney Jamie Boyd in 1977. According to Deputy U.S. Marshal Ray Muzquiz, Judge Wood was strict but fair. Muzquiz was the court security coordinator for Western District of Texas, and would be among the closest deputies to the judges.[25]

Boyd sent Assistant U.S. Attorney Jim Kerr to direct the criminal investigation around El Paso, allegedly associated with Chagra. A gunman nearly killed the prosecutor November 21, 1978, while he drove his car to work just outside San Antonio. Kerr's instincts saved his life. He spotted a rifle barrel emerging from a parked van and immediately slid to the floor as a gunshot rang out. Following this incident, the Marshals Service placed the Assistant U.S. Attorney and Judge Wood under a protective detail for three months.[26]

Muzquiz reported that the deputies accompanied the judge around the clock, even to a vacation home near Rockport, Texas. Deputies took up residence across the street from the judge as part of the protective detail. After several months, the judge ended the detail against the advice of his protectors. Western District of Texas U.S. Marshal Rudy Garza tried to convince him to continue it, reminding the judge that Kerr remained under 24-hour protection. However, the judge carried his own gun, an old .38 revolver, and felt the detail was no longer necessary. Garza and Muzquiz pleaded with Wood, but his mind was made up about ending the detail.[27]

Garza suggested that the judge alter his usual routes, though Muzquiz doubted there could be significant variation. A supervisory deputy marshal kept surveillance on Judge Wood for several weeks to "transition out" of the detail. A car checked on the residence and the surrounding neighborhood. However, this trailed off as grand jury proceedings continued against Chagra and other defendants.[28]

On the morning of May 29, 1979, tragedy struck. An assailant shot Judge Wood as he opened his car door at home. The assassin took advantage of the additional moment it had taken the judge to enter his vehicle, because he paused to notice a flat tire on his wife's vehicle. Judge Wood sustained gunshot wounds to his back and chest. Deputies arrived within minutes. U.S. Marshal Garza himself lived just a few blocks away. However, the judge died a short time later.[29]

Law enforcement reacted instantly to Judge Wood's murder. U.S. marshals placed all U.S. district judges under protection, and added extra measures of protection to the detail of AUSA Kerr. The search for Judge Wood's killer resulted in the arrest of Charles Harrelson. Law enforcement arrested Chagra's wife Elizabeth for delivery of payment to the assassin. In a series of legal moves, Jimmy Chagra entered the Witness Security Program in exchange for vital testimony against Kerr's attacker and leniency for his wife. Harrelson died in prison. For the U.S. Marshals Service, the murder meant the beginning of an enhanced protection program for the federal judiciary.[30]

THE MEMORANDUM

The decade's biggest change came in the form of a memorandum. On July 23, 1979, through a memorandum of understanding (MOU), Deputy Attorney General Benjamin Civiletti reassigned apprehension responsibility for most federal escapees and parole violators from the FBI to the U.S. Marshals Service. Not since the closing of the Old West had the U.S. Marshals handled a wide-ranging fugitive warrant program. The MOU spelled out clear guidelines and exceptions for both agencies, and became effective October 1, 1979.[31]

The advent of the MOU dated back two years. In November 1977, under the pressures of an increased workload involving complex cases, the FBI sought a solution for dealing with cases stemming from court actions. They looked to the U.S. Marshals Service. Deputy Director Twomey helmed negotiations for the Service. He knew much about escapees from his days as a warden in Illinois. Howard Safir, chief of WitSec, joined him.[32]

Some 15,000 cases resulting from court actions had pushed the resources of the FBI to their limit. Transferring enforcement of these actions to the Marshals Service seemed natural.[33] Civiletti, who became Attorney General in August 1979, wrote:

> The apprehension of fugitives is vital to maintaining the integrity of the federal criminal justice system and I am confident that our U.S. Marshals will discharge this mission with professionalism and diligence. This program is of great personal interest to me and I expect you to ensure that it is carried out as a high priority by each and every district.[34]

In June 1979, a conference of FBI, Marshals Service and DOJ officials recommended permanent transfer of the fugitive apprehension authority to the U.S. Marshals. The MOU literally changed the way business was done in law enforcement.[35]

The MOU also provided the nucleus of an enlarged fugitive apprehension program that grew steadily for the next 30 years. With careful planning by Safir and his successors, the Fugitive Apprehension Program became a major function of the agency. The new focus also served to remove the glare caused by past controversies, and took some heat off Director Hall.[36]

A NEW STAR WITH NEW DUTIES

Many deputy marshals held a negative view of the second nationwide issue badge introduced in 1970. Later dubbed the "Patty Hearst" badge and long associated with the trial proceedings of the Symbionese Liberation Army, the badge had been worn nationwide by deputies for just nine years. Director Hall sought a badge design to reflect the agency's expanding missions while staying grounded in the historic legacy of the U.S. marshal.[37]

Hall tapped Deputy Director Twomey to head a committee to create a new design. In June 1979, Twomey sent a letter to each U.S. marshal and chief deputy U.S. marshal to explain the project with a ballot and pictures attached for two proposed badge varieties and inscriptions. The first choice was an encircled star; the second a six-pointed variety. They could choose the wording for the face of the badge from two possibilities: "United States Marshal" or "United States Marshals Service." A separate credential case would reference the Department of Justice.[38]

The committee completed the process of changing the badge by the end of the year. Hall publicized the badge and credential in the agency's magazine *The Pentacle* in the August-September 1979 issue. The circle and star design echoed the past, but included modern flourishes. In the center of the star rested an eagle, and engraved on the ring of the badge were the words "United States Marshal." On August 2, 1979, a memorandum from Director Hall announced the new design, selected by more than 60 percent of survey participants, with the wording "United States Marshal" preferred by nearly 95 percent. U.S. Marshals received gold badges of the same design. Hall asked each U.S. Marshal to inform individual staff members about the new badge and its availability on October 1, 1979. The third nationwide issue badge remains the one used by all marshals and operational employees today.[39]

Mariel Boatlift

In April 1980, another challenge awaited the agency from a country south of Florida. From the beginning of his long term in office, Cuban president Fidel Castro sought to ease the tensions of his island nation caught between two cultures. Capitalism, in the form of foreign investment in its sugar and gaming industries, comprised one of the cultures. The other took root in the nation's rural existence, based on socialistic principles. With the radical differences and changes taking place, many Cubans wanted to leave the country. A thriving Cuban community in Miami consisted of many former citizens who had left Cuba when Castro ousted President Fulgencio Batista in 1959, including many with relatives back in their native country.[40]

In April 1980, Castro announced that anyone who wanted to leave Cuba would be allowed to, by boat from the port of Mariel and heading to the United States. However, this was a partial ruse. Castro allowed prisoners and patients from mental institutions to leave the nation as well, in what became known popularly as the "Mariel Boatlift." At once, the United States faced a flood of immigrants launched from the seaside town of Mariel. In all, an estimated 125,000 refugees arrived on the shores of Florida.[41]

The U.S. news media dubbed the makeshift fleet of boats the "Freedom Flotilla." The country had not prepared for the mass exodus from Cuba, which formally ended in October 1980, and the arrival of so many people seeking freedom and a new start in America. Although the armed forces, notably the Coast Guard, along with the Florida National Guard, piloted safety procedures, they were overwhelmed. The federal government called on the Marshals Service to maintain order and assist in the processing of the new arrivals into the United States.[42]

The Special Operations Group encamped at Florida's Eglin Air Force Base and a location in Key West in May 1980. Both places converted into giant shelters for the processing of the refugees. A refashioned aircraft hangar in Key West provided bed space for thousands of people. Eglin was a more difficult environment. The deputies sweltered in 100-degree-plus temperatures to provide order in makeshift barracks.[43]

Deputy U.S. Marshal Joseph Tolson spent many hours on the road during the Mariel Boatlift operation, providing logistics support and purchasing equipment for the mission. As the refugees arrived, he observed, "They would get off these makeshift boats, two or three hundred at a time."[44]

According to Tolson, the refugees slept on folding cots in the hangar. Crime was difficult to control, even with extra deputies on duty. The numbers of refugees swelled, and it became apparent that the encampment became a nightmare for law enforcement.[45]

SOG Commander Joel Wetherington policed the camps while coordinating with other agencies, such as the Marines and Air Force. Using riot control techniques, SOG worked as a unit to provide instructions to the refugees and search living quarters when necessary. The deputies worked 12-hour shifts, seven days a week, for two consecutive weeks. While not an easy workload, most made the best of it. Deputy U.S. Marshal Floyd Johnson became a community ambassador to Cuban refugee children. He often let them ride on his transport vehicle around Elgin. The grateful Cubans named their residential section "Johnsontown, USA," as a tribute to his kindness. Others made outreach efforts like Deputy Sidney Johnson, who conducted Taekwondo demonstrations for the refugees.[46]

The deputies faced an unusual situation. Spanish-speaking members of SOG conducted the interviews. SOG utilized informants within the large numbers of refugees to report any crimes or weapons. The worst offenders stayed in the "bull pen," which held violators in isolation in a small room in the Air Force police security tent. Law enforcement officials assessed each case to determine an appropriate course of action, usually deportation. SOG members were asked to be "stern, compassionate and curious" in the course of their public relations.[47]

In late September, Wetherington wrote Director Hall with a recommendation to remove SOG from Eglin, and replace them with regular deputies. The refugee camps split into smaller units to facilitate faster processing.[48]

The criminals Castro allowed to flee to America were eventually located. Conversely, U.S. Marshal Don Forsht of the Southern District of Florida, a veteran of the Civil Rights Era, went to Cuba to secure the safe transfer of 30 American prisoners jailed there as hijackers and parole violators. He took nine deputies with him to receive the prisoners. No prisoner objected to the transfer. One even stated, "We're just as happy being with you, Marshal. This is a thousand times better than Cuba!"[49]

Deputy Joseph Tolson oversaw the refugee moves to the smaller camps. The Fort Walton Beach facility, or "Camp Libertad," was the largest. Additional sites included Fort Chaffee in Arkansas, Fort McCoy in Wisconsin, and Indian Gap in Pennsylvania. Tolson recalled, "[The] command decision was made to move them to Fort Walton Beach."[50] Though not without challenges, deputies kept order and sifted out criminals from the general population much more easily at the smaller camps.

By decade's end, more senior staff and functions shuffled in and out of Headquarters. In late 1979, Ben Butler became Director Hall's special assistant. Julie Dubick became General Counsel in August 1977 after transferring from the Department of Justice's Civil Division. In March 1979, the National Prisoner Transportation System (NPTS) inaugurated a series of expanding plans in airlifting, busing, and housing prisoners. In June 1979, the Prisoner Transportation Division anchored in Kansas City.[51]

The seventies drew to a fevered close. The struggles of a growing Headquarters found some resolution by the end of the decade. With the structural cohesion of internal matters, the United States Marshals Service was poised for an effective start to the 1980s.

PHOTO GALLERY

Photo 1. Salvatore Andretta, who oversaw the formation of the Executive Office for U.S. Marshals.

From 1948-1949 yearbook of the National Association of Deputy United States Marshals. USMS Collections.

Photo 2. Deputy U.S. Marshal Training Class, Colorado, 1958.

USMS Collections.
As riot control came more in focus, classes proliferated. The main trainers in the front row, kneeling, are: Don Forsht, Al Butler, Ellis Duley, Jr., and Jack Cameron. Not pictured was Frank Noe.

Photo 3. Chief U.S. Marshal Clive W. Palmer and Eugene Matchett.

USMS Collections.
Clive Palmer (front row, left) and Eugene Matchett (front row, right) attend a meeting with deputies in the field, ca. 1960.

Photo 4. U.S. Marshals Prison Bus, 1960s.

USMS Collections.

Photo 5. Three surveillance snapshots from operations in Montgomery, Alabama, May 1961.

USMS Collections.
From top: Baptist Church where Dr. Martin Luther King, Jr. spoke; the city park directly across the street from the church, which was used by rioters; 6th Avenue and 17th Street North, at the border of the city park. Another strategic area of concern to deputies guarding Dr. King and the "Freedom Riders" in Montgomery.

Photo 6. U.S. Marshal Luke C. Moore (D/DC) shakes hands with Attorney General Robert F. Kennedy.

USMS Collections. Courtesy of Patricia Diggs and the Moore family.
Chief U.S. Marshal James J.P. McShane stands at center.

Photo 7. The U.S. Marshals visit the courtyard of the Department of Justice, 1964.

USMS Collections/ U.S. Department of Justice
In the front on either side of Attorney General Robert F. Kennedy are Chief U.S. Marshal James J.P. McShane (left) and Deputy Attorney General Nicholas Katzenbach. At far right, the lone female in the picture is Counsel Delores Klajbor.

Photo 8. The Official Seal of the United States Marshals, as painted by U.S.
Marshal Robert Morey.

Courtesy of the Morey Family. USMS Collections.
Morey, who was an artist himself, was chair of the committee to create the seal. This
became official in December 1968.

Photo 9. The flip side of the Norman Rockwell work *The Problem We All Live With.*

Courtesy of the late Fred Oczkowski and the Morey family. USMS Collections. This photo shows that life imitated art as well as the reverse. Here is the artist, second from left with, left to right: U.S. Marshal Robert Morey of Massachusetts, Deputy U.S. Marshal Fred Oczkowski, and Deputy U.S. Marshal William Baldwin, at Rockwell's Stockbridge home on October 6, 1963. Both Oczkowski and Baldwin were artist models for the famous depiction of headless deputies escorting a young Ruby Bridges to school in New Orleans three years earlier. The painting was published in *Look* Magazine on January 14, 1964.

Photo 10. The second nationwide issue U.S. Marshals badge.

USMS Collections.
Issued from 1970 until 1979, this was nicknamed the "Patty Hearst badge" because it was prominently seen during our duties in that case.

Photo 11. Director Wayne Colburn poses with staff and a group of U.S. Marshals, ca. 1972.

USMS Collections.
To the Director's right: William Hall, Ben Butler, and Donald Hill.

Photo 12. Reis Kash, a key leader in the agency, teaches a course on security, ca. 1972.

USMS Collections.

Photo 13. Map depicting a situational portion of Wounded Knee, South
Dakota, 1973.

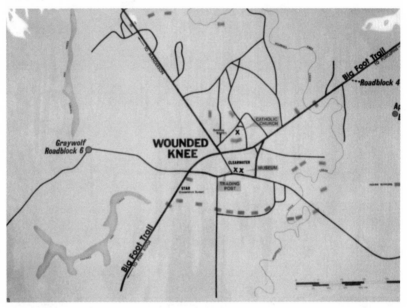

USMS Collections.

Photo 14. Gary Mead.

USMS Collections. Photo by Craig Crawford.
From his arrival in the USMS in 1974 until his departure in 2000, he served in a host of positions in Headquarters.

Photo 15. Director William Hall helmed the U.S. Marshals through much of its early transition.

USMS Collections.
Entering as General Counsel, he became Director in 1976.

Photo 16. Plaque ceremony honoring U.S. Marshal Frederick Douglass.

USMS Collections.

In 1979, the USMS, with permission of the District of Columbia, placed a ceremonial plaque to honor U.S. Marshal Frederick Douglass, the first African American U.S. Marshal. From left to right: Then-Mayor Marion Berry; Assistant Director Ben Butler; Director William Hall; and U.S. Marshal J. Jerome Bullock.

Photo 17. Deputies with the Special Operations Group on duty in Florida during the Mariel Boatlift, 1980.

Photograph by USAF 5383 80. Courtesy of U.S. Air Force.

Photo 18. Medina, North Dakota, February 1983.

USMS Collections.
U.S. Marshal Ken Muir and Deputy U.S. Marshal Robert Cheshire died while confronting militant tax protestors.

Photo 19. Director Stanley Morris (left) is sworn in by Chief Justice of the Supreme Court Warren Burger, October 1983.

USMS Collections. Photo by Craig Crawford.
Between them are Attorney General William French Smith (second from left) and outgoing Director Bill Hall.

Photo 20. A call is received in the Communications Center, ca. 1986.

USMS Collections.
The 24-hour, 7-day-a-week facility had its origins in the 1970s.

Photo 21. Mug shot of Alphonse "Allie Boy" Persico, Eastern District of New York.

UNITED STATES MARSHALS SERVICE

WANTED
BY U.S. MARSHALS

NOTICE TO ARRESTING AGENCY: BEFORE ARREST, VALIDATE WARRANT THROUGH NATIONAL CRIME INFORMATION CENTER (NCIC).

UNITED STATES MARSHALS SERVICE NCIC ENTRY NUMBER: (NIC/___W2346_____).

NAME: ALPHONSE CARMINE PERSICO

AKA(S):   "ALLIE BOY"

DESCRIPTION:
SEX:	MALE
RACE:	WHITE
PLACE OF BIRTH:	BROOKLYN, NEW YORK
DATE(S) OF BIRTH:	DECEMBER 6, 1929
HEIGHT:	6 FEET
WEIGHT:	225 POUNDS
EYES:	BROWN
HAIR:	BLACK/GRAY (SALT & PEPPER)
SKINTONE:	OLIVE
SCARS, MARKS, TATOOS:	SCARS LEFT SIDE OF FACE - TATOO
SOCIAL SECURITY NUMBER(S):	"Al" RIGHT HAND BETWEEN THUMB AND
NCIC FINGERPRINT CLASSIFICATION:	FBI #263 INDEX FINGER

ADDRESS AND LOCALE: According to investigative agencies, Alphonse Persico is the reputed underboss for an organized crime family. This crime family has connections throughout the United States and abroad.

WANTED FOR: FAILURE TO APPEAR FOR SENTENCE AND BOND DEFAULT
  WARRANT ISSUED: EASTERN DISTRICT OF NEW YORK
  WARRANT NUMBER: 4705 (79 CR 592)
DATE WARRANT ISSUED: JUNE 23, 1980

MISCELLANEOUS INFORMATION: Alphonse Persico was convicted of murder in 1953 and served 20 years in the New York State Prison System. He is considered armed and dangerous. On May 1, 1980, Persico was found guilty
VEHICLE/TAG INFORMATION: of conspiracy and extortion.

IF ARRESTED OR WHEREABOUTS KNOWN, NOTIFY THE LOCAL UNITED STATES MARSHALS OFFICE,
   (TELEPHONE:___212-330-____).
IF NO ANSWER, CALL UNITED STATES MARSHALS SERVICE COMMUNICATIONS CENTER IN WASHINGTON, D.C.
   TELEPHONE___703-285-_____: NLETS ACCESS CODE IS DCUSMOOOO.
        (24 Hour telephone contact)

FORM USM -132
(EST. 5/79)

USMS Collections.

Photo 22. Sculptor Dave Manuel with *Frontier Marshal*, 1988.

Photo by Walter W. Klages.
The statue greets employees and visitors alike at USMS Headquarters.

Photo 23. U.S. Marshals Service Director K. Michael Moore headed the agency from late 1989 to 1992.

USMS Collections. Photo by Craig Crawford.

Photo 24. Early Mobile Command Center.

USMS Collections.
Beginning with the oversize Red October, the idea of integrating a mobile office stemmed from the 1980s. They became prominent while on assignments after several major hurricanes, and as educational centers across the country.

Photo 25. Deputy U.S. Marshal William Degan.

USMS Collections.
He was in service as part of the Special Operations Group when he met his death at
Ruby Ridge in August 1992.

Photo 26. U.S. Marshal Jim Propotnick in Antarctica.

USMS Collections/Jim Propotnick.
The USMS maintains law enforcement jurisdiction for our citizens there, which is ironically out of the District of Hawaii.

Photo 27. Director's Awards, ca. 1993.

USMS Collections. Photo by Craig Crawford.
Left to Right: Deputy Director for Operations James Roche; Director Henry Hudson;
U.S. Marshal Tony Perez.

Photo 28. Director Eduardo Gonzalez and Human Resource's Chief Joseph Moy.

USMS Collections.
Director Eduardo Gonzalez (right) and Human Resources Chief Joseph Moy with memorial stone for the tragedy in Oklahoma City.

Photo 29. John W. Marshall being sworn in as Director of the U.S. Marshals
Service, 1999.

USMS Collections. Photo by Craig Crawford.
At right is Attorney General Janet Reno.

Photo 30. Benigno G. Reyna.

USMS Collections. Photo by Craig Crawford.
President George W. Bush appointed Texan Benigno G. Reyna as director in 2001. He
served until the summer of 2005.

Photo 31. Invitation to the 40th Anniversary Observance Ceremonies at the Department of Justice.

You are cordially invited to
attend the observance of

The 40th Anniversary of the
Integration of the
University of Mississippi

Tuesday, July 15, 2003

Reception Brunch
U.S. Marshals Service
Media Center
10:00 –12:00 p.m.

40th Anniversary Observance
Symposium & Ceremony
Robert F. Kennedy Building
U.S. Department of Justice
The Great Hall
1:00 –4:00 p.m.

USMS Collections.

Photo 32. Two pictures from the July 2003 40th Commemoration Ceremonies of the Integration of the University of Mississippi.

Department of Justice. Photos by Craig Crawford.
Top, James Meredith speaks to reporters. Bottom, retired deputies who manned the lines during the riots, and family members, respond to a portion of the ceremony.

Photo 33. USMS Director John F. Clark, with Attorney General Alberto Gonzales (left) at the Department of Justice's Great Hall, 2006.

USMS Collections and Department of Justice. Photo by Craig Crawford.

Photo 34. Promotional Poster for the Witness Protection Program, 2012.

Design by Shane McCoy. USMS Collections.
The public continues its fascination with the program.

SECTION FOUR—The Eighties: Redefinition

CHAPTER 11

STRIKE TEAMS AND HIGH-PROFILE PRISONERS

The 1980s began warily for the United States Marshals Service as it adapted to the reorganization. New duties tested the agency, especially in the area of fugitive apprehension. Additionally, deputies faced striking miners, organized ideological groups, and even foreign dictators. The agency created a process for evaluating threats to the federal judiciary. The U.S. Marshals again redefined themselves while taking on the new demands of this decade.

CLIPPING THE WINGS OF THE FALCON

In 1977, a court convicted Christopher John Boyce of espionage and sentenced him to 40 years in prison. He served his time at the Lompoc Correctional Institution in California. A former aerospace technology employee, Boyce had sold information to the Soviet Union through a friend named Andrew Daulton Lee during the 1970s.[1]

Boyce possessed an incredible memory, an unusual skill set, and a love of falconry. The latter earned him the nickname "Falcon" during his trial.

He used some of his inventiveness to escape from Lompoc on January 21, 1980. Several inmates assisted Boyce by hiding him in a drainage valve hole and providing "makeshift snips" and a ladder. After clipping his way through the fence wire, the Falcon took flight as a fugitive.[2]

The 1979 agreement with the FBI gave the marshals priority in the manhunt, and the Boyce escape presented a real test for the agency. Finding the Falcon would provide a difficult task. Time was crucial.

The investigation fell to Chief of Enforcement Operations Thomas "Chuck" Kupferer Jr., a well-travelled deputy who had served in six different postings in 10 years. Although he knew California well, having joined the U.S. Marshals there in 1969, his expertise in managing tough operations landed him the job.[3]

The sightings of Boyce were endless, and marshals conducted individual interviews worldwide. "One individual claimed he was a gun-runner, and that Boyce was in Costa Rica. [I] came to find out he never flew an airplane in his life," recalled Kupferer.[4]

In August 1981, credible information came to Kupferer that Boyce was in the state of Washington. According to Deputy U.S. Marshal Marvin Lutes in a *Pentacle* article from 1981, a local deputy marshal named Jim Maji caught a break on one of the many leads. During a painstaking review of possible clues, Maji uncovered a driver's license that Boyce had used under an assumed name. Agency leadership immediately convened a task force of 19 deputy marshals, eight FBI agents, and an agent from the Border Patrol. Among the deputies were Chief Deputy U.S. Marshals Bob Christman and Bob DeGuerra; Deputy U.S. Marshals Denny Behrend and Jack Cluff; and Supervisory Inspector Dave Neff.[5]

After months of searching, the FBI referred a call from an informant to Neff, who was on duty in Denver. He taped an interview with the informant once they met at a local destination. Neff recalled later, "I just took the tape recorder out, met him, and recorded what he had, and then brought him down to the office here with me..."[6]

Neff informed Bob Dighera at Headquarters, who compiled a list of 60 questions to ask the informant. The answers convinced investigators that the informant had good information on the actual location of Boyce. "We had word that he might be at a wedding in Idaho, so we went to Idaho and back over to Seattle and back over to Port Angeles. Inevitably we caught up with him at Port Angeles. A day before he was going to leave."[7]

Chief Deputy U.S. Marshal Bob Christman met with Neff, Kupferer, Behrend, Cluff, and other members of the team as they converged on Port Angeles, Washington. On August 21, 1981, they knew of several locations Boyce frequented, including supermarkets and restaurants. They split up into four surveillance teams. One team set up on the Pit Stop Restaurant and Drive-In. Around 8:30 p.m., they observed a lone Oldsmobile parked there. The deputies carefully approached the car. If Boyce looked up, he could still escape. The command phrase "Let's do it!" signaled all hands to surround the car as Boyce sat reading a mechanical guidebook. He looked up and said, "Who are you guys?"[8] The Marshals had their man.

FISTs of the US Marshals

Beginning in 1977, President Jimmy Carter's Reorganization Project criticized the jurisdictional overlap among federal agencies in the execution of warrants. In June 1978, marshals launched "Operation Noriega," a pilot program designed to decrease the number of warrants in the Central District of California. Named after the first U.S. marshal for the Southern District of California, Pablo Noriega, the operation proved to be a template for future enforcement actions. Deputies turned to local law enforcement agencies for assistance. The immediate goal of the operation was to clear warrants, but long-range goals were to "increase apprehension for Federal violations by 10% in three months. To reduce outstanding Federal warrants by 15% during the first two years. To establish a continuity cooperative program for the apprehension of fugitives."[9]

During "Operation Noriega," Marshals Service personnel reviewed warrants with the clerk of the U.S. court, and highlighted parole and probation violations as arrest priorities. Deputies classified each fugitive's original offense, and entered the names into a central database. Investigators contacted the originating agencies for leads.[10]

The investigative processes created for the four-month operation resulted in 282 arrests and a reduction in investigative hours per case, from 20 to 13.8 hours. Investigators utilized 39 informants during Noriega.[11]

The use of named operations, and the accompanying press interest, was relatively new to the agency. The Marshals Service had historically retreated from the news organizations due to the negative coverage of events in the past. However, the advantages were not lost on management. They built the foundations of a solid fugitive program and embraced more publicity. The agency did not want to lose the duties of fugitive hunters, and get "pigeon-holed" as guards or bailiffs:[12]

> When the Attorney General transferred responsibility for the investigation of certain Federal [sic] fugitives from the FBI to the Marshals Service in October 1979, fugitive operations began to come alive throughout the Service. As a result, 105 Deputies were selected for advanced training as Enforcement Specialists dedicated to overseeing the investigation and apprehension of Federal fugitives within their respective Districts [sic] and nationwide.[13]

Howard Safir knew how to find high profile cases to justify the widening scope of the fugitive mission. His previous experience at the Federal Bureau of Narcotics and the Drug Enforcement Administration had taught him the value of pursuing big names. In search of a winning combination, Safir and his contemporaries combined savvy tactics with regionalized or localized lists of fugitives. A 1980 study conducted by Safir's office highlighted a disturbing statistic: almost 13 percent of defendants who committed a felony and were granted bail ended up getting re-arrested in the period before trial. Effective policing required concentrating apprehension efforts in a specific area to dismantle supporting criminal elements. Marshals wanted to close as many outstanding warrants as possible in a stipulated period of time. They created the FIST (Fugitive Investigative Strike Team) concept as the solution.[14]

In October 1981, marshals conducted the first FIST in Miami and netted 76 wanted persons. A second FIST in Los Angeles captured 102 fugitives. In L.A., the operation used only Marshals Service personnel and pursued only federal fugitives, with the exception of a few state and local warrants in the immediate Los Angeles area. In April 1982, FIST III began the modern trend of using multi-jurisdictional personnel and cases. New York City detectives teamed with deputy U.S. marshals to specifically target fugitives in the city and its immediate suburbs. Two months later, investigators counted 303 fugitives arrested, all described as "USMS Class I" and "career criminals."[15]

The multi-jurisdictional teams changed the perception of the U.S. Marshals Service and the FIST formula impressed the Department of Justice, who embraced the concept. As a result, more FIST operations ensued.

In August 1982, U.S. Marshal Jim Moyer and the District of Colorado started a 10-week operation with the Denver Police, Lakewood Police and Arapahoe County Sheriff's Department to take 92 fugitives off the streets. Its importance was highlighted in the subsequent press conference at its conclusion. William P. Tyson, the Director for the Executive Office for U.S. Attorneys, attending on behalf of Attorney General William French Smith, answered press questions about the operation.[16]

The warrants targeted changed with each operation and jurisdiction, based on the criminal activity of the geographic area. FIST VI, conducted in California in 1984, included the California State Police, Los Angeles Police Department, and 24 other local jurisdictions to find fugitive segments of the "Marielitos." Named for their place of origin in Cuba, these former detainees and their followers committed violent crimes such as rape, robbery, and narcotics distribution. Many mixed in the general population after the Mariel Boatlift. By January 1984, the LAPD

attributed multiple murders to them. As a direct result of the FIST, 13
Marielitos wanted for murder were arrested.[17]

U.S. News & World Report profiled the value of FIST operations in the
New York area in late 1984. "An eight-week drive that ended November
20 netted 3,309 persons wanted in eight Eastern states. Atty. Gen. William
French Smith proclaimed it 'the largest and most successful fugitive
manhunt in law-enforcement history.' "[18] The article stated that the
number "nearly matched" the 3,500 fugitives caught in all six previous
FIST operations. During the sweep, the coordinating deputies worked
long shifts out of Fort Totten in Queens. Deputy U.S. Marshal Dave
O'Flaherty noted in the article, "If we can get him off the street for a
week or even a month, that's one murder or robbery he may not be
able to commit."[19]

FIST IX, the last numbered operation, took place in 1986. The success of
these round-ups garnered instantaneous media attention and publicity.
In fact, the positive press led to enthusiasm among law enforcement
agencies. The new tactics proved original and legal.[20]

As cooperative efforts developed, an equally impressive program
for apprehending high-profile fugitives began alongside it. The U.S.
Marshals worked with international law enforcement agencies such as
INTERPOL. It was a duty of deputy U.S. marshals to "apprehend fugitives
wanted by foreign nations and believed to be in the United States."[21] In
order to enhance this relationship, deputies began details in France's
INTERPOL offices. Meanwhile, fugitives from overseas expanded the
agency's frontiers once again.[22]

International interests in the United States were also of a protective
nature. U.S. Marshal Tench Ringgold protected a visiting Marquis de
Lafayette from France while in the nation's capital. Deputy U.S. marshals
protected foreign diplomats at the United Nations in September and
October 1980. Director Hall received a letter from Deputy Assistant
Secretary of State Karl Ackerman praising the unit from the U.S. Marshals
Service on this mission. The United Nations detail comprised over

20 deputies. Over time, deputy marshals served behind the scenes of many international events, from Olympic Games to worldwide judicial conferences.[23]

WOULD-BE PRESIDENTIAL ASSASSIN

John Hinckley, Jr. achieved infamy for one event: his attempted assassination of President Ronald Reagan on March 30, 1981. Marshals handled the infamous prisoner, taking responsibility for his housing, transportation and safety, from April 2, 1981, until his transfer to St. Elizabeth's Hospital.[24]

Assistant Director for Operations Safir and the U.S. Marshal for the District of Columbia J. Jerome Bullock took no chances with Hinckley. They secured a team of witness security specialists, like the Eastern District of Virginia's Jack Braxton and Southern New York's Jack Walsh, for the extended protective detail that produced the defendant for hearings and other court proceedings.[25]

The specialized prisoner movement for the first hearing in the matter proved secure, albeit arcane. Hinckley's transport to federal trial in D.C. involved a helicopter flight from Quantico Marine Corps Base in Virginia to Fort McNair in Washington, followed by an armored car motorcade to the court, supported by deputies, Park Police, and Metropolitan Police Department officers. All the while, Hinckley remained handcuffed.[26]

After the hearing, Safir and Bullock personally oversaw the safe evacuation of Hinckley to a waiting Marine helicopter bound for the Federal Correctional Institution in Butner, North Carolina. This ended the special detail in the public eye, but not in reality. Deputies assigned to the Hinckley detail looked after him long after the initial hearing, and took special measures to bring him from detention facilities to court.[27]

According to former Acting Director Louie McKinney, who was one of the deputies on the security detail, officials remembered what happened to Lee Harvey Oswald shortly after killing President John F. Kennedy. The assassin was killed while being transported by authorities. Attorney General Smith "didn't want history to repeat itself."[28]

According to McKinney, the high level of news media interest in the case forced frequent changes to Hinckley's moves. In November 1981, marshals housed Hinckley in the stockade at Fort Meade, Maryland, where he attempted to hang himself.[29] An official news account followed the attempt:

> With the door lock jammed, U.S. marshals reached in the window of John W. Hinckley Jr.'s prison cell and cut down the accused presidential assailant as he tried to hang himself with a rolled-up jacket, the Justice Department says.[30]

McKinney, in his biography *One Marshal's Badge*, reported that "Hinckley jammed his cell door by reaching around the bars and putting the cardboard top from a box of crackers into the lock mechanism. Even though our deputies could put the key in the lock, it refused to budge."[31] He further noted that Deputy U.S. Marshal Roger Mullis ran outside to the cell window and cut Hinckley down. The fire department used bolt cutters to open the cell door to get him to the hospital. It was his second suicide attempt—the first occurred in May while under evaluation at FCI Butner. He tried to overdose on Tylenol and valium.[32]

Despite these episodes, Hinckley's trial began on April 27, 1982, and lasted several tense weeks. Seated close to the United States Attorney's table throughout the proceedings was Supervisory Deputy U.S. Marshal Robert Reid. A court sketch artist, Freida Reiter, caught Reid in a watchful pose.[33]

Hinckley stayed in a specially renovated cell while he was on trial. Inspector Ken Barry, who had spent much of his career in Washington State, observed that Hinckley appeared docile at the beginning of the trial. On his two-week detail, Hinckley requested him to play multiple games of gin rummy. "After he lost three hands, he expressed his displeasure by hitting the bottom of the card table, and the cards would go flying." Still, Hinckley would later ask Barry to play cards with him.[34]

The court found Hinckley not guilty by reason of insanity. At the conclusion of trial, the Marshals Service tabulated the costs of the specialized measures and protective details at close to $1 million. Hinckley officially transferred to St. Elizabeth's on June 22, 1982.[35]

Attorney General Smith wrote Director Hall, "I want to thank and congratulate you personally for your outstanding performance in response to the crisis arising from the attempted assassination of the President. The emergency situation required thoughtful judgment, yet demanded immediate response and flawless execution. You and your subordinates provided precisely that in an exemplary fashion."[36]

John W. Hinckley Jr. seemed linked to the U.S. Marshals Service for years. Every time he attended a court hearing, deputies brought him to the proceeding. In December 2011, *Washington Post* reporter Petula Dvorak wrote a column entitled, "It's Nuts to Spend so Much Time and Money on John W. Hinckley Jr." Dvorak wrote about one hearing that there were "at least seven lawyers on the clock, one federal judge, court clerks, and a few U.S. marshals."[37] While her point of view as a taxpaying citizen saw the actions as a waste of time and money, the case required these extraordinary circumstances.

15 Most Wanted Fugitives

In July 1982, Hall, Safir, and Inspector Robert Leschorn of the Enforcement Operations Division came up with an angle to publicize high-profile fugitive cases: to bring back the feeling of wanted posters of the past as part of a national program. They selected 15 fugitives based on their past criminal charges and history of violence, and put them on official posters for public display. Headquarters printed publication USM-132 for display purposes in district offices and elsewhere. The most wanted fugitives represented the most difficult of cases.[38]

Leschorn drew the first draft of the Fifteen Most Wanted posters on agency letterhead. He set the format for descriptions and cases, and added a thumbnail mug shot, cut from copies of pictures. His sketch originated the Fifteen Most Wanted program.[39]

The Marshals Service's Fifteen Most Wanted was little different from the FBI's existing Top Ten program. Both focused on the "worst of the worst" fugitives, and utilized the program to motivate and generate interest in the press and the public. Safir and Leschorn added the first names in February 1983. Alphonse Persico made the first list, which gave the U.S. Marshals an additional tool for gathering intelligence on the fugitive.[40]

By December 1987, the Service had placed 66 names on the list. Deputy marshals arrested 42 of them, while other agencies arrested 11. Two of the fugitives had died while "on the lam," and one was removed. By September 1989, the program had closed 87 high-profile cases.[41]

Fifteen Most Wanted cases received constant investigative review and publicity, translating into a higher level of vigilance by investigators and state and local law enforcement, as well as the general public.

A 1989 informational handout gave an overview of criteria to make the list. The publication, entitled *Fifteen Most Wanted Program*, stated,

> Each district's submission is reviewed by Enforcement Operations to determine if it meets the stringent requirements of the program. Many of the fugitives on the list have a history of violent behavior and are wanted for such heinous crimes that their continued status as a fugitive would pose a serious threat to the public. Because of these stringent requirements, only one out [of] every thousand fugitives is accepted as a "15 Most Wanted."[42]

Between 1983 and 1988, most of the fugitives placed on the "Fifteen Most Wanted" were suspects in homicides or armed robberies. However, by May 1988, the most wanted shifted toward fugitives involved in the narcotics trade. The Enforcement Operations Division found that the "majority of the well-organized and wealthy drug fugitives rarely have well-documented criminal histories."[43] A graph within the handout, entitled "Criminal Cases Pending by Offense in the U.S. Attorney's Offices," reflected the same. Controlled substance cases rocketed to 36.5 percent of the caseload.[44]

The Enforcement Operations Division updated the case submission guidelines in September 1994 to reflect their burgeoning caseload. Those guidelines reflected the changes made by 1989, and emphasized the "Fifteen Most Wanted" posters. The popularity of the program fared well, and although many of the profiled fugitives remained on the district notice boards for years, they were never forgotten.[45]

Gordon Kahl

In February 1983, the dangers of the job of deputy marshal became apparent in Medina, North Dakota. Gordon Kahl, a well-known tax protester and powerful personality, had formed a militant ideological group called "Posse Comitatus." His magnetic personality matched his ideology, and he possessed a vehement antipathy towards the federal government. Kahl lived in Heaton, North Dakota, and had led a similar group in Texas.[46]

The marshals held a federal arrest warrant for Kahl because he violated his parole. A federal court convicted him for not paying his federal taxes and he served time in prison in the 1970s before getting out on parole. However, Kahl violated the conditions of his release. In April 1981, he failed to report to his probation officer, and a warrant was promptly issued.[47]

Nonetheless, Kahl had attracted a core group of sympathizers and like-minded tax protesters. Local law enforcement received information about a Posse meeting and the U.S. Marshals Service planned to serve the warrant following the meeting on February 13, 1983.[48]

U.S. Marshal Kenneth B. Muir, 63, a career deputy who had served during the riots in Oxford, understood the dangers of facing ideologically charged opposition. Knowing that Kahl might not go quietly, he assembled a team of local law enforcement and Deputy U.S. Marshals Robert Cheshire, James Hopson, and Carl Wigglesworth. They planned to arrest Kahl after setting up a roadblock just outside of town and after Kahl attended the meeting. Local authorities somehow knew the protester's regular driving route, and he appeared to be following it. None of Muir's team suspected Kahl already knew about the warrant and intended to surprise him to avoid violence.[49]

Cheshire received the call from the sheriff about the meeting and set off from Bismarck with Hopson, while Marshal Muir and Wigglesworth drove from Fargo. Just as the meeting ended, Muir and his men arrived in the area. They decided to set up the roadblock on a road just outside Medina. One of the local officers arrived to assist them in his vehicle, and they positioned Muir's Dodge Diplomat in front. A second car, with Hopson, Cheshire, and the sheriff as the occupants, was the chase vehicle.[50]

The plan went amiss. Kahl changed clothing with his son Yorivon and rode with another group member instead of his own car. Because the local police vehicle had a flashing light, both Kahl and his companion vehicle saw it. They turned into a driveway to head back towards Medina when Cheshire's car pulled in. Because the roadblock proved ineffective, Muir and the local policeman drove towards the standoff. Kahl and his son both held semi-automatic rifles, and the latter aimed his weapon at Cheshire. Muir stopped his car and tried to negotiate with Kahl's group. According to Wigglesworth, the attempt at negotiation lasted approximately nine minutes. An affidavit revealed Yorivon fired the first shot that hit Deputy U.S. Marshal Cheshire. An intense firefight between the parties ensued, which claimed the lives of Muir and Cheshire, and wounded Hopson, the two local policemen, and the younger Kahl. The rest of his group returned to the meeting location, and Gordon Kahl fled.[51]

Reaction to the deaths of Muir and Cheshire was swift and severe. Attorney General Smith was outraged. He released a press statement the next day that stated in part, "In a nation governed by law, there is no greater tragedy than the loss of those killed while trying to enforce and defend that law. We all owe a great debt, which we can honor, but never fully repay, to these brave men who died trying to enforce our law and protect us..."[52] A day later, approximately 100 law enforcement officers converged on North Dakota.[53]

President Ronald Reagan spoke at a special memorial at the Department of Justice's Great Hall to honor all lives taken in the line of duty. The images of Cheshire's young widow and three small children along with an aged Mrs. Muir only redoubled the efforts to find Gordon Kahl.[54]

However, locating Gordon Kahl was not easy. Chief Deputy U.S. Marshal Ron Evans received hundreds of leads across the region. Enforcement Chief Chuck Kupferer and Deputy U.S. Marshal Roger Arechiga coordinated the leads and search warrants. A $25,000 reward was offered for information leading to Kahl's capture. Deputies arranged for Gordon Kahl's wife, Joan, to appear on television from the old federal building in Fargo. She asked her husband to give himself up. The FBI and state troopers searched his former residence days later, but there was no sign of Kahl. On February 15, his associate Scott Faul carried a letter written by the missing man, a "confession" of some type, when he voluntarily surrendered in Fessenden, North Dakota. In the message, Kahl took full responsibility for the deaths of U.S. Marshal Muir and Deputy U.S. Marshal Cheshire.[55]

Chuck Kupferer set up a makeshift headquarters in Jamestown, North Dakota, that he described, as a "fifty man unit—25 deputy marshals... and 25 FBI... in February, it was brutal."[56] The task force followed hundreds of leads that produced nothing helpful in the case.

In June, investigators received word that Kahl was hiding in the farmhouse of friends in Smithville, Arkansas. Apparently there was a hideout on one side of a hill, where provisions and arms awaited him.

In the course of conversation, a family member overheard a discussion about Kahl's presence, and contacted police. The task force approached carefully. Roger Arechiga called for an airplane to Little Rock, and he, Kupferer, and several others from headquarters left for that location. They met a number of local police, including the sheriff of Lawrence County, Arkansas, Harold G. Matthews.[57]

Kahl prepared to die fighting. Law enforcement encircled the hideout, but he was well-armed. Casualties were probable. Arechiga saw that the roof of the hideout was easily accessible and made of sod, and surmised officers could force Kahl out with smoke. Sheriff Matthews, who unbeknownst to the others suffered from terminal cancer, decided to face down the fugitive from the front. While Kahl's attention was drawn toward the advancing Matthews, Arechiga and a constable climbed to the roof without being observed. They hoped to smoke him out, and lobbed gas canisters down the chimney of the structure. However, the dwelling's material was too flammable and the gunfire originating from inside started a blaze. Sheriff Matthews and Kahl exchanged rounds, and both fell mortally wounded. However, the policeman managed to get outside the building. The remainder of the officers and deputies concentrated their fire, but the heat of the rising blaze kept them back. They expected Kahl to jump out of the burning structure, but the fire consumed it with no sign of Kahl after his gunfire ceased.[58] Chuck Kupferer said, "His corpse was found by the window—incinerated from the heat of the fire."[59]

At the Conference of the Arkansas' Sheriffs Association, the Executive Director of the National Sheriffs' Association presented the 12-year-old son of the late Sheriff Matthews with the Medal of Valor for his father. Although Sheriff Matthews had made it to the hospital, he died three hours later. Gordon Kahl claimed his last victim, but the actions of the "Posse Comitatus" foreshadowed ideological struggles in the decades to come.[60]

CHAPTER 12

THE DEVELOPMENT
OF A GOLDEN AGE

The upper ranks of the United States Marshals Service reshuffled in the early 1980s. Jack Cameron retired for good in 1982, having witnessed the agency's designation as a Department of Justice bureau and the formation of its official headquarters. Director Bill Hall left after six years; DOJ tapped him as Assistant Associate Attorney General for Law Enforcement Training. He officially resigned as USMS Director. Deputy Director Twomey and younger assistants like Mead and Safir guided the Service during this transition. Soon, the position of Director of the Marshals Service would be filled with a presidential appointee, just like the U.S. marshal for each district.[1]

On October 25, 1983, Stanley Morris became the next director. Morris had been an associate deputy attorney general at the Department of Justice. Born in California in 1942, he received a Master's degree in public law and government from Columbia University in 1966. After an internship at the Department of Health, Education, and Welfare, he rose to the position of director of Operational Planning. He moved on to the White House Office of Management and Budget, where he was the deputy associate director for Economics and Government from January 1973 through October 1977. He served as deputy associate director for Regulatory Policy and Reports Management until 1979. Two years later, Morris joined the Justice Department.[2]

At the Marshals Service, Morris hit the ground running. Ably using the agency's magazine *The Pentacle* as a primary communications vehicle, he conveyed messages across the agency on a regular basis. In the November-December 1983 issue, he shared his hallmark vision. The first portion reads:

> As this issue of the **Pentacle** goes to press, I will have been Director for one month. Although this is a short time given the colorful 194-year history of this unique agency, I am enthusiastic to be joining it at a time when it is evolving still—as a top-notch professional law enforcement organization with a definite role in the nation's future.
>
> For many years, I have been a strong supporter of the Service, and have been personally involved in a number of special projects which have shaped its future... I have always been in your corner.[3]

Director Morris chose his language carefully, because he believed his responsibility included shaping the agency's future and making it whole. He wanted the employees to understand he was coming from a position of knowledge and trust already.

In his introductory message, he rolled out his four primary goals. First, he sought to improve the quality of work and enhance the morale of employees. Second, he wanted to increase appreciation and understanding for the essential law enforcement role played by employees in the federal criminal justice system. Third, he encouraged new, innovative ways to carry out critical responsibilities, noting the "can do" attitude of employees. Finally, he envisioned a Marshals Service with resources and grade levels appropriate for carrying out its mission.[4]

He continued the annual Director's Awards, which had begun in the fall of 1982 under Director Hall and commended employees nationwide for their achievements. In addition, he sought further morale-boosting initiatives in new exercise programs and historical celebrations.[5]

Deputy U.S. Marshal Henry Ohrenburger, a six-year employee of the U.S. Marshals Service at the time Stanley Morris arrived, stated later, "He was a take-charge guy, knew what he wanted to do."[6] He remembered that during a speech in those first few years of Morris' term, he said, "Look, you're Marshals out there and you have to understand our most important asset is not the gun on your hip or the car you drive to and from work, it's the people."[7]

Director Morris implemented work life improvements such as the Fitness-in-Total Program. In an effort to ensure better productivity, three hours of duty time per week were allowed for physical fitness. In July 1984, operational personnel were required to participate, while administrative participation was voluntary. He also had big plans for the agency's bicentennial in September 1989. Similarly, he harbored big ambitions for the Fifteen Most Wanted Program, as well as new initiatives in threat analysis, seized assets control, and programs involving the Special Operations Group and court security. He also began an initiative to better align deputies' salaries with their law enforcement duties.[8]

He championed the centralized communications center, which had its origins in the 1970s and greatly aided response time for operational missions. By 1983, four computer terminals, considered cutting-edge technology at the time, linked the U.S. Marshals Service to local law enforcement agencies and the FBI's National Crime Information Center. Internally, the terminals connected necessary elements of the Witness Security Program and administrative systems.[9] As stated in *The Pentacle* from 1983:

> All District offices have access to this communications system. The technology used in the Communications Center today has dramatically improved communications capabilities for the U.S. Marshals

Service. Simply in speed, reliability, accessibility, and quantity the Communications Center has come a long way since the teletype machines which were used throughout the U.S. Marshals Service less than three years ago.[10]

The Office of Internal Inspections was formed in early 1983. The burgeoning number of employees required more careful internal controls and auditing. The functions already existed, but in separate offices. Chief Inspector Donald Hill managed the Office of Field Management Services for a time, while Inspector Art Daniels led the Office of Internal Audit, and Chief Inspector Robert Schmidt helmed the former internal investigations unit. Schmidt was placed in charge of all three functions under his jurisdiction, with branches in the Headquarters building, Chicago and Burlingame, California. Daniels stayed at Headquarters with three inspectors, two auditors, and two administrative employees.[11]

> Complaints of misconduct or audit concerns will be directed to the OII Chief, who will consult with Director William Hall and Deputy Director John Twomey and make decisions concerning internal investigations and audit. He will then assign the case to one of the three Branch [sic] offices for handling... Approximately 36 routine and special audits will be conducted each year with a projected completion time of 30 days per audit.[12]

The Procurement and Property Management Division formed under the direction of Chief Robert T. Pandolfo. In actuality, the two functions related only because they both involved property. Chief James M. Coulter led the acquisition side, called the Procurement and Contracting Branch. The branch interpreted the legal processes associated with contracts. Brenda M. Shortt and Elizabeth Howard were both contracting officers. The other branch, Property Management, was headed by Chief James P. Mulcahy. His specialists included Mike Spearman, Mischalle W. Bush, and Carleton R. Parish, who for many years supervised warehouse operations.[13]

Headquarters remained in the Tyson's Corner mall building. Employees worked in space on the upper floor while shoppers browsed below. Oddly, the warehouse and additional office functions operated below the shopping level. Gary Mead recalled that by 1988, "Tyson's Corner was getting ready to expand itself, and wanted us out of there."[14] Director Morris wanted to leave the mall location and give the U.S. Marshals its own building. Mead noted that the Deputy Attorney General showed interest in pursuing a Department of Justice campus.[15]

Seizing Assets

Congress applied seizure and forfeiture of a criminal's property as an allowable sanction in the 1970 RICO (Racketeer Influenced and Corrupt Organization) statute (18 U.S.C. 1961 *et seq.*). By 1983, amendments linked seizure of property to the illegal drug trade. An explanation of one such amendment noted that the "authority to reach the profits and financial underpinnings of organized criminal activity through forfeiture is a necessary part of effective law enforcement in this area." Through the Comprehensive Crime Control Act of 1984, the Department of Justice designated the Marshals Service to manage property seized and forfeited by other DOJ law enforcement agencies until its final disposal.[16]

With the law enforcement focus on narcotics trafficking, commonly called the "War on Drugs," in full swing, the U.S. Marshals Service seized property once federal courts decided there was a "nexus," or a connection of an asset to criminal activity. Director Morris and Associate Director for Operations Safir saw the advantage of fighting crime in a whole new way.[17]

"The goal of this critical and powerful tool is to dismantle the economic power of drug enterprises," Safir stated. "It deprives the criminals of many of the resources—houses, aircraft, businesses—that are essential to the continued operation of illegal activities. When criminals get out of jail, they can't return to a high lifestyle if their assets have been seized."[18]

U.S. Marshals auctions were not new. Since the beginning of their existence, the Marshals auctioned forfeited property that fell into federal hands by court order. A provision in the Comprehensive Crime Control Act of 1984 allowed the sharing of forfeited assets through the Assets Forfeiture Fund, a fund controlled by the Department of Justice into which the proceeds of sales and money forfeited were deposited. The Equitable Sharing Program formalized the cash distribution of auction proceeds to law enforcement programs of all jurisdictions with a role in seizing and forfeiting proceeds of criminal activity. It really showed that "crime doesn't pay." The program was particularly effective in New York, where U.S. Attorney Rudolph W. Giuliani and U.S. Marshal Romolo J. Imundi sought to stem the continued flow of drug assets to criminals.[19]

Government agencies and news media scrutinized every case involving high-profile assets. If government disposed of an asset for less than its perceived worth, negative publicity ensued. The General Accounting Office submitted reports; news outlets wrote articles. In 1991, a reporter erroneously stated that the U.S. Marshals Service "mismanaged" assets totaling $1.4 billion, when addressing a specific $1.5 million dollar real estate sale.[20]

The complicated legal process of forfeiture sometimes made the job of the U.S. Marshals more difficult. For example, in one case, the court order only allowed for the seizure and sale of land but left out a business on the property. Bills for utilities went unpaid for a year because the government did not own the business, and in the end, the agency's ability to obtain a higher return or profit on the seized asset was reduced by the need to pay such past due bills. In the early days of this Marshals Service program, many seizures and disposals of forfeited assets presented the Service with unique circumstances and challenges.[21]

THREAT ANALYSIS

The Threat Analysis Group, or TAG, formed within the Office of the Assistant Director for Operations. Its formation represented a new tier of duties, providing both protective and support roles on fugitive cases and high-risk trials through assessments. Headquarters introduced TAG in 1983 as a resource to field investigators, rather than requiring them to use it. After the death of Judge John Wood, federal law enforcement proactively sought techniques to stop individuals from carrying out threats against the federal judiciary. TAG collected valuable law enforcement intelligence and other information about potential threats. Analysts formalized the information into assessments, and quickly shared the findings with deputies working cases in the field. TAG assisted investigative, judicial, and witness security functions.[22]

Eventually, the group developed into a division with streamlined practices.[23] TAG became the Threat Analysis Division, or TAD. A number of experienced leaders developed the new function—at first Chief Robert Liebscher, then Tony Odom. By the late 1980s, TAD concentrated on drug-related organizations and gang activity. The demand and output increased steadily for detailed assessments, and the burgeoning files required more personnel. The staff expanded to 14, among them longtime investigators such as Les Smith, Ron Collins, and administrative analysts such as Tina Kannapell. Because of the heavy reliance on intelligence-gathering databases, technical staff was added. Smith remarked, "There is sometimes a misconception that we have a staff of 125 people."[24]

Tony Odom had started with the U.S. Marshals in 1974, and served in five districts before returning to Headquarters to lead threat analysis in April 1987. He had a Master's Degree in criminology, and although he never received formal training in threat assessments prior to attaining the post, he noted there "were great similarities in working fugitive investigations and working court security details in the field and witness security details with threat analysis."[25]

In 1985, the District Threat Coordinator Program expanded through its training curriculum. By March 1990, 145 deputy U.S. marshals were trained to assess threats, and had provided 338 intelligence briefs. The briefs focused on both national and local events, and coordinated information with law enforcement partners like the Bureau of Prisons and the FBI National Crime Intelligence Center. The importance of intelligence reports was on the rise.[26]

Still, threat analysis remained uncharted territory. Odom shared the following:

> there was no way that we could determine if we had worked on somebody before. There was no way that we could develop a portfolio of affiliations. In other words, it came about in the Gordon Call [sic] shooting in North Dakota, where the deputies got killed, and went up through when Call [sic] was killed... our people turned around and said, what about the Posse Comitatus? And nobody knew. We didn't have anything that we could pull out and say, "Here's a history of them. Here's where they've been. Here's what they're doing now..."[27]

TAD gathered information from multiple sources, contacted other agencies, and asked other divisions for assessments on high-risk trials. In the 1980s, computers for analysis were a luxury. According to Odom, the first TAD computers remained in boxes for a time. It took some time to transition from a paper-based system to one automated by computers. "They had filing cabinets full of files of assessments that they had done, but nobody knew about TAD."[28]

From the piles of paper assessments, a computer program was developed. In the three and a half years under Odom's leadership, TAD analysts accumulated "100,000 records in the system on people, groups, affiliations that people may have with different groups, weapons that people had used, types of threats that they had made, explosive devices that may have been made."[29]

The basic underpinnings of threat analysis remained the same, even as the function evolved in the new millennium. The role of the intelligence analyst became more complex, but added a new and helpful dimension to the missions of the Marshals Service.

MENGELE

In January 1984, the *Washington Post* published an article about doctor Josef Mengele, infamously known during World War II and beyond as "the Angel of Death" of Adolf Hitler's Nazi regime in Germany. His human experiments on Jews and others in concentration camps were grotesque and cried out for punishment. He evaded all attempts to arrest him after the war, although there appeared to be evidence that he was under watch for a time. The *Post* article suggested that Mengele escaped after a short detention by American soldiers, and fueled renewed interest in the case from the Simon Wiesenthal Center, an organization dedicated to the prosecution of former Nazis accused of war crimes.[30]

Mengele moved around periodically to avoid capture for his war crimes. News sources and informants reported sightings in Argentina, Bolivia, Brazil, Paraguay, and Uruguay from 1949 through 1985.[31]

The Justice Department's Office of Special Investigations concentrated on locating former Nazis such as Mengele, and having them expelled from countries to face trial for war crimes in Europe. According to a statement by Associate Director for Operations Howard Safir, Attorney General William French Smith directed the U.S. Marshals to join the Office of Special Investigations in the hunt for Josef Mengele on February 11, 1985. The Department's Criminal Division Assistant Attorney General Stephen S. Trott sent a formal letter eight days later to Director Morris. Safir focused on the investigation.[32] The letter stated in part:

> Our first initiative was to learn as much about Joseph Mengele as possible: His background, his family, and any other possible support mechanisms that existed. It was our theory that rather than

immediately begin searching for Mengele in South America, that
a careful and deliberate review of the German support mechanism
would be the place to start. In February of this year, personnel of
this service proceeded to Frankfurt, Germany....[33]

The search for Mengele began in earnest. Ralph Zurita, Safir's deputy
chief, recalled that the hunt for Mengele took unprecedented international
steps. He went to Frankfurt and spoke to the German prosecutor, Hans-
Eberhard Klein, who provided 7,000 pages of loaned material on the case.[34]
In late April, the *New York Times* reported that deputies were sent to West
Germany to "question several jailed drug smugglers said to have been
close to Dr. Mengele in Paraguay, his last confirmed residence."[35] Safir
skillfully brought press attention to the investigation and, indirectly, to
the entire investigative program. The article quoted Safir that "the force of
2,400 marshals—Federal sheriffs, he called them—had extensive experience
here and abroad..."[36] The press not only followed the investigation, but
actively assisted. On March 26, 1985, the *Washington Times* announced
a $1 million reward for evidence leading to the arrest and conviction of
Mengele. Editor-in-Chief Arnaud de Borchgrave voluntarily passed any
information collected by the newspaper to the Marshals Service, which
made for an unusual partnership.[37]

While the Office of Special Investigations remained the primary
investigative agency, deputies followed the trail to recap Josef Mengele's
movement in Europe and South America. After a meeting in Frankfurt,
Safir relayed that Germany, Israel, and the United States would share
information on the case. Nazi hunter Simon Wiesenthal filled in the
gaps of information on possible associates. Safir met with German
and Israeli representatives in May, and found that the West German
police re-interviewed a longtime employee of Carl Mengele & Sons, the
family agricultural machine works company in Gunzburg. The employee
admitted that he met Josef Mengele several times in Argentina, and the
last of these visits occurred in 1960. In May, an authorized search of the
employee's home uncovered lengthy correspondence between the two.
In fact, one of the letters from a family friend revealed that Mengele

drowned while swimming in 1979. The employee also kept a directory with names and addresses of connections to Mengele in Germany and South America. The clues pointed to Sao Paulo, Brazil.[38]

By early June 1985, investigative activity focused on Brazil. The German authorities, along with the deputy marshals, interviewed a large number of witnesses before sending agents abroad. They attempted to interview Mengele's first wife and son. German agents found there were three families of couriers going between Gunzburg and Sao Paulo. In a short time, the Germans, working with the Brazilian authorities, located a possible burial site—albeit under the name of a deceased family friend, Wolfgang Gerhard. Three medical experts and three document experts were selected by the U.S. Marshals Service to work with Brazilian authorities in confirming information. They included a specialist in pen and ink writings and a forensic anthropologist. Both the Wiesenthal Center and German authorities provided medical experts.[39]

The body buried in Embu, Brazil, was fully examined. The team of American experts handling the exhumation and examination process opined in a June 21, 1985, preliminary report, that "the exhumed remains are definitely not those of Wolfgang Gerhard. It is further our opinion, that this skeleton is that of Josef Mengele within a reasonable scientific certainty."[40]

The Germans, Brazilians, and Americans examined related documents and unanimously agreed the writing belonged to Mengele. Brazilian authorities interviewed European expatriates from the town of Nova Europa, and from them learned that their quarry was seen at several social functions in 1959. Mengele spoke Portuguese, and as a farm manager was notably hard on the other employees. Apparently, the Gerhard family, with whom Mengele resided, moved to a farm in Serra Negra that year and hardly left the property. The real Wolfgang Gerhard died of cancer in the early 1970s. Mengele changed addresses several times before drowning in February 1979. Even when he was dead, the U.S. Marshals found their fugitive.[41]

Despite these conclusions, the Office of Special Investigations continued its search of Mengele. In fact, a final report on Mengele's death was not released until Germany and Israel officially accepted the conclusions in late 1992. Former Director Stanley Morris stated that the results "were absolutely clear to us over six years ago."[42]

TWO MOVEMENTS: SEDITION AND THE RAJNEESH CASES

The proliferation of ideological and religious groups reached new heights in the 1980s. Memories of the Jonestown, Guyana, mass murder-suicide of followers of Reverend Jim Jones in 1978 still hung in the air. Threats of bombings not seen since the days of Symbionese Liberation Army and the Weathermen grew.[43]

"The Covenant, The Sword and The Arms of the Lord," sometimes known as the "CSA," was an offshoot of an "order"called the Aryan Nations. The members of these organizations engaged in various illegal activities. Ideologically charged by white supremacy movements in the American northwest, branches of the group appeared in rural areas. In August 1983, the "CSA" emerged in Arkansas, and gained notoriety after they firebombed a Jewish community center in Indiana. Later that year an enclave was discovered near Fort Smith, Arkansas, where in November they set off a bomb on an electrical transition line.[44]

"CSA" was a throwback, a Klan imitator with overt political ambitions. Their goal was to bring down the government by force and racially "purify" society. A CSA member killed an Arkansas state trooper and allegedly murdered a Jewish pawnshop owner in 1985 in Texarkana. Mostly, members committed robberies and engaged in illegal firearms transactions. These actions followed the murder of Denver radio personality Alan Berg in June 1984 by an alleged white supremacist member. In Arkansas, in April 1985, CSA leader James Ellison and a number of the membership were arrested in their compound.[45]

The Aryan Nations railed against ZOG, an acronym for "Zionist Occupation Government." They decried the pending indictments against Ellison and the others as an extension of the original "Sedition Act." Attorney General Edwin Meese III and law enforcement agencies worked with a common goal of halting the violent acts of such groups.[46]

In April 1987, a federal grand jury in Fort Smith, Arkansas, charged 10 members of the Aryan Nation with conspiracy to overthrow the United States Government. The jury indicted leaders Richard G. Butler, Robert E. Miles, Jr., and Louis R. Beam, Jr., and the prosecution proved they financed their sedition operations through counterfeiting.[47]

The trial tested the U.S. Marshals, who had learned much about improved court security functions during a number of high-profile trials involving Columbian drug lord Carlos Enrique Lehder-Rivas, the Puerto Rican extremist group Los Macheteros, and organized crime trials like the "Pizza Connection" case.[48]

By this time the Marshals Service was adept at planning security for high-risk trials. Dave Neff recognized the vital aid of the Special Operations Group while producing prisoners for trial. They did so in several trials involving the Order and its kind.[49]

Director Morris explained, "With a total of about 1,900 operational employees, the Service is responsible for the security of 483 Federal facilities throughout the nation. In addition, it provides for the personal safety of 1,742 judicial officers and, when necessary, hundreds of jurors, witnesses, U.S. Attorneys, spectators, and trial participants."[50]

On August 8, 1985, U.S. Marshal Kernan H. Bagley of the District of Oregon wrote Director Morris a letter, with enclosed articles, about a guru named Bhagwan Shree Rajneesh. An immigrant from Poona, India, Rajneesh had a large following in Oregon. Apparently the settlers clashed with local authorities and citizens, which made the newspapers. Marshal Bagley wrote:

> I believe that this group has the potential for another Jonestown type massacre when and if substantially confronted by the federal government. There are many law suits pending against the Bhagwan Shree Rajneesh, Rajneesh Foundation International, and eight other Rajneesh organizations which were founded on August 3, 1965. Because the state of Oregon is there [sic] international headquarters, and they have made enemies with the people of the state, it's only logical that the differences will have to be settled in the federal courts.[51]

Bhagwan Shree Rajneesh and his followers purchased Big Muddy Ranch, east of Portland, Oregon, for almost $6 million in July 1981. Decades later, reporter Les Zaitz of the *Oregonian* recalled the scene with information obtained from former followers. The mysterious bearded leader arrived shortly after the ranch purchase and began his own city, putting him at odds with Oregon's Attorney General. Thousands moved to work in the new jurisdiction—some had been homeless. Zaitz revealed it was a tactic to increase the number of votes. Worse yet, a number of people in a nearby community suddenly contracted salmonella in September 1984 from eating at local salad bars. It was reported that a number of Rajneeshees may have been responsible.[52]

The situation became untenable as time passed. The Rajneeshees battled with an environmental group, according to Zaitz. After meeting wealthy donors, the guru rode in Rolls-Royce automobiles and wore jeweled watches. However, the guru's expansion plans stalled because of actions taken by several of his aides against investigating officials. Eventually, several of them spoke to state and federal officials about wiretaps, arson, fraud, and worse.[53]

By September 1985, most of Rajneesh's top aides fled or turned on him, so he attempted to flee as federal prosecutors closed in. A federal grand jury indicted him on 35 counts of mostly immigration fraud. He tried to escape to Bermuda by means of charter planes, but deputy U.S. marshals worked with the Immigration and Naturalization Service and found him first. Two jets landed at Charlotte, North Carolina, on October 28, and Chief Deputy U.S. Marshal Raymond Abrams and his deputies were waiting; they apprehended him. By early November, Rajneesh was on his way back to Oregon.[54]

Deputy marshals arrested Rajneesh and detained him for a time in the medical section of the Mecklenburg County Jail. Photographs of Rajneesh in handcuffs and restraints grabbed headlines in newspapers across the country. The guru's colorful garments accentuated the restraints.[55]

The guru complained about his treatment. Refusing to take the robes off, he required special arrangements for his meals and medical treatment. Until extradited to trial in Oregon, his arrest and detention caused major challenges and headaches for the Marshals Service.[56]

Disparate cases involving ideology and organized criminal activity foreshadowed the heightened challenges for the agency in the years to come. New obstacles would arise, but the agency developed effectively and met their goals consistently.

CHAPTER 13

UNIQUE ENFORCEMENT OPERATIONS

PERSICO AND RELATED MOBSTERS

Carmine Persico was an "old school" mobster. In 1957, he and another man received an order to kill one of the deadliest mob figures ever, Albert Anastasia, the leader of Murder, Inc. In that early "hit," the two men riddled Anastasia with bullets as he sat in a barber's chair.[1]

"[Persico] was one of the worst," said retired Inspector Bob Leschorn. "He was part of the Columbo crime family."[2] The inspector worked in the Eastern District of New York, home of one of the largest Mafia syndicates in the country. In 1980, Leschorn received the assignment to investigate crimes allegedly committed by the Persico family; he specialized at setting up high-profile stings.[3]

Shortly after the U.S. Marshals received the formal authority to pursue fugitives, among the first to cross his desk was Alphonse "Allie Boy" Persico, son of Carmine. The federal government wanted to prosecute the son for extortion, among other charges.[4]

With the approval of Chief Deputy U.S. Marshal Michael Pizzi, Leschorn planned a long-term operation to find the chink in the Persico armor. Along with Inspectors Victor Oboyski and Mike Moriarty, he spent long hours of surveillance at "Allie Boy" Persico's property. They set up in the woods near the home and purposely cut down trees to get a better view and send the fugitive a clear message. When the deputies received word of a meeting involving Persico, excitement about a bust filled their thoughts. At a meeting site, the deputies made one of the biggest busts in agency history, dramatically decreasing organized crime in the area for a time. Unfortunately, Allie Boy evaded capture and stayed in the wind.[5]

Leschorn transferred to the Headquarters Enforcement Division, and Persico's New York network disintegrated because its members were constantly in hiding. Several of Persico's group mysteriously died after the big bust, supposedly in retaliation for their failure to spot the deputies. However, Allie Boy Persico remained on the lam. Leschorn worked with Pizzi and others to create a plaster of Paris bust of the elusive fugitive. It was then that the team brought in valuable assistance.[6]

In 1985, the team brought in a young deputy marshal from Connecticut, Arthur Roderick, who was well-versed about mob activities in St. Louis. In early 1987, he hit the trail of Salvatore "Mickey" Caruana, a known member of the Patriarca Family and a 15 Most Wanted fugitive. Roderick waited at one of Caruana's known hideouts, and seized a bag of trash deposited at the curb. He found "chocolate-covered strawberries, receipts, the place had been completely cleaned out."[7] However, leads pointed investigators to the Marvin Hagler-Sugar Ray Leonard boxing match in Las Vegas on April 6, 1987. Caruana was an avid boxing fan, and the investigators expected him to attend the fight. Roderick worked with several deputies brought in from other operations to assist. They mixed with the crowds at the event. "He didn't go to the fight... he was in Connecticut," recalled Roderick. Apparently, the fugitive watched the fight on pay-per-view at a theatre.[8]

Within a month, deputies developed information on the existence of an apartment and storage facilities belonging to Caruana. They located a cache of arms both at the storage facility and a hotel room. The deputies obtained a search warrant for his living quarters in Groton, Connecticut, where more clues surfaced. Among them was a dated milk carton, which revealed that an occupant had recently stayed there. Deputies also found a number of stuffed animals from machines at truck stops. They released the information to the television show *Unsolved Mysteries*. Unfortunately, not much came from the publicity.[9]

While the marshals were working the Caruana case, however, Allie Boy Persico's name resurfaced. Roderick said investigators "kept hearing about this guy Persico, that was in Connecticut, hiding out in Connecticut."[10] In early 1988, Pizzi summoned Roderick to the Eastern District of New York. Roderick learned about an intense investigation. While many thought Persico had died in a boating accident, deputies had reason to think he still lived.[11]

Roderick quietly combed Coast Guard stations and state logs across Connecticut and Rhode Island, but found nothing. He turned to records of possible car accidents and liquor distributors for purchases of Persico's favorite brand of Cutty Sark scotch. At Connecticut's Division of Motor Vehicles, Roderick found the vital clue that led him to Alphonse Persico.[12]

"The fact was whenever he used an alias name, he used a vowel... I spent three weeks at the DMV," said Roderick.[13] He researched thousands of records and narrowed possibilities using dates and descriptions. He found 200 names in Connecticut. "Frank Bender was an artist out of Philadelphia, did a bust of Persico, did two different versions," recalled Roderick, who began carrying around a notebook with photos of the bust —some with possible disguises. He began reconciling possible hideouts among the residences of the 200 individuals. Finally, Roderick came across an apartment complex in West Hartford, near Persico's old stomping grounds. The female superintendent looked at one of the photos in

Roderick's notebook, and said in a thick European accent, "Oh yeah, that's Al Longo."[14]

Roderick realized he had found Persico. He called Oboyski, and waited for what seemed to him a long time before back-up deputies arrived.[15]

"We just knocked on the door," Roderick said. A frail-looking Persico answered, shaking because he thought someone was there to assassinate him. In his hand was a wooden spoon; he was making tomato sauce for spaghetti. The case was over.[16]

Roderick's notebook contained information that shut down much of the Connecticut mob's activity. Eventually, he learned the fate of Mickey Caruana. Sometime in May 1987, the mobster had met some of his associates, and was shot in the head. Apparently the heat was too close. Roderick believed that Caruana's burial spot, although never fully verified, was initially in a garage behind the home of a convicted bank robber. He stated the same location was used for several bodies, including that of Theodore Burns, a Massachusetts hotel executive Caruana thought was having an affair with his wife. Further, Roderick believed that some of the bones were removed from that location.[17]

THE GREAT CHICKEN STING

Stings and ruses were sometimes a necessary practice. In one of his earlier cases, Bob Leschorn had used a phony food delivery sign to surprise several unsuspecting fugitives in New York. Enforcement Chief Chuck Kupferer confided that one of the greatest ruses the Service ever played on fugitives came about by observing agents from other agencies using disguises. Other law enforcement agencies commonly used disguises:

> I think it was in Buffalo with an ATF agent [who] had a relative who was a postal service carrier. [He] borrowed his uniform, went up to a door with a brown-looking envelope containing a check

from the Internal Revenue Service a refund check... go to the door and ask for the suspect.[18]

Kupferer's observation became the impetus for "Operation Flagship." In late November 1985, the marshals sent 5,117 letters to the last known addresses of 3,000 wanted fugitives. Each letter included an invitation and prize notification from a fictitious organization named "Flagship International."[19]

Deputy U.S. Marshal Mark Shealey assisted the facilitation and execution of Operation Flagship. He said, "[t]he invitations were part of a promotional offer by Flagship International Sports Television," or FIST, the acronym used for nine fugitive operations designated for multi-jurisdictional Fugitive Investigation Strike Teams. The invitations were signed by Michael Detnaw ("wanted" spelled backwards).[20] Shealey recalled that the "invitees" called a specified telephone number to confirm their attendance, and could hear the 1966 Bobby Fuller Four song "I Fought the Law" playing in the background.[21]

Operation Flagship exceeded expectations. The prize offered by FIST consisted of tickets to a football game between the Washington Redskins and the Cincinnati Bengals. Marshals received 167 positive responses to the letters that contained instructions to collect their prizes at the Washington Convention Center.[22]

On December 15, 1985, the planners set up 150 chairs in two sections of the convention center, one area to greet "guests" and another for arrests. In total, more than 140 law enforcement officers from the Marshals Service and Metropolitan Police Department in Washington, D.C., worked the sting operation. Rodney Johnson, Bill Degan, and Bobby Banks supervised 64 deputy U.S. marshals, many from the Special Operations Group, as the primary arrest unit, along with a special operations unit of the Metro PD. Units with radios took positions near the arena.[23]

Operational personnel unfamiliar with the area were utilized as the ushers and other role players. Deputy U.S. Marshal Louie McKinney served as master of ceremonies and Stacia Kirk as one of the ushers. (Ironically, each would serve as director of the Marshals Service later in their careers.) Leschorn took the role of sales manager, while another official served as the Redskins fan mascot, "Chief Zee." Undercover officers mingled in the lobby as decoy "winners" of tickets to reduce suspicion. As a last minute thought to create an excited and festive atmosphere, Deputy U.S. Marshal Tom Spillane donned a San Diego Chicken costume and revved up the enthusiasm. A television played the 1982 Super Bowl while deputies served a buffet lunch.[24]

The anticipated crowd of fugitives gathered at the center. Joe Tolson handled logistics for the operation that day. Fugitive names were called out after each one signed in. Once a large crowd gathered, McKinney, dressed in a tuxedo and top hat, greeted the crowd with a short speech. The deputies discreetly separated the "lucky recipients" from others in the arena. The deputies serving food joined the ushers and a 14-person special operations team. On a pre-arranged signal, the arrest team swarmed the "winners," identified with color-coded name tags, handcuffed them and led them out of the building to waiting buses.[25]

Leschorn remembered one memorable comment from an arrestee: "Can I still have my tickets?"[26] Shealey added, "and the free transportation was a prisoner bus ride to D.C. Jail."[27]

Director Morris wanted news coverage of the sting to be as deliberate as the actual takedown. Marshals opted for the *Los Angeles Times* and CBS as the main media outlets to publicize the story. Morris stated, "That one happened because I had friends in the press... that I trusted... and I brought 'em in."[28] Morris believed the front page *LA Times* article raised the profile of the organization.[29]

WANT

In 1982, the Attorney General formed Organized Crime Drug Enforcement Task Forces (OCDETF) to combat the burgeoning narcotics trafficking industry fueled by savvy cartels exporting dangerous drugs to the United States. The U.S. Marshals took their position on the front line of the war on narcotics trafficking after the passage of the Comprehensive Crime Act of 1984, because of the high number of fugitives from drug-related cases. A comprehensive report retrospectively noted fugitive cases increased 24 percent, while arrests lagged behind. Marshals Service leadership considered ideas to address the backlog. From these discussions, the agency formed Warrant Apprehension Narcotics Teams, or WANT, specifically to address narcotics fugitives during a 10-week pilot project. Federal law enforcement realized that traffickers moved quickly with ready access to abundant cash reserves. The Service needed new innovations to counter their advantages. A key breakthrough came in a computer database.[30]

Computer analyst Ron Wutrich created a database called "Scorecard" to help deputies find clues to the criminals they chased. The database consisted of a unique electronic indexing system, and it linked relationships among clues. The program didn't replace police instincts, but uncovered relational links between places and people. Safir saw the technology as an asset and huge benefit for the U.S. Marshals Service.[31]

In 1987, Safir queried U.S. Attorneys and the Drug Enforcement Administration about "lines," or connections, among existing trafficking operations. Marshals Service enforcement units integrated Scorecard in a new series of warrant sweeps that "followed the money."[32]

By March 1, 1987, WANT was fully functional, with teams in eight cities: San Francisco, Los Angeles, Las Vegas, Houston, Chicago, Miami, Baltimore, and New York. Safir gathered a list of 700 suspects. Quickly realizing this would be an international operation, he worked with personnel in other countries.[33]

Using Scorecard and applying FIST tactics, the deputies rounded up 210 federal fugitives, and cleared an additional 324 warrants, including individuals already serving prison time on other charges. The deputies seized weapons, drugs, cash, and property valued at more than $1 million.

From March 3 through May 8, Operation WANT provided greater results than expected by Morris and Safir.[34]

Time magazine covered the new computer innovation in May 1987, and Safir told the magazine, "if a drug trafficker was out [free and on the run] more than 48 hours, he was basically home free."[35]

Unfortunately, WANT attracted some unwanted attention as well. *Los Angeles Times* staff writer Ronald J. Ostrow reported on January 12, 1988, that a "turf war" had emerged between the FBI and the U.S. Marshals over the burgeoning fugitive program. In actuality, the "turf war" was little more than a redefinition of scope. They objected to the expanded program with the DEA.[36]

The U.S. Marshals Service viewed WANT as innovative, but FBI Director William S. Sessions felt it created safety concerns and overlapped his agency's jurisdiction. Director Morris disputed the claims. Attorney General Meese ended the dispute by limiting the U.S. Marshals' role in both foreign and organized crime operations.[37]

The dispute with the FBI effectively ended the first WANT experiment. However, the Marshals Service soon created WANT II, under the sponsorship of the DOJ National Asset Seizure and Forfeiture (NASAF) Program. The new operation was composed of deputy marshals and specially deputized DEA and Internal Revenue Service agents joined by state and local police. From August to November 1988, investigators targeted areas in Alabama, Florida, Louisiana, and Texas. Deputies utilized "Scorecard" and made arrests without worries of jurisdictional overlap. NASAF funded the entire effort with the ill-gotten gains forfeited from drug offenders. WANT II resulted in 218 arrests and the seizure of $1.3 million in assets.[38]

From May 15 to 22, 1989, through an offer of assistance from the agency to the Department of Justice and National Drug Policy Director William J. Bennett, the Marshals Service completed 209 drug-related evictions in the District of Columbia and made a wide number of seizures.

A news release dated May 23, 1989, noted that as a result of this WANT operation, deputy marshals conducted evictions where "suspected illegal drug activities were occurring."[39] Negative news stories reported that the poor were unfairly targeted. Of the total evictions, 112 locations were unoccupied dwellings. Just 10 families faced actual eviction. The U.S. Marshals arrested drug offenders and continued to leverage their multi-jurisdictional strategy.[40]

CHAPTER 14

THE U.S. MARSHALS IMPROVEMENT REVOLUTION

.

Director Morris assumed the helm of the Marshals Service with a number of unique ideas to develop and improve the organization. He visited districts to assess the way local leaders implemented programs and missions. He stressed their important role in federal law enforcement, and especially their close relationship with the federal district judges. Morris valued the deputies' responsibility with the federal judiciary, and hated hearing about deputies tasked with trivial work by judges.

One respected jurist made deputy marshals carry his bags. Morris called the district judge and told him the practice had to end. His message was "Marshals can't carry bags... [because] they can't protect you [while carrying them]."[1]

FOCUS ON TRAINING

The Marshals established a full staffing level at its training academy in Glynn County (Glynco), Georgia, building from a temporary staff in 1976 to one with 20-30 deputy marshals working full time, according to

Gary Mead.[2] Morris entrusted training academy improvements to two able assistants, Wayne "Duke" Smith and Doug Wiggs, both longtime deputies with a passion for training future deputies. The director disliked too much swagger, and stated the most important weapon the deputies possessed "wasn't on their hip... it was between their ears."[3]

In 1984, in a *New York Times* profile on the U.S. Marshals, Morris emphasized the 13-week training program, noting that three-quarters of the incoming basic deputy candidates possessed college degrees. He also indicated that most had a state or local law enforcement background, adding value to the agency with knowledge at all levels of law enforcement.[4] Court Security Inspector Henry Ohrenburger ruminated on the improvement, calling it "Kennedy-esque." He appreciated how Morris hired folks to get the job done and refused to let the agency stumble along. He further opined that the director's most notable hires as problem solvers were Howard Safir and Chuck Kupferer. Morris took an idea about the agency "and made everybody want to do it."[5]

In the Morris era, deputies got fitter, younger, and more self-reliant. He emphasized training and focused on complete fitness, cutting down the chances of fatalities due to heart attacks. The Fitness-in-Total program followed personnel from the academy to the streets, and assured that deputies could chase their fugitives if necessary.[6]

In the mid-1970s, the government retirement system compensated operational employees for hazardous duty, setting a maximum age to enter service. Gary Mead recalled, "We had a lot of retirees, some in their late 40s, early 50s... [The] average age began plummeting... began to focus on [those in] college." He added, "The Marshals Service of 1970 was totally different than the Marshals Service in 1980."[7]

BRANCHING OUT

The agency made improvements in the areas of prisoner transportation and tactical equipment as well. The days of using personally owned vehicles (POVs) to transport prisoners ended by the 1980s with the arrival of the vehicle fleet system. Additionally, the agency ended the practice of borrowing radios from the FBI or other local jurisdictions.[8]

Bill Hufnagel and Bob Bouffard founded the Electronic Surveillance Unit (ESU) in 1988 to make innovative use of specialized equipment. ESU inaugurated the Marshals Service expertise to intercept certain video and audio transmissions. Hufnagel and Bouffard introduced cutting-edge technology and methodology vital to the agency's growth. Their vision and dedication led to extensive reviews and approvals of the modes of surveillance to be employed by the Service. They utilized electronic devices to aid the work of deputies.[9]

Although its implementation began before his term, Morris ushered in the Court Security Officer (CSO) Program in 1983. Associate Director Safir and James O'Toole, the chief of Court Security, developed the program to eliminate some of the rudimentary, security related tasks assigned to deputies, so they could concentrate on other duties such as prisoner transportation and judicial threat investigations. The CSOs would provide basic security at key entrances of court facilities, wear distinctive blue jackets, and display specially designed badges. Morris pitched the idea of having retired police officers and deputies become CSOs as contract employees to Justice Department officials. Tapping retirees as CSOs did not sit well with everyone, however. Even Deputy Director Twomey, naturally skeptical as a former warden, had to be convinced the idea could work.[10]

The Office of Equal Employment Opportunity solidified during the 1980s too, wrestling with an ongoing lawsuit about race and position within the agency from the mid-1970s. Former Director Hall, Special Assistant to the Director Ben Butler, and EEO Officer Kip Williams had stressed the need for communication in June 1980. Hall had stated, "The worst thing is for people to bottle up their frustrations and stop talking to each other."[11]

While prior leaders offered seminars and educational programs, Morris focused on work life. Under Mead, he targeted urban areas and historically black colleges and universities with criminal justice programs to increase diversity as part of the cooperative education program. Mead recalled, "Students could enroll in two seminars initially [in noted schools with criminal justice programs], to gain excepted service to be a deputy U.S. marshal."[12]

In the January 1987 *Pentacle*, Director Morris devoted a good portion of the issue to the cell-space crisis. He sounded the warning alarm to employees and lawmakers alike:

> Jail overcrowding can no longer be ignored. Our nation's jails are bulging—the prisoner population has grown more than 40 percent in the last five years. Because of insufficient jail space, America's criminal justice system is in imminent danger of breaking down in many areas.
>
> The jail crisis began when the courts or state governments mandated population ceilings for jails. This situation was aggravated by the slowness or unwillingness of state and local governments to provide funds for jail construction. As a result, the construction of new state and local jails has not kept pace with the rapid prisoner population growth over the past five years.
>
> What does that mean to the average citizen? It means that "least risk to society" offenders are being released back into the community because there's no room in jails and prisons. And studies show that many of these offenders are returning to lives of crime, preying on their communities once again.[13]

Prisoner transportation costs were significant, as was the demand on deputies. Overcrowded conditions at federal facilities made it necessary to utilize state and local cells. Therefore, the agency competed for the same cells as state and local authorities. The space was also costly. Per diem rates and fees to house federal prisoners in county and municipal facilities varied from facility to facility, creating management and planning challenges for the Marshals Service. From 1979 to 1987, work hours devoted to transporting prisoners from jail to court increased 102 percent. The Cooperative Agreement Program, or "CAP," allowed the Service to negotiate prices with state and local jail facilities for the detention of federal prisoners awaiting trial or sentencing, called "pre-trial detainees," with those facilities. Instituted in 1982, CAP helped but didn't solve the problems of housing pre-trial detainees for the Marshals Service. The price of housing prisoners was only part of the problem. In time, the agency would revisit the issue of jail space.[14]

NEW HEADQUARTERS, NEW RECOGNITION

In early 1988, the U.S. Marshals headquarters personnel moved into Lincoln Place, one of two 12-story buildings across Interstate 395 from the Pentagon in Arlington, Virginia. The structure boasted rose-colored granite and large, dark windows. The idea of an agency campus remained, but the new headquarters space was shared with the Drug Enforcement Administration. The U.S. Marshals Service occupied just five floors of one tower, while the DEA occupied the remaining 19 floors in both. Both agencies shared the cafeteria and gym in the Marshals Service building. Director Morris and his DEA counterpart, Administrator Jack Lawn, raised their agency flags at an August 9, 1988, ceremony,[15]

> This new, modern headquarters reflects the high level of professionalism that is the hallmark of today's Marshals Service... It also accomplishes a joining-together of the "oldest" and the "newest." We in the Marshals Service are extremely pleased to be co-located in this facility with the headquarters of the Drug Enforcement Administration.... We look forward to many opportunities for cooperation—both as sister law enforcement agencies and as neighbors—in the months and years ahead.[16]

The United States Marshals Act of 1988 (Public Law 100-690) was Director Morris' capstone. The statute finally and officially established the agency as a bureau of the Department of Justice. It ended the days of uncertainty between different authority structures. In fulfilling what former Director Colburn envisioned, an organizational issue was resolved. The days of drifting between the authority of the U.S. Marshal and the Director ended with the Act. The legislation stated that the Director would be appointed by the President of the United States, and that individual U.S. Marshals "shall serve under the direction of the Director."[17]

The significance of the law and its enactment nearly flew under the radar, as it was only one part of a much more comprehensive drug enforcement bill. Nonetheless, it was a triumph for the agency. The law addressed other issues, such as the pay of the Director and the role the Service would play in the Department of Justice's Asset Forfeiture program.[18]

WITNESS SECURITY IMPROVES

In the *Director's Report* for Fiscal Year 1989, the overly simplistic description given in the overview for "Witness Security" was: "Witness protection, relocation, and child visitation services in return for testimony" for appropriate criminal cases.[19] The time spent on this function represented just 10 percent of the agency's workload. In fairness, no mission component occupied more than 19 percent of time allocation. Information on the program was scarce but its significance grew—especially in the public eye.[20]

Today the program has earned a respected place in law enforcement and in the mind of the American public. Its secrecy harkens back to memories of mob movies and other dangerous possibilities. Hollywood and news media added to the lore, creating an image of a secretive and complex program through movies, books, and news coverage that persists today. In reality, the Witsec program bears little resemblance to how it is depicted in the media.[21]

In the mid- to late-1980s, law enforcement agencies arrested many key figures of traditional crime families, bringing those illegal enterprises under siege. As the concentration of law enforcement changed from mob families to drug cartels, the composition of protected witnesses changed to reflect that shifting priority.

In Fiscal Year 1989, the number of program participants increased by 14 percent to just under 2,000. The Witness Security Program succeeded, as the testimony of protected witnesses led to the conviction of 89 percent of the defendants they faced.[22]

JUDGE VANCE

In December 1989, a man named Walter Leroy Moody Jr., mailed four separate packages containing explosive devices to officials in the 11th Circuit. His appeal to expunge his criminal record had been denied by judges within the circuit, including U.S. Circuit Court Judge Robert S. Vance.[23]

Judge Vance received a package and opened it without any suspicion. The resulting explosion killed him and injured his wife. A neighbor called the fire department. By the time the fire fighters reached the home, the fire chief realized it was a crime scene and called for assistance. U.S. Marshal Thomas Greene of the Northern District of Alabama arrived at the judge's residence in 40 minutes. Greene recalled, "Chief [of Mountain Brook, Alabama, Police Martin] Keely told me that he [Judge Vance] had opened up a package that had a pipe bomb in it loaded with nails, and that they opened up and killed him."[24]

Official reaction to the explosion was swift. The Bureau of Alcohol, Tobacco, and Firearms and the FBI took charge of the scene. Judge Vance's wife suffered a serious wound from a nail that entered her liver. In her panic, she had not noticed the injury to herself while attending to her husband.[25]

U.S. Marshals knew all the judges in the circuit; they ensured their safety. This incident struck with little warning. Judge Vance was known as a friendly jurist in Birmingham. Marshal Greene confirmed that the judge had never received any threat in his district, but he had denied a former defendant a motion to petition the court. Judge Vance had not been alarmed by it.[26]

In Boston, Court Security Inspector Henry Ohrenburger's phone rang while he was at home watching television. Court Security Inspector Steve Gill was on the line. He informed Ohrenburger about the death of Judge Vance and that Court Security Division Chief Ralph Zurita ordered him to report to Jacksonville, Florida, to meet with U.S. Circuit Court Judge Gerald Tjoflat. Understandably upset, Judge Tjoflat wanted a court inspector with legal training "in the room" when the jurist consulted with the Director and Attorney General. All 11th Circuit judges were placed under protective detail.[27]

Two days later, a similar package appeared in the mail in the 11th Circuit headquarters in Atlanta, addressed to the clerk of the court. Court security officers knew the hallmarks of the package that killed Vance, and immediately called for bomb technicians from the Atlanta Police Department. The U.S. Marshals perceived a wide range of potential victims, as no specific addressee was on the package. Bomb technicians defused the device.[28]

Not all the explosive devices mailed by Moody targeted federal jurists. An identical device felled African-American lawyer Robert Robinson at his law office in Savannah, Georgia, on the same day the Atlanta device arrived. Shortly after, the NAACP offices in Jacksonville, Florida, received a similar package; it was not opened. In the meantime, deputies continued the protective details on 29 federal judges. The FBI homed in on the similarities of the incidents, and arrested Moody 18 months later.[29]

THE MINE STRIKE

The history of strikes involving the U.S. Marshals date from the 1890s, when they guarded rail cars containing U.S. mail during the Pullman

Strike. For instance, on July 15, 1894, Special Deputy U.S. Marshal Robert Pate was mortally wounded while guarding the rail system near Little Rock, Arkansas.[30] Continuing their involvement, in September 1974, U.S. Marshal Irwin W. Humphreys served temporary restraining orders on coal mine picketers at 20 locations in three West Virginia counties. Violent protests ensued as picketers armed with baseball bats and 2 by 4 planks damaged property and assaulted people.[31]

The United Mine Workers (UMW) went on strike at the Pittston Coal Mine Company on April 5, 1989, protesting a sharp reduction in health benefits of former employees. The strike grew in size, and law enforcement authorities began making arrests later that month.[32]

U.S. District Judge Glen M. Williams issued an injunction, effective June 7, 1989, to maintain order during the strike in Virginia's western mountains. In early July, a special team consisting of more than 90 deputies from many districts rotated through the protest assignment. U.S. Marshal Wayne Beaman paired some deputies with Virginia State Police for 12-hour shifts, six days a week.[33]

> Deputies were called to intervene in offenses such as mass pick- eting, the physical blocking of ingress and egress points of coal mine and coal preparation sites, arson of buildings and vehicles, small arms fire directed at occupied dwellings, vehicles, and commercial buildings, bomb explosions at mine sites, private residences and public utility installations, general vandalism, and threats of physical violence. Each of these examples very frequently was accompanied by strong verbal abuse directed at law enforcement officers.[34]

The worst situation occurred in the Southern District of West Virginia on July 17, 1989. Word passed among strikers that deputies were to only observe, and that the picketers should "run off the U.S. Marshal" as they had local authorities. On July 21, 1989, the U.S. District Court issued a restraining order for protesters possessing "jack rocks," converted nails or spiked objects used to flatten tires, and blocking avenues to coal transport in the Logan County, West Virginia, area.[35] Beginning in late August, a series of intimidating and violent actions by mine employees prompted law enforcement to act. Members of the United Mine Workers routinely blocked access routes for coal shipping, prompting instructions to the deputies by U.S. District Judge Dennis Knapp to "exercise such action as is reasonably necessary to enforce the order."[36] The October 24, 1989, *Charleston Daily Mail* reported that picketers "threatened to physically assault and/or shoot an undercover U.S. Marshal."[37]

Judge Knapp asked U.S. Marshal Walt Biondi to proceed peacefully. Striking miners blocked the right-of-way on the railroad line, so Biondi publicly announced the violation in hopes they would leave. Still, on October 25, Biondi and his deputies arrested two miners after they refused to move off the railroad tracks. A number of them made a human chain across the tracks. Chief Deputy U.S. Marshal Jesse South handed out copies of Judge Knapp's order and asked them to move off. In response, some of the picketers littered the access road with debris and jackrocks.[38]

In December, tensions resurfaced when the striking miners blocked an entrance to the Elkay Mine in Slab Fork, West Virginia. Citing the violation of Judge Knapp's order, deputies and Bureau of Alcohol, Tobacco, Firearms, and Explosives (ATF) agents arrested five of them. A number of jackrocks were confiscated as evidence. U.S. Marshal Biondi videotaped a rock-throwing incident to prove intent to harm his deputies. This led to the arrest of 20 offenders, and consideration of an around-the-clock patrol of the area.[39]

Judge Knapp enacted more restrictions on the picketers to no avail. Several non-union trucks rammed into vehicles blocking the road. Another picketer assaulted a deputy. With the direct assistance of state police and the National Labor Relations Board, renewed discussions began to end the impasse. Although the chain of incidents seemed endless, final discussions in early 1990 brought the stand-off to an end. The U.S. Marshals began to withdraw. On February 19, 1990, the Virginia strike was over.[40]

HURRICANE HUGO

On September 18, 1989, a massive Category 4 hurricane wreaked havoc through the Caribbean. The worst hit was St. Croix in the U.S. Virgin Islands. The pervasive damage hampered communications and assistance to the approximately 50,000 residents. The *Des Moines Register* reported that "Hugo's winds on Sunday night and Monday destroyed or damaged 90 percent of the buildings on the Virgin Islands."[41]

Indeed, homelessness led to lawlessness. The situation created rife conditions for looting and violence, and fanned fears soon after the winds of Hugo headed north. President George H.W. Bush ordered U.S. military police to the Virgin Islands to help restore order. The same news source reported that "Attorney General Dick Thornburgh said that he ordered 100 U.S. marshals and FBI agents to St. Croix."[42]

The Special Operations Group sprang into action. Once they arrived in St. Croix, Deputy U.S. Marshal William Degan organized them into small teams. Some of these groups conducted law enforcement operations, while others evacuated stranded tourists. A news report announced that 145 St. Croix tourists arrived in Miami on a flight arranged by U.S. marshals.[43]

Looting subsided, but Hugo's damage to infrastructure called for further attention from the U.S. Marshals Service. U.S. Marshal John Washington visited Headquarters on October 11, 1989, "with a three-page list of supplies he needed for our employees and their families to help keep operations going in the District."[44] In response to the need, employees "tied up a check-out line for two hours as they purchased and hauled away about eight tons of goods. Curious store employees and other customers praised the Service when they learned what our people were doing."[45]

The Virgin Islands employees received these supplies by C-130 transport aircraft from Andrews Air Force Base on October 19. Warehouse supervisor Carl Parish and his employees prepared the shipments, while the Employee Development Division's Joe Tolson and John Pierce, along with the Special Operation Group's Ed Farley, arranged the transit. It was a large-scale humanitarian operation undertaken by Headquarters, requiring many hands to achieve.[46]

The reaction by the U.S. Marshals Service to Hurricane Hugo showed the American public another side of the agency. The Special Operations Group and its impressive cooperation with the Federal Emergency Management Agency and other agencies built good relationships and a solid reputation. Headquarters replaced its bureaucratic image with one in which they rolled up their sleeves to serve its employees far away. Most of all, the Hugo response provided a blueprint for other disasters.[47]

"JUST CAUSE"

At the close of 1989, a select group of Special Operations Group deputies embarked on one of the most ambitious missions of the decade, participation in Operation Just Cause, the U.S. military invasion of Panama. The DEA enforcement action to bring Panamanian strongman Manuel Noriega to justice on drug trafficking charges proved intricate and complex. It required cooperation and careful planning among an array of jurisdictions, domestically and internationally.[48]

Tony Perez, chief of the Major Case Investigations Branch of the Enforcement Operations Division, and a team of SOG members received a briefing from Howard Safir before departing for Panama in December 1989. They all realized the steep restrictions on their activities in a foreign country and their role in support of the Drug Enforcement Administration.[49]

The U.S. Marshals had staffed a district office in the Canal Zone until its closure in 1984, so they knew the topography of Panama. They also knew that vital American interests remained in the area. Perez and Deputy U.S. Marshal James Rankin flew to Howard Air Force Base in Panama on December 22.[50]

Unfortunately, Perez had to fight jurisdictional battles immediately upon arrival. The FBI maintained ties to the local military command. As the DEA and the FBI worked different areas of enforcement, the local military was unaware of the presence of Marshals personnel. Perez recalled the initial clash with the local military leaders at the base. "They just said, 'Stand over here, because we don't know what you're doing here. We don't know who you are,' and all that stuff. So we're in a corner of the airport, trying to make contact with these people."[51]

Eventually, Perez convinced the military commander in charge that deputies were present to accompany DEA agents in gathering, processing, and extraditing prisoners. His team constructed a makeshift radio, known as a "Misty," to contact headquarters. Several hours later, the Attorney General clarified the U.S. Marshals' role in Operation Just Cause.[52]

At the SOG compound near Alexandria, Louisiana, Task Force Commander Keith Erni selected four members for the task force to enter Panama shortly after Perez's team. The four were Richard Lymburner, Francis "Mike" Hammer, Mariano "Mickey" Rellin and Mike Cameron.[53]

According to the notes of Deputy U.S. Marshal Mel McDowell, who was involved in the operation with Perez, the group advanced in full gear to Panama, "Our basic instructions were to support and provide protection for the Drug Enforcement personnel also assigned to the mission, and to further assist these agents in searching for and gathering evidence in the development of their case against Manuel Noriega and conspirators."[54]

Lymburner and Hammer accompanied military and DEA personnel to a small fishing village named La Palma, located on Panama's west coast. Intelligence reports revealed an airstrip and tower there used by planes carrying narcotics in and out of the country. A Panamanian military compound was located adjacent to the airport. Both SOG operators stayed with their assigned DEA agent, and expected to gather evidence. After the DEA secured the compound, Lymburner and Hammer searched and photographed the facility, where they found a cache of weapons and ammunition. The newly constructed tower held the most evidence of interest to U.S. investigators, who found a record of flights with identifying information of planes. This record traced specific flights into the U.S., and proved to be a key piece of evidence against Panamanian leader Manuel Noriega. Their mission completed, the SOG deputies departed La Palma on December 31, 1989.[55]

Meanwhile, Perez and his cohorts kept a watchful eye on Noriega's movements and coordinated related actions. On Christmas Eve, the dictator found temporary sanctuary with the papal nuncio, the official diplomat of the Pope. The American military surrounded the complex and blared heavy-metal music to force his surrender through sleep deprivation.[56]

The other duties of the deputies in Panama were rounding up fugitives who attempted to leave. However, once at the Omar Torrijos International Airport, the operation became a nightmare. A firefight had taken place in the airport, and panicked refugees mixed in the crowd with pro-Noriega opposition. Perez knew the job was going to be difficult. He recalled, "We've got people stranded there. There's blood and guts, because they had fought in the airport, and there were chunks of flesh and all still in the bathrooms... They blew them up, so they had to clean up the stuff and get the operations moving, get people out of there."[57]

Perez and the SOG deputies ran all security operations at Torrijos International Airport throughout the crisis. They conducted screens, and a list of USMS fugitives was cross-referenced with each departing passenger. They coordinated with the agency's communications center to run detailed checks of criminal history. They also carried the military's listing of top Noriega officials, and a half-dozen of them were caught as they tried to leave the country. At their temporary refugee camp, they found several high-profile fugitives from the United States. Deputies brought the famous leader to the Southern District of Florida.[58]

BICENTENNIAL

If the headquarters move and U.S. Marshals Service Act of 1988 served as the capstone for Director Morris, the celebration of the agency's bicentennial (officially observed September 24, 1989) provided a fitting legacy. He began planning bicentennial events from the time he took office. He hired Ted Calhoun as the agency's first historian and went to work on an agenda. An internal body was formed, called the Bicentennial Working Committee, and met on December 6, 1984, to discuss a museum exhibit, the status of an historical association, and documentary materials. Attendees of the initial meeting included Deputy Director Twomey, chair; Calhoun; Special Assistant to the Director Jack McCrory; Public Affairs Chief Werner Koehler; Public Information Officer Bill Dempsey; along with Reis Kash, Edna Dolan, Mike Adams, and Gary Mead.[59]

The minutes expressly stated the purpose of the working committee:

> The purpose of the USMS Bicentennial Working Committee is to provide advice and policy direction to guide the Historian in preparing bicentennial commemorative museum exhibits for public display across the country in 1989. The minutes of Committee meetings will be used to keep the Director officially informed of the progress in developing exhibits.[60]

Two big priorities of Morris' plan included a new, book-size publication, or history book, and a special, traveling exhibit. They developed a schedule that incorporated other aspects of the agency's celebration, like commemorative items, a "U.S. Marshal's Posse," an official political declaration, and local events at district offices.[61]

The agency issued a news release, dated November 23, 1988, entitled "U.S. Marshals/Smithsonian Exhibit Opening at Supreme Court Building Kicks Off Year-long Nationwide Bicentennial Observance of U.S. Marshals." The exhibit opened December 9, 1988, at the Court with a ceremonial ribbon cutting by former Chief Justice Warren Burger, Chief

Justice William Rehnquist, and actor James Arness. The exhibit plan scheduled exhibit stops in 13 cities, with an ending planned in May 1991.[62]

The Smithsonian Institution's news release, dated August 25, 1988, stated:

> Comprised of more than 200 objects, "America's Star" traces the history and contemporary duties of the U.S. Marshals and their impact on law enforcement from the nation's early days to the present. The story is recounted in the exhibition with such items as the re-creation of a marshal's office, circa 1900, complete with jail cell; weapons used by marshals, deputies and outlaws; badges and law enforcement equipment; original documents—"Wanted" posters and warrants; works of art, and vintage photographs.[63]

The United States Constitution Bicentennial Committee, led by Burger after his retirement from the Court, designated "America's Star" as an official project. While the agency maintained its interest in the exhibit, the Smithsonian Institution Traveling Exhibition Service organized and physically handled the travel and installation. The exhibit cases showcased a combination of loaned and permanent agency artifacts. The 13 stops of the "America's Star" tour were the Supreme Court, Oklahoma City's National Cowboy Hall of Fame, the Indiana State Museum in Indianapolis, Philadelphia's Independence Hall, Nashville's Tennessee State Museum, the Seattle Center, the Colorado Historical Society in Denver, the Louisiana State Museum in New Orleans, St. Louis' Jefferson National Expansion Memorial, the Dallas Historical Society, the California Railroad Museum in Sacramento, California, the Gene Autry Western Heritage Museum in Los Angeles, and Federal Hall in New York City. By the end of the tour, "America's Star" actually made 14 stops. The last display took place at the Museum of Florida History in Tallahassee, Florida, and ended in June 1991. At the conclusion of its run, the Service arranged to have the USMS Collections and extended loans of privately owned artifacts displayed in Laramie, Wyoming.[64]

DEPARTURE OF A GIANT

At the height of the bicentennial year of the U.S. Marshals, Director Stanley Morris left the agency in October 1989. Attorney General Edwin Meese had left the Justice Department in July 1988, and his successor, Richard Thornburgh, had fundamental differences in outlook for DOJ. On October 23, 1989, Morris assumed new duties as deputy director for Supply Reduction in the Office of National Drug Control Policy. Just three days prior, the Senate Judiciary Committee held a confirmation hearing for the new nominee for Marshals Service director, K. Michael Moore.[65]

In mid-November, Moore and Morris presented key remarks at the Marshals National Conference in Oklahoma City. With former director Bill Hall in attendance, the U.S. Marshals Foundation announced an estimated $7 million memorial to honor the USMS fallen, to be located adjacent to the National Cowboy Hall of Fame.[66]

In his final speech to the Marshals, Morris stated:

> You have prepared me well for my journey. The men and women of the Service have given me new insights into the real meaning of the words on your official seal—justice, integrity, and service. You've given new meaning to the simple words "duty" and "courage"; and you've shown me what innovation and creativity can accomplish.[67]

Director Moore was equally effusive in his praise of the organization, but hinted at changes:

> In a nationwide organization like the Marshals Service, with a variety of complex responsibilities that must be carried out day-after-day, good, clear and candid communication is extremely important. And I want you to know that I will do everything possible to keep the lines open between us.

> Over the next several weeks, I will be examining the details of headquarters and field operations and I intend [to] press forward in the search for solutions to the critical issues—like the terrible

shortage of jail space—that are high on everyone's list. I'm sure we will be in close touch on a variety of matters within a short time.[68]

It was a sign of things to come. The agency grew stronger during the 1980s, referred to by many employees as the "golden period" of the Marshals Service.

SECTION FIVE—THE NINETIES: WANDERLUST

CHAPTER 15

THE TERM OF K. MICHAEL MOORE

In October 1989, Director Stanley Morris departed the Marshals Service and ended his tenure full of successes, technological advances, and increased morale. Director K. Michael Moore, a serious but amiable man, ushered in the 1990s. Well connected, the 38-year-old prosecutor had served as the United States Attorney for the Northern District of Florida, and as a member of the Attorney General's Advisory Committee of U.S. Attorneys. He had graduated from Fordham Law School in 1975.[1]

On December 6, 1989 while a crowd of 125 people including Senate Judiciary Committee member Sen. Strom Thurmond of South Carolina watched, U.S. Attorney General Richard Thornburgh administered Moore's oath of office.[2] The Moore Era began in earnest within days of the ceremony, as marshals were immersed in "Operation Just Cause." Deputy U.S. marshals secured former Panamanian dictator Manuel Noriega in a Florida federal prison. The numbered FIST operations morphed into named operations, like "Southern Star," "Sunrise," "Trident," "Olympus," and "Gunsmoke." Prison overcrowding ushered in the idea of using private detention facilities to house Marshals Service prisoners. Structural and management changes foreshadowed broader changes.[3]

On November 8, 1989, the U.S. Marshals Foundation announced plans to construct a 7.7-acre memorial park for the agency, adjacent to the National Cowboy Hall of Fame in Oklahoma City. At the center of the star-shaped garden stood a 10-foot bronze statue by Oregon artist and sculptor Dave Manuel called *Frontier Marshal.* Director Moore and former directors Hall and Morris placed a star-shaped wreath at the foot of the statue to commemorate the second phase of construction of the memorial. The Oklahoma governor and a former New Jersey governor spoke at the dedication event. Before Morris made his remarks, Director Moore read a message from President George H.W. Bush,[4]

> For 200 years, United States Marshals and their Deputies have courageously enforced the laws of our Nation and defended the rights guaranteed to individuals under the Constitution. During their two centuries of service to our country, hundreds of marshals have given their lives in the line of duty. The National Memorial dedicated here today is a fitting tribute to the courage and sacrifice of those marshals who made the ultimate sacrifice to uphold the laws we cherish.[5]

In May 1990, Moore created two deputy directors, a first for the Marshals Service. John Twomey became deputy director for Administration, while James B. Roche, the U.S. marshal for the District of Massachusetts, assumed duties as deputy director for Operations. Roche came from Massachusetts, where he had served in the state police and as U.S. Marshal from 1983. Each of the deputy directors oversaw two associate directors.[6] G. Wayne "Duke" Smith became the associate director for Operations. Smith had begun his Marshals Service career as a deputy in the Middle District of North Carolina in 1974. Gary Mead transitioned from associate director for Administration to associate director for Operations Support. His directorate maintained the National Asset Seizure and Forfeiture Division and the Prisoner Transportation Division. Ken Holecko became associate director of Human Resources. Joseph Enders became associate director for Administrative Services.[7]

The annual "Director's Report," issued in 1992, explained the reasoning for the larger leadership structure:

> The Office of the Deputy Director for Administration and the Office of the Deputy Director for Operations provide overall guidance to the Headquarters divisions. The Deputy Directors assist in the establishment of policy, goals, and objectives; approving specific policy guidelines; overseeing internal control review activities; and assuming the functions of the Director whenever necessary. The Deputy Director for Operations also exercises overall executive direction and supervision of U.S. Marshals.[8]

The new senior positions reflected the rapid growth of Headquarters. Henry Ohrenburger recalled, "Things were changing at a fast pace."[9]

New Implementations and Old Issues

Director Moore continued or extended some of the internal structures set by Morris. However, the relationship between Headquarters and the districts cooled. Part of the reason was generational: the deputies who had joined the Service in the 1960s and early 1970s began to retire. The field offices orbited outside the politics of Washington, D.C., but bore the brunt of decisions made inside the Capital Beltway. This was not the fault of the new director, but rather concerns over resources.

When he first arrived, Moore had noted the need for clear communications between field offices and Headquarters. To meet this need, he tapped U.S. Marshals James Roche and Wallace L. McLendon of the Northern District of Florida to serve as liaisons. Although these positions were for a term period, Roche remained at Headquarters after the assignment ended and became deputy director for operations. Moore used the agency newsletter, "FYI," to explain their duties to employees. "Their duties will include providing me with input and ideas from field offices as well as providing information to the field regarding Marshals Service policies."[10]

One primary problem was jail space. By 1990, the burgeoning problem led to consideration of private sector solutions. The first contract jail for U.S. Marshals Service prisoners was under construction in Leavenworth, Kansas. To meet specifications, the prison needed 24-hour medical coverage, the ability to facilitate visitors and educational programs, and access to legal representation. While not a perfect solution, private jails gave law enforcement another option to house detainees. However, challenges littered the path on which the Service was headed.[11]

Director Moore addressed jail overcrowding again in early 1991 in *The Pentacle.* He stated, "Our nation's jails are bulging—the prisoner population has grown more than 250 percent in the last ten years. In many parts of our country, there is no place to put new prisoners."[12] In four years, the number of prisoner productions for court proceedings increased from 298,000 to a projected 559,000. The deputy U.S. marshals making long trips from distant jails to courts suffered under the strain to find prison space. For example, deputies in Philadelphia traveled 800 miles to a facility at Alderson, West Virginia, with no other viable option. The long prisoner movements prevented deputies from performing other duties. Deputy Director Twomey admitted districts shifted personnel at times to keep up with the pace.[13]

In late 1990, Moore reconstituted the U.S. Marshals Advisory Committee, composed of 12 presidentially appointed marshals from around the country. U.S. Marshal Brian Joffrion of Western Louisiana chaired the committee, and U.S. Marshal Al Solis of New Mexico served as vice-chairman. They drilled down on issues, and recommended an array of policies changes that reflected the needs of the field. Each committee member contributed local perspectives.[14]

The field was also bound by one of the last achievements of the bicentennial. *The Lawmen: United States Marshals & Their Deputies 1789-1989*, a history book authored by Ted Calhoun, was published by the Smithsonian Institution Press. Hired as the agency's first historian, Calhoun worked extensively on the book, which chronicled the roots of the U.S. Marshals. Penguin Books published a paperback version two years later that found more access onto bookstore shelves. About the same time the new printing was released, new hiring standards were being set for the field.[15]

In June 1991, one of the most enduring decisions for operational personnel happened. The Attorney General set the maximum age at which an applicant could begin service as deputy U.S. marshal at 37 years of age. The exceptions were few and only attainable through the Assistant Attorney General for Administration, and none past the age of 40.[16]

BIG OPERATIONS AND BIG TRIALS

The numbered FIST efforts ceased, replaced by enforcement operations with imaginative, memorable names. In 1989, the Street Terror Offender Program, or "STOP," resulted in 456 fugitive arrests. Working with familiar law enforcement partners like the Metropolitan Police Department and 10 other agencies, the Washington-based operation focused on violent offenders and those influenced by the drug trade.[17]

From August 6 to October 17, 1990, "Operation Southern Star" targeted fugitives wanted in five cities in the southern and southwestern United States. It employed a multi-jurisdictional task force composed of federal, state, and local authorities and focused on clearing warrants related to violent offenders and drug-related crimes. The Marshals Service identified cities for Southern Star based on the President's National Drug Control Strategy and the Anti-Drug Abuse Act of 1988. The cities represented High Intensity Drug Trafficking Areas (HIDTA) sites and included Miami, Houston, San Antonio, San Diego, and Los Angeles. Deputy marshals along with their cohorts made arrests at an average cost of $742 per arrest. The seizures of property and cash offset the expenses for the operation. Art Roderick, Joe Lucero, and Ed Stubbs oversaw the operation, coordinating personnel from 28 different jurisdictions.[18] Director Moore and Attorney General Thornburgh announced the results of Operation

Southern Star on October 24, 1990. The account in the *FYI* newsletter
stated, "The project, a 10-week drug fugitive manhunt, resulted in the
arrests of 3,743 criminals and the seizure of more than $5.5 million in
cash and property in five major metropolitan areas. Guns, drugs, and
other contraband valued at approximately $7.2 million were also seized
during the Operation."[19]

The Marshals Service conducted "Operation Sunrise" over 10 weeks,
from August to October 1991, in Atlanta, Boston, Miami, New York,
and the Baltimore-Washington area. The criminal investigators targeted
violent criminals and drug traffickers who had previously proved elusive.
In the end, the multi-jurisdictional teams arrested nearly 1,500 fugitives.[20]
The agency stepped up its efforts to reach the general public via the news
media during Operation Sunrise. Each location issued customized news
releases, emblazoned with the operational logo, and closed the operation
with a local news conference to highlight significant cases of interest
to the specific geographic area. In New York, fugitive Victor Bautista
made the highlight reel.[21] In Miami, fugitive Manuel Menocal received
particular attention for the way he tried to elude investigators and
because he was wanted in Sweden for international cocaine trafficking.
In Atlanta, violent gang kingpin Jeffery Lee's run ended when deputies
arrested him while he played tennis.[22]

During this time, operational leadership changed at headquarters.
Howard Safir retired in 1990; he would become the New York City police
commissioner in 1996. Jim Roche departed in February 1991, tapped by
Massachusetts Governor-Elect William Weld as the state's secretary of
Public Safety. Tony Perez became the chief of Enforcement and Don
Horton, a supervisory deputy U.S. marshal in Washington, D.C., moved
into the office of chief of Court Security. Joseph Lucero took over as chief
of the Threat Analysis Division. Challenges tested the new leaders early.[23]

Chief Horton prepared for the trial of former Panamanian leader
Manuel Noriega, who was indicted in February 1988 on 11 counts,
including racketeering and drug smuggling. Costs for court security

measures quickly mounted, projected to top $2 million. Deputies protected witnesses and rotated through 24-hour details. Problems and motions in the case delayed the start of the trial until September 3, 1991. The *Washington Times* reported 60 prosecution witnesses were set to testify on Noriega's role in drug-related offenses, including incarcerated former Medellin cartel leader Carlos Lehder (also known as Lehderer-Rios).[24]

In the Southern District of Florida, U.S. Marshal Daniel Horgan set up a second metal detector outside the courtroom. He told reporters, "It serves a greater purpose than seeking weapons. It gives us time to slow people down, to count the people going in.... We are making some special security arrangements. Those I won't discuss. We do have extra personnel; I won't say how many. And we do have additional firepower, and I won't say what kind."[25]

The jury found Noriega guilty on eight counts on April 9, 1992. He received a sentence of 40 years in July 1992. It was historic: he was the first foreign leader convicted for breaking U.S. law in his own country.[26]

WICHITA

U.S. Marshals historically found themselves at odds with segments of the public who objected to the enforcement of certain federal laws. Laws protecting reproductive rights, related to *Roe v. Wade*, thrust deputy marshals in the position opposite protestors once again.[27] U.S. District Judge Patrick Kelly of Kansas ordered deputies to guard entrances to two specific clinics after protestors from "Operation Rescue" blocked access to them.[28] Kent Pekarek held the position of U.S. marshal for the District of Kansas for a decade and knew about riot control.[29] He recalled the build-up in Wichita:

> In May or June [1991], Operation Rescue national leaders went to Wichita, and had their meetings with the top-level city officials, and were going to show up in Wichita for a week or two, and that was it. In fact, the abortion clinics closed for those two weeks

so there would be no problems... This just mushroomed into a huge, huge media event.

At that point in time, they decided to stay. Because then it was a national event. After the second week, it became a national event. Everybody was watching it on television... Then towards the end of July, the police department were making a lot of [arrests.]... Then the clinics opened back up the second week. That's when they had their large crowds of hundreds of people, who then were blocking the entrances to the clinics.[30]

The strain on local resources from continual arrests and divided local sympathies on the matter of legalized abortions added stress to Pekarek's situation. Judge Kelly signed a preliminary injunction based on a Virginia case, *Bray v. Alexandria Clinic,* but the clinics requested more law enforcement presence in August.[31] Pekarek said, "I went down to Wichita and talked to the judge, and the judge told me some things that he was told. That's basically how the U.S. Marshals got involved in it."[32]

On August 9, 1991, Pekarek set up a line of deputy marshals between the clinic doors and the protestors. The line allowed public access to the clinics, but highlighted their presence in a defensive posture. Pekarek reasoned that under the glare of cameras, the presence of deputies translated positively to local and national viewers. It also gave the demonstrators the opportunity to openly provoke the deputies, who in turn arrested them.[33]

The risk of an attack grew with the crowd size, so Pekarek pulled the deputies back to the gates of the clinic. The demonstrators surged forward and blocked access to the gate. They were arrested and loaded on waiting buses to be processed. "In fact, one day, we arrested 76 people. They blocked the gate. We arrested them, handcuffed them, and had them gone in 46 minutes," said Pekarek.[34]

Many of Operation Rescue's leaders were arrested, and the organization noticed the media coverage favored the U.S. Marshals Service. About 40 disorganized protestors tore down fencing and entered the facility grounds. Deputies moved quickly to detain them, as another surge of protestors blocked the gate. Pekarek recalled that some of the demonstrators intentionally scraped their heads against the cement to make it look as if the deputies bloodied them. However, news media caught this tactic on camera.[35]

In the end, Pekarek felt that the leadership of Operation Rescue wavered due to its lack of control over protestors and negative coverage in the news. The marshals protected the clinics and Judge Kelly, and enjoyed a favorable public opinion. The numbers of protestors dwindled, and eventually dispersed.[36]

DEPARTURE

In February 1992, Director Moore departed the agency to become a federal district judge. His term was active but brief, lasting just over two years. News stories had circulated about his nomination as federal district judge as early as August 1991. By the time of his confirmation for the bench, a number of operational successes overshadowed any negative criticism.[37]

In his final communication, he wrote in *FYI*,

> I am deeply honored by my nomination by the President and confirmation by the Senate as a federal judge. I am at the same time saddened that in accepting the honor I will be leaving the best law enforcement organization in the world... It has been my pleasure to work with some of the most talented and professional people in the government.[38]

Chapter 16

A Dramatic Era

Henry Hudson Takes Over

Henry E. Hudson assumed duties as Acting Director of the U.S. Marshals Service on February 24, 1992. Known for his toughness as U.S. Attorney for the Eastern District of Virginia, Hudson immediately canvassed the agency and installed new personnel in key positions. Katherine K. Deoudes took over the Office of Congressional and Public Affairs, which became the Office of Policy and Communications. Kristine M. Marcy, a former associate deputy attorney general, arrived to fill the position of acting associate director for operations support, which included prisoner operations and seized assets. Karin B. Alvarez, from the Naval Investigative Service, became the chief financial officer. General Counsel Larry Gregg replaced Charles Currin. Gary Mead became the associate director for administration, while Joseph Enders became assistant director of research and development. Ken Holecko remained the leader at human resources. Hudson quickly established his leadership team for the next 18 months.[1]

Director Hudson introduced a new internal publication. The *Marshals Monitor* newsletter replaced the *Pentacle* magazine in November 1992.

Printing and publishing costs were scrutinized, so the newsletter published in black and white, instead of full-color, but retained a magazine-style layout. The content of the *Monitor* focused on recent news, events, and achievements, publishing stories nearly monthly. The old *Pentacle* magazine was heavy on photographs and was published quarterly, at best. Early versions of the newsletter sported some blue color in the banner, but changed to all black and white. Directors used the *Monitor* as an official communications vehicle to the agency's employees, providing their voices in regular columns. The agency even distributed copies to retired deputies. It ceased regular production in 2006.[2]

Hudson desired to raise the agency's visibility among its peers, and to "achieve parity" with other federal law enforcement entities. The U.S. Marshals provided an overseas representative to INTERPOL in France, but the director wanted to commit a higher-ranking official for the post. He tapped Jim Sullivan, formerly a supervisory deputy in California and a member of the Special Operations Group, for the job. Although the position rotated periodically, the move would benefit and strengthen the agency's international efforts for years to come.[3]

CHICAGO

On July 20, 1992, Hudson faced his first formidable challenge leading the agency. Jeffrey Erickson, a Marshals Service prisoner on trial in Chicago for eight bank robberies and assault on a police officer, was among nine prisoners preparing to return to the Metropolitan Correctional Center. He managed to kill a young deputy and a court security officer in a desperate attempt to escape.[4]

The official district statement by U.S. Marshal Marvin Lutes read in part:

> Erickson, 34, succeeded in removing his handcuffs, wrestled the service revolver from Special Deputy (WAE) Terry Pinta, and

used that weapon to fatally wound Deputy U.S. Marshal Roy "Bill" Frakes.

Court Security Officer Harry A. Belluomini, 58, who was at his assigned post in the basement garage of the Dirksen Building, was confronted by subject Erickson after hearing shots fired. Belluomini and Erickson simultaneously fired, with Belluomini being hit in the chest with two bullets. Belluomini fired and hit Erickson in the back as he exited the garage. The bullet passed through Erickson's lung and severed his aorta. This would probably have proven fatal. Erickson then turned the gun on himself and fired into his head.[5]

Erickson had freed himself from his handcuffs with a smuggled key. Terry Pinta later testified, and the *Chicago Tribune* reported, that "she noticed as the elevator rode to the basement on July 20, 1992, that Erickson had moved from the front of the inmate section to the back."[6] He was the last inmate in the elevator and came at the special deputy with his arms raised, grabbing her by the throat. According to her testimony, Erickson pushed her to the elevator wall, grabbed her arms, punched her in the face, and went for her gun.[7]

According to Lutes, the other prisoners scattered as Erickson moved to a van parked outside the sally port. Pinta shouted a warning to her partner, Deputy U.S. Marshal Roy Frakes, who stood between the prisoner and the van. There was no time for Frakes to react before Erickson shot him. As he ran towards the entrance, he shot the deputy a second time. The noise brought him face to face with Court Security Officer Harry Belluomini. "Then he saw [Belluomini]. They were toe to toe almost... shot at each other," Lutes continued. "It killed Harry, shot him in the heart."[8]

The loss of two members of the Chicago office resonated deeply and many questions remained. Director Hudson designated the funeral date of both men, Friday, July 24, as an official day of mourning for the Marshals Service. A full investigation ensued, followed by a review of policies regarding transporting prisoners. News stories focused on Pinta, but she was cleared of wrongdoing. In time, the mystery surrounding the smuggled key was solved. During a trial 10 years later, the court convicted another inmate for giving the key to Erickson.[9]

The Marshals Service memorialized the two victims killed in the line of duty. The agency named an air operations hangar facility for Deputy U.S. Marshal Frakes; an annual award for bravery by a court security officer bears the name of Belluomini.[10]

Ruby Ridge

Only weeks after the Chicago deaths, and prior to his confirmation as director, Hudson faced another tragic event in the history of the Marshals Service that evokes many emotions and memories in the American public. "Ruby Ridge," a remote, mountainous area in northern Idaho where federal marshals located a cabin occupied by federal fugitive Randy Weaver, is the common name of the incident in which a SOG member and two of the fugitive's family members died.

To some elements of the public, the name "Ruby Ridge" represents a warning of the overzealousness of federal law enforcement. To federal law enforcement, it recalls the extremes to which protectors and enforcers of the law will go to effect lawful court orders. In the end, it reminds everyone about the tragic results that can occur.

News stories reported the unfolding events of the incident without the benefit of the full slate of facts, many of which were revealed years later. Unfortunately, under the crush of public opinion and politics, the account most people finally accepted was rather weighted in one direction. One fact was that the deputies were not ruthless, uncaring people. They were highly trained and seasoned deputy U.S. marshals placed in a precarious situation on a remote mountain. As dedicated deputies, they sought to enforce a lawful order of the court and bring a wanted person to justice. However, confusing orders from Boise and Washington and a compromised operation led to death. The FBI replaced the deputies and fared no better.

Randall Weaver, charged with a weapons violation, had failed to appear in the Moscow, Idaho, courthouse on February 19, 1991. The first unfortunate miscue: a typographical error generated confusion about the scheduled trial date. U.S. District Judge Harold Ryan, with no knowledge of the clerical mistake, issued a bench warrant on February 20. After discovering the error, the court relented from taking further action until a corrected letter was sent to Weaver. The U.S. Marshals agreed that any attempt to execute the bench warrant would take place after March 20. However, U.S. Attorney Maurice Ellsworth was convinced that Weaver had no intention of appearing in court at all.[11]

According to Deputy U.S. Marshal Dave Hunt, the U.S. Attorney received several letters signed by Vicki Weaver, the suspect's spouse. Hunt noted two other letters addressed to the "Servant of the Queen of Babylon," dated January 22, 1991, and February 3, 1991. The U.S. Attorney forwarded the letters to the U.S. Marshals Service to determine the level of possible threat or inappropriateness to the federal judiciary. According to Hunt, Deputy U.S. Marshal Warren Mays felt there was no "overt" threat, but the writer knew minute details of the Randall Weaver case and used angry rhetoric towards authority. The agency determined the letters originated with Vicki Weaver.[12]

Deputy Hunt remembered, "As a result, I quite naturally began to look at Weaver a little closer. At this time, I also learned that Weaver had failed to maintain his contacts with Pretrial Services. My position was to let Pretrial Services solve that problem."[13] He also learned of Weaver's anti-government ideological leanings and noted, "This is borne out by, among other things, the 'Babylon letters' wherein he considered the USA [the U.S. Attorney] as well as other government employees [as] servants of a 'lawless government.' Furthermore, it also became apparent that any attempt by the USMS to enforce a bench warrant could possibly result in a violent reaction on the part of Weaver."[14]

Subsequent interviews with associates and friends of Weaver confirmed Hunt's suspicions, and weighed on any actions to resolve the situation.

Through one of the fugitive's friends, the U.S. Marshals attempted contact with Weaver on March 5, 1991. As he knew the subject would be armed, Hunt refrained from entering the Weaver property. The following day, a signed letter from the Weavers arrived. It stated, "whether we live or whether we die, we will not obey your lawless government."[15] Despite the message, the U.S. Marshals gave him another chance to surrender. Hunt attempted mediation through family members and ideological associates. Weaver's neighbors told Hunt that he planned to resist arrest by force of arms. Time passed as the deputies hoped he would tire of the situation and surrender. By the following spring, further surveillance was needed to determine whether or not Weaver was moving off the mountain residence.[16] Over time, options to end the standoff with Weaver closed for the district office and Headquarters became more involved. A team from the Electronic Surveillance Unit assessed the need to track Weaver's movements on the mountain and a team of deputies from the Special Operations Group arrived to watch the residence. According to Art Roderick, they needed to ascertain his movements and find out if he was still present. The team moved closer to find out.[17]

Between March and August 1992, Randall Weaver displayed an increasing degree of paranoia. According to an interview, an armed Weaver stopped two civilians, forced them out of their vehicle, and demanded to know if they were deputy marshals. The May 3, 1992, *Bonner County Daily Bee* quoted him as saying, "Right now, the only thing they can take away from us is our life. Even if we die, we win."[18]

Supervisory Deputy U.S. Marshal Larry Cooper had joined the Marshals Service in 1978. In August 1992, he joined other SOG team members assigned to Ruby Ridge. Cooper recalled, "In or about May or June 1992, I reviewed some surveillance tapes that were sent to me, tapes that showed Randall Weaver and his family regularly carrying firearms in the immediate vicinity of their cabin. It was not until mid-August 1992 that I was actually notified of my assignment."[19]

Like Cooper, the other members of the surveillance team were well trained and experienced. Art Roderick worked in the Enforcement Division. Bill Degan tracked fugitives in the District of Massachusetts, and had experience operating in remote areas and planning rescue operations. Dave Hunt, Joe Thomas, and Frank Norris were all seasoned deputies.[20]

After several days of planning, the SOG deputies arrived to begin surveillance on Ruby Ridge in the early morning hours of August 21, 1992. Two trails merged at a place designated as the "Y"; the six deputies split into two groups, posted on different sections of the mountain, but stayed away from the residence and off the Weaver property. They observed that the family and their longtime friend Kevin Harris were present and armed. They hoped that Weaver could be apprehended alone, and worried about any confrontation.[21]

Deputies Hunt, Thomas, and Norris were the observation team and followed a trail to a previously used site for that purpose. From that point, they were about a half mile from the Weaver cabin. Roderick, Cooper, and Degan, as the forward team, headed for an area where Weaver had stopped approaching vehicles in the past. The site was a rock outcropping about 250 to 300 yards from the edge of the driveway leading to the cabin. Roderick knew the location, and warned Cooper and Degan about the topography and ways to approach to prevent discovery. They checked in with the observation group by code on the radio. They heard the family dogs bark, but this was not unusual. Roderick wanted to gauge the reaction of the dogs to random sounds, so he threw several rocks in the general direction without stirring the residents. As dawn approached, the forward team moved back to the "Y" to figure out the next course of action.[22]

Roderick recalled the reconnaissance team went forward again the next morning to scout a garden and spring house below the residence. Before they moved, Roderick informed the observation team of their plans. Upon reaching the garden and pointing out several possible positions, Thomas radioed that several of the Weavers suddenly ran out of their cabin—armed. They heard an approaching vehicle, but the deputies never heard a vehicle pass them. However, their equipment at the "Y" was in view and may have been spotted. At first, Roderick was not worried as the Weavers appeared at the rock outcropping. This was a pattern they followed in the past. However, several figures ran past the outcropping and headed towards their position. Roderick saw Harris and a large Labrador retriever approaching them.[23]

The reconnaissance team immediately pulled back. They ran through the woods, making a great deal of noise. They were being chased, as the dog had their scent. The three deputies ran into a fern field for cover, but the pursuers gained on them. Reaching a cluster of trees near the "Y," they feared being shot in the back, and decided to stop running and prepared to face their pursuers. At that moment, Randy Weaver appeared from a second trail. To the deputies, it was a trap and they were being hunted.[24]

Initial efforts to diffuse the situation failed. Cooper shouted, "Back off, U.S. Marshals!" The dog circled him, growling, and then passed him, launching towards Roderick. Cooper was more concerned with Harris, who faced his front. Randall Weaver spotted Roderick, who was at the "Y," and shouted at him. Roderick shouted, "Stop! U.S. Marshal." Then shots rang out.[25]

Versions of the initial shooting differ, with both sides blaming each other. Samuel Weaver, Randy Weaver's son, appeared near the fern field and was in the area of the initial melee. The deputies testified that Harris fired after hearing Degan behind him. Harris and Weaver stated Roderick fired first. The *Washington Post* reported that the jurors "according to interviews after the trial," believed the dog was hit by the first bullet.[26]

Bill Degan was positioned behind a tree stump, and was detected by Harris, who wheeled around and shot his rifle. Degan fell wounded. According to the deputy marshals, Harris aimed at the wounded deputy after he fell. Cooper fired three times from his pistol. Roderick heard the exchange and saw the dog heading straight for him. He was unsure of Randall Weaver's location, and the dog would expose or attack him.

Given the danger, he raised his rifle and shot the Labrador retriever. According to Cooper, Sam Weaver cursed angrily and fled.[27]

Death visited both camps. Deputy U.S. Marshal Degan was shot in the chest and died within minutes, his arm still in the rifle sling. Cooper informed Roderick by radio. Meanwhile, the deputies did not realize Sam Weaver was shot. He died from a bullet that had entered his back.[28]

The danger increased after the initial volley of gunfire. The deputies were pinned down with Degan's body, in horrible weather. They could not predict the reaction from the Weaver household. Later in the afternoon, a massive law enforcement presence reached the deputies and took control of the situation. Members of the FBI's hostage rescue team, a larger contingent of Special Operations Group deputies, and the Idaho State Police moved in and cordoned off the area. Once the initial team departed, the U.S. Marshals officially turned over the situation to the FBI.[29]

After the departure of the deputies, the situation deteriorated further. An FBI sniper shot and killed Vicki Weaver, the fugitive's wife. The sniper believed that the family had fired guns at a helicopter, and Vicki Weaver was caught in the crossfire. Harris was also badly wounded. A negotiator arranged for the surrender of Harris, the removal of Vicki Weaver's body, and eventually, an end to the standoff by September 1. However, the public relations fallout was enormous. News coverage depicted the anger of the local populace towards the federal government. Between the news coverage, court cases, and Congressional inquiries, the remnants of Ruby Ridge remained an on-and-off challenge for years.[30]

CHAPTER 17

THE BUSY SEASON

Ruby Ridge generated a great deal of negative press for the agency. However, the Marshals Service response in the wake of Hurricane Andrew did shine a positive light on the agency. The storm devastated portions of south Florida on August 24, 1992, leveling the town of Homestead. Due to fears of looting and an immediate need of support, Governor Lawton Chiles requested support from the U.S. Marshals, to whom he granted peacekeeping authority. On the same day, U.S. Attorney General William Barr approved Chiles' request. Chief Deputy U.S. Marshal James Tassone headed the Hurricane Andrew Response Task Force, which worked around the clock.[1]

The Marshals Service Mobile Command Center, a monster of a vehicle capable of comfortably transporting ten people with computers and office space, parked near Florida City. A 1991 Kenworth tractor, forfeited in a New Jersey drug operation, the command center was equipped with Citizen's Band (C.B.) and law enforcement radios, and had 40-kilowatt generators to provide power. The trailer was self-contained for operational travel, and included computer, camera, and telephone equipment. If needed, it contained expandable side units.[2] Dubbed "Red October," both for its color, black and red, and the month of use in the aftermath of Hurricane Andrew, the mobile command center found its way to the Marshals Service out of necessity for special operations that allowed full functionality on the road. While rudimentary, "Red October" was the forerunner of more practical vehicles used today. Nick Prevas, who worked with the Seized Assets Division, recalled its simple origins, "The tractor truck wore out. At that time, we had trucks seized, waiting for forfeiture... It was fine, totally legal."[3] While it was certainly primitive by later standards, a supporting telephone system for 50 external lines with secure receivers and computers was then a rarity in a mobile setting. The visible presence of Red October, and more importantly, its successors, brought a new dimension of public image to the USMS.[4]

Deputies provided security to responding medical and Federal Emergency Management Agency teams. They guarded temporary bank sites and patrolled tent cities of stranded residents. When President George H.W. Bush visited, the task force augmented his security detail. The Air Operations Division moved 1,402 prisoners from the devastated Miami Metropolitan Correctional Center to a number of facilities in and out of Florida. Some prisoners neared the point of dehydration for lack of water. By October 15, when the task force dismantled, it was then considered the largest humanitarian relief effort in the nation's history.[5]

More agency pride and enthusiasm emerged when the Special Operations Group cut the ribbon on its new headquarters and training center on January 8, 1993, at the Army National Guard facility in Camp Beauregard, Louisiana. Although the compound had been SOG's headquarters since 1984, the new installation was named the William F. Degan Tactical Operations Center and dedicated in March 1993. The surrounding training compound is still utilized by the Army National Guard, but the agency's Degan Center encompasses 37,000 square feet of office and training space.[6]

By spring 1993, after the Oklahoma City memorial project fell victim to financial woes, the headquarters building gained possession of the 1,300-pound statue called *Frontier Marshal*. Designed by Oregon sculptor

Dave Manuel, the impressive work of art arrived to occupy a prominent location in the lobby at Lincoln Place in Arlington, Virginia, and greet employees and visitors. It took over 10 people, and the temporary removal of doors, to bring the bronze statue to its resting place.[7]

On March 3, 1991, four Los Angeles Police Officers were videotaped subduing an African American man named Rodney King. In April 1992, the four officers were tried and acquitted in state criminal proceedings. The verdict triggered angry riots in Los Angeles, in which 53 people died and over $1 billion of property damage.[8]

On February 25, 1993, the civil rights trial against the four officers commenced in federal court in Los Angeles.[9] Careful plans were made to avoid rioting or violence during their second trial. The U.S. Marshals issued press and public passes to the proceedings. The Office of Policy and Communications explained the public affairs measures taken for the high-profile trial in Los Angeles:

> At the request of the U.S. Marshals in these districts and the Court Security Division, a public affairs specialist from the Office of Policy and Communications (OPC) traveled to Los Angeles and San Antonio to coordinate media relations during these trials. The specialists responded to media inquiries about trial procedures under USMS responsibility, coordinated media inquiries with the judge and the prosecution team, established an allocation scheme to fairly and equitably distribute the limited amount of passes for courtroom seating among the media requesting to cover the trial, established and monitored a press room equipped with audio feed from the courtroom to accommodate reporters who did not get courtroom seating passes, assisted court security personnel with public and VIP seating, and organized a press conference after the verdict so that the prosecution and defense attorneys could make statements and answer reporters' questions in a secure and controlled setting.[10]

Public Affairs Specialist Bill Licatovich handled the press involving the King trial. He later recalled to a reporter in Florida, "It was such a big case that I made several two-week trips out there while the trial was going on."[11] Guilty verdicts against two of the four officers quelled potential civil unrest and rendered further procedures unnecessary.[12]

The role of U.S. marshals piqued the interest of Hollywood, as it had many decades before. The public flocked to see the movie version of the old television series, *The Fugitive*. In 1993, Warner Brothers released their blockbuster, which cast fictional pursuer Samuel Gerard as a U.S. marshal.[13]

Marvin Lutes, only a few months removed from the deaths of Frakes and Belluomini, responded to a call from Warner Brothers with Chief Deputy Jim Tantillo. Lutes said, "They said they wanted to talk to somebody from the Marshals Office because they wanted to talk about a movie."[14] Prior to the early 1990s, the U.S. Marshals generally avoided any involvement with production companies or movie studios. Rules regarding official participation in entertainment media projects were undefined at the time. Lutes and Tantillo erred on the side of caution and took personal leave in order to meet studio representatives at the Four Seasons Hotel to get the particulars of the proposal. They met with a producer, director, and screenwriter who wanted to know what deputy U.S. marshals did. Lutes would provide details, and the screenwriter periodically left the room. He was rewriting new concepts in place of old descriptions under which he had operated. The studio team offered the real marshals a full review of the script. As Lutes and Tantillo left the hotel, they were introduced to a bearded man—actor Harrison Ford. The studio cast the actor to play Dr. Richard Kimble.[15]

The producer invited Lutes to the sound stage, located south of Chicago. Lutes brought his copy of the script, with "a considerable amount of changes" to go over with them. Intending only to watch, Lutes spent two to three hours editing the script with actor Tommy Lee Jones, who played Deputy U.S. Marshal Samuel Gerard. He pointed out operational issues in the original script. For example, deputies would never fire a gun in a crowded hotel lobby, as the initial script indicated. He told them, "We would catch him another time."[16]

Following wise counsel, retired deputy Jim McLaughlin took on the role of advisor to the filmmakers. McLaughlin advised the crew on the duties of deputy marshals that are carried out regardless of jurisdiction or circumstances. Arguably, no other film about U.S. Marshals utilized more "hands-on" involvement by the agency than *The Fugitive*. When *U.S. Marshals*, the sequel to *The Fugitive*, was filmed, official agency participation was limited.[17]

Marshals Service's Office of Public Affairs received numerous requests by media representatives for various projects. Most popular were "ride along" requests on prisoner transportation airplanes, used by the agency as part of the Justice Prisoner and Alien Transportation System, or JPATS. These aircraft were passenger airliners retrofitted to securely move detainees to and from all parts of the United States. Dubbed "Con Air" by the news media at some point, screenwriters scripted the flights into a movie by the same moniker that was released in 1997. Hollywood adapted Elmore Leonard's novel *Out of Sight*, a fictional journey into what he called the Witness Protection Program, into a screenplay for a movie released in 1998. If movies about the USMS served as a barometer of the public's sentiment toward the agency, then its public image in the 1990s improved significantly.[18]

Other significant transitions took place during the 1990s. In the February-March 1993 issue of the *Marshals Monitor*, Maureen Pan of the Information Technology Division wrote that a new communications network was "being installed in 21 district offices, six remote headquarters offices, and 16 divisions and offices at headquarters… these network users can send electronic mail (email) messages…"[19] Email rendered handwritten or typewritten products obsolete. In addition, advances in information technology ushered in improvements to the electronic system that tracked Marshals Service detainees, known as the Prisoner Tracking System, or PTS. Ron Pautz, who worked in Resource Analysis, recalled, "When I came on board it was ADP [computers]... everything was main frame" and done at the department level.[20]

CRISIS IN TOPEKA

System improvements and positive media attention buoyed an agency often overlooked in modern, federal law enforcement. Still, Director Hudson faced constant crises throughout his tenure.

In August 1993, a former employee of the Santa Fe Railroad, 37-year-old Jack Gary McKnight, entered the fourth floor of the Frank Carlson Federal Building in Topeka, Kansas. He arrived for a hearing regarding his sentence on drug and weapons charges, harboring darker plans. He approached the security checkpoint and fired one of several handguns on his person, while outside, McKnight's car exploded in the parking lot. In addition, explosives were strapped to his body. He approached the metal detector and 61-year-old Court Security Officer Gene Goldsberry, at the checkpoint on the fourth floor of the courthouse. McKnight shot him dead and wounded attorney Terry Morrow, who was standing nearby. McKnight, slowed but undeterred, headed for the district court clerk's office. Employees hid, but McKnight intended a massacre. He threw several detached pipe bomb explosives. SWAT teams deployed quickly. However, McKnight never intended to leave alive; he died after an explosive detonated around his waist. In the process, three people fell injured from the blasts. U.S. District Judge Sam Crow was scheduled to preside over the sentencing and was likely McKnight's primary target. Deputy marshals and court security officers followed their training and emergency operational plans and immediately evacuated the judges and their staffs. The courts and halls were sealed, so McKnight had nowhere to go.[21]

Hudson, in a memorandum to all U.S. Marshals, stated: "I am very proud of the professional reaction of our people. As a result of their actions, no federal judge or their staff members were harmed during this incident."[22]

For Director Hudson, Topeka represented the last crisis of his tenure. The political party at the White House changed with the elections of 1992, along with myriad political appointments. President William Jefferson Clinton nominated his choice for the next Marshals Service director in the summer of 1993; Hudson remained until October, after which, Attorney General Janet Reno designated John Twomey as acting director for several weeks, pending Senate confirmation of the president's nominee. Henry Hudson later became a federal district judge.[23]

Eduardo Gonzalez and the Realignment

In June 1993, President Clinton nominated Eduardo Gonzalez, the Chief of Police of Tampa, Florida, to replace Hudson. He was appointed after the President received the advice and consent of the Senate, on November 19, 1993.[24]

In November 1993, *America's Most Wanted*, a popular television show that focused on fugitive cases, aired an account of the "Escape from Alcatraz" case. Three prisoners, Frank Lee Morris, John William Anglin, and Clarence Anglin, had tunneled their way out of the maximum security prison in June 1962. The three escapees made their way to the roof, hopped a barbed-wire fence, and ventured into the San Francisco Bay using a makeshift raft from interwoven raincoats.[25]

New information about the escape came from a reliable source. Thomas Kent, a fourth inmate at Alcatraz who backed out in the final moments of the escape plan, was paroled in 1965. Kent's account of the escape from Alcatraz was featured on *America's Most Wanted*. Acting Director John Twomey admitted the escapees might have survived in the cold water and strong current. The new account brought attention to the cold case.[26]

Twomey retired a short time later. Since his arrival at the Marshals Service, he had worked to unify administrative and operational components of the agency. At nearly 60 years old, Twomey went out on top.[27]

On November 19, 1993, Eduardo Gonzalez, 51, was sworn in as director of the U.S. Marshals Service. The Tampa native had graduated from Florida International University in 1974 with a degree in Criminal Justice. His mother worked in one of the city's famed cigar factories, and was a staunch union supporter, who influenced her young son. While he was working in his uncle's Miami liquor store, an armed robbery convinced Gonzalez to pursue a career in law enforcement. Throughout his career in Florida, Gonzalez included community involvement as an active element to policing. He began work with the Dade County Public Safety Department in 1965. He rose through the ranks and became the deputy director of the Miami-Dade Police Department 21 years later. Tampa hired him as its police chief just a year and a half before he joined the U.S. Marshals. A strong believer in organizational affiliations, his core aim was to link the Marshals Service with local law enforcement. Given the traditional nature of the agency, he had a tough road ahead.[28]

"When I arrived at the Marshal[s] Service I was briefed by the various unit chiefs and as one would expect to find in any organization, some were pretty good, some were ok, and some I should have replaced as soon as whatever the time was I had to keep then [sic] ran out," reflected Gonzalez.[29]

Gonzalez set three priorities as director: reorganization, budget, and professionalizing U.S. marshal appointees. He also made the protection of the federal judiciary a priority over fugitive investigations. Gonzalez believed that "chaos … occurs in many countries when the judiciary breaks down, often because of the numbers of threats they receive while enforcing the laws of the country."[30]

Gonzalez put a new management team in place to help him steer the new course for the U.S. marshals. Francis J. "Frank" Martin was a broad-shouldered attorney from the Department of Justice, a physical giant of a man with extensive experience in a number of disciplines. Larry Mogavero, in charge of printing and publications, remembered Martin from his days at the Department and was impressed by the amount of his experience in different duty areas. George R. "Ray" Havens arrived on February 25, 1994, to become deputy director. A protégé of Attorney General Janet Reno, the tall, bespectacled Havens had served as chief investigator for Florida State Attorney's Office for the 11th Circuit for 13 years. Richard "Rick" Smith, hired as a consultant, assisted Gonzalez with an extensive realignment process for the agency.[31]

The incoming management team possessed the qualifications for their jobs, but lacked familiarity with the federal culture and the Marshals Service. The agency was still resistant to change. Headquarters had grown steadily from the 1960s, but directors met with limited success in previous attempts to affect budgetary efficiency by merging functions or making sweeping organizational changes.

Director Gonzalez joined an agency with approximately 3,500 employees and an operating budget of $333 million. In Tampa, he had approximately 1,000 employees and a budget of $58 million, and his focus on economy and efficiency of missions worked well there.[32]

In an interview for the February 1994 issue of the *Marshals Monitor*, Director Gonzalez provided a blueprint for his directorship and articulated the most important challenges facing the Marshals Service at that time:

> Certainly the problem we are having with the budget is an important issue for the entire Marshals Service. But aside from that, I think the need to further professionalize the Service is important. That includes looking really hard at the position of U.S. Marshal in regards to the appointment process. At a minimum, we need to strengthen the requirements for the position.

> The challenge will be to help us get away from the "us versus them" mentality—both as it applies to USMS headquarters and the field, and also between the Service and other law enforcement agencies, especially within the Department of Justice. I think there is a great need for everybody to recognize that we all must work together if we are going to have any degree of success.[33]

Director Gonzalez embraced the reinvention of government based on Vice-President Albert V. Gore, Jr.'s National Performance Review. Gonzalez stated, "if I can convince everyone here that we need to get on the reinvention bandwagon. I was very enthusiastic about the reinvention concept when I first read about it and I remain enthusiastic about it."[34]

The first signs of Gore's concepts appeared as a regular feature in the *Marshals Monitor*, "Reinvention Corner." Director Gonzalez implemented alternative work schedules that provided employees with flexible options to accomplish 80 work hours in each pay period.[35]

REORGANIZATION

The reorganization Gonzalez sought to implement proved to be a hard adjustment for the rank and file employees. Most Headquarters employees were in the middle of their careers and accustomed to the status quo. With few retirements and little turnover, Gonzalez needed buy-in from employees for his staffing changes. The gregarious Director, who had an open door policy and regularly chatted with employees, forged ahead.[36]

However, the 1994-95 reorganization stalled. New titles for managers and supervisors, like "team leader," confused the rank and file, as did the "PIT" concept, which established numerous employee-based "process improvement teams." Designed to work on specific projects across work disciplines, each "PIT" included members from operational and administrative mission areas. Likewise, a divisional improvement reinvention team, or "DIRT," allowed for employee input as a means to eliminate bureaucracy. Rick Smith managed the teams, and he sought membership from different corners of the agency. In the eyes of many, the reorganization results reflected decisions made by people with little expertise or knowledge in specific areas of specialty of the USMS.[37]

APPROPRIATIONS

The annual appropriation was an immediate concern. The Office of Management and Budget and an Executive Order reduced the 1994 appropriation of $360 million by $20 million, while new tasks and costs increased. Everyone in the agency felt the pinch. To keep the books balanced, several of the Director's top assistants—particularly Smith and Joe Enders, a longtime employee—planned an organization and cost-saving streamline in Headquarters. Rumors circulated among Headquarters employees that, if there was no budgetary need for a person's position, it meant possible job elimination or movement. Despite attempts to dispel the rumors, the message spread. In the March 1994 *Marshals Monitor*, most of the first two pages addressed the subject of rumors.[38]

Understanding employee reluctance to change, and given time, Director Gonzalez adjusted his reinvention strategy. He realized some successes —such as the increased employee participation and suggestions and the search of accreditation. Because of these more subtle changes, the agency's overall effectiveness was increasing. Although painful to divisional and district budgets, savings were being realized.

Director Gonzalez wrote numerous articles in the *Marshals Monitor* on reinvention, stressing increased structural efficiency. After a year, he wrote: "I can promise you this—the Service will *not* just sit there in 1995. I believe that we are on the right track to a better agency and we will work together to stay on track and move forward at a steady pace."[39]

PROFESSIONAL MARSHALS

Director Gonzalez believed strongly that a U.S. Marshal should be appointed based on professional experience rather than purely for political reasons. In early 1994, Director Gonzalez reached out to the National Organization of Black Law Enforcement Executives (NOBLE), in hopes of gaining support. In the letter to its executive director, Gonzalez provided some of his thoughts on the subject:

> As the former Chief of the Tampa Police Department and as the Deputy Director of the Metro-Dade Police Department, I never encountered a situation where I was not in control of all my high ranking staff officers, and had to yield to the power of managerial persuasion. I can't conceive of the Federal Bureau of Investigation or the Drug Enforcement Administration functioning with this type of management arrangement.[40]

The proposal to make Marshal appointment based on career law enforcement experience alarmed the sitting U.S. Marshals, who benefitted from the current confirmation process. This led to inevitable conflict.[41]

ASSETS AND ABORTION CLINICS

The landmark transfer of a 1948 Tucker automobile, seized as part of a 1992 Drug Enforcement Administration case in California, from the Marshals Service to the Smithsonian Institution provided a bright spot for a program under assault. In a rare move, the Seized Assets Division decided not to sell the valuable, forfeited asset—number 39 of the 51 Tucker autos ever produced. The Smithsonian received the vehicle for exhibition in the National Museum of American History.[42]

Jim Herzog, the agency employee who handled the exchange, recalled the special arrangement: "Once it was forfeited we contacted the Smithsonian and started to negotiate with Roger White [curator at the Smithsonian's Museum of American History]. Once we agreed on the transfer, they submitted the requested paperwork. DOJ approved and we waived all expenses. They paid for the transport from the Southern District of California to their storage facility... The whole thing took about 6 mos or so to complete."[43]

This transfer occurred in October 1993. However, it coincided with the Division's attempts to sell a forfeited California-based casino called the Bicycle Club. Since its seizure from two Florida drug traffickers in 1990, the business was on Marshals Service books. By law, the marshals kept the enterprise operating until it could be sold. However, the sale proved burdensome and gave the program a bad image in the news media. Additionally, Director Gonzalez wanted to change the way the agency handled seized assets.[44]

Gonzalez reflected, "I thought the Seized Assets folks experienced a lot of trouble managing the assets, both big and small and many of our audits revealed that properties frequently slipped through the cracks."[45] He added that the field staff and Headquarters lacked sufficient communications on assets.[46]

In March 1995, the *Legal Times* reported that Attorney General Reno approved a reorganization of the USMS "that will virtually disband the [Seized Assets] division, folding much of its staff into other branches of the service and devolving responsibility for government-owned assets to regional offices."[47] The news account shocked many employees who were unaware of the plans. In the end, regional offices were restructured, but the seized assets function was not eliminated.[48]

The Freedom of Access to Clinic Entrances (FACE) Act of 1994 brought the U.S. Marshals back in the discussion about reproductive health facilities. This Act prohibits, among other things, violence and intimidation against persons seeking reproductive health services and their providers. As a result of the Act, the federal government has a responsibility to protect a person's rights to access clinics for this purpose. It fell to the Marshals Service to protect such access. Since the Wichita incident, the Department of Justice formed a special task force on violence against abortion providers made up of personnel from the FBI, ATF, USMS, and DOJ attorneys. In March 1993, Florida provider Dr. David Gunn had been shot to death. In August 1993, an activist shot and wounded Dr. George Tiller outside his clinic in Wichita. In December 1994, in Brookline, Massachusetts, a man named John Salvi shot and killed two receptionists and wounded five other people at two abortion clinics. There was an escalating cycle of violence directed at reproductive health clinics and doctors performing abortions.[49]

Director Gonzalez recalled, "I do remember at Justice that I agreed with the notion of protecting clinics immediately after an attack, but also arguing that at some point in time the clinics needed to assume responsibility for their own protection and hire their own security."[50] The subject was a longstanding political quagmire.[51]

CHAPTER 18

THE CHANGING LANDSCAPE

OKLAHOMA CITY

Of the high profile events that occurred under the term of Director Gonzalez, one stood above the others. At about 9:00 a.m. on the morning of April 19, 1995, Supervisory Deputy U.S. Marshal Jamy Murphy felt the blast as he sat in his office in the courthouse across the street from the Alfred P. Murrah Federal Building in Oklahoma City. His chair rolled back towards the wall, and he sprang to his feet and looked out of a window. Across the street, he saw a crumbled portion of the interior wall of the Murrah building. In the nearby squad room, some of the light fixtures came loose. Murphy noted, "All the windows were blown out. Devastation was actually two blocks. Photos hardly do it justice."[1]

Murphy's first concern was for the building occupants. As he rushed toward the Murrah building, smoke and dust choked the air. The building, with its insides exposed, clearly lacked stability. Murphy ran into the building's garage, which was pitch black. He recalled seeing eight office workers who looked "almost like zombies."[2]

U.S. Marshal for the Western District of Oklahoma Patrick Wilkerson was attending an event for Special Olympics that morning. Chief Deputy

Brad Miller sent a message to his pager: "911... USM... Major explosion in federal building... 911... Authority... Brad."[3] As Marshal Wilkerson drove back to the district office, he telephoned Murphy and asked which floor exploded. Murphy answered, "Boss, it's the whole building. It's bad. It's bad."[4]

By the time other deputy U.S. marshals joined Murphy, they all feared a total collapse of the building. They quickly canvassed the structure and accounted for and evacuated judicial personnel.[5]

Communications were in a horrible state, as the area was devastated. Murphy set up a command post at a dry cleaning store. From there he reached Art Roderick, then working in the Investigative Services Division (which replaced the former Enforcement Division) at Headquarters. According to Murphy, the telephone connection between him and Roderick represented one of the first communications after the bombing between that section of Oklahoma City and Washington, D.C.[6] Then-Chief of Court Security Programs Stacia Hylton (later director) coordinated the command post at Headquarters. She recalled they were "running phone lines like there was no tomorrow."[7] Murphy maintained the makeshift command post and coordinated aid operations until the Federal Bureau of Investigation established its post later.[8]

By 9:45 a.m., Marshal Wilkerson arrived on the scene. A deputy took him up a back staircase to the site of the Secret Service offices. There was little left of them. As Wilkerson described it, "A narrow slice of the office remained, and only silence greeted us as we hollered out names. It took 20 minutes to work our way across what was left of an office where 12 people had worked."[9] Wilkerson recalled stepping over motionless bodies to reach the injured. After evacuations of survivors, deputies guarded the crime scene.[10]

Director Gonzalez was in Chicago, preparing to board a plane back to Washington, when he learned of the bombing. He called Deputy Director Havens, who clarified erroneous news reports that the courthouse was bombed. In the May-June 1995 *Marshals Monitor*, Gonzalez recalled, "He

[Havens] said that initial reports were that our folks, the judges and their staff all seemed to be safe, but that the blast had been devastating and casualties were expected to be high. We agreed that it would be best for me to alter my flight plans and head to Oklahoma City."[11]

An Air Operations plane brought Director Gonzalez to Oklahoma City only five hours after the first news reports. He was the first major official from Washington on the ground there. The director arranged the quick transfer of deputies to aid the district.[12]

Wilkerson remarked, "No question, he was a very welcomed sight. He didn't come in giving orders, or questioning actions. He just asked us what we needed to do our jobs, and he provided it."[13]

Gonzalez summed up his thoughts that day:

> I was grateful that we didn't lose any Marshals Service members in the federal courthouse as a result of the explosion at the Murrah Building. I remember speaking with CSO's working in the lobby area and they reported on how some of their colleagues were sucked out of the building. I remember touring the Courthouse and finding windows blown out and offices in shambles... I remember seeing our Deputies out on the streets, trying to help who they could, some with blank stares on their faces as they tried to digest what had happened.[14]

Wilkerson and his deputies tried to get their offices in working order four days after the bombing. The volunteers and assistance from other districts was vital.[15]

The vehicle-borne bomb killed 168 people, including 19 children in the building's day care center. One of the most personal losses to the USMS was Katherine Ann Finley, the wife of Riley Finley of the Air Operations Division.[16]

Although captured quickly, the domestic terrorist Timothy McVeigh faced trial for years. Deputies transported McVeigh to and from court. The agency dealt with the change of venue, from Oklahoma City to

Denver, and bore the increased costs of housing and security. After more than two years, the total expenses to the U.S. Marshal Service for his prosecution exceeded $6 million.[17]

As the head of court security programs, Stacia Hylton led a federal working group that developed a groundbreaking report and investigative approach for addressing building security issues. She recalled that approximately a month after the Oklahoma Bombing Deputy Director Havens told her the "President of the United States has asked the Attorney General to assess the security at all federal facilities. And the Attorney General said the Marshals Service has the person to do it."[18] The report, "The Vulnerability Assessment of Federal Facilities," was released in late June 1995, recommended minimum standards and suggested specific improvements for building construction and safety. After noting their involvement in security teams around the trials after the first attempt to bomb the World Trade Center and the Oklahoma bombing trials, the U.S. Marshals were in a better position to assess safety in preparation for crisis situations. In April 1996, Acting Associate Director for Operations Eugene Coon addressed the House Transportation and Infrastructure Subcommittee on Public Buildings and Economic Development. Coon explained that two working groups "conducting a two-track study" developed questionnaires and set standards for federal facilities. The study was repeatedly requested and utilized, even decades later.[19]

Overtaken by Events

By September 1995, Director Gonzalez refocused on agency reinvention and announced that a reorganization plan was under review by Congress. Additionally, under the direction of the Attorney General, the air fleets of the Immigration and Naturalization Service (INS) and the Marshals Service Air Operations Division merged to form the Justice Prisoner and Alien Transportation System (JPATS). Designed to control costs and create efficiencies between two DOJ entities performing similar activities, it became a major factor in mass deportations and prisoner movements.

Thomas Little Jr., who served with the INS Air Transportation Branch, was promoted to division chief and led JPATS.[20]

The Office of District Affairs was formed under the Gonzalez watch. The office provided guidance and support to the field on a variety of issues, from the newly enacted Law Enforcement Availability Pay (LEAP) to Special Operations Group deployments. Two chief deputy U.S. Marshals, Al Matney and Mary Wong, managed District Affairs under the supervision of the Deputy Director. Matney coordinated the eastern half of the country and Special Operations, while Wong handled the western half and special assignments.[21]

In another change, the Analytical Support Unit in the Investigative Services Division replaced the former Threat Analysis Division, with analysts working with the operations threat desk in the Judicial Services Division. The new unit produced reports and analytical research. Debra Jenkins, a longtime employee with Enforcement, led the unit.[22]

Acting Chief Donald Ward replaced Tony Perez in the Enforcement (later Investigative Services) Division, and General Counsel Deborah Westbrook took over for Larry Gregg. In January 1996, Jim Sullivan, chief of the Office of Policy and Communications and former Chief Deputy U.S. Marshal for the Northern District of California, became director of the United States National Central Bureau at INTERPOL.[23]

On May 12, 1995, Director Gonzalez sent a memorandum to all employees regarding the Ruby Ridge incident. The prolonged 1993 trial reopened old wounds of personnel across the agency. The participating deputies grappled with a maze of legal issues. In the memorandum, Gonzalez noted the various investigations restricted his discussion of the matter with employees and his own review of the actions at Ruby Ridge,

> I, along with senior Marshal's Service staff, carefully reviewed the report and all other available material regarding these events, which totaled over 1000 pages... I concluded that the use of deadly force by Marshals Service personnel was entirely justifiable.

Moreover, I found that the actions of Marshals Service personnel during these events were proper and courageous at all times.[24]

Congress planned full hearings on the incident. The Department of Justice investigated the roles of both the U.S. Marshals and the Federal Bureau of Investigation. Ward turned over everything to investigators as requested. He believed the last thing the agency needed was to be accused of a cover-up. In August 1995, Deputy Attorney General Jamie Gorelick asked Senator Arlen Specter of Pennsylvania, chairman of the Senate Subcommittee of Terrorism, Technology, and Government Information, to delay the Ruby Ridge hearing until the completion of the internal DOJ investigation on the use of deadly force. In their conclusions, the DOJ task force cleared the deputies and agents, but newspaper reporters probed the decision-making process.[25]

The deputy U.S. marshals at Ruby Ridge appeared before the Senate Subcommittee on Terrorism, Technology, and Government Information on September 15, 1995. As expected, there was plenty of scrutiny, but the deputies held their own. By the time of the hearings, the Ruby Ridge incident was three years old. Although the agency went through an intensive self-examination during this period and updated certain operational procedures, the U.S. Marshals Service moved forward. Director Gonzalez recalled:

> Ruby Ridge was an unfortunate situation for all involved. Bill Degan was a hero whose life was ended tragically on the hill. I thought that Art Roderick and Larry Cooper displayed heroism in remaining with Deputy Degan's body not knowing if more militia were on the way or already on the ridge. They were nominated for a bravery award during my tenure and I was happy that I was the one that had the opportunity to approve them and present them.[26]

The U.S. Marshals turned the corner with new special assignments, including the response in the aftermath of Hurricane Marilyn which hit the U.S. Virgin Islands in September 1995. Attorney General Janet Reno requested the agency's assistance in maintaining order and working with the Federal Emergency Management Agency (FEMA). The hurricane extensively damaged many homes and businesses on St. Thomas, and left local authorities with no working motor vehicles. The many extraordinary humanitarian efforts of deputy U.S. marshals to assist the population of the Virgin Islands, along with several levels of law enforcement specially deputized for this purpose, fostered a positive image for the Service and proved uplifting to its employees in the wake of Ruby Ridge criticism.[27]

Unfortunately, federal budget woes dampened the enthusiasm. A congressional showdown created a logjam and led to a federal government shutdown. U.S. Marshals Service employees were furloughed. In fact, the action occurred twice, the first in November and again in December of 1995.[28]

A continuing resolution finally passed in early January 1996, but a snowstorm prevented re-opening business in Washington for several more days. This was followed by yet another blizzard. Even furloughs could be overtaken by natural events.[29]

THE NEW COURSE

From 1995 through 1998, the agency saw many new faces in key leadership positions. Most of the initial hires who arrived with Director Gonzalez moved on or shifted roles within the organization. Three important leadership roles went to people from outside the agency, and all of them impacted the direction of the organization.

Gonzalez appointed Robert J. Finan II as assistant director of Executive Services in May 1996. He brought executive and legislative experience. After 20 years with the Secret Service, he became an assistant director with the Naval Criminal Intelligence Service (NCIS). In addition, he once worked on the personal staff of Senator Dennis J. DeConcini of Arizona. After three years at NCIS, he moved to the U.S. Marshals Service to oversee functions in Congressional and Public Affairs, Internal Affairs, Equal Employment Opportunity, and Special Deputations.[30]

Suzanne D. Smith became assistant director of Human Resource Management, where she'd spent five years as a personnel officer. Previously, she was director of Employment Policy at the General Services Administration.[31]

In April 1997, G.H. "Gil" Kleinknecht, former director of Enforcement Support for the Immigration and Naturalization Service, joined the U.S. Marshals as the assistant director of Investigative Services. He replaced Al Solis, an administrator and former U.S. Marshal, who assumed duties as the assistant director for Prisoner Services.[32]

Kleinknecht, like Director Gonzalez, had served at both local and federal levels. In addition, he was invested in the idea of accreditation. The Commission on Accreditation for Law Enforcement Agencies (CALEA), founded in 1979, provided a grading system through professional standards. A team would assess compliance with these standards, and through this process the USMS would become the first federal law enforcement agency to achieve accredited status.[33]

U.S. Marshal for the Eastern District of Virginia John Marshall, the younger son of Supreme Court Justice Thurgood Marshall, credited Gonzalez for his willingness to experiment with new ideas. While participating on a panel for new deputy U.S. marshal applicants, it occurred to Marshall that a committee composed of U.S. Marshals could provide a strong voice when discussing the needs of district offices. He suggested the idea to the Director Gonzalez, who asked him to draw up a plan.[34]

Marshall composed a model and Director Gonzalez made it a reality. The director later added chief deputy U.S. marshals to the committee, as he reasoned they ran most day-to-day affairs within the districts. The "Marshals and Chiefs Committee" became the "Leadership Council." Marshall served as the first chair of the new entity.[35]

Director Gonzalez sought legislation to convert the U.S. Marshal position from political appointment to career status. He sought support from professional police organizations, like the National Sheriffs Association and the International Association of Chiefs of Police (IACP),

> I remember going to speak with both groups. While the Chiefs would not support a total elimination of political appointments, they did pass a resolution supporting the notion that all appointees should have some law enforcement background. The Sheriffs would not even consider that proposition. Many of these individual[s] retire from their positions and aspire to gain one of the appointments.[36]

He formed an "ad hoc" committee, composed of personnel from Headquarters components, to prepare language for a bill to articulate the changes. Background paperwork from the committee outlined several goals. Among them were:

> Only experienced career managers from within the Marshals Service will become U.S. Marshals via merit promotion. This will ensure that individuals being considered for the position of U.S. Marshals will be selected on the basis of what they know, not who they know.

> Career U.S. Marshals will [be] subject to the same disciplinary actions as the employees they supervise.

> Middle management positions can be downsized. There will be no need for the extra positions currently needed to support the political U.S. Marshals.

> A number of USMS national programs can be delegated to the field offices where an experienced career U.S. Marshal can oversee its operation.[37]

The notes suggest U.S. Marshals functioning more like Chief Deputy U.S. Marshals. Gonzalez argued the changes would make the agency more efficient, while trimming the opportunities for political deals.

After a number of attempts, the House of Representatives passed bill H.R. 927, known as the *United States Marshals Service Improvement Act of 1997.* The legislation carefully phrased that existing U.S. Marshals would not be affected, and could serve until they resigned or were removed by the President.[38] Under H.R. 927, the Attorney General would appoint new U.S. Marshals, rather than the President. After a long struggle, the *United States Marshals Service Improvement Act of 1997* passed the House on March 18, 1997.[39]

Director Gonzalez felt many chief deputies stayed silent on the subject. Chairman of the Chief's Advisory Committee, Chief Deputy U.S. Marshal Marvin Lutes, clearly stood in support. On his own time, he contacted his fellow chiefs and asked them to support the "de-politicization" of the U.S. Marshal position. In doing so, Lutes risked angering many Presidentially appointed U.S. Marshals. Looking back, Lutes felt the initiative faltered internally because many chiefs worked daily with the appointed marshals and demurred to them on political matters. Some didn't want to risk standing against their own bosses. Others just simply opposed the concept.[40]

The House resolution reached the Senate, and Director Gonzalez addressed the Committee on the Judiciary March 10, 1998.[41] He recalled the hearing, entitled "United States Marshals Service: A Selection Process for the 21st Century," as a "great achievement, and one I think displeased many as by then this item had fallen off the radar screen for the reinvention project."[42]

He stated that his predecessors and the Department of Justice supported the initiative. He argued that the long history of a changing and growing U.S. Marshals Service justified the Improvement Act.[43]

Gonzalez later recalled, "While a couple of the House members and Senators understood the difficulties in managing an organization where your senior leaders in the field are Presidential appointees who can only be disciplined through the President... the majority were more intent in maintaining the senatorial candy aspects of these nominations."[44]

Although the United States Marshals Service Improvement Act of 1997 never became law, there was general internal agreement that the positions of U.S. Marshal should be filled with professional law enforcement personnel. Applicants faced a higher bar for future appointments as U.S. Marshals. Despite the attempts of Director Gonzalez, legislation never went far in the Senate. It brought attention to the subject of professionalization of U.S. Marshals, but stopped short of changing the process of appointment.[45]

Director Gonzalez turned his focus on long-term planning and professional accreditation. A booklet, "Marshals Service 2000," outlined this strategic vision, comprised of three different plans: tactical, strategic and business. The tactical plan consisted of goals to be achieved within three years. The strategic plan required a list of no more than eight goals to achieve in the shorter term. The business plan outlined "multiple measurable targets" to directly meet the goals set in the other two plans. The director wanted to capture the costs associated with each stated goal as proof of fiscal integrity and documented justification for expending appropriated funds.[46]

Director Gonzalez distributed the strategic plan on March 12, 1997.[47] Now revised, the publication clarified mission and vision statements for the agency. "The mission of the United States Marshals Service is to protect the Federal courts and ensure the effective operation of the judicial system."[48] The vision stated, "The Marshals Service: Committed to Excellence as We Cross the Bridge to the Twenty-First Century."[49] The second publication listed six overarching goals: maximizing effectiveness of missions, cost effectiveness, diversity, investment in infrastructure, multi-jurisdictional coordination, and educating through an information strategy.[50]

The detailed tactical plan was distributed to employees in July 1997, with revisions in March 1998. Objectives placed below the major goals helped management to figure out their needs and to identify milestones on the way to achieving the larger goals. In the updated tactical plan,

Director Gonzalez announced that 16 of the "sub-goals" were already completed. The publication touted the success of JPATS and noted reductions in costs during the conversion, and earned the agency one of Vice President Al Gore's Golden Hammer awards.[51]

The business plans proved more complex. Each district had a performance management plan, or PMP, to guide their spending and objectives. Unexpected events or unforeseen expenses completely changed the goals. However, the real value of the business plan was tracking expenses. If an expense could be explained to an official or to Congress, funding decisions could be more easily justified.[52]

Another organizational shuffle occurred between 1997 and 1998. It would be the last under the leadership of Gonzalez. The Deputy Director handled the districts, the Judicial Security Division, the Prisoner Services Division, and the Investigative Services Division. The Associate Director for Administration oversaw the remaining components. In July 1997, the Equal Employment Opportunity Team, previously in the Executive Services Division, moved under the Deputy Director. The move favored a strong, independent EEO Office and a commitment to diversity. Assistant Directors Finan and Kleinknecht swapped components—with Finan moving to Investigative Services and Kleinknecht to Executive Services.[53]

Frank Martin, who oversaw several components at Headquarters, left the agency. Assistant Rick Smith departed after setting up the DIRT and PIT, the employee-focused teams created to bridge operational and administrative differences. Joe Enders took this reinvention function in the new Office of Organizational Development. Perhaps the hardest blows to the agency came from funding shortfalls. Despite cost reductions across the agency, unexpected operational expenses and the inability to reprogram funding clearly took its toll. As added assignments piled up, financial woes continued.[54]

Gonzalez restated his argument for professionalism in the October 1998 issue of *Police Chief* magazine. In March 1999, he hosted a town hall meeting for agency personnel in the Drug Enforcement Administration's auditorium. The meeting was filmed for agency-wide distribution and took on the appearance of a pep rally. The director and each assistant director presented key achievements, but still fielded tough questions from the rank and file. The March-April 1999 issue of the *Marshals Monitor* contained a reprinted article from David Ignatius of the *Washington Post.* The subject of the story was taking risks. It outlined differences between Washington, D.C., and Silicon Valley. Ignatius concluded that great innovations went through trials and even failure. Whatever the message intended, it marked one of the director's last appeals for organizational change.[55]

On June 18, 1999, Director Gonzalez departed for Florida. He had served nearly six years as Director of the U.S. Marshals Service.[56] Some of his achievements brought accolades. In 1997 and 1998, Director Gonzalez received the honor of being named twice by *Hispanic Business* magazine as one of the 100 most influential Hispanic leaders in America. He championed a diverse work force. Accreditation was closer to reality.[57]

Gonzalez's departure left the agency in the hands of Acting Director Ray Havens. Before the final year of the decade closed, though, the President tapped U.S. Marshal John W. Marshall for the top job.[58]

CHAPTER 19

THE NEW "MARSHALL"

FIVE MONTHS IN 1999

Ray Havens became acting director until the appointment of his successor. The Miami native led an agency with many missions and skyrocketing costs. As chief investigator for the Office of State Attorney for the 11th Judicial Circuit in Miami-Dade, Florida, for 13 years, Havens knew the expectations of judges. Eugene Coon, formerly the assistant director of the Judicial Security Division, became acting deputy director.[1]

Acting Director Havens reframed agency goals in his first message in the *Marshals Monitor* July-August 1999 issue:

> Our number one priority must be to obtain the staffing and budget resources we need to get through the remainder of the fiscal year and into the future. As we move toward the next century, we must be prepared to accomplish our mission... Threats to judicial officials are increasing, as are the number of high threat trials we secure. Our prisoner population grows daily while the number of available jails to house them is shrinking. The number of violent fugitives we apprehend is also growing and removing them from the streets is an integral part of the overall crime control strategy. By emphasizing these vital responsibilities, I am confident that,

working with the Department of Justice and the Congress, we can get the resources we need to do our job.[2]

Havens' message confirmed that conflicts between burgeoning duties and a stagnant budget threatened the missions of the agency. While Director Gonzalez had achieved some lasting and important reforms, particularly in granting LEAP (Law Enforcement Availability Pay) to deputies in 1994, which helped stem runaway overtime costs, Acting Director Havens had a full plate, and little time for new initiatives.[3]

Immediately, Havens had to deal with two sensitive events: mounting tensions in Vieques, Puerto Rico, and the awkward seizure of documents from the FBI pertaining to the Branch Davidian activities in Waco. In both cases, he relied on his experienced subordinates. Acting Deputy Director Coon and the Special Operations Group (SOG) dealt with the Island of Vieques, and Assistant Director Robert Finan approached the FBI.[4]

The U.S. Navy conducted military exercises on Vieques through a 1983 memorandum of understanding with the Commonwealth of Puerto Rico. As on Culebra Island, the testing of armaments and bombshells on Vieques created anger in the region. During training exercises in April 1999, two bombs accidentally detonated off target, killing a security guard and wounding four others. The public reaction in Vieques and Puerto Rico forced the Navy to temporarily cease activity while authorities investigated. On August 20, 1999, Coon, SOG Commander Scott Flood, General Counsel Deborah Westbrook, and Special Investigations Chief Darrell Williams met with representatives from other federal law enforcement agencies. They worked on a plan to secure the range area, approximately an hour from the main body of Puerto Rico. Two-thirds of the island was owned by the United States Navy. Two installations, Roosevelt Roads and Camp Garcia, housed a small number of military personnel. The most populous portion of Vieques was Isabel Segunda, a fishing village on the island's northern coast.[5]

The accident strengthened the claims of protest groups and dissident political parties. The history of protest over Vieques had peaked in 1984,

when disruption led to an order from U.S. District Court Judge Juan R.
Torruella. His ruling, Civil Injunction 79-259, restricted unlawful entry
of protestors into the exercise zone. After the ruling, any positive relationships between residents, protestors, and the military disintegrated.
After the 1999 accident, demonstrators reappeared and used civil disobe-
dience to prevent further exercises. The U.S. Marshals were drawn in by
Judge Torruella's original injunction. Although the Navy ceased using
the training range in April, deputies were initially asked to assist with
expected protestors. Eventually, an investigating panel recommended a
phase-out of Navy exercises over a five-year period.[6]

In September 1999, Attorney General Janet Reno ordered the U.S.
Marshals to seize evidence from FBI headquarters about their actions
involving the Branch Davidian Compound in Waco, Texas, six years
earlier. It was a unique request, as deputies were required to go into FBI
offices and physically carry out the evidence from a sister DOJ agency.
As the FBI and U.S. Marshals often work together, tact was vital. Though
news outlets reported widely on the action, what actually took place
demonstrated the professionalism of both organizations.[7]

The *Washington Post* reported that evidence was found in the case that
required the transfer of records to the Department of Justice after the FBI
Director ordered an internal search of the Hostage Reserve Unit offices.
Officials from the FBI voluntarily reported this evidence had been found.
At the same time, Attorney General Reno wanted an external presence
conducting the transfer. The U.S. Marshals retrieved the evidence boxes
from the J. Edgar Hoover Building. The records were to be made available
to investigators on the case.[8]

The task of retrieval fell to Assistant Director of Investigative Operations Robert Finan. To maintain the integrity of the evidence, he recalled
it was necessary for the USMS to be involved in the chain of custody.
Unlike the overblown reports, complete with a political cartoon that
showed Old West deputies carrying nineteenth-century rifles outside
FBI Headquarters, the transaction was uneventful. Finan made a round

of phone calls, met with the lawyers from the FBI's General Counsel's Office, and on September 1, 1999, brought two deputy marshals to pick up the evidence. He quipped, "The only thing consistent with the cartoon is that there were three of us. That was part of the agreement."[9]

The U.S. Marshal's "Marshall"

In early August, President William J. Clinton announced his selection of John W. Marshall, 41, as the next Marshals Service director, but the political process delayed confirmation for months. Finally, on November 18, 1999, the U.S. Marshal for the Eastern District of Virginia became the first African American to be appointed as director. Son of the late Supreme Court Justice Thurgood Marshall, John Marshall brought optimism for the future to the agency. Prior to his appointment as U.S. Marshal in June 1994, he had served 14 years as a Virginia state trooper, attaining the rank of sergeant in the Northern Virginia field division. He had also served as a special agent in Virginia's Bureau of Criminal Investigation.[10] Director Marshall said in his initial press release, "As Marshal for Eastern Virginia, I've seen first hand the dedication and professionalism of Marshals Service employees, and I'm enthusiastic about leading such a quality organization into the 21st century."[11]

In a message to employees, Director Marshall announced that Attorney General Reno appointed the former U.S. Marshal for the Central District of California, Michael Ramon, as deputy director. He established goals of steering through the budget shortfalls and hiring freezes that plagued the agency, improving relationships between Headquarters and the districts, and the realignment of functions.[12] Director Marshall felt he and Ramon had the necessary experience to meet those goals. He later recalled, "Mike and I served together on the Marshals Advisory Committee and the Leadership Council."[13] In fact, Ramon had served in the agency since 1979. After a stint in the Air Force, the Missourian had begun his career as a deputy U.S. marshal in the Southern District of Alabama.

In 1989, a promotion brought him to California. He was later tapped as a U.S. marshal.[14]

The two talked about their respective strengths and they established an informal division of labor. Ramon preferred administrative duties at Headquarters, while Marshall liked in-person communications with the field to discuss USMS priorities and get to know personnel. The deputy director began crafting a justification for additional deputy hiring. Marshall explained the quandary that in the past, a marshal might ask for more deputies without a clearly articulated basis. The need was often based on anecdotal information rather than justifiable facts.[15]

As the new leadership team launched into action, they completed one of the major goals begun by former Director Gonzalez. The Commission on Accreditation for Law Enforcement Agencies (CALEA) conducted a final assessment of the agency from October 2 to 7, 1999. At the conclusion of the long process and assessment, CALEA officially accredited the U.S. Marshals Service, and it became the first federal law enforcement agency to receive the designation. To both Directors Gonzalez and Marshall, accreditation provided an undeniable quality checkmark for the U.S. Marshals.[16]

Still, Director Marshall had to deal with fundamental "here and now" problems, including a hiring freeze. Perhaps the most unique issue he faced at that time was public concern about "Y2K," the technological challenges associated with computer programs and their internal calendars not moving beyond the year 2000. People feared Y2K would cause massive systems failures and disruptions of service. The prevailing nightmare scenario portended a massive computer and network failure when the date changed to January 1, 2000. Without some manual intervention, the fear of the unknown was real. In preparation, federal courthouses placed additional security systems in readiness. Director Marshall maintained a vigil in Headquarters on New Year's Eve, just in case there was a need. Thankfully the event passed without issue.[17]

Although he had already been in office for months, the director's formal installation ceremony occurred on February 1, 2000, at the Crystal Gateway Marriott in Arlington. A number of impressive guests gave remarks, including Supreme Court Justice John Paul Stevens, Attorney General Janet Reno, Deputy Attorney General Eric Holder, and Virginia Senator Charles Robb. The same Bible that was used at the swearing-in of his father as Justice to the Supreme Court was used for John Marshall's installation ceremony. In a rare display of public emotion, the director described their close relationship. He said during the ceremony, "I know that he hears me when I say, 'Thanks Dad, I miss you and I love you.'"[18]

Former Director Gonzalez returned for the installation and awards ceremony, where the agency received recognition for the CALEA accreditation. He recalled, "Director Marshall was kind enough to invite me to the awards ceremony at which the Agency received their certificate, and I was pleased to be on the stage with the members who worked so hard to achieve that status."[19]

Rightly or wrongly, many officials and onlookers expected much of "Marshal Marshall," or "Marshal Squared," as he was humorously called for years by both employees and the media. He wasted no time and gave an interview in the February 2000 newsletter of the Administrative Office of the U.S. Courts, *The Third Branch*. This was followed by an appearance on the Federal Judiciary Television Network (FJTN) and an April 2000 article in *People*.[20] Marshall spelled out the challenges he immediately faced in the new century:

> Without a doubt, internally, the greatest challenge that I'm dealing with is our budget. Last year we were faced with a budget shortfall, which included a hiring freeze that has affected all of our offices... This year, we've started a whole new budget review process we're calling a bottom-up review... Externally, we're trying to be as proactive as we can with regard to our primary mission of protecting the federal Judiciary.[21]

In stressing the importance of protective missions, Marshall recalled, "One thing I'd learned in the district in particular was the importance of the judicial mission. That is the primary [agency] responsibility."[22]

With a chance for a fresh start, Director John Marshall and the U.S. Marshals Service cured a long-term case of wanderlust. After a long hunt for stability and a search for their identity through several leaders and after a series of course-changing events, the largest period of self-examination ended and an internal figure was selected from the field. His stature as a son of a civil rights icon gave reason for optimism. However, many more challenges appeared on the horizon of the next decade.

SECTION SIX—THE NEW CENTURY: RENEWAL

CHAPTER 20

A BOY NAMED ELIAN

The Marshals Service's path in the 1990s included four different directors, two acting directors, three large-scale reorganizations, and unprecedented growth in both missions and personnel. After a long period of self-examination and transition in philosophy and outlook, Director John Marshall cleared the field for a hopeful return to optimism and growth. But first, as with many of his predecessors, the director faced a controversy almost immediately.

OPERATION QUINCY

On Thanksgiving Day, 1999, fishermen rescued three survivors of a Cuban boat wreck just off the Florida coast near Ft. Lauderdale. One of them was a six-year-old boy named Elian Gonzalez. Ten others, including the boy's mother, had drowned before being rescued. The U.S. Coast Guard received the three survivors and turned them over to the Immigration and Naturalization Service (INS). In turn, INS temporarily placed the child with relatives in Miami, until the U.S. government determined his status. Ultimately, the federal courts sided with the child's father, who allegedly opposed his emigration to the U.S. from Cuba. Juan Miguel Gonzalez claimed custody of Elian from abroad. Elian's parents were divorced, and his mother's relatives lived in Miami and opposed returning the boy.[1]

Though the INS placed Elian in the physical custody of the Miami relatives, a federal court in March 2000 dismissed Elian's asylum petition filed on his behalf by attorneys and set in motion the boy's ultimate return to Cuba. The relatives appealed the decision and circulated a petition for Elian's political asylum, but it was rejected by the U.S. government. Juan Gonzalez flew to the United States to demand custody of his son. Attorney General Reno authorized the INS to take custody of the boy from his guardian-relatives. When a special INS tactical unit arrived to seize the boy from the uncle's Miami residence, news stories mistakenly identified the uniformed INS agents as deputy U.S. marshals. Headlines around the globe showed a picture of a fearful relative facing down an armed agent in tactical gear. The popular photo was reprinted and the mistake of identity repeated in new venues. Deputy U.S. marshals received the boy from INS. However, no personnel from the U.S. Marshals Service entered the home to take custody of the child. Deputy marshals had provided a continuous protective detail for Elian's father since his arrival in the United States, and this expanded once the INS transferred the boy to federal custody.[2]

The transfer and care of Elian Gonzalez was an unscheduled and expensive endeavor. The case had cost the agency $161,000 by April 24. After the news media reported that the 11th U.S. Court of Appeals had rejected emergency motions by the Miami relatives, it became prudent to move the pair to a controlled environment from a temporary residence on the grounds of an estate in northwest Washington, D.C. Indeed one of the cousins had attempted to enter their temporary residence four times. During this tense period, Director Marshall carried two cell phones and frequently met with Attorney General Reno on decisions involving the boy. Assistant Director Finan secured accommodations on the Eastern Shore of Maryland.[3]

USA Today reported on April 25:

> Elian, his father, stepmother and half brother were moved today from nearby Andrews Air Force Base to an undisclosed location, the Marshals Service announced. There has been speculation the family would be taken to the secluded Wye Center on Maryland's Eastern Shore to await court action over whether Elian should be allowed to return to Cuba. The Marshals Service remained with the family for protection, said Marshals spokesman Drew Wade.[4]

Officials felt the Carmichael Farm, a 300-acre estate about 70 miles east of Washington, D.C., provided a more secure location to house the family until the matter was finally resolved. According to a May 7, 2000, article in the *Florida Times Union*, Nina Houghton, widow of an heir to the Corning Inc., glassmaking fortune, offered use of the private residence to the Gonzalez family. The farm, lined by mature evergreen trees, was part of the Wye River Conference Center, where Israelis and Palestinians had met in 1998. Meanwhile, a protest of almost 200 women dressed in black gathered outside the Justice Department's main building. There was additional fear of an armed attack.[5]

In April and May, while the domestic and international politics revolved in Washington, the deputy marshals on the protective detail, known as "Operation Quincy," continued their work. The expansive property was ideally located but required special measures to secure. The Electronic Surveillance Unit set up sensors along the perimeter of the farm to alert deputies of unwanted visitors. Those and other precautions went largely unnoticed by the family members and news media posted at the gates of the property.[6]

Four Cuban children arrived as playmates for Elian—they rode bicycles and used the swing set. Nearly all the deputies on the detail "entertained" the energetic Elian. Inspector Mike Pyo got along famously with the boy. He recalled, "It's hard not to get attached to the kids. They're just like my nieces and nephews..."[7]

The deputies and inspectors on the detail were well-prepared for the mission. In fact, Pyo was one of the deputies who picked up Elian Gonzalez from Andrews Air Force Base, evading a press barrage in the process. He conducted some of the vital site surveys to make sure the perimeters were secure at Wye. It seemed surreal for Pyo to be setting up a command post one minute, and playing ball with Elian the next. He added, "two Witsec inspectors and two SOG guys were on the kid 24-7."[8]

Not only was it an unconventional detail, protecting the family also took its toll on the protectors and protectees. A psychiatrist visited the boy on a weekly basis. The pastoral environment, while beautiful and relaxing, confined the elder Gonzalez too much, and he requested more outings away from the compound.[9]

According to public affairs specialist Drew Wade, Rev. Pat Mahoney of the Christian Defense Coalition requested permission to hold a vigil for the Liberty for Elian Alliance at the Carmichael Farm. Denied by the Marshals Service, he instead conducted a protest by boat at the back of the property from the Wye River. At 7:05 p.m., Sunday, April 14, 2000, Mahoney and 23 other adults arrived on the river adjacent to the farm onboard the boat "April M" of Grasonville, Maryland. With megaphones, they pleaded in Spanish and English for the release of Elian to his Cuban relatives in America. They offered a prayer, released balloons, and spread carnations on the water, then departed at 7:30 p.m. Unfortunately for the protestors, the river bank lay 50 feet down an embankment bordered by trees and open fields. The family, nearly a half mile away on the property, could not hear or see the party.[10]

Though media outlets set up a tent and pool coverage from just outside the farm gates from April 26 until the family departed a month later, news coverage proved minimal. Even with powerful telephoto lenses on their cameras, the media had no clear line of sight from their outpost and little chance to capture images of Elian or his family at the farm. At least two media representatives arrived each morning and left around 8:00 p.m. each night. The journalists caused minimal distraction, only needing to be rebuked once for attempting to film into the windows of cars driven by Marshals Service inspectors.[11]

On May 26, Elian and his father were moved to new quarters at Rosedale, an eighteenth-century farmhouse in Washington, D.C. Youth for Understanding, an international educational exchange, owned the property on Newark Street in northwest Washington, D.C. The property rested in the heart of the city and presented different security challenges for the Marshals Service. However, its location offered more convenient entertainment and activities for the Gonzalez family. It was a "diplomatic" trade off. News media and private citizens set up cameras on the fence line with a clear line of view to the residence of the family.[12]

The appeals by the Florida relatives of Elian Gonzalez kept Operation Quincy active until June 28, 2000. The Supreme Court declined to hear the case, and the previous ruling stood. The boy returned to Cuba on a Cuban-chartered plane. While it was the conclusion of a unique protection detail for the U.S. Marshals Service, the agency proved up to the task again.[13]

TRAGEDY AND CHANGE

While Operation Quincy was transpiring, the U.S. Marshals lost one of their own in a tragic accident. On June 8, 2000, Deputy U.S. Marshal Pete Hillman, 47, a 14-year veteran who worked out of the Eastern District of California's Fresno office, was in the process of transporting prisoners to a county jail. With him were Special Deputy U.S. Marshal Mike Delpupo and three prisoners. While on the highway, the van was hit by a tractor-trailer in traffic near South Bakersfield, California. It was reported that the tractor-trailer blew a tire, hit another car, and went airborne before landing on the van. Hillman and the three prisoners died instantly. Somehow, Delpupo crawled out the side window. It was the first line-of-duty death since 1993.[14]

Pete Hillman had started his career in the Northern District of California, where he earned the nickname "Hillmanator" for his dogged

pursuit of fugitive drug offenders. He worked a number of special assignments, including Operation Sunrise. Given his popularity, it was not a
surprise that 400 people attended his funeral in Fresno. Director Marshall
also attended, and stayed nearly three days.[15]

In a special ceremony at the National Law Enforcement Officers
Memorial, Assistant Director of Prisoner Services Jay Frey and his
longtime friend Deputy Dave Hiebert spoke to Washington, D.C. area
personnel. Hillman posthumously received the "Fallen Hero Award," and
an overpass in California was named in his honor.[16] Director Marshall,
saddened by the tragedy, made an important observation:

> The bottom line is this: we stand together as Marshals Service
> employees no matter what our job. When tragedy hit the Eastern
> District of California with the death of Deputy Peter Hillman,
> it became evident to me that the entire district was genuinely
> united. It was a perfect example of the fact that we in this agency
> are all one family.[17]

DEPARTURES AND BEGINNINGS

Deputy Director Ramon assembled a large working group to create a
nationwide formula for district spending. Director Marshall recalled that
Ramon "even had a big table moved into his office" which resembled
"a war room" with all the flip charts. Although his efforts made strides
towards a spending model, internal issues came to the fore. The intensity
ended when, on July 31, 2000, Deputy Director Ramon was reassigned as
a Special Assistant to the Director. Nearly 13 years later, Ramon recalled,
"I still see myself as a deputy marshal and always will. Once a deputy,
always a deputy."[18]

Several changes occurred during this time. Most immediately, Louie T.
McKinney, who had recently reappeared as special assistant to Director
Marshall, became acting deputy director. The veteran began his career
with the U.S. Marshals in 1968. Over the years, he held a number of senior

leadership positions, including Chief of Enforcement, Deputy Chief of Witness Security, and U.S. Marshal for the Virgin Islands. Although he retired in 1994, McKinney honored the request of Marshall to return. "I needed him, needed that wise counsel," Marshall recalled years later.[19]

The Director's Office added a permanent support position. David Musel became the first Chief of Staff for the agency in the summer of 2000. The former military officer brought ample legal experience; he had served as appellate counsel among his past positions. The immediate reinforcement he provided to the Office of the Director eased pressures.[20]

Another organizational change also provided additional support. The Presidential Threat Protection Act of 2000 enlarged the scope of the Marshals Service task force. The Act created regional fugitive task forces which had been, until then, local endeavors. The new task forces had multi-state jurisdictions and broader law enforcement participation. The transition began with the New York-New Jersey Regional Fugitive Task Force and extended to Washington D.C. and Chicago. By 2003, four regional fugitive task forces operated.[21]

Another innovation sprang from a casual idea. While on the road with the Special Operations Group, Mike Pyo suggested the idea of a K-9 unit to Commander Scott Flood. He never thought the suggestion would be seriously considered, but Flood liked the idea. Pyo recalled, "He [Flood] said, 'Do it right, do the research.' "[22] That was all the incentive he needed. Pyo contacted the Bureau of Alcohol, Tobacco and Firearms, the Treasury Department law enforcement agency that oversaw the explosives detection canine program at the federal level. In the summer of 2000, the ATF program manager encouraged Pyo to submit a formal proposal. Somewhat surprised with the cooperation, Pyo said, "A simple thirty second phone call turned [the program] into what it is today."[23]

Agency management created the position of Comptroller in 2000 to better direct budgetary resources. Ed Dolan transferred from the Department of Justice, Justice Management Division, to fill the position.

John Marshall remembered, "Ed had the DOJ perspective. I had to sell this to DOJ, so I played this like a chess game."[24]

There were more moves in that chess game. Director Marshall's message in the September-October 2000 *Marshals Monitor* addressed salary decentralization to the districts. "By 2002, the districts will be responsible for 40 percent of this agency's funds, as compared to four percent in the past," Marshall wrote. "This initiative will require cooperation, and I am confident that I can count on your support to make this a success."[25]

Although not the most senior official present during the August 9, 2000 ceremony, Director Marshall made key remarks after Deputy Attorney General Eric Holder bestowed the title of honorary deputy U.S. marshal on Mrs. Ruby Bridges at the Corcoran Gallery of Art in Washington, D.C. With the backdrop of Norman Rockwell's iconic painting, *The Problem We All Live With*, the moment buoyed agency spirits.[26]

His short term as director ended after a divisive presidential election between Democratic candidate Al Gore, Jr. and Republican challenger George W. Bush. The Texas governor took the White House in 2001, and ushered major leadership changes at Executive Branch agencies headed by holdovers from the Democratic president. President Bush's clean slate meant a new bend in the Marshals Service's long road of constant renewal.

CHAPTER 21

THE MCKINNEY INFLUENCE

One of the most ironic moments of Director Marshall's term occurred at a U.S. Marshals Service Holiday Party. For years, U.S. Senator Strom Thurmond of South Carolina had visited Headquarters on special occasions. He was a regular presence at the annual Director's Awards, which had included an award in his name. The aged politician looked frail, and at one point leaned too far. The director instinctively supported him, guiding him back upright. Director Marshall remembered that the two always got along, although Thurmond did not support his father's appointment to the Supreme Court. The unexpected moment at the party represented trust. "People change," Marshall said.[1]

THE TEXAS SEVEN

On December 13, 2000, seven violent inmates of the Connally Prison Unit in Kenedy, Texas, escaped after gaining access to the repair shop. They took hostages, changed into maintenance personnel attire, and took weapons before leaving in a prison vehicle. From a command post, the Texas Department of Criminal Justice (TDCJ) worked with the USMS, particularly the Investigative Services Division and the Gulf

Coast Fugitive Task Force, to locate the escapees. The net widened to other states, and over 5,000 leads were investigated. Although the seven fugitives were unknown to each other prior to their imprisonment, they stayed together for a time after the escape.[2] Senior Inspector Bill Sorukas, who was one of the key personnel coordinators for the USMS, remarked, "At that point, they were pretty much gone."[3]

By Christmas Eve 2000, the trail of the seven escapees went from San Antonio, Houston, and finally to the Dallas area. There they robbed a sporting goods store, killed a policeman, and obtained semi-automatic weapons. After the murder, the leads went as far as New York. The Electronic Surveillance Unit traced their movements, and the unit set up 35 different operations by court order. Deputies fanned across the country, tracing the origins of all seven escapees, while coordination centered through Investigative Services—particularly Sorukas, Investigative Operations Chief Art Roderick, Senior Inspector Keith Braynon, and Domestic Investigations Chief John Clark. The television show *America's Most Wanted* featured the first of four timely segments on the escapees.[4]

Ultimately, it was the television segments that ended the manhunt. A couple at a Woodland Park, Colorado, RV park recognized the fugitives and notified the county sheriff. In turn, the USMS District of Colorado office moved in. Deputy U.S. Marshal Gerard McCann, working with the TDCJ, was already running down leads. With the FBI and Teller County Sheriff's Office personnel, and with other deputies across the state, they converged within hours at the Coachlight Motel and RV Park. By January 22, 2001, four of the seven were captured in the area and another committed suicide. The two remaining men fled in a van to Colorado Springs, where they surrendered after a standoff with police.[5]

The Texas Seven case was one of the largest fugitive operations involving the U.S. Marshals in years, rivaling the mass effort in the searches for Christopher Boyce and Gordon Kahl. It also brought renewed focus on the Investigative Services Division and multi-agency operations.

As the Texas Seven case ended, there was also a focus on leadership. The Supreme Court resolved the election of 2000 in favor of George W. Bush, and a change of political parties usually meant a leadership turnover. In Director Marshall's case, the decision to remove him arrived quickly. Acting Deputy Director Louie T. McKinney officially took over as acting director of the U.S. Marshals Service on February 16, 2001.[6]

A Good Man in a Storm

McKinney was calm and friendly. The agency was fortunate for his presence during this transition. McKinney's personality and professionalism steered the Marshals Service forward until the White House nominated a new director. Almost everyone in the agency knew him. The agency had grown rapidly during his career, which started in a deputy position in 1968. He obtained managerial experience in witness security, enforcement, and as the U.S. marshal in the Virgin Islands.[7]

Stacia A. Hylton, the first female deputy in the Special Operations Group, joined him as the acting deputy director. She had led the DOJ team responsible for assessing federal building security after the Oklahoma City bombing and was known for hard work and willingness to take on new roles. She also had a strong family connection to Marshals Service leadership. Her husband, Isaac (Ike) Hylton, Jr., formerly served as a chief deputy U.S. marshal and her father-in-law, Ike, Sr., had been the U.S. marshal for the Eastern District of Virginia. For three months between February and May 2001, Acting Deputy Director Hylton maintained the complex day-to-day details of the agency until a permanent appointment was made. Afterward, she returned to operational duties.[8]

McKinney's term as acting director began with a task reminiscent of the first challenge the U.S. Marshals had as an organization—the Whiskey Rebellion of 1794. In that early test, an unpopular federal excise tax on whiskey was violently challenged. U.S. Marshal of Pennsylvania David

Lenox rode alongside President George Washington to serve summons on the leadership of the resistance. The root of resentment was federal taxes.[9]

Acting Director McKinney and U.S. Marshal Frank Anderson of the Southern District of Indiana began dealing with the seizure of Indianapolis Baptist Temple on February 13, 2001. The leadership of the Temple argued that religious law and the First Amendment trumped federal taxation, and they ceased paying federal income taxes and Social Security (FICA) from its employees' paychecks in 1984. Even churches who registered for exemption status had to pay FICA. The Indianapolis Baptist Temple had never registered, and its leadership refused to do so. The amount of tax debt had bloated to $6 million dollars, and the Internal Revenue Service sought to collect.[10]

The U.S. Marshals entered the picture when a federal court ordered the agency to seize the properties of the church to satisfy the tax lien. After this decision, the Indianapolis Baptist Temple took their argument to the Supreme Court, but lost its case in January 2001. The agency planned to avoid events like those at Waco or Ruby Ridge. U.S. Marshal Anderson, a former deacon, understood the legalities, sensitivities, and his role. However, the Temple's leadership planned to resist any seizure. A small number of congregants and the church leaders had maintained a "vigil" for 91 days inside the church. The well-traveled Art Roderick of the Investigative Services Division worked with the Special Operations Group and the Southern District of Indiana to formulate a "low key approach" to seize the church properties.[11]

Anderson and Roderick waited for the initial wave of anger to diffuse, and selected the best moment to seize the building. On February 13, 2001, SOG deputies entered the structure. Indianapolis Police barricaded roads two blocks away, which kept nearly 50 supporters fenced out, and fire and rescue units stood ready to respond. The deputy marshals quietly and peacefully secured the Indianapolis Baptist Temple and a nearby parsonage—the best possible result. "I can say personally," U.S. Marshal

Anderson told the press, "this has been as difficult a task as I've had in my 37 years of law enforcement."[12]

In June 2001, Oklahoma City bomber Timothy McVeigh faced federal execution in Terre Haute, Indiana. Since his trial, conviction, and death sentence pronouncement in 1997, the infamous prisoner had dwelled in maximum security conditions. McVeigh showed little concern or sympathy. The *New York Times* disclosed he told reporters Lou Michel and Don Herbeck (who later co-authored *American Terrorist: Timothy McVeigh and the Oklahoma City Bombing*) that he had no sympathy for the dead children in the Murrah Building. To him, they were "collateral damage."[13]

In 1999, McVeigh was on death row at the U.S. Penitentiary, Terre Haute, in Indiana, which had a newly built wing. All federal executions moved to this facility as a result. As the date of execution neared, the media inquiries increased along with worries about disturbances by protestors. This motivated the Bureau of Prisons (BOP) to request assistance from the U.S. Marshals. McVeigh's was the first federal execution since that of Iowa murderer Victor Feguer in March 1963. The historic duty of the U.S. Marshal at federal executions was to be present and give assent to carry out the sentence.[14]

For the McVeigh execution, Supervisory Deputy U.S. Marshal Richard Burton of the Southern District of Indiana coordinated with the BOP to set perimeter security during the final weeks leading up to the date to carry out the sentence.[15]

Timothy McVeigh and Juan Raul Garza, a former drug dealer responsible for three murders in the United States, waited in the special confinement unit for their executions, June 11 and June 19, respectively. Prior to the execution date, 200-300 people gathered in opposition to the death penalty, and approximately 40 people protested in support of the executions. U.S. Marshal Frank Anderson, who months earlier had handled the seizure of the Indianapolis Baptist Temple, took on the official role in support of BOP. He provided a realistic assessment of the duty. Anderson said, "The world was looking at us [as officers] to perform what we have been ordered to do."[16]

Anderson's role in the chamber was more than ceremonial. He called the Department of Justice's Command Center on legal matters, primarily to check on a stay; then he gave the official permission to Terre Haute's warden to carry out the execution by lethal injection. Although Marshal Anderson displayed no emotion at the time, he later described the moment. "It is something that is very sobering... you're dealing with human life."[17]

A MOVEMENT REVISITED

A debate about human life was also at the center of another controversy in Wichita, Kansas. Activists planned a week's worth of protests to mark the tenth anniversary of 1991's "Summer of Mercy," when an estimated 30,000 pro-life supporters converged on the city in peaceful protest. In 2001, the Department of Justice worried about unknown threats against abortion clinics and their staffs. The sponsor of the weeklong series of activities, Operation Save America, successor to Operation Rescue, regularly targeted the clinic of Dr. George Tiller, whose facility had been bombed in 1985. Further, he'd been shot by an anti-abortion activist in 1993. His clinic performed late-term abortions and was the lone facility in Wichita in 2001. Given the previous violence, there was ample concern for safety.[18]

U.S. Attorney General John Ashcroft realized the potential danger. He ordered the U.S. Marshals to provide "door-to-door" protection for Dr. Tiller and a security plan to complement those of the local police. Ashcroft wanted limited presence from Washington to keep public opinion neutralized. The deputies assigned to the detail endured chides by the protesters, led by Rev. Philip "Flip" Benham. The 1994 Freedom of Access to Entrances to Clinics Act (FACE) limited protest alternatives and created a prominent role for federal marshals during the "Summer of Mercy."[19]

Wichita was prepared for the July 2001 protests. Local police fenced off space and minimized chances of direct confrontations at the clinic. The city refused a permit for the groups to march on Tiller's clinic. Despite setbacks, the protesters gathered at other locations, including the Reformation Lutheran Church attended by Dr. Tiller. Protesters won a court ruling to march on the clinic two times a day for an hour time period.[20]

The controversy and anger against the doctor lasted beyond the presence of the marshals and the weeklong protests. Eight years later, while serving as an usher during church services on May 31, 2009, the 67-year-old doctor was shot and killed by Scott Roeder. His assailant was sentenced to life in prison with no chance of parole for 50 years.[21]

Clayton Lee Waagner was a fugitive with determination. In September 1999, he was arrested during a routine traffic stop by the Illinois State Police. His RV was a stolen vehicle, and inside were a number of semi-automatic handguns. Three states had warrants on him. On February 22, 2001, Waagner was in the DeWitt County Jail awaiting his sentence in federal court. By use of common household items, he opened a lock and climbed through the jail's roof. Waagner stole a truck and escaped, triggering a manhunt. The U.S. Marshals added him to the 15 Most Wanted list on March 9.[22]

When he was initially caught, Waagner's computer had contained "a list of abortion clinics, a weapons manifest and contacts with fringe, anti-abortion groups."[23] When arraigned, he expressed regret he could not carry out his "mission from God" to kill abortion clinic doctors. After Waagner's escape, there was every reason to believe he would try again.[24]

Waagner surfaced again in May, when he was filmed on a surveillance camera in the act of robbing a Harrisburg, Pennsylvania, bank. However, he managed to stay ahead of his pursuers by constant travel in remote areas and changes in his personal appearance. As long as Waagner remained at large, the deputies could not let any intensity slip in the search for him.[25]

Arguably, considerable challenges faced Acting Director McKinney and the U.S. Marshals Service in the summer of 2001. It was nothing compared to what awaited America only months later. The agency would be tested as never before.

CHAPTER 22

A TIME OF TERRORISTS

VIEQUES REVISITED

CNN correspondent Paul Courson reported April 26, 2001, that "A federal judge rejected Puerto Rico's request for an emergency injunction to stop the U.S. Navy's training shelling on the island of Vieques. The decision by U.S. District Court Judge Gladys Kessler clears the way for the Navy to resume its drills on the island, which have generated protests for more than a year."[1] The Navy desired a resumption of military exercises, and Judge Kessler's ruling triggered renewed protests regarding the safety of island residents outside the security zone and the noise caused by the explosions. The Justice Department sided with the Navy pending a resolution on the noise factor.[2]

Again, federal marshals were called in to keep demonstrators away from the naval range and maintain the peace on the island. It was a difficult task, as trespassing was common and deputy marshals sustained injuries from rocks, pellets, and nails, and had vehicles vandalized by protestors. One demonstrator held up a sign to the deputies that stated "Salir O Mir [Leave or die]" in Spanish.[3]

Ramping up operations in May and June 2001, a group of deputy marshals from the Special Operations Group detained those who breached the fence to the naval facility. The deputies continued the operation until the Bush Administration decided, in June, to phase out exercises in Vieques by 2003.[4]

By the end of the summer, Acting Director Louie McKinney had a new partner in leadership. A new deputy director, Donald Gambatesa, began work on May 29, 2001. A former officer in the U.S. Navy and a longtime employee of the Secret Service, Gambatesa ran that agency's training facilities and served in the Presidential Protective Division.[5]

Meanwhile, the U.S. Marshals badge made its way to outer space. On June 4, 2001, at NASA's Johnson Space Center in Houston, Acting Director McKinney presented Astronaut Jim Reilly with a badge and the credentials of an honorary U.S. marshal. Special Events Coordinator Garland Preddy masterminded a new and unique concept for a ceremony. Reilly, only the seventh recipient of an honorary U.S. marshal designation, took the badge and credentials into space on an orbiting mission.[6]

In July, President George W. Bush announced the nomination of former Brownsville, Texas, Police Chief Benigno G. Reyna as Marshals Service director. His experience included knowledge of a large prisoner workload and both federal and local border issues. However, the new appointee had to wait for confirmation, as the political wheels moved slowly. Congress prepared to go on its annual August recess. He was eventually appointed on October 30, 2001.[7]

As September 2001 approached, Acting Director McKinney and the U.S. Marshals Service fell into a holding pattern. Late summer meant vacations and things slowing down in D.C. However, all American lives changed abruptly on one September morning.

SEPTEMBER 11, 2001

Many people remember exactly where they were or what they were doing when a major crisis occurred. General Counsel Gerald Auerbach remembered driving down the George Washington Parkway just a short distance away from Headquarters, when he passed Arlington National Cemetery and saw a "plume of light smoke" rising in the air on a clear day.[8] In an Alexandria, Virginia, federal courtroom, Deputy U.S. Marshal Jeff Cahall was listening to opening arguments in a bank robbery case. "We're all in the court room... [got] a text message," he recalled. "Hold on your Honor. I need to approach the bench." The Judge flinched at the request, but Cahall persisted, "Your Honor, how many times have I approached?" With this comment, the Judge realized something was seriously wrong. After he reached the bench, Cahall divulged the attack on the World Trade Center. The Judge called a recess, and the court facilities were quickly locked down.[9]

September 11, 2001, began as a normal Tuesday morning, but descended into complete madness. Terrorists had hijacked four American airplanes, and guided them towards well-known landmarks. Only aboard one of the planes did some passengers understand what was taking place and rushed into action to avert a greater tragedy. That plane crashed in a farmer's field in Pennsylvania, killing all aboard. Those passengers potentially saved thousands of lives in Washington, where the hijackers planned to down the jetliner. That was the starting point for many individual acts of heroism that day.

Deputy marshals in the Southern District of New York reacted quickly after the first plane hit the World Trade Center, as their Manhattan office was only five blocks away. Deputy U.S. Marshals Dominic Guadagnoli and John Svinos had started their day in the district's warrant office. Looking back, Guadagnoli recalled, "when the first tower was attacked, the explosion actually shook our building and we thought either our building or one of the other prominent City or Federal buildings close by had been the target of a bomb."[10]

Instincts took over for the deputies. Guadagnoli and Svinos joined others as they grabbed their protective gear. A number of federal buildings lined the area. Peering out a window, Guadagnoli noted that "in less than a minute you could see all the paper and debris floating to the ground between our buildings. However, as close as we were, from the angle of the courthouse we could not see the Trade Center or the towers."[11] Stepping outside, they were informed by citizens that a plane had struck the World Trade Center. Deputy U.S. Marshal Bill Schuchact, Guadagnoli, and Svinos joined the wave of first responders who rushed toward the towers. Svinos recalled that in trying to reach the towers, "we had to fight our way down there past running screaming people."[12]

As the trio reached the base of the buildings, a second plane struck the south tower. Svinos spied a large number of people running from the revolving doors, which slowed traffic coming to the surface from the subway concourse below. Debris rained down, and they feared citizens would be trapped. Svinos and Schuchat broke open the revolving doors. They realized it was not just debris that was falling, but people who were jumping from the upper floors. Svinos recalled, "The initial wave of people were relatively unscathed. Then came individuals covered in soot and debris and wet from the sprinklers... As people descended [from] the higher floors, we saw more injuries and people were wet and bloody."[13]

When the plane hit the 78th floor of the south tower, Donna Spera and her fellow employees ran from their offices at the Aon Corporation, located on the 101st floor. Somehow Spera and 11 of her co-workers avoided death. Badly burned, she crawled over glass and dead bodies to the stairs. A co-worker assisted her and they descended flight after flight. After a seeming eternity of slowly making their way down, Spera saw Guadagnoli with his hat and jacket clearly marked. Unable to stand any further, she began to fall, but Guadagnoli caught her.[14]

"I've got you. You're going to be OK," he said as he carried Spera across the street. An Associated Press photograph captured the moment. The photograph appeared in countless newspapers, magazines, and television reports. It became a symbol of heroism, akin to Joe Rosenthal's iconic photograph of Marines pushing up the American flag at Iwo Jima. Guadagnoli gave no thought to the clicking cameras. His concern was Spera's safety. After ensuring she was in an ambulance, the deputy returned to the tower to assist other people.[15]

As Guadagnoli furiously pulled people out of rubble to safety, the tower collapsed. "I was able to run to the safety of a subway stairwell to avoid being buried alive," he remembered. "Moments later I realized my life had been spared but I was injured. Working on pure adrenaline, I returned to the remaining tower and continued helping people out. However I could not find my friends and feared that they were dead."[16]

Svinos found a former co-worker, New York City police officer Ramon Suarez. After they had assisted the wounded for a short time, they heard the rumbles in the building increasing. The two men felt the tower collapsing. As Svinos described, "It sounded like a thousand trains coming at you at once."[17] They ran, but a blinding pillar of smoke caught them. Svinos raised his hands above his head, and expected a fatal chunk of debris to hit him. Although he fell to the ground, he landed in one of the tower's enormous planters. He could not see anything, but the cover of the planter saved Svinos. Sadly, Officer Suarez was killed in the collapse.[18]

In the confusion and thick, black smoke, the deputies made their way back to their offices on Pearl Street. Schuchat was at the entrance to the subway concourse during the collapse. He found a bookstore from the tunnel access, and spied another exit door to the street, which he broke through. Despite a "calm cold silence," Svinos was covered in a tar-like substance. He threw up to get rid of substances coating his mouth making it difficult to breathe. Worried about the collapse of the one remaining tower, Svinos moved toward Pearl Street with another police officer. They cleared a few blocks when he heard the sound of the last tower preparing to fall. They paused at a side street and crouched for cover.[19]

Somehow all three deputies got back to the district office. It was buzzing with activity, as all were working rescue efforts. The unrecognizable

Svinos walked to a triage, where Supervisory Deputy Ralph Burnside took him inside St. Andrew's Church to wash away the thick coating of muck. Until he removed some of it, Burnside did not recognize his own subordinate. He and others, also busy being responders themselves, were setting up a rescue party for them. A short time later, Guadagnoli ran into the courthouse. Svinos concluded it "was one of the best moments of my life knowing he was alive. We made it into the office and we were told that Bill was OK as well, so we all made it out alive."[20]

U.S. Marshal Don Horton for the District of Columbia heard about the chaos over the television. He was responsible for the safety of two senior federal judges visiting the Capitol. "I got on my cell phone to the deputy who was in charge of the detail," Horton recalled, and instructed him to evacuate the judges from Capitol Hill. In this highly unusual situation, the deputy drove on the sidewalk as he navigated the gridlock in Washington, D.C. streets. While the judge was being transported, Horton and his assistant, Joanne Howdershell, were swearing in special deputies to aid the emergency efforts and trying to figure out how to get the court personnel home.[21]

Inspector Bill Sorukas was in Alexandria, Virginia, on the morning of September 11. He was startled to hear the ear-cracking roar of a low-flying jet. He recalled, "I remember seeing several people coming out of a balcony and looking at a plane flying in this area."[22] Sorukas could not see the Pentagon and concentrated on his tasks. After he finished, he took a call from his nephew. It was only then Sorukas discovered what was going on. When his panicked mother called, he remembered, "I'm trying to explain—I'm not near a TV. I don't know what's going on."[23]

Acting Director McKinney ordered that Marshals Service facilities, including Headquarters, be secured. Sorukas hurried back to his unit, housed a distance from the main offices. "I remember [Tactical Operations] David Robertson and [ESU leader] Bill Hufnagel, and myself all of a sudden having a meeting. We began to load a cargo trailer—with everything that we had—food, water, radio communications, firearms, and within an hour or so we were on our way to Marshals Service Headquarters."[24]

Across the agency, operational teams snapped into action within 24 hours of the attacks. Assistant Director Robert Finan recalled there was a strategic plan for national emergencies, but it was open-ended. "Certain things happened that day that required an immediate response, even though we didn't know what the long term [result] was going to be."[25]

Immediate needs placed the U.S. Marshals Service in the nation's airports and in support to the Federal Emergency Management Agency (FEMA) in New York. Both duties were areas of previous experience for the agency.[26]

The U.S. Marshals, assisted by U.S. Customs and Border Patrol, took the lead in securing the airports. Initially the Federal Aviation Administration and the Department of Justice selected 12 airports to open for public transportation, based on size and passenger volume. Two Washington, D.C., area airports opened with a large presence of armed deputies in full gear under the command of Chief Deputy U.S. Marshal Bill Snelson of the Eastern District of North Carolina.[27] Deputy Jeff Cahall started his assignment at Dulles Airport that same evening. There, he supervised magnetometers and X-ray machines, observed the surroundings, and discussed strategy with airport officials.[28]

On September 12, Acting Director McKinney issued a memorandum to the entire agency. It was three paragraphs in length, but answered the immediate questions most had:

> Fortunately, none of our employees was seriously injured as a result of yesterday's vicious terrorist attack on our country. As you know, the attack has initiated what is sure to be one of the most comprehensive criminal investigations in our history and the Attorney General has committed all resources of the Department of Justice to apprehend those responsible. Although we will probably be tasked with other responsibilities, thus far we have been directed by the Department to assist with security at 17

major airports around the country. We have been in contact with the Marshals of the districts involved and they are coordinating with local law enforcement officials and representatives of the FAA in their districts. The Border Patrol and U.S. Customs have also been directed to assist.

The Marshals Service has a long history of excellent performance during difficult situations and this is one of those times when we need to join together for the benefit of the Service and our nation. We appreciate all the calls and e-mail messages we have received from you offering support and we will undoubtedly be contacting you at some point for resources.

Please remain vigilant in your duties and thanks for your support in this time of great need.[29]

The words sounded a call to duty, although most employees already knew what they had to do. Their responses were almost automatic. The agency rallied to the country's defense.

Inspector Bill Sorukas and a dozen personnel from the Technical Operations Group reached New York on September 12. It was eerie and quiet for a city normally bustling with throngs of people. For the following two weeks, searches were made through the devastation for the living and identifying the dead. The technology they deployed was useful in locating both.[30]

Still, there was an emphasis on manual labor. With the rescue teams set up by FEMA and the New York Police Department, Sorukas recalled, "We helped haul debris out of certain areas as a part of a chain gang... We were moving five gallon buckets of debris from the front end of the line and they were just trying to find cavities [to search]."[31]

As the rescue teams combed the area, Sorukas saw little but devastation. He observed, "Two, hundred-story plus buildings and we were not seeing a desk or a chair or a file cabinet. There was nothing left."[32]

Despite the bleak circumstances, the need to restore normal travel conditions was a priority. The FAA gave clearance for diverted planes to finish their flights on September 12. Gradually commercial air traffic returned to normal.[33]

All the major networks wanted to interview a Marshals Service official about plane security and the past program run by the agency. Public Affairs Specialist Drew Wade lined up interviews with ABC, CBS, and NBC, one after the other on the same night. Deputy Director Gambatesa appeared on *ABC World News Tonight* with Sam Donaldson and on *CBS Evening News* with Dan Rather. "The appearances were a golden opportunity to highlight the expertise of the agency in protective operations and personal security," recalled Wade.[34]

The presence of the deputies at airports gave rise to speculation about the Air Piracy Program being reinstated by the agency. Later, any debate faded when the White House and Congress created the Transportation Security Administration (TSA). Realistically, the agency had too many other functions to take on comprehensive and permanent airport presence.

After 10 days, Bill Sorukas walked around looking for postcards to send to family. Finally locating a shop, Sorukas bought one for his niece. He later told reporter Bill Moor of the *South Bend Tribune* of the message he penned on the card. "Sent with love... from a place where hate did its dirty work... and then where hope and the human spirit quickly took over."[35]

The agency displayed hope and human spirit at 18 airports where they maintained security and at the Pentagon where they joined in recovery efforts.[36] Inspector Michael Pyo, with a newly graduated explosives detection canine, a black Labrador named Beacon, reported to the Pentagon days after the plane hit. The demand for K-9 assistance was high. First, Pyo and Beacon supported perimeter security, but eventually they sifted through wreckage. He remembered, "They had a morgue area set up. So they would bring in parts of the aircraft or the building and lay it out. They would bring cadaver dogs through, and then they wanted the bomb dogs to go through... so we did that for a while."[37]

JPATS flew over 18 missions in support of airport security and to transport over 800 federal law enforcement personnel. A class of deputies, just graduated from the academy in Georgia, experienced their first mission in New York. Surrounding districts, such as New Jersey, pitched in. At Headquarters, the Emergency Operations Center was fully staffed until November 1. The Special Operations Group assisted the extended operations at the Pentagon. As Protective Operations Program Chief Michael Prout stated, "The Marshals Service worked miracles... All over the place, greatness happened."[38]

Aside from airports, federal court facilities not directly affected by the attacks re-opened for business, but stayed on alert. In all instances, it was a transition made easier due to the agency's earlier efforts.[39]

On March 21, 2002, the Director's Honorary Awards recognized numerous heroes. The Robert Forsyth Act of Valor Award, a rare honor for select acts of exceptional courage in dangerous conditions, was presented to the three deputies from the Southern District of New York: Dominic Guadagnoli, William Schuchat, and John Svinos. The Harry Belluomini Memorial Court Security Award went to Court Security Officer Joseph Carrieri for his leadership in evacuating federal facilities in Manhattan. Distinguished Group Awards highlighted the sheer number of employees involved in recovery efforts. There were also several Special Achievement Awards and three districts—Southern and Eastern New York, and New Jersey—all shared the Large Distinguished District Award. Related assistance garnered the Eastern District of Wisconsin the Small Distinguished District Award.[40]

The Associated Press photograph of Guadagnoli and Spera symbolized not only this heroic deputy, but all of the other deputies and employees who performed magnificently and tried to provide comfort and assistance to others in one of the darkest moments in American history.[41]

ANTHRAX AND RESPONSE

The country was still reeling from the shock of the 9/11 terrorist attacks when anthrax-laced letters were discovered. Five letters addressed to three major television broadcast companies and two newspapers had postmarks from Trenton, New Jersey, on either September 17 or 18, 2001. A Florida photo editor received one of the letters, saw powder in the envelope and accidentally inhaled some of it. Several weeks later, the editor died. The letter contained anthrax, a deadly spore. According to the FBI, two other letters delivered a few weeks later to U.S. Senators Tom Daschle (South Dakota) and Patrick Leahy (Vermont) contained anthrax. More than 30 staffers tested positive for exposure. Two postal employees in the Brentwood, Maryland post office, near Washington, died of anthrax poisoning by October 22.[42]

Chief of Printing Larry Mogavero oversaw the mail for the Marshals Service. At the time, DOJ routed U.S. mail to its components through a joint-use facility. Mogavero recalled, "There was an anthrax letter to the Attorney General... had anthrax in it. And that was found in our warehouse."[43]

The warehouse immediately shut down. Acting Director McKinney suspended mail service at Headquarters on October 19. Safe mail handling procedures were distributed to administrative officers throughout the nation. Acting Senior Inspector of the Eastern District of Virginia Kevin Combs, the designated point of contact for chemical and biological issues, prepared protocols for the emergency, as employees used e-mail and faxes instead of letters.[44]

The agency was in a quandary. Large amounts of mail required screening on a daily basis. One short-term measure was to sort mail in a large vehicle, by a person wearing the appropriate safety clothing and using special equipment. Mogavero opposed this idea, and it lasted just a short time. For a time, the agency routed its internal mail to a "central mailbox" under an alternative name with no reference to the U.S.

Marshals Service. Unfortunately, employees unwittingly compromised the box on several occasions.[45]

Finally, DOJ ordered that mail to its agencies be processed through a contracted facility, where it was irradiated. The drawbacks: mail took longer to be delivered and the process caused certain pieces of mail to stick together. Still, "frying" the mail (as employees referred to it) became a normal state of affairs for some time.[46]

Despite the presence of foreign and domestic terrorism, the agency adapted and responded as strongly as ever. The country needed recovery, and the coming years proved vital ones for the employees of the U.S. Marshals Service.

CHAPTER 23

DIRECTOR REYNA AND
THE AFTERMATH OF 9/11

The nation remained focused on the search for terrorists involved in the attacks of September 11, 2001, and on providing suitable security on airplanes. Amid considerable speculation about training and arming airline pilots with guns to thwart mid-air threats, the U.S. Marshals remained in the conversation. It was in this environment that the next director began his term.[1]

A CONSTITUTIONAL DIRECTOR

President George W. Bush appointed 44-year-old Benigno G. Reyna as director on October 29, 2001. Director Reyna had completed a 25-year career with the Brownsville, Texas, Police Department. Six of those years he spent as chief of police. He had attended the University of Texas-Pan American in Brownsville. In 1997, he was appointed to the Texas Commission on Law Enforcement Officer Standards. From 1998 to 2001, he served as regional advisor with the White House Office of National Drug Control Policy through its Counter Drug Technology

Assessment Center. Reyna was prepared for the transition to federal law enforcement.[2]

As the agency bounced back from September 11 and the anthrax attacks, it needed a morale boost like so many others left emotionally drained by the ordeals. A ceremonial swearing-in was scheduled for December 5, 2001.[3] In his first message to agency employees, three weeks prior to the ceremony, Director Reyna conveyed his respect for the U.S. Marshals as legendary law enforcers. His heroes were America's founding fathers, and his frame of reference often came from the U.S. Constitution:

> "United States Marshals are indispensably necessary as a shield to our fellow citizens." The simple truth of those words spoken by President Thomas Jefferson hasn't dimmed in 200 years. Today, as our country moves forward from September 11, our accomplishments at the Marshals Service will help make the U.S. a stronger nation. We must continue to carry out our vital mission each and every day.[4]

Director Reyna pledged "to use all my skills and energy to help shine a light on your dedication to service." He wanted a return to a simpler, straightforward management style, saying, "I am not an advocate of 'name brand' or fashionable management philosophies."[5]

Political muscle attended Director Reyna's swearing-in ceremony December 5 at the Crystal City Sheraton. U.S. Attorney General John Ashcroft, Deputy Attorney General Larry Thompson, and White House Chief of Staff Andrew Card were there, along with Reyna's wife Maria and son Michael. Attorney General Ashcroft administered the oath of office.[6]

Reyna used the forum to announce the capture of 15 Most Wanted fugitive Clayton Lee Waagner. The FBI added him to their Ten Most Wanted on September 21, 2001, and while this intensified investigative efforts, Waagner ran out of time. Deputy marshals developed information that the fugitive frequented Kinko's copy store locations. They passed out wanted posters at a shop in Ohio, and a clerk recognized the fugitive as a recent customer. Working with local police, federal marshals captured the man who threatened to bomb abortion clinics and mail anthrax-laced packages to individuals. To cap the announcement, Reyna penned the word "Apprehended" in black marker across a giant poster of Waagner on the stage.[7]

The year ended with a flurry of activity. In December 2001, the Marshals Service made plans to handle the high-profile trial of terrorist suspect Zacarias Moussaoui. In November an American citizen, John Walker Lindh, had been captured on the battlefield in Afghanistan and many speculated that he too would be tried in U.S. federal court. Many in the Marshals Service prepared to provide extensive support to the Secret Service, charged with securing the upcoming February 2002 Olympic Winter Games in and around Salt Lake City, Utah.[8]

Since 1991, the non-profit Wyoming State Territorial Park had housed the U.S. Marshals Museum and the agency's main artifact collection. Despite the attractive surroundings and initial strides, expectations fell short. Attendance dropped sharply. The original plan for the museum included a sizable stand-alone building, but that never materialized. Director Reyna decided to move the agency artifacts. In February 2002, the crated artifacts went into storage in the Cheyenne, Wyoming, district office. The artifacts would remain there until a decision was made to move the agency museum to Fort Smith, Arkansas, in January 2007.[9]

The acting chief of Protective Operations, Mike Prout, led a team of more than 100 deputy marshals who augmented security at the 2002 Winter Olympics in February. Operational personnel conducted visible and inconspicuous duties throughout the duration of the games. They were assigned to various Olympic venues in Utah by the Secret Service and the Public Health Service.[10]

In May 2002, Director Reyna received a letter from Attorney General Ashcroft congratulating the agency on a "clean" financial audit for Fiscal Year 2001. The audit without significant deficiencies represented a milestone. In addition, the agency made fixing large districts with historical budget issues a priority. These districts had a high volume of work and expenses. The achievement particularly gratified Comptroller Ed Dolan, Assistant Director of the Management and Budget Division Broadine Brown, and the Office of Finance's Robert Whiteley. They met a major goal to correct audit deficiencies of the past.[11]

Mike Pyo's suggestion to create a Marshals Service canine program became a reality in June 2001. However, after his assistance at the Pentagon, the fledgling Explosives Detection Canine Program went into overdrive. Pyo and Beacon, the three-year-old black Labrador trained to find 19,000 different kinds of explosives, provided critical support after 9/11. Their accomplishments with this new dimension of law enforcement added capability. It was rewarded because the agency expanded the program over time.[12]

Pyo and Beacon made the rounds at airports and the U.S. Supreme Court. Pyo recalled one incident when he and the canine sat exhausted, after hours of security checks at the airport. Art Roderick, the newly installed chief of staff, called Pyo and asked, "Did you meet a lady and a little girl in the airport?" Pyo answered, "Probably. Did someone complain?" Roderick said a congressman's wife and daughter complimented the agency because of the calming effect of the dog at the airport.[13]

Shortly thereafter, two more deputies in Eastern Michigan and Southern California completed the explosives detection canine and handler training. By the time a formal policy was drafted for the program in 2004, six more K-9s worked for the U.S. Marshals.[14]

The Hazardous Response Unit (HRU) officially began in September 2002, in response to the terrorist attacks and anthrax scares the year before. Bill Snelson, chief of the new Office of Emergency Preparedness, headed the 11-person unit that had educational and protective components. HRU provided training dealing with weapons of mass destruction (WMD), emergency medical care, and judicial protection in terrorist-related trials. The K-9 program assisted with the explosives detection mission.[15]

Politicians questioned the HRU mission because of its expense. By 2004, it was being phased out. HRU became the Office of Emergency Management (OEM), which included national programs like the USMS Emergency Operations Center and the Continuity of Operations (COOP), the program that outlines procedures and personnel needed to maintain critical government functions during an emergency, as well as providing training to employees involved with COOP. Pyo credits Snelson for the innovation that began with HRU: "He saw the big picture."[16]

THE D.C. SNIPER CASE

By October 3, 2002, a three-week flurry of investigations commenced when six people were gunned down by "the D.C. snipers," John Allen Muhammad and Lee Boyd Malvo, in Washington, D.C., nearby suburbs in Montgomery County, Maryland, as well as in Fairfax, Prince William, and Spotsylvania Counties in Virginia. On October 4, tactical units in the area gathered in Maryland. Federal and local law enforcement established a command post to coordinate resources. Bill Sorukas, working with the Technical Operations Group, recalled, "While we were being briefed, another shooting was happening in Fredericksburg [Virginia] in a shopping center."[17]

Thereafter, the participation of the U.S. Marshals Service quietly increased. Chief Inspector Mike Earp coordinated staffing and resources. Sorukas was joined by deputy marshals from all affected jurisdictions and support units, like the New York-New Jersey Regional Fugitive Task Force. When the assailants shot and wounded a 13-year-old boy at the Benjamin Tasker Middle School near Bowie, Maryland, the press followed closely and the public panicked. Law enforcement wanted fast investigative results.[18]

It was at Tasker Middle School that U.S. Marshals personnel found vital clues that ultimately led to an arrest. Mike Pyo and his canine Beacon arrived at the school with a large multi-jurisdictional army of law enforcement units. He viewed the terrain strategically. "To the left of me was the woods, and beyond that was a parking lot. So, some of the guys came up and said, 'the way the victim fell there was only one way... it had to come from the woods."[19] Pyo and Beacon worked a grid based on an estimated location a sniper might use. As they passed under a large branch, Beacon looked up alertly and tugged on his leash. The Labrador sniffed, and then sat down, a sure signal he found something. Pyo rewarded the dog, and watched for Beacon's next move. The canine sat again.[20]

"We called the forensic guys, the ATF chemist," Pyo said. The area was immediately cordoned off, as teams began combing the area. Pyo was not present during this phase. However, he found out just hours later that the very spot where Beacon sat was where the shell casing had ejected. In the immediate area were two to three casings, but only one mattered.[21]

A partial print was found on one casing, which eventually was matched with one of the perpetrators. In fact, there were more clues. Investigators found a tarot card, which was a message. Sorukas said of the criminals, "They were seeking credit for what they were doing."[22]

From October 9-19, three more people died and another was wounded, all in Virginia, at the hands of the snipers. Fear crippled the national capital region as people literally ran in and out of gas stations and stores, fearing the assailants might shoot them. A clergyman in Ashland, Virginia, just north of Richmond, received a call on October 18 from a male claiming to know about the sniper. The caller mentioned a specific piece of information regarding Montgomery, Alabama, and quoted directly the same message from the tarot card found at the Benjamin Tasker School.[23]

The information from Alabama pointed authorities to Tacoma, Washington. Although initially dismissed by some, Sorukas credited the U.S. Attorney in the District of Maryland, Thomas DiBiagio, with giving his team approval to follow up a vital lead on Malvo. "We began to pull files," Sorukas said, from the state of Washington. Additional research forwarded to him yielded another name, John Allen Williams, who was using the surname Muhammad. Muhammad and Malvo had a "father-son" relationship. In addition, the older man had ties to the Washington, D.C. area and the military. Other suspects were eliminated from inquiry.[24]

Although there was initial reluctance, the sniper task force concentrated on Malvo and Muhammad. Although they were looking for a white van based on tips, new information pointed the task force to a 1990 blue Chevrolet Caprice. There was resistance to adjusting the information, but Sorukas, fearing for officer safety, was able to send out an informational bulletin. He said, "A very observant truck driver heard that broadcast, and saw that car at a rest area in northwest Maryland."[25]

The long three weeks ended at a rest stop in Myersville, Maryland. At 3:30 am on October 24, 2002, law enforcement found the blue Caprice parked there and its occupants were surrounded by the multi-jurisdictional force. They found a Bushmaster XM15 rifle and located two holes in the vehicle's trunk. One hole was used for the gun's scope and the other for the barrel. By folding or moving the back seat, they shot without being seen.[26]

By no means did the U.S. Marshals crack the D.C. Sniper case on their own. But without a doubt, the agency's investigators quietly contributed significant and vital information that led to the arrests of the D.C. Snipers. The trail they left behind was indeed a bloody one, but while Muhammad had domestic problems, the Jamaican-born Malvo was an enigma. He moved around a bit, got into minor scrapes with the law, but only after he paired with Muhammad in Washington State did his behavior become violent. Drifting across the country committing robberies and murder, the pair had killed 10 people by the time they were caught. Muhammad was sentenced to death, and was put to death on November 10, 2009. Malvo, a juvenile at the time of the murders, will never leave prison.[27]

A RETURN TO MISSISSIPPI

Forty years after 127 full-time deputy U.S. marshals had faced mobs at the University of Mississippi on the night spanning September 30-October 1, 1962, the institution and the town of Oxford extended an olive branch and invited them back. The surviving deputies, long-since retired and all almost 80 years old, joined anniversary activities at Ole Miss. Director Ben Reyna and members of the Public Affairs staff received invitations, and joined the retired deputies at the recognition ceremony.[28]

The agency commissioned an "abstract art" poster, by artist Jeffrey Batson, for this anniversary to symbolize the clouds of tear gas rounding the columns of the Lyceum and newspaper headlines about the riots. Centered at the base of the columns, a dark figure stands alone with a long path of red behind it. The print graces many walls in the offices of the agency's employees.[29]

Director Reyna presented a framed Batson print to Ole Miss Chancellor Robert Khayat in the shadow of the Lyceum, still pocked with dents and holes from projectiles thrown at the deputies during the riots 40 years before. Present among the retired deputies were Al Butler and Don Forsht, who had led the front line defense; Gene Same, who had sustained near mortal wounds from the buckshot; and Charlie Burks, the deputy who had escorted Ruby Bridges into a New Orleans school in 1960. Other brave and accomplished retired deputies from that Ole Miss integration operation who joined the 40-year celebration included: Bud Staple, Bill Banta, Ernie Mike, Eric Jonesson, Duane Caldwell, Carl Ryan, Marvin Morrisett, and Herschel Garner. Oxford Mayor Richard Howorth presented them with keys to the city. In 2002 the University of Mississippi was composed of a student body that was 13 percent African-American. One of those students said to a visiting retiree, "I wouldn't be here without you."[30]

Author William Doyle, who wrote about the Ole Miss riots in his book *An American Insurrection*, Mississippi Governor Ronnie Musgrove, and James Meredith, the very man the deputies protected, all addressed the crowds.[31]

However, and more importantly, Meredith met personally with the retired deputies. They had not seen each other since that troubled time long ago. In the privacy of a courthouse, they shook hands and talked about those days. As Director Reyna later stated in the *Marshals Monitor*, "Let us honor them for their brave actions—and for what they stood for and defended. They safeguarded the U.S. Constitution and protected the rights we enjoy today."[32]

CHAPTER 24

EPILOGUE

Although the modern history's main narrative ends in 2002, it necessitates a brief description of highlights since that time. The following epilogue bridges the years from 2003–2014.

FUTURE PLANS

The USMS, with its long history and expertise in fugitive apprehension, routinely locates and arrests violent fugitives wanted by state and local law enforcement based on agreements with these entities that the latter will seek extradition and pay for the transportation of the fugitives back to their own jurisdictions. The success of U.S. Marshals Service joint apprehension initiatives, combined with the outstanding relationships forged with other law enforcement agencies, led to the formation of permanent fugitive task forces, as well as *ad hoc* task forces in response to unique cases that pose immediate threats to the public.

The Presidential Threat Protection Act of 2000 gave the Marshals Service authority to establish permanent Regional Fugitive Task Forces (RFTF) consisting of federal, state, and local law enforcement authorities.

Specifically, RFTF target fugitives wanted for violent crimes against persons, weapons offenses, felony drug offenses, failure to register as a sex offender, and career criminals.[1]

Initially, the Senate provided for two RFTFs—one on each coast. The New York/New Jersey RFTF in New York City and the Pacific Southwest RFTF in Los Angeles were first. By 2003, the following RFTFs joined the list: Great Lakes in Chicago, Southeast in Atlanta, and Capital Area in Washington, D.C. By 2011, RFTFs in Orlando (Florida Caribbean) and Birmingham, Alabama (Gulf Coast) rounded out the seven permanent units.[2]

Naturally, the energy and focus on investigations ramped up during this period. The cost reductions and efficiencies of the RFTFs benefitted all. Southeast Regional Task Force Commander Buck Smith, marveling at the success of the concept, noted, "All five of the regional task forces have been more successful than I think any of us could have imagined."[3] Pacific Regional Task Force Commander John Clark (no relation to Director John F. Clark) stated, "We don't get these cases until other agencies have exhausted all their resources—so we've become the agency of last resort."[4]

In 2003, international investigations increased in visibility with the presence of three permanent USMS overseas offices in the Dominican Republic, Jamaica, and Mexico. These three countries were chosen for USMS foreign field offices to deal with the many fugitives who flee to these jurisdictions to evade capture and prosecution, and this active presence supports many extraditions from those countries.[5]

The agency continued its trajectory into new frontiers and mission areas in law enforcement. With the advent of Regional Fugitive Task Forces and international offices, the agency was poised for the main course of its future.

THE WINDS OF CHANGE

Looking back over four decades of service, longtime employee Elizabeth
Howard reflected, "I can see that the Marshals Service over the years has
gotten more professional in dealing with changing criminal elements in
our culture."[6] No statement could have been more accurate about the
modern history of the USMS.

With historical deference, the U.S. Marshals Service watched the
creation of an external entity of one of its old initiatives. When the
Department of Homeland Security formed, creating the Transportation
Security Agency and the "Air Marshals," the latter was an historical
nod to the deputies in the old "Sky Marshals" program. Although the
name of this TSA program initially confused the public into thinking it
was a USMS program, many of its training programs were conducted
by former agency employees.[7]

In July 2003, the Department of Justice invited retirees from the 1962
riots to the commemoration of the 40th anniversary of the integration
of Ole Miss at the Great Hall. Of the 127 deputies, 29 appeared with
their families to take part. The day started with a breakfast discussion at
Headquarters. At the Great Hall, the agency participated in a joint ceremony. Following a panel discussion featuring James Meredith, Attorney
General Ashcroft and Director Reyna presented silver medallions to each
attending retiree.[8]

In October 2003, Director Reyna, Deputy Director Gambatesa and
America's Most Wanted's John Walsh jointly celebrated the nation's oldest
existing task force. Formed in 1983, long before the regional fugitive
task force concept, the Eastern Pennsylvania Violent Crimes Task Force
arrested over 13,500 fugitives in its 20 years of existence. In Benjamin
Franklin's home on Chestnut Street, Director Reyna swore in John Walsh
as the eighth Honorary U.S. Marshal in history.[9]

In December 2003, Attorney General Ashcroft signed off on a new
organizational chart that consolidated a number of offices. JPATS, which

was formerly under the Prisoner Services Division, became a separate entity. The Office of Equal Employment Opportunity moved under the Director. The most significant change occurred with the position of Comptroller. In April 2001, this position was considered a powerful one, equal to an associate director. Two years later, the position still existed but was further internalized, and it vanished from the chart.[10]

Special Operations Group deputies rotated on six-month shifts to support the fledgling Iraqi courts beginning in March 2004. After the fall of former President Saddam Hussein, an eight-person team assisted its Iraqi counterparts. Supervisory Deputy Eric Kessel noted, "They either had old Russian guns that rarely worked, or they had no gun at all."[11] Deputies overcame many obstacles, and the Iraqi Ministry of Justice thrived with the training and protection provided by SOG. Even during the trial of Saddam Hussein and his subsequent execution, the professionalism of the U.S. Marshals Service made the difference between order and potential chaos. SOG Deputy Greg Ray recalled that one judge was attacked four different times, and was saved because he was transported out of danger in one of the agency's armored vehicles. The missions of the U.S. Marshals Service moved far beyond United States borders.[12]

2005: HURRICANES, A JUDICIAL TRAGEDY, AND FALCON

In many ways, the arrival of 2005 signaled a watershed year. Director Reyna, who revered the agency's history, celebrated the 215th anniversary of the U.S. marshals with a special rodeo in Cowtown, New Jersey, on September 18, 2004. Despite the festivities, the anniversary foreshadowed a difficult period for the agency.[13]

On February 28, 2005, U.S. District Judge Joan Humphrey Lefkow returned home from the federal courts in Chicago to a horrifying scene. Her 89-year-old mother Donna Grace Humphrey, and her 64-year-old husband Michael Lefkow lay dead in the family residence. Neighbors heard her screams from the street, and detectives appeared quickly. The

Chicago Tribune reported entry was forced, probably through a broken window.[14]

The tragedy at the Lefkow home was also devastating for the U.S. Marshals Service. Although the agency responded immediately, the fallout lasted long afterward. Questions arose regarding security systems installed at the residence in response to a 2003 threat assessment. The *Chicago Tribune* reported information that a former defendant, Matthew Hale, solicited Judge Lefkow's murder. Hale was the leader of a radical ideological group, and his ties to the Aryan Nation gang seemed credible. Cameras and block guards were set around the residence, but with Hale's April 2004 conviction, extra measures receded—according to neighbors. However, the public rarely sees or knows all measures of protective details, which are constantly assessed and re-assessed. Many federal judges receive inappropriate communications that get scrutinized rigorously. It was not uncommon for a judge or prosecutor to be threatened multiple times.[15]

Law enforcement did not expect the person who turned out to be the killer of Judge Lefkow's husband and mother. Bart Ross, 57, claimed responsibility for the murders in a letter that was received on March 9, 2005, at a Chicago television station. Judge Lefkow had dismissed his lawsuit against doctors in an area hospital, who he blamed for disfiguring his appearance and causing the loss of teeth during cancer treatment in the early 1990s.[16]

After Ross killed the family members, he claimed he hid in the basement of the home for hours before fleeing. Law enforcement followed up on the letter. However, Ross committed suicide after being pulled over by police in Wisconsin. A second note was found in his van.[17]

The spotlight of the criminal act against a federal judge shone brightly on a very sensitive part of agency work. Although judicial security was a foremost focus of the agency, renewed emphasis ranged from assessing threats and inappropriate communications to installing residence alarms.

Fiscal restrictions curtailed wholesale changes, so the agency upgraded its existing assessment system.[18]

However, damage was done. The murders aroused fears in the legal and legislative communities. Criticism was swift, as the federal judiciary wielded considerable power in pushing for improved security. Director Reyna and U.S. Marshal Kim R. Widup of the Northern District of Illinois faced a firestorm.[19]

In May 2005, the Senate Judiciary Committee heard from Judge Lefkow and U.S. Circuit Judge Jane Roth, who was chair of the Judicial Conference Committee. Director Reyna testified about the importance of judicial protection, but his words failed to shield him from criticism. Judge Roth felt the agency's resources were not adequate for the mission, and that the judiciary needed greater protection. Magistrate Judge Samuel Alba felt assessments on residential alarm systems were uneven. Millions in supplemental funding allowed the agency to begin installing security systems in homes of the federal judiciary.[20]

No matter his assurances, Director Reyna faced powerful currents pushing for change. The *Washington Post* reported that "leaders of the federal judiciary," including Judge Roth, approached Attorney General Alberto R. Gonzales with their concerns. Although USMS leadership insisted the agency's overall performance was sound, there was clear disagreement over direction. Director Reyna resigned on July 31, 2005, after nearly four years at the helm of the Marshals Service. The Lefkow murders were certainly a factor for his resignation. The following day, John F. Clark was sworn in as acting director of the U.S. Marshals Service.[21]

There were many changes in judicial protection. In one of his last duties before retirement, Don Horton helmed a new Office of Protective Intelligence that refined and guided assessments of threats and inappropriate communications. He consolidated the judicial threat function into the Judicial Security Division, formed a network of liaisons with other agencies, and set the stage for a "sensitive compartmented information facility," or SCIF, to house operations. The U.S. Marshals Service dedicated the Threat Management Center, of which the SCIF was a part, on September 14, 2007.[22]

Prior to the Congressional hearing on the Lefkow murders, Reyna got to oversee Operation FALCON (Federal and Local Cops Organized Nationally). From April 4-10, 2005, the "national roundup" paired deputies with officers from 959 agencies of all jurisdictions. In all, law enforcement partners arrested 10,499 violent criminals and cleared 14,085 warrants. The round-up complemented National Crime Victims' Rights Week. Chief Deputy U.S. Marshal Brad Miller, the first FALCON commander, commented to the *Marshals Monitor*, "When the first e-mail went out, the chief deputies responded one after another that they were short of funds and deputies, but they would give it their best shot."[23]

A second initiative that year broke new law enforcement ground. Fugitive Safe Surrender, a concept by U.S. Marshal Peter J. Elliott of the Northern District of Ohio, created a novel deterrent to violent confrontation. The idea originated from tragedy. In June 2000, Cleveland patrolman Wayne Leon, the marshal's family friend, was killed after pulling over a dangerous fugitive.[24] Elliott recalled, "I was at the hospital with his family the night he died."[25] Elliott, a third-generation law enforcement officer, was affected deeply by Officer Leon's death.

"Desperate people commit desperate acts with tragic circumstances," he reasoned, and many tragedies could be averted by a peaceful surrender before the fugitives feel cornered. By utilizing the neighborhood staples of church and community, Elliott aimed to reach fugitives non-violently. By making a "temporary courthouse" out of a religious building, Marshal Elliott effectively created a safe way to surrender. He partnered with the local police, Cuyahoga County Attorney, the media, and church leadership to pull the operation off.[26]

Reverend C. Jay Matthews opened the Mount Sinai Baptist Church for the first Fugitive Safe Surrender operation. Even former football legend Jim Brown assisted in the effort. Elliott worked on the arrest and processing guidelines, which highlighted community volunteers and a low-stress environment. In a four-day period from August 3-6, 2005, 850 people voluntarily surrendered. From this, 340 felony cases were closed.[27]

Given the success of this concept, Congress authorized funding for Safe Surrender for three more years. Some states adopted the program on their own.[28]

The biggest test of 2005 came in September. Deputies flocked to the Gulf Coast to aid beleaguered communities in the wake of Hurricane Katrina. The Emergency Operations Center deployed other deputies to the area to assist, too. They worked 16-hour days, bringing a semblance of order to the region. Deputies did everything from working with FEMA and the Red Cross to securing communications and enforcing New Orleans' curfew order. They provided an escort for the staff of the Centers for Disease Control and Prevention. Most of all, deputies ensured the safety of the federal judiciary.[29]

SOG deputies used boats to find people and their pets. They went from house to house in several portions of New Orleans. Deputy Bobby Freeman told the *Marshals Monitor* they "rescued 12 people in five days of boat operations—and more animals than we could keep up with."[30]

JPATS moved more than 3,500 Hurricane Katrina refugees to five states. The Capitol Area Regional Fugitive Task Force searched the wreckage for bodies, finding more than they expected. The agency's response lasted until October in New Orleans and until December on the Gulf Coast.[31]

OLD PLACES, NEW HORIZONS

Deputy Director Donald Gambatesa departed in January 2006, and was replaced by Senior Counsel to the Deputy Attorney General Robert Trono. He had worked with the U.S. marshals in the Eastern District of Virginia, easing his learning curve.[32]

In March, John Clark received formal appointment as director of the agency. The mild-mannered Clark, a native of upstate New York, had worked with the U.S. Capitol Police and the Border Patrol before joining the U.S. Marshals Service in May 1983. Clark described his first and simple goal, "It's obvious we've got to grow."[33]

Growth meant meeting requirements of both the current missions and those of new programs. One piece of legislation guaranteed the latter. The Adam Walsh Child Protection and Safety Act of 2006 required convicted sex offenders to register their whereabouts in states where they resided. The law also called for the creation of a national sex offender register. The act gave the U.S. Marshals a new mission: to investigate for federal prosecution, failure on the part of sex offenders to register as such in the states of residence as required by this statute. The law impacted the agency as greatly as the 1979 Memorandum of Understanding between the U.S. Marshals Service and FBI, which made permanent the fugitive apprehension mission. The Adam Walsh Act was named after the young son of television personality John Walsh, who was abducted and murdered in 1981. The U.S. Marshals would enforce its requirements.[34]

In January 2007, after a year-long study by the U.S. Marshals Site Selection Committee under Assistant Director Mike Pearson of the Executive Services Division, Director Clark made history when he announced that Fort Smith, Arkansas, would be the site of a new U.S. Marshals museum. Organizers envisioned a groundbreaking in September 2014, and promised a structure worthy to honor the U.S. marshals past and present.[35]

THE BROWNS

In January 2007, Edward and Elaine Brown of Plainfield, New Hampshire, failed to appear during the fourth day of their trial after their indictment in April 2006 for failure to pay federal income taxes for many years. U.S. District Judge Steven McAuliffe issued arrest warrants for them, which drew threats against him and the prosecutor from the

Browns. U.S. Marshal Steve Monier of the District of New Hampshire understood the potential for a grave situation.[36]

Ideology pervaded this simple case of tax evasion, and drew outside elements. Yet again, the U.S. Marshals were thrust into a sensitive standoff. The elderly couple, each over 60 years old, was arrested on May 24, 2006, on charges of tax evasion. Although both were armed when arrested, they were released on condition they reported regularly to the U.S. Probation office and appeared at proceedings.[37] Although both appeared at the beginning of the trial, Edward Brown stopped attending. On January 18, 2007, the Browns were found guilty.[38]

On February 20, Elaine Brown defied her court-ordered conditions of confinement and cut off an electronic bracelet. Judge McAuliffe issued an arrest warrant for her. By late March, the Browns were joined at their compound by a number of sympathizers.[39]

In late March, the brewing tensions prompted the U.S. Marshals Service to assess this situation tactically. Images of the property revealed unique features such as an observation tower and windmill. The Browns could hold out a long time and, with increasing numbers of followers, could create a situation not unlike Ruby Ridge or Waco.[40]

The Browns failed to appear for sentencing on April 24, and received 63 months of incarceration from the court, *in absentia*. U.S. Marshal Monier drafted a letter to the couple, which expressed concerns and stated their options. It read in part:

> As you both know, there are outstanding warrants for your arrests. To date, you have made statements threatening law enforcement if attempts are made to serve those warrants. This creates a public safety concern for the community and subjects both you, and anyone who may be assisting you with this obstruction of justice, to further prosecution.
>
> 1. Contact us to make arrangements, and

2. Surrender peacefully to the United States Marshals Service.

You have my assurance that you will be treated professionally, with courtesy and respect. That is the right thing for you to do, and I encourage you to do it.[41]

With no resolution in sight, Chief Deputy Gary DiMartino and Chief Inspector Dave Dimmitt watched all movements in and around the compound. On June 7, advanced surveillance encountered Brown supporter Daniel Riley, who was walking a dog. The sight of deputies alarmed him, and Riley was detained for questioning. U.S. Marshal Monier reminded the press that "anyone aiding and abetting in their obstruction" could be arrested.[42]

Following the Riley arrest, Headquarters became more involved in the Brown standoff. The Special Operations Group, led by Commander Dave Robertson, began joint plans with Monier and Investigator Bill Sorukas, the incident commander.[43]

The press interest rose again after the seizure of Mrs. Brown's dental office. The media compared the Brown standoff to Ruby Ridge and Waco in articles and broadcasts; they caught the attention of Randall Weaver himself. By this time, Edward Brown spoke daily on a radio show from the compound. Supporters planned a music festival.[44]

U.S. Marshal Monier and Sorukas waited for the right moment to act. In October 2007, Edward Brown decided he wanted some property back that deputy marshals had seized from his wife's dental office. Sorukas arranged for "supporters" (undercover deputies) to fake a "break in" of the storage facility used to store the seized items. Three "supporters" purportedly breached the building, took the items that Brown asked for, and hauled the property back to the compound. A suspicious Brown, armed with an AK-47 rifle, warily let the undercover deputies unload the merchandise.[45]

Edward Brown offered to buy pizza, and the undercover deputies picked up several pies. When they returned, the deputies noticed handguns in both Ed and Elaine's waistbands instead of the AK-47. The Browns supplied the beer.[46]

At the command post, Sorukas and other leaders waited for a signal to advance with a large unit of deputies. When the Browns and their supporters were sufficiently distracted, the undercover deputies gave the signal. The deputies moved in and disarmed the Browns. Sorukas was shocked by the sheer amount of firepower they had. Pipe bombs were in the home and in the surrounding woods.[47]

The standoff with Edward and Elaine Brown was lengthy, but it showed Americans that the U.S. marshals could bring a dangerous situation to a bloodless conclusion. Internally, it helped the agency move beyond Ruby Ridge.

The Resilience

The demands of leadership in the U.S. Marshals Service are many. Forces pull at the director, as the head and face of the agency. Less recognized are the pressures on the deputy director. After Donald Gambetesa's departure, former prosecutor Robert Trono stayed only until June 2007. Director Clark appointed Brian R. Beckwith, a popular longtime deputy who headed the agency's training academy, to be deputy director. Beckwith's appointment by the Attorney General in August represented the first time career deputy marshals served together in appointed positions as director and deputy director.[48]

During this time, leadership realigned its strategic goals. FALCON saw its fourth iteration from June to September 2007. The total number of arrested fugitives decreased, but it remained an effective operation. Two more versions of FALCON, in June 2008 and 2009, focused on sex offenders and gang members. Operation FALCON 2009 utilized law enforcement officers from 42 federal, 209 state, and 1,973 local jurisdictions.[49]

In Witness Security, Assistant Director Sylvester Jones worked for pay parity for inspectors and increased exposure of the mission with an "International Symposium," chaired by longtime inspector, Joseph Paonessa. In recognition of the valuable role the agency played with witness protection, other countries, primarily in South America and the Middle East, requested U.S. Marshals share its expertise.[50]

Robert Finan became associate director for operations in March 2008. He explained that the U.S. Marshals Service "went from a director, deputy director, twelve assistant director-scenario to a director, deputy director, two associate directors—one for operations and one for administration, and then [assistant directors]."[51] The assistant directors reported to their respective associate director.

Deputy Director Beckwith retired in February 2009. Christopher Dudley, who served as chief of staff and as associate director for administration, found himself in the acting deputy director role most of that year. His knowledge of budgetary matters and calm personality gave him a natural edge for the job. The agency had long wanted the deputy director to be a career, not appointed, position. This would align it with the chief deputy U.S. marshal positions at the district level, who work for Presidentially appointed U.S. marshals.[52]

In September 2009, Dudley became the first non-appointive deputy director.[53] At that time, he stated, "It's an honor, strictly an honor. It's truly, from a guy who started in a cellblock in Atlanta, to be able to sit here, hopefully positively—it's just an honor."[54]

With the start of Director Stacia A. Hylton's term on December 31, 2010, the agency continued its vigorous growth, and sought ways to improve. The leadership shifted, with a combination of old and new faces. Deputy Director Dudley continued in his position, while Steve Mertens became associate director for administration. Associate Director for Operations Bob Finan retired, and David Harlow, Assistant Director of the Investigative Operations Division, replaced him.[55]

A DIRECTOR'S EXPERIENCE

Director Stacia A. Hylton knew the value of meeting a challenge. Long before her term as director, she had repeatedly challenged herself. In 1980, Director Hylton, then a Northeastern University criminal justice major named Stacia Kirk, took part in the agency's blossoming cooperative program. After a rigorous interview process, she arrived in the District of Columbia Office. She explained, "I went from Boston to D.C. every six months for three years."[56] During her second year, she witnessed deputies bringing John Hinckley, Jr. into federal court after his assassination attempt on President Ronald Reagan in March 1981. "He would never look up," she recalled. Completing her time in the program, Stacia Kirk was hired as a deputy U.S. marshal in 1983.[57]

Before she was formally hired, Director Stacia Hylton remembered meeting then-Director Bill Hall and pointing to a picture of a uniformed group of deputies in Special Operations. "I love the Marshals Service... I want to be in that group."[58] She was immediately hired. After graduating in a class of 24 people from the Training Academy in August 1983, Stacia Kirk tried to enter the membership of the Special Operation Group. "I think a hundred people applied, and sixty were selected... and eleven of us graduated."[59]

During a concerted fugitive operation in Miami, she was part of a six-person entry team. This was dangerous work, being on the front lines during raids and barricade situations. In 1985, she took part in the famous "chicken sting" operation that netted hundreds of fugitives who were lured in by the prize of football game tickets. She won over the respect of old school judges as an acting supervisor in Eastern Virginia, where she married Deputy U.S. Marshal Ike Hylton, Jr., the son of a longtime U.S. Marshal.[60]

The accumulation of experience that Deputy U.S. Marshal Stacia Hylton acquired during the course of her career was impressive. She became a training instructor at the Academy for nearly four years, then worked with recruiting staff in Human Resources, followed by three years as a Witness Security Inspector. In 1992, Hylton started a long stint with the Court Security Division. Headed by Assistant Director Don Horton, she saw the inside of judicial protective details, the Court Security Officer program, for which she had direct responsibility; and facility safety. After the Oklahoma City Bombing, Deputy Director Ray Havens asked her to find a way to assess security at all federal facilities.[61]

Hylton's career experience took even wider turns. After three more years with the Court Security Division, she became chief deputy U.S. marshal in the District of South Carolina. Then, in 2001, she became acting deputy director of the agency when Louie McKinney called. A few years later, she was literally drafted to lead a new agency—the Office of the Detention Trustee. She did not want to leave the U.S. Marshals Service, and asked Director Ben Reyna to write a letter to allow her "to return home" if she needed to use it.[62]

Stacia Hylton did return home. After serving five years as head of the Office of the Detention Trustee, she retired for sixteen days. Then, she received a call to be Director of the U.S. Marshals Service. Knowing the strengths and weaknesses of the agency, she worked on refining our business culture and missions.[63]

Director Hylton's term began with many challenges. In the first three months of 2011, she dealt with the tragic line-of-duty deaths of two deputy U.S. marshals: Derek Hotsinpiller on February 16 and John Perry on March 8. To add to the grief, the agency lost six special deputy U.S. marshals on task forces that same year. Still, the agency found its way through these dark periods.[64]

Hylton commissioned a comprehensive review of apprehension protocols and instituted revolutionary training for deputy marshals and task force officers based on risk mitigation and active shooter scenarios. She said, "Budget challenges cannot impede our focus on the safety of our law enforcement personnel."[65]

The High Risk Fugitive Apprehension (HRFA) training course represented the largest training initiative in the history of the Marshals Service. It standardized a tactical-based curriculum with the simple goal of enhancing arrest protocols while mitigating risk. The goal of the training is to keep operators in the mindset of "staying in the game" during fluid, unpredictable situations. HRFA training stressed advanced tactics, operational planning, communications, and trauma medic procedures. It incorporated real-life situations to challenge participants to develop the right mindset when in a potential gun battle or fight to save their partners' lives or their own.[66]

Tragically, Deputy Director Dudley, 46, took his own life on November 23, 2012. His death created a gloomy period for the Marshals Service. It was the first time the agency had lost a director or deputy director while in office, since James McShane in 1968. The agency grieved together, and conducted a special ceremony at Alexandria's Masonic Temple to celebrate Dudley's life and his many contributions to the Marshals Service. Director Hylton gave an inspired address, and a slideshow displayed Dudley's past and brought tears to nearly every eye. The USMS Critical Incident Response Team (CIRT) aided employees in the following months.[67]

Despite tragedy, the agency's resilience and dedication set it upright in time. Despite the scars, the U.S. Marshals moved forward on its mission. Still small enough to feel like an extended family of sorts, the agency operates today with the same *esprit de corps* of its predecessors. Each new class of deputies graduating from the Training Academy realizes the big shoes they must fill. Both administrative and operational staffers continue to uphold "America's Star," and their dedication keeps the machine running. They all remember, appreciate, and learn before moving on to the next test. After all, there will always be a new challenge for the U.S. Marshals Service.

A Last Word: Down the Road

There are assurances of historical continuity in the U.S. Marshals Service. Names and faces will be different, but the mission and its historic importance will remain. There is simply nothing comparable to any other federal organization. History is interwoven in the fabric of the organization, and it becomes part of every employee who walks through the door. People seek employment with the U.S. Marshals Service for different reasons, but for many it is the fulfillment of a lifelong dream or goal.

Down the road, the agency will transform with its missions and regenerate itself as needed. While no law enforcement agency escapes scrutiny, the U.S. Marshals Service learns from its mistakes and adapts to the environment required. Historically, today, and tomorrow—there is a constant: U.S. Marshals Service employees will be called to duty in situations that are not popular with certain segments of society. When they do, they should remember Al Butler's motto: "you put on the badge, do the job." Just like the generations before them, they will do the job whatever that may be.

Appendix

Directors Since 2005

Eastern District of Virginia U.S. Marshal John F. Clark, a career deputy who had served in a number of agency roles, including chief deputy U.S. marshal, took the reins of the Marshals Service as acting director in August 2005. He was appointed director in March 2006. Clark proved popular, particularly among fellow deputies, as he increased enforcement initiatives like FALCON and focused on the agency's fugitive investigations mission. Despite a change in political parties at the White House, Clark stayed on as director until 2010.

Stacia A. Hylton took the helm of the agency in December 2010 and began the arduous task of balancing operational and administrative responsibilities while trying to restore the agency to a sound financial footing. She was a career deputy marshal, who knew her agency and its various duties based on her own diverse experiences. Past leaders in the Marshals Service and Department of Justice had tapped her for numerous special projects.

With the retirement of Director Hylton in July 2015, Acting Director David Harlow has been in charge of the agency. He started his career with the agency in 1983, and became Deputy Director in 2014.

Deputy Directors Since 2005

Robert E. Trono of the Justice Department succeeded Donald Gambetesa in January 2006. Following the end of Trono's term, longtime deputy U.S. marshal and the assistant director of the Training Academy, Brian R. Beckwith, assumed the job of acting deputy director in July 2007 and the full appointment less than a month later.

Beckwith retired in 2009, and Christopher Dudley joined the leadership team first as acting deputy director in March. He became deputy director in September. Dudley, with a congenial style, became extremely popular as a leader with a strong connection to the rank-and-file. He first served in Investigative Services or Enforcement, and like Director Clark before him, was chief of international operations there. His first top management positions were chief of staff and Associate Director of Administration.

With the passing of Deputy Director Dudley in November 2012, James A. Thompson became Acting Deputy Director. Having served as U.S. Marshal for the District of Utah, his leadership greatly aided Director Hylton during this difficult period.

In February 2014, David Harlow, who had formerly served as assistant director, Investigative Operations Division and associate director for Operations, became deputy director.

EXECUTIVE MANAGERIAL STAFF SINCE 2005

The organizational structure of the agency has shifted frequently since 2005. Structurally, it reverted to two associate directors: one for operations and another for administration. The number of assistant directors fluctuated and increased over time. Below is an abbreviated chronology of leadership shifts at the associate director levels from 2005 and assistant director levels at specified dates until 2012:

Associate Director for Operations (ADO):

- In April 2008, Director Clark selected Robert J. Finan II, formerly Assistant Director for Judicial Security, Investigative Services, and Executive Services Divisions, to become the Associate Director for Operations.
- In March 2011, Assistant Director of Investigations T. Michael Earp became Associate Director for Operations.

- Assistant Director, Asset Forfeiture Division Eben Morales served as Acting Associate Director for Operations in January 2012 after the retirement of Associate Director Earp.
- In October 2012, Director Hylton tapped David Harlow as the Associate Director for Operations.
- In March 2014, Assistant Director William D. Snelson served as the Associate Director for Operations.

ASSOCIATE DIRECTOR FOR ADMINISTRATION (ADA):

- In April 2008, Director Clark appointed Chris Dudley the Associate Director for Administration.
- Effective December 2009, Director Clark tapped Donald S. Donovan as Associate Director for Administration.
- In July 2011, Hylton hired Steven M. Mertens, as the Associate Director for Administration. He joined the Marshals Service executive team after many years at the White House Office of Management and Budget.
- After Associate Director Mertens retired, Principal Deputy General Counsel Lisa Dickinson became Acting Associate Director for Administration in June 2013.
- In February 2014, Assistant Director for JPATS David Musel became Associate Director for Administration.

WITNESS SECURITY DIVISION:

- Over the years, the Witness Security Division had been paired with Investigative Services for a time, then with Prisoner Services. Eventually, the agency separated it from the other divisions, letting it stand independently. Sylvester Jones became assistant director of WitSec in June 2004, when it was still combined with Prisoner Services.
- The current assistant director, as of March 2015, is Michael Prout.

JUDICIAL SECURITY DIVISION:

- In 2001, Sylvester Jones became the first African-American career deputy marshal selected to the Senior Executive Service at the Marshals Service, when selected as the Assistant Director of the Judicial Security Division. He moved to the Witness Security Division.
- In 2005, Marc A. Farmer became Assistant Director for the Judicial Security Division.
- Bob Finan served as AD of JSD from 2006 until April 2008.
- In August 2008, Director Clark tapped Michael Prout as its Assistant Director.
- Carl Caulk assumed the reins of JSD in March 2012, at the behest of Director Hylton.
- Noelle Douglas became Assistant Director after the departure of AD Caulk, and served until late 2015.
- The current Acting AD is Thomas Wight.

PRISONER OPERATIONS DIVISION:

- In August 2008, Clark selected Candra S. Symonds as Assistant Director for the Prisoner Operations Division.
- David Musel became Acting Assistant Director of Prisoner Operations Division in October 2012.
- Eben Morales is the current Assistant Director for Prisoner Operations Division.

MANAGEMENT SUPPORT DIVISION:

- Director Clark appointed Donald S. Donovan the Assistant Director of the Management Support Division in October 2008.
- In January 2011, Hylton appointed Shannon Brown to lead MSD.

- Long-time Chief Deputy U.S. Marshal Aldean Lee became its Assistant Director in November 2012.
- The current AD for Management Support Division is Thomas Sgroi.

ASSET FORFEITURE DIVISION:

- In June 2010, Clark chose Eben Morales as the Assistant Director of the Asset Forfeiture Division.
- After AD Morales moved to the Prisoner Operations Division, Kim Beal served as AD until August 2015.
- Acting Assistant Director Timothy Virtue currently leads the Asset Forfeiture Division.

INFORMATION TECHNOLOGY DIVISION:

- In October 2008, Clark hired Lisa M. Davis as the Assistant Director for the Information Technology Division.
- Hylton moved Shannon Brown to the position of AD of ITD in January 2011. She had been the Chief Information Officer for the Office of Federal Detention Trustee at DOJ.
- The current AD is Dr. Karl Mathias.

FINANCIAL SERVICES DIVISION:

- In September 2009, Clark hired Albert D. Hemphill II as the agency's Chief Financial Officer and Assistant Director for the Financial Services Division.
- Holley O'Brien took over the dual position when selected by Hylton in 2012.

HUMAN RESOURCES DIVISION:

- In September 2008, Darla Callaghan was hired as Assistant Director for the Human Resources Division.
- In December 2012, Hylton brought Katherine "Kat" Mohan, who had previously served as the USMS Personnel Officer, back to the agency to lead HRD.

TRAINING DIVISION:

- In the first of three executive moves in a relatively short period of time for the career deputy, Chris Dudley became assistant director for Training at the behest of Director Clark in April 2008.
- In August 2010, Vernon Johnson became Acting Assistant Director.
- In January 2011, Director Hylton made William Fallon the Assistant Director of the Training Division.

JUSTICE PRISONER AND ALIEN TRANSPORTATION SERVICE:

- Scott C. Rolstad was Assistant Director for JPATS from 2006 until 2011.
- Dave Musel, the first chief of staff for the agency, was tapped to lead the Justice Prisoner and Alien Transportation Service in 2011.
- Shannon Brown is the current AD for JPATS.

TACTICAL OPERATIONS DIVISION:

- In August 2008, William D. Snelson became Assistant Director for the Tactical Operations Division (TOD). Note: TOD functions included special deputations, badges and credentials, the Critical Incident Response Team, Special Operations Group, Communications Center, and continuity of operations, along with the agency's security of the Strategic National Stockpile, the nation's supply of emergency medicine and medical supplies in a crisis.

- Both Thomas E. Wight and Derrick Driscoll served as Acting Assistant Directors.
- The current AD for Tactical Operations is Neil K. DeSousa.

INVESTIGATIVE OPERATIONS DIVISION:

- Under Robert Finan, Investigative Services increased its role. However, he was promoted to Associate Director for Operations (ADO) in 2008, and replaced by Michael Earp.
- Director Hylton named David Harlow as Assistant Director of Investigative Operations Division in March 2012.
- The current AD for Investigative Operations is Derrick Driscoll.

ENDNOTES

NOTES TO INTRODUCTION

1. Charles Warren, "New Light on the History of Federal Judiciary Act of 1789," *Harvard Law Review* 37, no. 11 (1923): 49; Author, "Setting the Record Straight—USMS Is Nation's First Federal Law Enf.[orcement] Agency," *Marshals Monitor*, Spring 2004, 3-4; Frederick S. Calhoun, *The Lawmen—United States Marshals and Their Deputies, 1789-1989* (New York: Penguin Books, 1991), 2, 12-15. The U.S. Marshals were the first federal entity formed for law enforcement purposes. It was found that deputies served on revenue cutters in the early days of the nation, and also trained other organizational personnel when exchanging a duty. Prime examples of this can be found at the Office of Instructions and Mail Depredations in 1830, which later became the Postal Inspection Service. See J. Holbrook, *Ten Years Among the Mail Bags: or, Notes from the Diary of a Special Agent of the Post-Office Department* (New York: J.C. Derby, 1856), 25-28, and the Secret Service, who assumed duties on pursuing counterfeiting from our personnel.

2. "An Act to Establish the Judicial Courts of the United States," in *Statutes at Large*, Session 1, Chap. XX, Section 27, September 24, 1789.

3. Calhoun, *Lawmen*, 14-15; U.S. Marshal James Plousis and David S. Turk, "The Measure of a Law Enforcement Icon: The History of the New York/New Jersey Regional Fugitive Task Force," USMS Collections; David S. Turk, "Billy the Kid and the U.S. Marshals Service, *Wild West* 19, no. 5 (February 2007).

4. Calhoun, *Lawmen*, 12-13.

5. "An Act to Establish the Judicial Courts," in *Statutes at Large*, Session 1, Chap. XX, Section 28, September 24, 1789; "Setting the Record Straight," *Marshals Monitor*, Spring 2004, 3.

6. Calhoun, *Lawmen*, 15-16, 55, 136, 139.

7. Calhoun, *Lawmen*, 192-194; Ben T. Traywick, *Marshal of Tombstone— Virgil Walter Earp* (Tombstone [Sierra Vista], Arizona: Red Marie's, 1985), 6-7; David S. Turk, "Billy the Kid and the U.S. Marshals Service, *Wild West* 19, no. 5 (February 2007); "Bloody Battle Pits Deputies Vs. the Wild Bunch," *Marshals Monitor*, November-December 2000, 6-7; "Wyatt Berry Stapp Earp," in Dan L. Thrapp, comp., *Encyclopedia of Frontier Biography, Volume I A-F* (Glendale, CA: The Arthur H. Clark Company, 1988), 448-449; "James Butler (Wild Bill) Hickok," in Dan L. Thrapp, comp., *Encyclopedia of Frontier Biography, Volume II G-O* (Glendale, CA: The Arthur H. Clark Company, 1988), 658; "In the Old West, Bass Reeves Was Unparalleled," *Marshals Monitor*, January-February 2001, 13; "John R. (Catch-'em-alive Jack) Abernathy," in Thrapp, comp., *Encyclopedia of Frontier Biography, Volume I*, 3-4. For a detailed study of Deputy U.S. Marshal Bass Reeves, see Art T. Burton, *Black Gun, Silver Star* (Lincoln: University of Nebraska Press, 2006).

8. The FBI's predecessor, the Bureau of Investigation, was founded in 1908. The Federal Bureau of Narcotics was founded in 1930, but its predecessor organizations date to 1915. Although the first income taxes originated in 1862, the modern version of the IRS began in 1918. See FBI.gov, Archives.gov, and IRS.gov. See Calhoun, *Lawmen*, 18-19.

9. Notes, Poster Plan File, "Now Showing: 'Passing of the Oklahoma Outlaws,'" USMS Collections.

10. "'Bat' Masterson is Dead," *Kansas City Star*, October 25, 1921; Elmo Scott Watson, "When Tombstone, Ariz. was 'Helldorado,'" *Blockton News*, April 4, 1929; "Evett Dumas Nix," in Dan L. Thrapp, comp., *Encyclopedia of Frontier Biography, Volume II*, 1058. U.S. Marshal Evett D. Nix of the Oklahoma Territory from May 1893 to February 1896, wrote *Oklahombres,*

published in 1929. Despite a wave of interest previously, books about Jesse James and Billy the Kid were resurgent in the late 1920s.

11. Alexander Holtzoff to Attorney General, October 8, 1936, Classified Files, Record Group 60, National Archives and Records Administration. See also Calhoun, *Lawmen*, 248.

12. Calhoun, *Lawmen*, 248.

13. Copy, Office of Public Affairs, Fact Sheet, "Facts and Figures 2013," Revised January 10, 2013.

14. Calhoun, *Lawmen*, 6; Copy, Press Release, Department of Justice, December 17, 1956.

15. Ray Sherrard and George Stumpf, *Badges of the United States Marshals* (Garden Grove, CA: RHS Enterprises, 1991), 44; Calhoun, *Lawmen*, 250. There is a photograph which might indicate a first nation-wide-issue badge from 1937, but more research is needed to determine if this was the same variety.

16. Interview, Director Stacia A. Hylton, August 19, 2013. See e-mail, Director to USMS-ALL, "Message from Director Hylton—Re: Farewell," July 20, 2015.

Notes to Chapter 1

1. "U.S. Deputy Marshal Slain Making Arrest," *San Francisco Examiner*, November 25, 1937; "Slayer Sent to Hospital," *San Francisco News*, February 24, 1938; "Military Funeral for Raoul Dorsay," *The Recorder*, November 27, 1937.

2. Appointments for U.S. Marshal were made by the President with the advice and consent of the Senate. Senators provide the name of the candidate to the President, which exercises local appointment advisory power.

3. *Register of the Department of Justice and the Courts of the United States, 42nd edition* (Washington, D.C., 1955), 8. Another long-term employee, Eugene J. Matchett, was chief of the accounts branch from 1944. Author also communicated with Mr. Andretta's son Gage.

4. Copy of Draft, Attorney General Frank Murphy to "My dear Mr.," May 18, 1939, USMS Collections. Also, see Calhoun, *Lawmen*, 136.

5. Calhoun, *Lawmen*, 248. See the Appropriations Act of 1937, U.S. Statutes, 279; "An Act Further Defining the Number and Duties of Criers and Bailiffs in United States Courts and Regulating Their Compensation," 1944, U.S. Statutes, 796.

6. John Kobler, *Capone: The Life and World of Al Capone* (New York: Putnam Publishing Group, 1971), 342; see also Mike Marsh, " 'Scarface' Al Capone and U.S. Marshall [*sic*] Henry C.W. Laubenheimer, Chicago, Illinois, May 4, 1932," describing picture taken on that date, commentary posted from December 31, 1969, and displayed on www.cigaraficionado.com website. U.S. Marshal Laubenheimer was at the helm of the Northern District of Illinois from 1928 to 1934.

7. Copy, NARA (Archivist) to William Dempsey, Public Affairs Officer, ca. 1980, USMS Collections; Copy of Release, William Dempsey, "A U.S. Marshal for China?," January 4, 1980; Calhoun, *Lawmen*, 174-175; Copy of Oath, Edward L. Faupel, July 5, 1934, Record Group (RG) 527, National Archives.

8. Edward L. Faupel to S.A. Andretta, September 4, 1937, RG 527, National Archives.

9. Interview, Judge Gordon Campbell, August 20, 1993, USMS Collections.

10. Ibid.

11. Ibid.

12. Ibid.

13. Ibid.

14. Ibid.

15. Ibid.

16. Calhoun, *Lawmen*, 250.

17. Ray Sherrard and George Stumpf, *Badges of the United States Marshals* (Garden Grove, CA: RHS Enterprises, 1991), 43-45.

18. Copy, E.R. Butts, General Agent to T.D. Quinn, Administrative Assistant to the Attorney General, "Memorandum for Mr. T.D. Quinn Administrative Assistant to the Attorney General," October 23, 1941, General File, New York, USMS Collections

19. Copy, E.J. Matchett, Chief, Division of Accounts to Mr. S.A. Andretta, Administrative Assistant to the Attorney General, Memorandum, March 18, 1946, USMS Collections; Copy, S.A. Andretta to U.S. Marshal James E. Mulcahy, March 21, 1946, USMS Collections.

20. Notes, Billy Williamson, January 12, 2003, USMS Collection; "History —A Visit to Chief Deputy U.S. Marshal Helen Crawford, Retired," Web Article from usmarshals.gov, with notes of visit by author with Helen Crawford, July 14, 2008. Billy Williamson's father, Shirley, was a deputy in 1942. Specifically, because of his skills as a trapper, he obtained the duty of tracking down draft dodgers in the District of Utah during this time.

21. Copy, Unknown Deputy U.S. Marshal's Journal, 1943-48, Northern District of New York, USMS Collections.

22. Ibid.

23. Robert W. Welkos, "Scripting a Scandal in Hollywood," *Toronto Star*, August 27, 1992; "Charlie Chaplin's Women," *Sunday Mail*, April 9, 1989; Civil Case No. 15135, *Carol Ann Berry, a Minor, etc., Respondent, v. Charles Spencer Chaplin*, Appellant, May 27, 1946; Julien Cornell, *The Trial of Ezra Pound* (New York: The John Day Company, 1966), 1-3.

24. Carol Ann Berry, etc., *Respondent, v. Charles Spencer Chaplin,*
Appellant, May 27, 1946; "Charlie Chaplin's Women," *Sunday Mail,* April
9, 1989; J.Y. Smith, "Charlie Chaplin, Comic Actor Famed for Role as
'Tramp,' Dies," *Washington Post,* December 26, 1977; Welkos, "Scripting
a Scandal," *Toronto Star,* August 27, 1992. Note: "Berry" is the spelling on
the documentation, while "Joan Barry" was the name used by the actress.

25. Cornell, *The Trial of Ezra Pound,* 6-7, 12-14, 21-23.

26. *Deputy United States Marshals' News of the National Association of
Deputy United States Marshals* 1, no. 1 (January 1947): 1.

27. Copy, Roy H. Webb to President (Harry S. Truman), July 6, 1947,
USMS Collections.

28. Edward M. Ranson, United States Marshal, "Our United States
Marshal," *The Nevada Peace Officer* 11 (1948): 33-34.

29. Copy, "National Association of Deputy United States Marshals
Constitution," USMS Collections; E. Norris Becker, ed., *Year Book National
Association of Deputy United States Marshals* (Baltimore, MD: French-
Bray Company, 1950).

30. Copy, Notes in File, National Association of Deputy United States
Marshals, USMS Collections.

NOTES TO CHAPTER 2

1. "Collazo in Plot at Blair House," *Washington Post,* November 11,
1950; "Assassin Transferred From Gallinger to District Jail," *Times Herald,*
November 10, 1950.

2. "Hiss in Handcuffs on Way to Jail," in *Coshocton Tribune (Ohio),*
March 23, 1951. The prisoner who hid was Eddie Jones, sentenced for
mail theft.

3. "Chronology of Events," in John Wexley, *The Judgment of Julius and
Ethel Rosenberg* (New York: Cameron & Kahn, 1955), xii; Copy of Receipt

of Prisoner, Ethel Rosenberg, April 11, 1951, Records of U.S. Attorney, National Archives and Records Adminstration. See also Calhoun, *Lawmen*, 255-256.

4. "Chronology of Events," Wexley, *Judgment of Julius and Ethel Rosenberg*, xii-xiii.

5. Copy, U.S. Marshal William A. Carroll to H.D. Quigg, January 2, 1953, USMS Collections.

6. David Snell, "Spies Take Secrets to Grave," *New York World-Telegram Sun*, June 20, 1953.

7. Calhoun, *Lawmen*, 256.

8. "Feuger Quiet on Trip Back to Iowa Prison," *Dubuque Telegraph Herald*, March 6, 1963; Copy, "Notes on Federal Executions," USMS Collections.

9. Copy, William P. Rogers to the Attorney General, August 6, 1956, USMS Collections; Copy of Attachment, Report of Sal Andretta, in Rogers to the Attorney General, August 6, 1956, USMS Collections.

10. Ibid.

11. Ibid.

12. Ibid.

13. Ibid.

14. Copy, (Attorney General) Brownell, Jr. to Mr. (William P.) Rogers, August 15, 1956, USMS Collections.

15. Ibid.

16. Copy, Press Release, Department of Justice, December 17, 1956.

17. Ibid. Copy, Newsletter, Department of the Justice Recreation Association, "Just-Us," August 3, 1959. See Letter, Larry Palmer to Author, May 22, 2005.

18. Copy, Memorandum, Clive W. Palmer, Assistant to the Deputy Attorney General to William P. Rogers, Deputy Attorney General, January 9, 1957, USMS Collections.

19. Ibid.

20. Executive Office for United States Marshals, *Summary of Notes of the Six Regional Conferences of United States Marshals March-June 1957,* 1-2, 3-8.

21. Copy, Hometown News Release, Questionnaire, 1982, USMS Collections; Copy, Biography, John W. Cameron, USMS Collections; *United States Marshals Bulletin,* No. 79, December 15, 1965, flyleaf page.

22. Copy, Memorandum, Clive W. Palmer to William P. Rogers, January 9, 1957, USMS Collections; Copy, Response dated January 23, 1957, USMS Collections.

23. Copy Release, Department of Justice, December 29, 1958, USMS Collections.

24. Copy of Program, *Deputy U.S. Marshal Training Program,* ca. 1959, USMS Collections; Calhoun, *Lawmen,* 257-258.

25. "Meyer Takes Office as Federal Marshal," *Arizona Star,* April 13, 1954.

26. Copy, J.W. Sefton to Mr. A.M. Meyer, April 19, 1954, USMS Collections.

27. Calhoun, *Lawmen,* 257-258; "Carlton Beale Named D.C. Postmaster," *Washington Evening Star,* December 2, 1958.

28. Interview, Robert Haislip, November 6, 1985, USMS Collections.

29. Ibid.

30. Interview, Frank Vandergrift [sic], July 10, 1985, USMS Collections.

31. Ibid.

32. Interview, Robert Haislip, November 6, 1985, USMS Collections.

33. Undated Interview, Bud Staple.

34. Interview, Frank Vandergrift [*sic*], July 10, 1985.

35. The legal citation for *Brown v Board of Education* is *347 U.S. 483 (1954)*.

36. "Report of Special Activities United States Marshal Eastern District of Arkansas August-December 1958," ii, USMS Collections.

37. Ibid.

38. Ibid.

39. Ibid. In 1957, the use of military forces brought about the mention of the Posse Comitatus Act, which began in 1877 and disallowed nearly all use of the military against civilians. The U.S. Marshal deputized a number of people for the task, mostly local officials.

40. Ibid.

41. Ibid.

42. Ibid.

43. Ibid., 2-4.

44. Ibid., 4-5.

NOTES TO CHAPTER 3

1. James Baldwin, *The Fire Next Time* (New York: The Dial Press, 1963).

2. Edward Emerine, "You Should Know Louisiana," *Farmington Times-Hustler*, March 1, 1946; Ralph Wheatley (AP), "Death of Long Leaves Regime Without Rudder," *Monroe [Louisiana] News-Star*, September 10, 1935; "Assassin's Bullet Fatal for Huey P. Long," *Monroe [Louisiana] News-Star*, September 10, 1935.

3. Copy, Clive W. Palmer to Byron R. White, "Report of the Activities of the Executive Office for United States Marshals for the Months of October, November, December 1960, and January 1961," February 13, 1961, USMS Collections; Calhoun, *Lawmen,* 262.

4. Copy, John W. Cameron Notes, New Orleans File, USMS Collections; Copy, Palmer to White, "Report," February 13, 1961, USMS Collections.

5. Interview, William Shoemaker, August 30, 2011, USMS Collections.

6. Copy, Cameron Notes, New Orleans File, USMS Collections; Copy, Palmer to White, "Report," February 13, 1961, USMS Collections.

7. Copy, Cameron Notes, New Orleans File, USMS Collections.

8. Copy, Cameron Notes, New Orleans File, USMS Collections; Copy, Palmer to White, "Report," February 13, 1961, USMS Collections.

9. Al Butler, Notes from Telephone Interview, January 31, 2007; Cameron Notes, New Orleans File, USMS Collections.

10. Copy, Cameron Notes, New Orleans File, USMS Collections. The National States Righters were mentioned on November 13, 1960.

11. Cameron Notes, New Orleans File, USMS Collections; Interview, Al Butler, August 30, 2011, USMS Collections.

12. Cameron Notes, New Orleans File, USMS Collections.

13. Ibid.

14. Ibid. The four deputies were Park, Bryant, Dorsey, and Allen.

15. Ibid.

16. Ibid.

17. Ibid.

18. Ibid.

19. Ibid.

20. Ibid.

21. Ibid.

22. Ibid.

23. Ibid.; Copy, Palmer to White, "Report," February 13, 1961, USMS Collections.

24. Report of Deputy Charles D. Burks, November 16, 1960, in Cameron Notes, New Orleans File, USMS Collections.

25. Cameron Notes, New Orleans File, USMS Collections; Palmer to White, "Report," February 13, 1961, USMS Collections.

26. Interview, Al Butler, August 30, 2011; Notes from Telephone Interview, Michael Buckheim to author, 1991. Buckheim was Norman Rockwell's neighbor and owned the famous painting.

27. Notes, Ralph Oczowski to Author, January 31, 2003. The rules were arranged by Rockwell with Morey, and after he finished, Mrs. Oczowski took photographs that confirmed the connection to the painting. Additional information was provided by U.S. Marshal Morey's daughter, Sheila Diskes, and grandson, Jon Morey.

28. Ibid.; Jane Allen Petrick, "Lynchburg Woman Was Child Model for Rockwell Painting," *Lynchburg News and Advance*, October 9, 2011; Copy, Buckheim to Author, 1991.

29. Entries on U.S. Marshals Carlton Beall and James J.P. McShane, *United States Marshals: 1789 to Present.*

30. Interview, Michael J. McShane, Alexandria, Virginia, June 13, 2003.

31. Known as the "Senate Select Committee on Improper Activities."

32. Interview, Michael J. McShane, Alexandria, Virginia, June 13, 2003; Copy, Press Release, Department of Justice, May 8, 1962.

33. The citation for *Boynton v Virginia* is 364 U.S. 454.

34. Associated Press, "Racial Clash Threatens in Alabama City," *Lowell Sun*, December 5, 1955; Copy, "Statement by Attorney General on Behalf of the United States in Support of Petition for Rule Making," Docket No. MC-C-3358, *In the Matter of Discrimination in Operations of Interstate Motor Carriers of Passengers*, Interstate Commerce Commission, in Records of Burke Marshall, Attorney, Civil Rights Division, RG 60, Box 1, National Archives; Raymond Arsenault, *Freedom Riders—1961 and the Struggle for Racial Justice* (New York: Oxford University Press, 2006), 95-96, 98.

35. Arsenault, *Freedom Riders*, 141-146, 195-199, 202-204; Copy, Press Release, Department of Justice, May 20, 1961, Record Group 60, National Archives.

36. Entry for McShane, *United States Marshals: 1789 to Present*; Copy, Notes of Paskal Bowser, USMS Collections; Entry for William M. Parker, *United States Marshals: 1789 to Present*.

37. Copy, Notes of Paskal Bowser, USMS Collections; Copy of Memorandum, James McShane to Byron R. White, May 25, 1961, USMS Collections.

38. Copy, Statement of William D. Behen, Assistant Supervisor In Charge, Alcohol and Tobacco Tax Division, Jacksonville, Florida, May 29, 1961, USMS Collections.

39. Ibid.; Copy, Report on Montgomery, Deputy U.S. Marshal Warren S. Emmerton, June 13, 1961, USMS Collections.

40. Copy, Statement of William D. Behen, May 29, 1961.

41. Ibid.; Copy, Statement of Deputy U.S. Marshal R.E. Moore, June 12, 1961, USMS Collections.

42. Copy, Statement of William D. Behen, May 29, 1961.

43. Ibid.

44. Copy, Statement of Deputy U.S. Marshal Raymond C. Pope, Undated, USMS Collections.

45. Ibid.

46. Interview, Herschel S. Garner, July 8, 1985, USMS Collections.

47. Ibid.

48. Copy, "Ann" to Marshal McShane, May 19, 1961, USMS Collections; Statement by the Honorable Robert F. Kennedy Attorney General of the United States Issued At 11:00 A.M., May 24, 1961, in Files of W. Wilson White, Civil Rights Division, Record Group 60, Box 1, NARA.

49. Copy, Typed Notes on Phone Conversation, May 25, 1961, USMS Collections.

50. Copy of Letter to Harold F. Reis from Richard Berg, in Files of W. Wilson White, Assistant Attorney General, Civil Rights Division, Record Group 60, Box 1, NARA.

51. Calhoun, *Lawmen*, 128-130. The 1890 case was resolved in the Supreme Court in favor of Neagle.

52. Entry of McShane, *United States Marshals: 1789 to Present;* Interview, Michael J. McShane, Alexandria, Virginia, June 13, 2003.

53. Calhoun, *Lawmen*, 262; Interview, Michael J. McShane, June 13, 2003.

54. Interview, Michael J. McShane, June 13, 2003.

55. Ibid.

56. Copy, James Meredith, *Remarks for United States Justice Department Celebration of the 40th Anniversary of the Integration of Ole Miss—15 July 2003.*

57. Copy, Script, "40th Commemoration Symposium Observance July 15, 2003," USMS Collections; Copy, Notes dated "9/20 3:15", "9/24 9:50 p.m.," "9/25 12:20 p.m, in "Phone Calls," from Transcripts from Conversations between Governor [Ross] Barnett and Robert F. Kennedy, USMS Collections. Originals in R12(B3), John F. Kennedy Library. These were

handwritten notes taken from transcripts with exact dates and times, participants, and summations or direct statements.

58. Helen M. Emmerton to author, May 13, 2003.

59. Ibid.

60. Interview, Cecil Miller, July 9, 1985, USMS Collections.

61. Ibid.; Interview, Robert Courtright, October 6, 1993, USMS Collections.

62. Interview, Robert Courtright, October 6, 1993, USMS Collections.

63. Interview, Cecil Miller, July 9, 1985, USMS Collections; George B. Leonard, T. George Harris and Christopher S. Wren, "How a secret deal prevented a massacre at Ole Miss," *Look*, December 31, 1962.

64. Interview, Herschel Garner, July 8, 1985, USMS Collections.

65. Denzil N. "Bud" Staple, "Forty Years Ago 1962 'Ole-Miss'—Oxford, Mississippi."

66. Interview, Robert Courtright, October 6, 1993, USMS Collections.

67. Ibid.

68. Ibid.

69. Ibid.

70. Interview, Willard McArdle and Al Butler, October 1, 2003, USMS Collections.

71. Copy, Notes of John "Jack" Cameron, USMS Collections; Interview, Willard McArdle and Al Butler, October 1, 2003, USMS Collections.

72. Interview, Robert Courtright, October 6, 1993, USMS Collections; "40th Commemorative Observance," USMS Collections.

73. Interview, McArdle and Butler, October 1, 2003, USMS Collections.

74. Ibid.

75. Ibid.; "40th Commemorative Observance," USMS Collections; Copy, Notes of Jack Cameron, USMS Collections.

76. Interview, Bill Banta, September 21, 2008, USMS Collections.

77. Ibid.

78. Copy, Notes of Cameron, USMS Collections; "40th Commemoration Observance," USMS Collections; Calhoun, *Lawmen*, 268-270; Copy, E-Mail, Graham "Gene" Same to Author, July 29, 2002.

79. "40th Commemoration Observance," USMS Collections; Interview, McArdle and Butler, October 1, 2003, USMS Collections; Calhoun, *Lawmen*, 269-271.

80. Interview, McArdle and Butler, October 1, 2003, USMS Collections.

81. "40th Commemoration Observance," USMS Collections; Interview, McArdle and Butler, October 1, 2003, USMS Collections; Calhoun, *Lawmen*, 269-271.

82. Interview, Bill Banta, September 21, 2008, USMS Collections.

83. Ibid.

84. Calhoun, *Lawmen*, 271-272; Interview, Cecil Miller, July 9, 1985, USMS Collections.

85. "40th Commemorative Observance," USMS Collections. Both Staple and Hopper related these accounts, which were formally documented at the 40th Commemorative Symposium, held in Washington, D.C. in July 2003.

86. Ibid.

87. Ibid.; Interview, Herschel Garner, July 8, 1985, USMS Collections.

88. "40th Commemorative Observance," USMS Collections. The family name was spelled without the letter "u." The famous author William Faulkner added it. Murry Cuthbert Falkner (1928-2004) was the son of John Faulkner, also an author.

89. Calhoun, *Lawmen*, 271-273; "40th Commemoration Observance," USMS Collections; Copy, Notes of Cameron, USMS Collections. Dunn, who was stationed in California, and lived in Texas, never met Deputy Same again. However, he attended the 50th anniversary ceremonies of the riot in Oxford, Mississippi in 2013.

90. Calhoun, *Lawmen*, 270; "40th Commemoration Observance," USMS Collections.

91. James Meredith met with twelve visiting retired deputies, ten of whom served during the night of the riots, in the federal courthouse during the City of Oxford's 40th commemoration ceremonies in October 2002.

92. Interview, Robert Courtright, October 6, 1993, USMS Collections; Interview, Al Butler and Willard McArdle, October 1, 2003, USMS Collections.

93. Newsletter, "Rebel Underground," Vol. 3, No. 2. Notes on the envelope revealed that a university professor turned over the letter, composed sometime just after the riots, to Deputy U.S. Marshal C.A. Smith on February 26, 1963, during the Meredith detail. State or local warrants were issued for several leaders during the Ole Miss crisis, including Chief U.S. Marshal McShane and Al Butler.

94. Ibid.; James E. Clayton, "Marshal McShane Freed After Arrest in Ole Miss Rioting," *Washington Post*, November 22, 1962.

95. "Owensville Resident Recognized for Part in 'Ole Miss' Integration," *Gasconade County Republican*, October 1, 2003. Retired Deputy U.S. Marshal Ernie Mike, who resided in Kentucky, also related to the author that family members were approached and threatened.

96. Copy, Pamphlet, Mississippi State Jr. Chamber of Commerce, Inc., *Oxford: A Warning for Americans* (Jackson, Mississippi: Electric Building, October 1962), USMS Collections.

97. Interview notes, Bennie Brake, June 25, 2008, USMS Collections.

98. Interview, Frank Vandergrift, July 10, 1985, USMS Collections.

99. Copy, Meredith, "Remarks For United States Justice Department Celebration—15 July 2003."

100. Copy, Memo, James J.P. McShane to Honorable Ray H. Hemenway, United States Marshal, St. Paul, Minnesota, July 24, 1963, USMS Collections.

101. Copy, Memo, Deputies P.D. Bowser and W.C. McArdle to James J.P. McShane, December 12, 1962, USMS Collections. Cameron's notations were initialed "JWC."

102. Copy of Memo, John W. Cameron, June 8, 1963, Tuscaloosa File, USMS Collections. Hood's name was also given as "Hunt."

103. Ibid.

104. Copy, Notes, John W. Cameron to Oxford File, August 19, 1963; Copy of Notes, John W. Cameron, June 11, 1963, Tuscaloosa File, USMS Collections. A comparison between rosters shows the similarities in personnel—likely based on experience.

105. UPI, "Wallace Prepares to Surrender to Armed Might of Federal Govt.," *Redlands [California] Daily Facts*, June 11, 1963; Editorial, "The Schoolhouse Door," *Independent [Pasadena, California]*, June 13, 1963.

106. Copy of Memo, John W. Cameron, June 20, 1963, Tuscaloosa File, USMS Collections; Copy, Notes behind copy of memo, June 20, 1963, Tuscaloosa File, USMS Collections; Copy of Memo, John W. Cameron, June 19, 1963.

107. Copy, Notes behind copy of memo, June 20, 1963, Tuscaloosa File, USMS Collections; Copy of Memo, John W. Cameron, June 27, 1963, Tuscaloosa File, USMS Collections.

108. Copy of Memo, John W. Cameron, June 28, 1963, Tuscaloosa File, USMS Collections.

109. Copy of Memo, Homer H. Henry, July 1, 1963, Tuscaloosa File, USMS Collections; Copy of Memo, John W. Cameron, June 28, 1963, Tuscaloosa File, USMS Collections.

110. Copy of Notes, John W. Cameron, July 2, 1963, Tuscaloosa File, USMS Collections; Copy of Memo, John W. Cameron, July 5, 1963, Tuscaloosa File, USMS Collections; Copy of Memo, John W. Cameron, July 15, 1963, Tuscaloosa File, USMS Collections. On July 18, Cameron was told that the Nigerian student would not go to summer school as originally thought, but would attend in the fall.

111. Copy of Memo, John W. Cameron, July 19, 1963, Tuscaloosa File, USMS Collections; Copy of Memo, John W. Cameron, July 22, 1963, Tuscaloosa File, USMS Collections; Copy of Memo, Dorothea M. Klajbor, July 30, 1963, Tuscaloosa File, USMS Collections; Copy of Memo, Dorothea M. Klajbor, August 5, 1963, Tuscaloosa File, USMS Collections; Copy of Memo, Dorothea M. Klajbor, August 12, 1963, Tuscaloosa File, USMS Collections. Note that that there were "15 or 16 crosses" burned in different places around Tuscaloosa.

112. Copy of Memo, September 18, 1963, Tuscaloosa File, USMS Collections; Copy of Memo, John W. Cameron, October 2, 1963, Tuscaloosa File, USMS Collections; Copy of Memos, John W. Cameron, October 3 and 4, 1963, Tuscaloosa File, USMS Collections; Copy of Memo, John W. Cameron, October 12, 1963, Tuscaloosa File, USMS Collections.

113. Copy of Memo, J.W. Cameron, October 14, 1963, Tuscaloosa File, USMS Collections; Copy of Memos, J.W. Cameron, October 17 and 18, 1963, Tuscaloosa File, USMS Collections; Copy of Memo, J.W. Cameron, October 21, 1963, Tuscaloosa File, USMS Collections; Copy of Memo, J.W. Cameron, October 28, 1963, Tuscaloosa File, USMS Collections; Copy of Memo, J.W. Cameron, November 8, 1963, Tuscaloosa File, USMS Collections.

114. Copy of Memo, J.W. Cameron, November 16, 1963, Tuscaloosa File, USMS Collections; Copy of Memo, J.W. Cameron, November 21, 1963,

Tuscaloosa File, USMS Collections. Dr. J. Jefferson Bennett, who served as an Assistant to the University President, did not report Governor Wallace's reaction to the bombing. He first served as a professor and assistant dean. He died in 2001, according to the *Tuscaloosa News.*

115. Copy of Memo, J.W. Cameron, December 3, 1963, Tuscaloosa File, USMS Collections; Copy of Memo, J.W. Cameron, December 10, 1963, Tuscaloosa File, USMS Collections; Copy of Memo, H.H. Henry, January 6, 1964, Tuscaloosa File, USMS Collections; Copy of Memo, J.W. Cameron, January 14, 1964, Tuscaloosa File, USMS Collections; Copy of Memo, Homer H. Henry, January 24, 1964, Tuscaloosa File, USMS Collections.

NOTES TO CHAPTER 4

1. Associated Press, "State Police and Treasury Agents Break Up Meeting of 65 Leading Members," [Helena, Montana] *Independent Record,* November 15, 1957; Associated Press, "Anastasia of Murder, Inc.—Overlord of Crime Slain," *Syracuse Herald-Journal,* October 25, 1957.

2. Associated Press, "State Police and Treasury Agents"; Orr Kelly, "How U.S. Blends Endangered Witnesses into the Landscape," *Washington Star,* April 25, 1975.

3. Notes, Telephone Interview with Ronald Messa, September 22, 2003; Copy, Timesheet dated June 18, 1970, Courtesy of Ronald Messa. Marcello was able to fight off any further deportation attempts.

4. Copy, U.S. Marshal Victor Wogan, Jr. to Chief, Executive Office for United States Marshals James J.P. McShane, April 8, 1965, USMS Collections; Copy of Memo, McShane to J.W. Cameron, April 11, 1965, USMS Collections.

5. Copy, "Foremat [*sic*] of Procedures Concerning Sequestered Jury – U.S.A. vs Carlos Marcello," Undated, USMS Collections; Copy, McShane to Wogan, May 7, 1965, USMS Collections; Copy, Wogan to McShane, July 13, 1965, USMS Collections; Copy, McShane to Wogan, July 2, 1965, USMS

Collections; Copy, Message, "JMcS" [McShane] to "JWC" [Cameron], Undated, USMS Collections; Copy, Wogan to McShane, June 23, 1965, USMS Collections.

6. Copy of Notes, Marcello Trial Sequestered Jury Detail, USMS Collections; Copy, Wogan to McShane, July 23, 1965, USMS Collections.

7. Copy of Note, Victor Wogan to McShane, Undated, Marcello Trial, USMS Collections; Copy, Layout of Rooms Assigned for Operation in the Royal-Orleans Hotel, Map, USMS Collections; Copy, "Foremat [*sic*] of Procedures Concerning Sequestered Jury – U.S.A. vs Carlos Marcello," USMS Collections.

8. Copy of Notes, Marcello Trial, USMS Collections; Copy, McShane to U.S. Attorney Louis C. LaCour, USMS Collections.

9. *Time* 52, no. 22 (November 29, 1948): 24-25; "Dave Beck to Start 5-Year Federal Prison Term Today," *Toledo Blade*, June 20, 1962.

10. Clark R. Mollenhoff, "Behind the Plot to Assassinate Robert Kennedy," *Look*, May 19, 1964, 49.

11. Mollenhoff, "Behind the Plot," 53.

12. Mollenhoff, "Behind the Plot," 53; Copy, Cameron Notes from "Nashville, TN Evidence Guard" File, USMS Collections.

13. Copy, Cameron Notes from "Partin File," December 13, 1966; See Copy, Cameron Notes from "Partin File," December 20, 1965; "Former U.S. Marshal Honored," *Taylorsville Times*, August 27, 2003.

14. Mollenhoff, "Behind the Plot," 53-54.

15. Copy, Homer H. Henry to Chattanooga File, February 4, 1964.

16. Ibid.

17. Copy, John W. Cameron to Baton Rouge File, March 9, 1964, USMS Collections; Copy, Cameron to Partin File, March 30, 1964, USMS Collections.

18. "Paskal Bowser, Ex-deputy Marshal, Dies," *San Diego Union*, February 14, 1985; Copy, Paskal Bowser to James J.P. McShane, April 6, 1964, Report of Special Assignment in Chicago, April 1-4, 1964, Re Selection and Summoning of Jurors for James R. Hoffa Trial, USMS Collections.

19. Copy, Bowser to McShane, April 6, 1964, Report of Special Assignment, Hoffa Trial, USMS Collections.

20. "Hoffa Is Sentenced to 5 Years, $10,000," Undated news clipping, ca. August 17, 1964; "Hoffa's Shadow Puts New Strains on Probe," *Washington Evening Star*, September 14, 1964.

21. Copy of Memo, Robert L. Carpenter and H.M. Henderson to Honorable J.P. McShane, September 7, 1964.

22. Ibid.

23. Copy, John W. Cameron to Partin File, September 23, 1964, USMS Collections; Copy, John W. Cameron to Partin File, September 24, 1964, USMS Collections; Copy, John W. Cameron to Partin File, September 28, 1964, USMS Collections.

24. Copy, James J.P. McShane to North Carolina Middle Louisiana Eastern File, October 14, 1964, USMS Collections; Copy, John W. Cameron to Partin File, December 9, 1964, USMS Collections.

25. Copy, John W. Cameron to Partin File, December 2, 1964, USMS Collections; Copy, John W. Cameron to Partin File, December 9, 1964, USMS Collections; Copy, John W. Cameron to Partin File, December 21, 1964, USMS Collections; Copy, Deputy U.S. Marshal Jesse W. Grider to Chief U.S. Marshal James J.P. McShane, December 28, 1964, USMS Collections.

26. Copy, Ed Partin to Deputy U.S. Marshal Dick Smith, as sent to Jack Cameron, December 21, 1964, USMS Collections.

27. Copy, John W. Cameron to Partin File, January 11, 1965, USMS Collections; Copy, John W. Cameron to Partin File, March 29, 1965, USMS Collections.

28. Copy, John W. Cameron to Partin File, March 29, 1965, USMS Collections.

29. Copy, John W. Cameron to Partin File, July 6, 1965, USMS Collections.

30. *Congressional Record*, Appendix, October 22, 1965, A6083.

31. Copy of Memorandum, Paskal D. Bowser to Request File, April 28, 1967, with Undated Clipping, USMS Collections.

32. Copy, Paskal Bowser to Special Assignment, May 4, 1967, USMS Collections; Copy, "Court Detail Hoffa Hearing," [U.S. Marshal Harry D. Mansfield], USMS Collections.

33. "Hoffa Sentenced to Five Years," *Arizona Republic*, September 23, 1967; Copy, Myrl E. Alexander, Dir., Bureau of Prisons to Warren Christopher, Deputy Attorney General, September 20, 1967, USMS Collections.

34. Copy, Report of P.D. Bowser, Chief Special Assignment Section, 19 June 1969, USMS Collections; Orville Trotter, "The 'Crime' of a Good Dinner," *Manchester Union Leader*, June 20, 1969.

35. "Threat to Kill Valachi at Hearings Revealed," *Milwaukee Journal*, October 8, 1963. A number of photographs reveal that McShane was seated next to Valachi in the Congressional hearings. For background, see "Joseph Valachi," *Encyclopedia Britannica*, www.britannica.com.

36. Photographer Thornell won the 1967 Pulitzer Prize for the photograph of Meredith. Caroline Kleiner Butler, "Down in Mississippi," *Smithsonian Magazine*, February 2005; Copy, John W. Cameron to James J.P. McShane, June 16, 1966, USMS Collections.

37. Copy, Cameron to McShane, June 16, 1966, USMS Collections.

38. Copy, Standby Emergency Group Listing, June 16, 1966, USMS Collections.

39. Nichalas von Hoffman and Dan Morgan, "Rally of 12,000 Ends Jackson March," *Washington Post*, June 27, 1966.

40. Copy, Certificate of Acceptance of Liability, AFR 76-28, USMS Collections; Copy, James J.P. McShane to U.S. Marshal Frank Udoff, District of Maryland, July 5, 1966, USMS Collections; Copy, James J.P. McShane to U.S. Marshal Luke C. Moore, Washington, D.C., July 6, 1966, USMS Collections.

41. Ibid.; "Rally of 12,000," *Washington Post*, June 27, 1966.

42. Ibid. Carmichael was one of the key leaders of the Black Panthers.

43. Copy, J.P. McShane to Honorable Silvio O. Conte, February 7, 1966, USMS Collections.

44. Copy of Release, "Text of Remarks by the President to U.S. Marshals Conference," Office of the White House Press Secretary, September 27, 1966, USMS Collections.

45. Ibid.

46. Copy, James J.P. McShane to Mr. Ramsey Clark, Acting Attorney General, October 13, 1966, USMS Collections.

47. "Nazi Leader Rockwell Shot Down by Sniper," *Harrisonburg Daily News*, August 26, 1967; Joseph E. Mohbat, "Order Halts Rockwell Rites," *Petersburg Progress Index*, August 29, 1967.

48. Copy of Special Assignment File, Paskal D. Bowser, "Funeral of George Lincoln Rockwell," August 29, 1967, USMS Collections.

49. Ibid.

50. Ibid.

51. Ibid.

52. Copy of Special Assignment File, Paskal D. Bowser to James J.P. McShane, August 30, 1967, USMS Collections.

53. Ibid.

54. Ibid.; "Army Prevents Rockwell Burial with Nazi Rites in Culpeper Grave," *Washington Post*, August 30, 1967.

55. Copy of Special Assignment File, Bowser to McShane, August 30, 1967, USMS Collections; "Army Prevents Rockwell Burial with Nazi Rites," *Washington Post*, August 30, 1967.

56. Ibid.

57. Copy of Special Assignment File, Bowser to Operation Pentagon, October 18, 1967, USMS Collections.

58. Copy, List of Assignment Personnel, Pentagon File, Undated, USMS Collections. The deputized female guards were also known as "matrons."

59. Calhoun, *Lawmen,* 279; Norman Mailer, *The Armies of the Night* (New York: New American Library, 1968); Press Release, Department of Justice, November 13, 1967, USMS Collections.

60. Copy, James J.P. McShane to Honorable George Bush, October 26, 1967, USMS Collections.

61. Copy, John W. Cameron to File, November 8, 1967, USMS Collections; Copy, P.D. Bowser to James J.P. McShane, November 1, 1967, USMS Collections.

62. Calhoun, *Lawmen,* 206-207.

63. See Mailer, *The Armies of the Night,* 144.

64. Ibid. Mailer noted on pages 146-147 about his actual arrest and his inquiry of the background of one of the deputies.

NOTES TO CHAPTER 5

1. Copy, Memorandum of Paskal D. Bowser, March 26, 1968, USMS Collections; Copy, U.S. Marshal Cato Ellis to Hon. James J.P. McShane, Memorandum, April 1, 1968, USMS Collections.

2. Bill Dries, "Judge Brown Dies; Ordered School Integration," *Memphis Commercial Appeal,* October 7, 2004; Lela Garlington, "Versatile, Busy Cato Ellis Was Once U.S. Marshal," *Memphis Commercial Appeal,*

September 22, 1995. U.S. Marshal Ellis' son informed the author that he felt "ambushed" by the photographers and was not happy being in the picture.

3. Copy, Civil Case C-68-60, United States District Court for the Western District of Tennessee, Western Division, April 5, 1968.

4. Copy, Notes of Cameron, Request File, Western District of Tennessee, April 6, 1968, USMS Collections.

5. Ibid.

6. Copy, Flyer,"Community on the Move for Equality," March 8, 1968, USMS Collections.

7. Ibid.

8. Copy, Notes of Cameron, Request File, April 6, 1968, USMS Collections.

9. Copy, Memorandum, U.S. Marshal Luke C. Moore to Honorable James J.P. McShane, April 11, 1968, USMS Collections; Denise Kersten Wills, "'People Were Out of Control': Remembering the 1968 Riots," *Washingtonian,* April 1, 2008; Daniela Deane, "H Street NE, the Next Hot Spot," *Washington Post,* June 12, 2004.

10. Associated Press, "Kennedy Is Dead from Killer Shot," *Southern Illinoisan,* June 6, 1968; Associated Press, "Kennedy Extremely Critical," *Findlay [Ohio] Republican Courier,* June 6, 1968.

11. Presentation, Al Butler, "Reflections on Two American Icons: Robert F. Kennedy and Martin Luther King, Jr. 1968-2008," December 3, 2008, Department of Justice. Al Butler was one of several speakers at this event.

12. Paul Clancy, "Fired up: Catonsville Files Plus Nine Hearts; 25th Anniverary of 'Suffering Love.'—May 17, 1968 Burning of Selective Service Records in Catonsville, Maryland," *National Catholic Reporter,* May 21, 1993; Edward Duff, "Why Are You Not Here? Bearing the Burden of the Berrigan Brothers," *New Republic,* March 6, 1971.

13. Jack Nelson and Ronald J. Ostrow, *The FBI and the Berrigans* (New York: Coward, McCann & Geoghegan, Inc., 1972), 50-51, 53-54; Duff, "Why Are You Not Here?"

14. Copy, Subpoena to Mrs. Mary E. Murphy, United States District Court, October 2, 1968, Friends of Catonsville Library Collection, Catonsville, Maryland; Nelson and Ostrow, *The FBI and the Berrigans*, 54-55; Daniel Berrigan, *The Trial of the Catonsville Nine* (Boston: Beacon Press), back cover, ix; Nelson and Ostrow, *FBI*, 55.

15. Robert Davis, "The Chicago Seven Trial and the 1968 Democratic National Convention," *Chicago Tribune*, September 24, 1969; Robert McG. Thomas Jr., "Mitchell Goodman, Antiwar Protest Leader, Dies at 73," February 6, 1997, *New York Times;* Book Review, "The Trial of the Boston Five," *Eugene Register-Guard,* September 14, 1969.

16. Copy of Contract, May 10, 1968 between U.S. Department of Interior and National Coordinator of Washington Poor People's Campaign and Southern Christian Leadership Conference; Copy, Blueprint of Plan, USMS Collections.

17. Copies of Memorandum, John W. Cameron to U.S. Marshal Luke C. Moore, May 13, 1968 and June 10, 1968, USMS Collections.

18. Ibid.; Copy of letter, *American People Should Know the Facts About the Treaty of Guadalupe Hidalgo*, USMS Collections.

19. Copy of Memorandum, Paskal D. Bowser to Poor People's Campaign File, June 20, 1968.

20. *United States Marshals Bulletin*, No. 79, December 15, 1965, flyleaf page; "Introduction," *United States Marshals Bulletin*, No. 81, January 1, 1969, 12; "Miss Klajbor Transfers to the L.E.A.A.," *United States Marshals Bulletin*, No. 81, January 1, 1969, 6. The Election of 1968, which brought about a Republican Administration under President-Elect Richard M. Nixon, was said to have further eroded McShane's authority. There were also rumors he would be replaced.

21. Interview, Michael McShane, June 13, 2003, USMS Collections; Associated Press, "Top Marshal Dies," *Tucson Daily Citizen*, December 25, 1968.

22. Interview, Michael McShane, June 13, 2003, USMS Collections.

23. Ibid.; Interview, Bill Hall, April 6, 2005, USMS Collections; "Ms. Klajbor Transfers to the L.E.A.A.," *United States Marshals Bulletin,* No. 81, January 1, 1969, 6. Jack Cameron was Acting Chief U.S. Marshal in the months-long gap between McShane and Turner. Cameron departed the agency in May 1969, but would return.

24. Press Release, Department of Justice, March 24, 1969, USMS Collections.

25. Copy, Carl C. Turner to Richard G. Kleindienst, March 28, 1969, USMS Collections; Copy, Carl C. Turner to Mark D. Biallas, May 7, 1969, USMS Collections.

26. Copy of Memorandum, Deputy Chief United States Marshals Donald A. Synnott to All United States Marshals, May 9, 1969, USMS Collections; Interview, Bill Hall, April 6, 2005, USMS Collections.

27. Interview, Bill Hall, July 30, 1986, USMS Collections.

28. Copy of Memorandum, Deputy Chief United States Marshal Donald A. Synnott to All United States Marshals, May 9, 1969, USMS Collections; Interview, Bill Hall, April 6, 2005, USMS Collections.

29. Interview, Bill Hall, April 6, 2005, USMS Collections; Copy, Carl C. Turner to John W. Cameron, May 5, 1969, USMS Collections. Hall was initially hired with Cameron as his supervisor, although Synnott's Memorandum of May 9, 1969 announced that he would assume Cameron's duties.

30. Release, "TITLE 28-JUDICIAL ADMINISTRATION CHAPTER I-DEPARTMENT OF JUSTICE, Order No. 415-69," May 21, 1969, USMS Collections. Another clipped version of a general release dated May 12 —probably by mistake—is often confused with this document.

31. Ibid.

32. Copy of U.S. Marshals Circular (USMC), 69-2 "The Road Ahead," June 12, 1969, USMS Collections; Interview, Bill Hall, April 6, 2005, USMS Collections. This was confirmed by numerous retirees from the era.

33. Copy of U.S. Marshals Circular (USMC), 69-2 "The Road Ahead," June 12, 1969, USMS Collections.

34. Ibid.

35. Ibid.; Interview, Bill Hall, April 6, 2005, USMS Collections.

36. Interview, Bill Hall, July 30, 1986, USMS Collections.

37. Interview, Al Butler and Willard McArdle, October 1, 2003, USMS Collections.

38. Ibid.; Interview, Bill Hall, April 6, 2005, USMS Collections; "Reis R. Kash Biographical Statement, November 1, 1975," Attachment to Kenneth C. Holecko to William E. Hall, December 1, 1975, USMS Collections; Copy, Deputy Chief U.S. Marshal Donald A. Synnott to All United States Marshals, April 2, 1969, USMS Collections.

39. Copy, Synnott to All Marshals, April 2, 1969, USMS Collections; Copy of Memorandum, Carl C. Turner to All U.S. Marshals, April 3, 1969; Interview, Al Butler and Willard McArdle, October 1, 2003, USMS Collections.

40. Copy, William J. Neptune to William H. O'Donoghue, August 5, 1969; Copy, Carl C. Turner to William H. O'Donoghue, August 22, 1969, USMS Collections.

41. Interview, Al Butler and Willard McArdle, October 1, 2003, USMS Collections; "Armed Forces: The Military Mafia," *Time*, October 17, 1969; Ramsey Clark, "Watergate: A Brush with Tyranny," June 4, 1973, *Nation* 216, no. 23.

42. Interview, Bill Hall, April 6, 2005, USMS Collections. A nearly exact account is presented in Calhoun, *Lawmen*, 292.

43. Ibid.; Copy, USMS Circular 69-7, September 3, 1969, USMS Collections; Stephen G. Tompkins, "Army Feared King, Secretly Watched Him," *Memphis Commercial Appeal*, March 21, 1993.

44. Richard Pearson, "Retired Army Carl C. Turner, 83, Dies," *Washington Post*, January 1, 1997; Record of Graves, Carl C. Turner, Arlington National Cemetery, Section 7, Site 10050.

NOTES TO CHAPTER 6

1. Copy, Department of Justice Order 415-69, USMS Collections.

2. "Californian Named Chief of Marshals," *Washington Star*, January 12, 1970; Synnott remained as deputy director until approximately February 1971. Although mentioned in the January 1971 newsletter, he departed soon after. See copy, United States Marshals Service Circular 71-5, February 8, 1971, USMS Collections.

3. "Director of the United States Marshals Service," in *United States Marshals: 1789 to Present;* Calhoun, *Lawmen*, 292.

4. "California Southern—Wayne B. Colburn," in "New Marshals," *United States Marshals Bulletin*, No. 80, April 1, 1967, Item 7; United *States Marshals: 1789 to Present.*

5. Copy, Release, Department of Justice, January 12, 1970, USMS Collections; Copy, Biographical Sheet, U.S. Marshals Service, 1970, USMS Collections; "Colburn Due for Job of U.S. Marshals," *San Diego Union-Tribune*, January 11, 1970.

6. Ibid.

7. Ibid.

8. Ibid.

9. Calhoun, *Lawmen*, 292-293. A great example can be found in the first independent newsletter of the USMS in September 1970, where

he introduced the newsletter with his statement that "communication between Washington D.C. and our 93 field offices has always been in my opinion a major weakness in our Service."

10. "U.S. Marshals Service New Headquarters Facility," *United States Marshals Service Newsletter,* Vol. 14, October 1971, 1.

11. Calhoun, *Lawmen,* 291-293.

12. "U.S. Marshals Service New Headquarters Facility."

13. Interview, Elizabeth Howard, January 29, 2013, USMS Collections.

14. Interview, Bill Hall, July 30, 1986, USMS Collections; Interview, Bill Hall, April 6, 2005, USMS Collections; "Californian Named Chief of Marshals," *Washington Star,* January 12, 1970.

15. Copy, United States Marshal Service Directive 70-8, September 2, 1970, U.S. Marshals Collections.

16. Ibid.

17. Copy, Memorandum, Charles M. Odell to Mr. O.T. Berkman, January 8, 1971, "Delegation of Authority"; Outline, "Personnel Office-U.S. Marshals Service."

18. Interview, Bill Hall, July 30, 1986, USMS Collections.

Notes to Chapter 7

1. "'Dynamite' Ruse Backfires," *Las Vegas Sun,* July 5, 1968.

2. Copy, U.S. Marshal Beverly W. Perkins to Chief, Executive Office for U.S. Marshals James J.P. McShane, July 5, 1968; "'Dynamite' Ruse Backfires," *Las Vegas Sun,* July 5, 1968.

3. Copy, U.S. Marshal Beverly W. Perkins to Chief, Executive Office for U.S. Marshals James J.P. McShane, July 5, 1968.

4. United States Marshal Service Directive 69-9, 24 October 1969. See also "USMS pioneered the Air Marshal Program," *The Marshals Monitor*, January-February 2002, 1.

5. Ibid.

6. Copy, Memorandum, John T. Brophy to Reis R. Kash, 10 June 1970, "PROPOSED USMS DIRECTIVE – Subject: Supplement to U.S.M.D. 69-9, Anti-Hijacking Support," USMS Collections. See also "USMS Pioneered the Air Marshal Program," *The Marshals Monitor*, January-February 2002, 1.

7. Glen D. King, "Guidelines Issued by FCC for Air Security," *Police Chief*, May 1971, 22; Copy, Memorandum, Wayne B. Colburn to All United States Marshals Concerned, April 23, 1971, "Anti-Air Piracy Personnel Policy," USMS Collections.

8. Copy, Memorandum, John T. Brophy to William E. Hall, January 7, 1971, "Concurrent Jurisdiction Anti-Air Piracy Program," USMS Collections; Copy, Memorandum, Wayne B. Colburn to United States Marshals, January 25, 1971, "Anti-Air Piracy Program," USMS Collections; Copy, Memorandum, John T. Brophy to William E. Hall, February 1, 1971, "Marshal support for Anti-air Piracy Program," USMS Collections; Copy, Memorandum, Wayne B. Colburn to All United States Marshals Concerned, April 23, 1971, "Anti-Air Piracy Personnel Policy," USMS Collections.

9. "Progress in War on Skyjackers," *U.S. News and World Report*, August 9, 1971, 25. The program involved both FAA and the USMS, and under the umbrella of the Secretary of Transportation. It drew sources from both organizations.

10. Ibid.

11. Copy, Director Wayne B. Colburn to General Benjamin O. Davis, September 14, 1971, USMS Collections.

12. *United States Marshals Service Newsletter*, October 1971, 3.

13. Ibid.

14. Interview, Dave Neff, May 1, 1991, USMS Collections.

15. Interview, Jesse Grider, September 20, 1991, USMS Collections.

16. Ibid.

17. Ibid.

18. *United States Marshals Service Newsletter,* November 1970, 1; Copy, "Talking Paper on USMS Witness Security Program, June 1996.

19. See Janet Maslin, "Eraser," *New York Times,* June 21, 1996; Gary Tischler, "James Gandolfini: More than Tony Soprano, and Yet," *Georgetowner,* June 20, 2013.

20. "O'Dwyer Goes Before Grand Jury in Brooklyn Today," *Lowell Sun,* via International New Service.

21. G. Milton Kelly, "Teamster Boss to 'Talk,'" *Nashua Telegraph,* November 16, 1957; "Valachi: Hoodlums could buy into Cosa Nostra for $40,000," UPI [ck], October 3, 1963; Interview, Butler and McArdle, October 1, 2003, St. Louis, Missouri.

22. Interview, Butler and McArdle, October 1, 2003, St. Louis, Missouri.

23. Copy, "Talking Paper on USMS Witness Security Program," June 1996 Revision. See Pete Earley and Gerald Shur, *WITSEC: Inside the Federal Witness Protection Program* (New York: Bantam Books, 2002); Fact Sheet on Witness Protection Program, USMS.

24. Earley and Shur, *WITSEC,* 55; Ibid., 59-62.

25. Orr Kelly, "How U.S. Blends Endangered Witnesses into the Landscape," *Washington Star,* April 25, 1975.

26. See Fact Sheet on Witness Protection Program, USMS.

27. Jerry Landauer, "Culebrians Fire Back: Islanders Seek to End Role as a Navy Target-Shells Fall Close to Governor of Puerto Rico," *Wall Street Journal,* June 10, 1970; Interview, Hall, April 6, 2005, USMS Collections; Calhoun, *Lawmen,* 297.

28. Interview, Hall, April 6, 2005, USMS Collections; Calhoun, *Lawmen*, 297.

29. "Culebra," in *United States Marshals Service Newsletter* 6 (February 1971): 2-3; Interview, Hall, July 30, 1986, USMS Collections.

30. Interview, Hall, April 6, 2005, USMS Collections; Calhoun, *Lawmen*, 297; Copy of Draft, Calhoun and Lou Stagg, "History of the Special Operations Group," October 17, 1994, USMS Collections.

31. Calhoun and Stagg,"History of the Special Operations Group."

32. Calhoun, *Lawmen*, 297; Calhoun and Stagg, "History of the Special Operations Group."

33. Interview, Hall, April 6, 2005, USMS Collections.

34. Ibid.

35. Interview, Hall, July 30, 1986, USMS Collections;*United States Marshals Service Newsletter,* Volume 14, October 1971, 2.

36. *United States Marshals Service Newsletter*, Volume 14, October 1971, 2.

37. Copy, Memorandum, John H. Lockie, General Counsel, to Director Wayne B. Colburn, September 4, 1973, USMS Collections.

38. Ibid. SOG can be utilized without a judicial order, but this particular instance included one.

39. "Transpo '72," *United States Marshals Service Newsletter*, June 1972, 6.

40. Copy, Marshal Raymond J. Howard to Reis R. Kash, October 12, 1970, USMS Collections; *Milwaukee Sentinel*, August 17, 1970.

41. Ibid.

42. "Deputies Seize $21 Million in Gems," *Pentacle*, June 1978, 8.

43. Copy, U.S. Marshal Gaylord L. Campbell to Director Wayne B. Colburn, October 20, 1971, USMS Collections.

44. "Public Information," *Marshal Today* 37 (November/December 1973): 15. Rice was a reserve Green Beret and former Vietnam veteran with the 101st Airborne Division. His official appointment date was November 12, 1973.

45. Copy, Christian H. Rice to Richard Landau, September 12, 1974, USMS Collections. See Copy, Edward Hymoff to Christian N. Rice, April 1, 1975, USMS Collections.

46. " 'Big Six' Henderson Retires," *The Gimlet Edmonson News*, October 2, 1975; James M. Day, *Captain Clint Peoples—Texas Ranger Fifty Years a Lawman* (Waco, TX: Texian Press, 1980), 162.

47. Richard Cox, "The Growing Role of the U.S. Marshall," *Los Angeles Herald-Examiner*, September 24, 1971.

48. "Public Information," *The Marshals Today* 37 (November/December 1973): 15; Ibid., 2; U.S. Department of Justice, *United States Marshals Bulletin*, No. 1, November 1, 1946; U.S. Marshals Service, Newsletter, Number 1, September 1970. *The Marshals Today* replaced the newsletter, but kept its numbering—so the first issue is Volume 37. *The Pentacle* began in January 1978.

49. *The Pentacle* began in 1978 with Susan Olson as editor. Beverly Dodd was first mentioned as managing editor in the January-February 1980 issue, although Olson remained as editor for a time. *The Pentacle* lasted until December 1991.

Notes to Chapter 8

1. Arthur T. Burton, *Black, Red, and Deadly* (Austin, TX: Eakin Press, 1991), 3, 144, 150-153.

2. Copy, Overview of Research Guide, "American Indian Movement (AIM)," Minnesota Historical Society Library; "Indians and Supplies Pouring Into Alcatraz," *Oakland Tribune [Sunday]*, November 30, 1969; Adam Fortunate Eagle, *Alcatraz! Alcatraz!* (Berkeley, CA: Heyday Books,

1992), 14-15, 17-18; F.J. Clauss, *Alcatraz Island of Many Mistakes* (Menlo Park, CA: Briarcliff Press, 1981), 55. The claim was based on the money offered to tribes in California after the Gold Rush, likely the Verona Band. The Sioux pressed the claim on behalf of those tribes.

3. Clauss, *Alcatraz*, 55-57; Fortunate Eagle, *Alcatraz! Alcatraz!*, 107-110.

4. "Report on the Reoccupation of Alcatraz by the United States Marshals Service on June 11," *United States Marshals Service Newsletter* 10 (June 1971): 23.

5. Ibid.

6. Ibid.

7. Ibid.

8. *United States Marshals Service Newsletter,* October 1971, 2.

9. Ibid., 7.

10. Ibid.

11. Interview Notes, Carl Parish, June 20, 2003, USMS Collections.

12. Copy, Memorandum, J.W. Cameron to Mr. Sidella, October 19, 1971, USMS Collections.

13. Calhoun, *The Lawmen*, 299; Peter Osmos and Raul Ramirez, "500 Indians Here Seize U.S. Building," *Washington Post*, November 3, 1972.

14. *Washington Post*, November 3, 1972.

15. Eugene L. Meyer, "Indians Seize Files as Some Go Home," *Washington Post*, November 8, 1972; Grayson Mitchell, "Indians Find Living in BIA 'Miserable,'" *Washington Post*, November 8, 1972. These two stories were moved to the "Metro" section of the newspaper, which was a marked shift from front page stories from November 3-7, 1972.

16. Osmos & Ramirez, "500 Indians Here Seize U.S. Building," *Washington Post*, November 3, 1972; Raul Ramirez, "Indians Continue Occu-

pation of BIA," *Washington Post*, November 4, 1972; Donald P. Baker and Raul Ramirez, "Officials, Indians Parley on Protest," *Washington Post*, November 5, 1972; Paul Hodge, "Another 'Wounded Knee' Was Feared Friday Night," *Washington Post*, November 5, 1972.

17. Interview, Reis Kash, February 7, 1985, USMS Collections; Calhoun, *Lawmen*, 299.

18. Telephone Interview, Bill Hall, January 25, 2005; Calhoun, *Lawmen*, 299.

19. "Indians, Historians Criticize Army Report on Wounded Knee," *The Daily [Fergus Falls, Minnesota] Journal*, December 30, 1975; Dee Brown, 'Lightning Crash' at Wounded Knee, 1890," *Journal [Hamilton, Ohio] News*, August 14, 1971. AIM also clashed with the management of the reservation and strongly opposed the tribal president. Some of the Sioux residing there agreed with AIM.

20. "Marshal Is Shot at Wounded Knee," *Stars and Stripes*, March 28, 1973; Frank Macomber, "Wounded Knee Impasse Hurts Tribe's Economy," *Colorado Springs Gazette*, April 12, 1973; Terry DeVine, "Wounded Knee Seige [sic] Ends," *Estherville [IA] Daily News*, April 6, 1973; Calhoun, *Lawmen*, 300-301.

21. Calhoun, *Lawmen*, 300; "FBI Battles with Indians," *Santa Fe New Mexican*, February 28,1973; Field Spotlight, *Pentacle*, November-December 1980, 13.

22. Telephone Interview, Bill Hall, January 25, 2005; "U.S. Marshal Wounded in Gunfight at 'Knee,'" *Indianapolis News*, March 27, 1973; "U.S. Marshal Is Shot in Chest in Wounded Knee Gunfire," *Rocky Mountain News*, March 27, 1973. See Copy, Susan L.M. Huck, *Renegades: The Second Battle of Wounded Knee* (Belmont, MA: American Opinion, April 12, 1973). According to news accounts, Wilcox was outspoken against AIM actions on the reservation. There was bodily trauma, but the car had no dents, only damage from the flames.

23. Calhoun, *Lawmen*, 302-303; Copy, *United States Marshals Service Newsletter* 31 (April-May 1973): 1. Calhoun noted that part of the settlement was to repair the trench work and bunkers built during the operation.

24. *United States Marshals Service Newsletter* 32 (June 1973): 1; Copy, Memo, John W. Cameron to Colburn, August 8, 1973, USMS Collections; Copy, Memo, Director Colburn to All United States Marshals, August 9, 1973, USMS Collections.

25. Copy, Copy, "Part II: Transition to Bureau Activities Background," USMS Collections.

26. Copy, Organizational Chart, ca. January 1974, USMS Collections; Copy of Message, Wayne B. Colburn to All United States Marshals, August 1, 1973, USMS Collections.

27. Copy, Memo, John W. Cameron to Colburn, August 8, 1973, USMS Collections; Copy, Memo, Director Colburn to All United States Marshals, August 9, 1973; Copy, Two Way Memo Colburn to All U.S. Marshals, May 22, 1973; "So Long," *United States Marshals Service Newsletter* 30 (March 30, 1973).

28. Ibid.

29. Copy, "The Saturday Night Massacre October 20, 1973," Retired Deputy U.S. Marshal Melvin McDowell, USMS Collections.

30. Ibid.

31. Copy, "Tocks Island Background Sheet," USMS Collections.

32. Ibid.

33. Ibid.

34. Copy, William C. Whitworth Memorandum 71-158-CD-20, August 30, 1971, USMS Collections.

35. "Squatters Evicted—Tocks Island Dam Project," *Marshals Today*, March/April 1974, 3; "U.S. Marshals Evict Dam Squatters," *Pittsburgh Post-Gazette*, February 28, 1974; "U.S. Marshals Evict Squatters From Tocks Island," *Philadelphia Inquirer*, February 28, 1974.

36. Editorial, "Tocks Island Niceties," *The Evening Bulletin [Philadelphia, PA area]*, March 4, 1974; "Squatters Evicted—Tock's Island Dam Project," *Marshals Today*, March/April 1974, 3; Copy, Press Release, Department of Justice, February 27, 1974; Copy, Letter of Information, USMS Collections; "Tocks Squatters were Lawless," *Philadelphia Inquirer*, March 16, 1974; "Tocks Island Facts," Letters to the Editor, *New York Times*, March 23, 1974.

37. "Squatters Evicted," *Marshals Today*, March/April 1974, 3; "U.S. Marshals Evict Squatters," *The Pocono Record*, February 28, 1974; "U.S. Ousts Tocks Squatters," *New York Daily News*, Undated Clipping, USMS Collections.

38. "Squatters Evicted," *Marshals Today*, March/April 1974, 3.

39. Interview, Donald Waite, August 30, 2004, USMS Collections; Copy, Letter, U.S. Marshal George K. McKinney to Donald Waite, December 9, 1974, USMS Collections.

40. Copy of Receipt, United States District Court for the District of Columbia, Miscellaneous No. 47-73, to Deputy U.S. Marshal Donald Waite, March 7, 1974. Courtesy of Donald Waite.

41. Ibid.

42. "As Marshal, Smith Part of History in Making," *Greenville News*, February 14, 2001.

43. *New York Times*, April 19, 1974.

44. "Md.'s New U.S. Marshal Takes Heat, Keeps Cool; He Once Delivered Watergate Tape Subpoena to Nixon," *Baltimore Sun*, October 23, 1995.

45. Ibid.

46. Ibid.

47. Copy, Reis R. Kash,"Cell Block Seizure," USMS Collections.

48. Ibid.; "Cellblock Takeover," *Marshal Today,* December 1974, 9-11; "2 Seize Hostages At Court," *Washington Post,* July 12, 1974.

49. Ibid.

50. Ibid.

51. Ibid.

52. Kash, "Cell Block Seizure"; "2 Seize Hostages At Court," *Washington Post,* July 12, 1974; "Deputy Marshal's Daring Plan Enabled 7 to Slip to Freedom," *Washington Post,* July 15, 1974.

53. "Deputy Marshal's Daring Plan Enabled 7 to Slip to Freedom," *Washington Post,* July 15, 1974; Kash, "Cell Block Seizure." Jones went to trial in December 1974, followed by Gorham in April 1975. See "Wilkerson Denies Kidnap in July Cellblock Siege," *Washington Star-News,* December 5, 1974; "Gorham Trial Opens Here," *Washington Star,* April 9, 1975.

54. "Cost of Cellblock Takeover Already Exceeds $300,000," *Washington Star-News,* July 18, 1974.

55. Copy of Release, Office of Senator Edward M. Kennedy, July 24, 1974; Copy, Senator Edward M. Kennedy to Chris Rice, July 25, 1974, USMS Collections.

56. *New York Times,* August 16, 1974; *New York Times,* August 17, 1974.

57. "Subpoena for Nixon Awaiting 'Time and Place,' Officer Says," *Los Angeles Times,* August 21, 1974.

58. *New York Times,* August 28, 1974; "Subpoena for Nixon," *Los Angeles Times,* August 21, 1974.

59. "U.S. to Pay Costs in Indians' Trial," *New York Times,* January 15, 1974; "Lawyers for Means, Banks to Seek Dismissal of Charges," *Minneapolis Tribune,* January 8, 1974; "AIM Defense to Watch Possible Jurors Closely," *Minneapolis Tribune,* January 8, 1974.

60. "Defendants Call Trial Focus of Indians' Struggle," *Minneapolis Tribune*, January 8, 1974.

61. Gerald Vizenor, "Those Searches at the St. Paul Trial," *Minneapolis Tribune*, January 30, 1974, attached to Copy, U.S. Marshal Harry D. Berglund to Office of the Director [William E. Hall, Deputy Director], January 30, 1974, USMS Collections.

62. Ibid.

63. Martin Waldron, "Witness Testifies No Firearms Were Found at Wounded Knee," *New York Times*, February 28, 1974; Dennis Cassano, "Marshal Testifies He Found 'Trip-bomb,'" *Minneapolis Tribune*, February 28, 1974.

64. "Lawyers for 2 Indians Seek Curbs on Marshals," *New York Times*, August 19, 1974.

65. "Defense Rests in Trail of 2 AIM Leaders," *Washington Post*, August 17, 1974.

66. "Mace Fired in Wounded Knee Trial," *Washington Post*, August 24, 1974.

67. Martin Waldron, "Dismissal Urged in Indians' Trial," *New York Times*, September 16, 1974; Martin Waldron, "Indians in Take-Over Free as Judge Criticizes F.B.I.," *New York Times*, September 17, 1974; Orr Kelly, "U.S. Appeals Indian Case," *Star-News*, December 20, 1974. The decision was upheld.

68. "40 Indians Accept Amnesty and End Plant Occupation," *New York Times*, March 4, 1975; Release, Department of Justice, Friday, May 23, 1975.

NOTES TO CHAPTER 9

1. Copy, "Regionalization: A Brief Review," in "Alternative Plan for Regionalization of the United States Marshals Service," William Hall to Attorney General Griffin B. Bell, undated, USMS Collections.

2. Copy, John W. Cameron, Associate Director for Witness Security to Donald D. Hill, Associate Director for Administration, June 17, 1974, USMS Collections.

3. Copy of Memorandum, Wayne B. Colburn to Attorney General Edward H. Levi, March 6, 1975, USMS Collections; Copy, "Introduction" in Department of Justice, Office of Management and Finance Task Force on the Regionalization of the U.S.M.S.[sic], *The Management, Staffing and Organization of the United States Marshals Service: A Critical Analysis,* USMS Collections.

4. Copy of Memorandum, Wayne B. Colburn to Attorney General Edward H. Levi, March 6, 1975, USMS Collections. Although largely planned, few moves happened. The only regional move that started was for the regional office located in Virginia.

5. Copy, "Regionalization: A Brief Review," in "Alternative Plan for Regionalization," Hall to Bell, Undated, USMS Collections; Copy, Cameron to Hill, June 17 1974, USMS Collections.

6. "Prisoner Coordination-1975," *The Marshal Today* 44 (September 1975): 3-4.

7. Ibid., 4-5.

8. Mitch Himaka, "3 Women Become First U.S. Deputies," *San DiegoUnion-Tribune*, August 10, 1971; Copy, Letter, Director Wayne B. Colburn to Mr. and Mrs. Ernest S. Mike, June 19, 1974; "Women in the U.S. Marshals Service," *Marshals Today*, May 1975, 4-7. Incidentally, Himaka was incorrect about the subject of his article as the first national female deputies. There were female deputies in the 1890s. Anna Ruth Mike passed away in January 2006.

9. "Prisoner Coordination—1975," *Marshal Today*, September 1975, 5; "New Prisoner Transportation Division Opens," *Pentacle*, June-July 1979, 1; "Focus on...the Prisoner Coordination Division," *Pentacle*, January-

February 1980, 8-9; "A Look at the New Prisoner Airlift Program," *Pentacle*, June-July 1979, 8.

10. Copy, "Wayne B. Colburn to Norman Carlson [Director, Bureau of Prisons]," January 23, 1974, USMS Collections; Copy, "Wayne B. Colburn and Norman A. Carlson [Director, Bureau of Prisons] to all U.S. Marshals and Federal Prison Wardens and Superintendents," Feb 4, 1974, USMS Collections.

11. "How U.S. Blends Endangered Witnesses Into the Landscape," *Washington Star*, April 25, 1975.

12. Ibid.

13. Ibid. The 90-day target was a goal, but not always a "one size fits all" strategy.

14. Paul Hoffman, "How the Cops Hide Mafia Informers," *Argosy*, May 1975.

15. Copy, Press Release, Department of Justice, July 9, 1975, USMS Collections.

16. Copy, Typed Notes, Jack Cameron, Guam File, Undated, USMS Collections; "201 Viet Refugees Start Return Trip," *Washington Post*, July 4, 1975.

17. Gary Comerford,"S.C. Marshal to Oversee Viet Security On Guam," *The Columbia Record*, July 17, 1975.

18. Norman Pearlstine, "Refugees Trying to Return to South Vietnam Wait on Guam and Blame U.S. for Long Delay," *Wall Street Journal*, August 28, 1975; "U.S. Marshals Injured by Viets," *Los Angeles Herald*, September 1, 1975; Pat McElroy, "Congressmen Talk To Refugees," *Pacific Daily News*, August 7, 1975.

19. "Guam Wants to Isolate Repatriates,"*Washington Star-News*, September 8, 1975;"Refugees to be flown to Guam," *Washington Star-News*, September 17, 1975.

20. Interview, Willard McArdle and Al Butler, October 1, 2003, USMS Collections.

21. Ibid.

22. Murrey Marder, "U.S. to Let 1,600 Return to Vietnam," *Washington Post*, October 1, 1975; "1,546 Vietnamese Go Home on a Vessel from Guam," *New York Times*, October 17, 1975; "Saigon to Accept Refugees," *Washington Post*, October 27, 1975.

23. Copy, Deputy Director Bill Hall to Mr. Roger Adams, General Counsel, Interagency Task Force on Indochina, Department of State, November 26, 1975, USMS Collections. No corresponding documentation was found to determine if the agency was fully reimbursed. The events at Guam, and its geographic importance, heightened its importance.

24. "Marshals in Boston," *The Marshal Today* 45 (July 1976): 10-11.

25. Ibid., 12.

26. Ibid., 12-13.

27. "Marshals to Police Busing Orders," *Washington Star,* July 31, 1975.

28. "For U.S. Marshal Grider, a Job at Home," *Louisville Courier-Journal*, August 25, 1975.

29. Ibid.

30. "Louisville Busing off to Violent Start," *Chicago Tribune*, September 5, 1975; Glenn Rutherford, "Marshal Makes Lone Stand at Building," *Louisville Courier-Journal,* September 5, 1975.

31. "Guardsmen Called Out After Louisville Rioting," *Washington Post*, September 9, 1975; "Last of Guardsmen set to exit Louisville today," *The Boston Globe*, September 16, 1975; Interview, Jesse Grider, July 12, 1985, USMS Collections.

32. Copy, Chief Judge U.S. District Court James F. Gordon to Honorable Wayne B. Colburn, September 23, 1975, USMS Collections; Copy, Attorney

General Edward H. Levi to Director Wayne B. Colburn, October 2, 1975, USMS Collections.

33. "Miss Hearst Was Set to Flee, Report Says," *Los Angeles Times,* March 29, 1976.

34. Ibid.; Tom Hall, "San Mateo Paid $599 a Day for Patty's Safe-keeping," *San Francisco Examiner,* November 5, 1975; Carolyn Anspacher, "Patty, Judge and Jurors Visit the Scenes of Her Capitivity," *San Francisco Chronicle,* February 17, 1976.

35. Steve Dunleavy, "Patty Hearst Jailer Signs $1m Book Deal," *The Star,* September 7, 1976.

36. Dunleavy, "Patty Hearst Jailer," *The Star,* September 7, 1976.

37. Ibid.; Janey Jimenez, *My Prisoner* (Mission, KS: Sheed Andrews and McMeel, 1977).

38. "Same Hotel for Zebra, Patty Juries," *San Francisco Examiner,* March 12, 1976.

39. "Patty Arraigned in L.A.," *Star News,* March 29, 1976.

40. "Patty's Fate Rests in Hands of Jury," *San Francisco Herald-Examiner,* March 19, 1976; "Hearst's Final Sentence Is Delayed," *Washington Post,* April 13, 1976; "Miss Hearst's Trial Put Off 6 Months but Her Lawyer Doubts He'll Find Jury," *New York Times,* July 27, 1976; "Death Will Postpone Sentencing of Hearst," *Washington Star,* June 15, 1976. Hearst was arraigned in Los Angeles court in late March 1976 on 11 felonies.

41. Copy, Teletype of Chief Deputy Pipkin, March 29, 1976, USMS Collections.

42. "Miss Hearst Transferred to San Diego for Mental Tests," *Los Angeles Times,* April 28, 1976.

43. "Hearst Released on $1.5 Million Bail," *Washington Post,* November 20, 1976; "Clinton grants more than 100 pardons," *The Sunday [Annapolis, Maryland] Capital,* January 21, 2001. [Knight Ridder]

44. Sherrard and Stumpf, *Badges of the United States Marshals*, 44-45.

Notes to Chapter 10

1. The USMS attained bureau status twice, regained in May 1974. It was further sought in Congressional reform. It was made permanent by section 7608 of the Anti-Drug Act of 1988.

2. Interview, Elizabeth Howard, January 29, 2013, USMS Collections.

3. Interview, Gerry Auerbach, May 11, 2005, USMS Collections.

4. Interview, Nick Prevas, Larry Mogavero, and Leon Roberts, April 17, 2013; Additional Notes, Nick Prevas, June 29, 2007.

5. Interview, Bill Hall, April 6, 2005, USMS Collections. Bill Hall also related in the July 30, 1986, interview that Colburn's health deteriorated rapidly due to a clot on his lung and circulatory problems.

6. Interview, Bill Hall, July 30, 1986; Calhoun, *Lawmen*, 305. The Black Deputy U.S. Marshals Organization, which monitored discrimination within the agency, won concessions from the Department of Justice following an Equal Employment Opportunity complaint in October 1973. The *Federal Times* reported in October 1975 that racial problems continued for Colburn. See *Federal Times*, October 29, 1975 and Undated Clipping, *Federal Times*, ca. October 18, 1973, USMS Collections.

7. Copy, Press Release, Department of Justice, May 19, 1976, USMS Collections; Copy, Announcement, Wayne B. Colburn, Director to All United States Marshals, August 1, 1973, USMS Collections.

8. Calhoun, *The Lawmen*, 306; Interview, Gary Mead, May 22, 2003, USMS Collections; "HQ Spotlight," *Pentacle*, January-February 1980, 4; Interview, Howard Safir, August 1, 2013, USMS Collections; Interview, Ralph Zurita, September 23, 2004, USMS Collections.

9. "T.P. McNamara Retires," *The Pentacle*, February 1978, 9; Tommy Witherspoon, "Century of Law-enforcement Tradition Riding off into

Sunset," *Waco Tribune-Herald,* May 6, 2003; Gary Cartwright, "The Last Posse," *Texas Monthly* (texasmonthly.com).

10. "Major Move Planned for Headquarters," *The Pentacle,* March 1978, 1.

11. Ibid.; "Update on Tyson's Corner Move," *The Pentacle,* May 1978, 3.

12. Interview, Bill Hall, April 6, 2005,USMS Collections.

13. Gary Mead, "Marshals' Training Moves to FLETC," *The Marshal Today* 45 (July 1976): 8; Frederick S. Calhoun, *The Trainers: The Federal Law Enforcement Training Center and the Professionalization of Federal Law Enforcement* (Brunswick, GA: FLETC, 1996), 22-25, 34, 63-66, 70-71.

14. "SOG Graduates 'Prepared for Any Mission,'" *The Pentacle,* July 1978, 1-2; "Hall Issues Sharp Rebuttal to Critics of Protection Program," *The Pentacle,* May 1978, 1, 4-5.This article was reprinted from *Law Enforcement News.*

15. "Hall Issues Sharp Rebuttal," *Pentacle,* May 1978, 1, 4-5; "Civiletti Pledges Support to WITSEC Grads," *The Pentacle,* August-September 1978, 1.

16. "Headquarters Spotlight: Ben Butler Chief, Court Security Division Headquarters," *The Pentacle,* July 1978, 5.

17. Herbert Spiller, "Nuclear Missile Escort," *The Marshal Today,* July 1976, 20-21; "The Missile Escort Program... Fulfilling One of the Service's Most Sensitive Missions," *Pentacle,* June-July 1979, 6-7. The USMS has since stopped this function.

18. Inderjit Badhwar, "Let Them Eat Cake," *Federal Times,* October 23, 1978.

19. Ibid.

20. Deputy U.S. Marshal Stanley Olivers,"Hard to Believe," *Federal Times,* November 13, 1978; Thomas C. Kupferer Jr., "Offensive Column," in *Federal Times,* December 4, 1978.

21. Badhwar, "Let Them Eat Cake," *Federal Times*, October 23, 1978; Michael Dobbs, 'Koreagate' Figure Tied to Oil-for-Food Scandal," *Washington Post*, April 15, 2005; Stephanie Mansfield, "Park Visits His Seized Belongings, *Washington Post*, October 20, 1978; "The Park Patrol," *Newsweek*, March 13, 1978; "Tongsun Park Booked to Leave for Washington," *Washington Post*, February 22, 1978.

22. "Summary of Background on Funding Authorization for Tongsun Park," Copy, USMS Collections; "The Park Patrol," *Newsweek*, March 13, 1978; Copy, Memo, Bill Dempsey to Mr. Robert J. Havel, September 7, 1978, USMS Collections.

23. Copy, William M. Dempsey to William E. Hall, August 29, 1978, USMS Collections; Copy, Memorandum, Leo C. Badart to William E. Hall, September 6, 1978, USMS Collections; Inderjit Badhwar, "Caviar and Champagne? U.S. Marshals Picked Up Huge Tab for Tongsun Park," *Federal Times*, September 4, 1978; "U.S. Spent $70,000 on Tongsun Park During Visit to U.S.," *Washington Star*, October 6, 1978; Stephanie Mansfield, "Park Visits His Seized Belongings," *Washington Post*, October 20, 1978.

24. Entry of John Howland Wood, Jr., *Biographical Directory of Federal Judges*, Federal Judicial Center (fjc.gov); Interview, Ray Musquiz, November 29, 1990, U.S. Marshals Service Collections.

25. Ramon Renteria, "Daughter Writes Manuscript about El Paso Personality Jimmy Chagra," *El Paso Times*, January 19, 2014; Interview, Ray Musquiz, November 29, 1990, U.S. Marshals Service Collections.

26. Interview, Ray Musquiz, November 29, 1990, U.S. Marshals Service Collections; "Ambush Prompts Police to Guard Judge, Lawyer," *Sandusky [Ohio] Register*, November 23, 1978.

27. Interview, Ray Musquiz, November 29, 1990, U.S. Marshals Service Collections; Steven R. Reed, "Deal with Feds Got Chagra in Witness Program Official Sees 'Rank Injustice' in Plot Figure's Plea Bargain," *Houston Chronicle*, April 23, 1989.

28. Interview, Ray Musquiz, November 29, 1990, U.S. Marshals Service Collections.

29. Maro Robbins and Guillermo Contreras, "Judge Wood's Assassin Dies of Heart Attack," *San Antonio Express-News,* March 21, 2007; Reed, "Deal with Feds," *Houston Chronicle,* April 23, 1989; Interview, Ray Muzquiz, November 29, 1990, USMS Collections.

30. Ibid.; "For Prosecutors, Wood Slaying a Crime that Had to be Solved," *The Paris News,* May 29, 1989.

31. Copy, Memorandum, Benjamin R. Civiletti, Deputy Attorney General to William H. Webster, Director, Federal Bureau of Investigation, and William E. Hall, Director, United States Marshals Service, July 23, 1979, with attached copy of Memoradum, USMS Collections; Agency Copy, Director, FBI to Deputy Attorney General Attn: Ms. Judith Bartnoff, June 29, 1979, USMS Collections; Calhoun, *Lawmen,* 306-307.

32. "Expanded Warrant Program Generates New Positions, Enthusiasm," *Pentacle,* November-December 1979, 1-2; Copy, "Biographical/Background Information," John J. Twomey, Deputy Director, USMS Collections.

33. Calhoun, *Lawmen,* 306-307.

34. "Expanded Warrant Program Generates New Positions, Enthusiasm," *Pentacle,* November-December 1979, 1-2.

35. Copy, Director, FBI to Deputy Attorney General, June 29, 1979, USMS Collections; Copy, Deputy Attorney General Civiletti to William H. Webster and William E. Hall, July 23, 1979, USMS Collections.

36. Calhoun, *Lawmen,* 307.

37. Sherrard and Stumpf, *Badges of the United States Marshals,* 44-45; Copy, Deputy Director John J. Twomey to U.S. Marshal Juarez, June 15, 1979, USMS Collections. Note this letter went to every U.S. Marshal and Chief Deputy U.S. Marshal.

38. Copy, Deputy Director John J. Twomey to U.S. Marshal Juarez, June 15, 1979, USMS Collections.

39. "Sneak Preview," *The Pentacle*, August-September 1979, 2; Copy, Memorandum, Director to All United States Marshals, August 2, 1979, USMS Collections. Note that personnel positions are issued on credentials. See Sherrard and Stumpf, 47-48.

40. "Freedom Flotilla Anchors in Florida," *Pentacle*, July-August 1980, 8-11.

41. Andrew Glass, "Castro Launches Mariel Boatlift, April 20, 1980," *Politico*, April 20, 2009 (Taken from Alex Lazelere, "The 1980 Cuban Boatlift"); "Freedom Flotilla Anchors in Florida," *Pentacle*, July-August 1980, 8-11; Copy, "Cuban Freedom Floatilla [*sic*] After Action Report, May 5, 1980 to September 26, 1980," United States Marshals Service, Special Operations Group.

42. Ibid.; Gena Parsons, "Marcotte Recalls Days of Mariel Boatlift," *The Citizen, keysnews.com*, November 11, 2014.

43. "Freedom Flotilla Anchors in Florida," *Pentacle*, July-August 1980, 8-11; Copy, "Cuban Freedom Floatilla [*sic*] After Action Report, May 5, 1980 to September 26, 1980," United States Marshals Service, Special Operations Group.

44. Interview, Joseph Tolson, April 20, 2004, USMS Collections.

45. Ibid.

46. "Freedom Flotilla," *Pentacle*, 9-11; Copy, Memo to Director John J. Twomey, September 5, 1980, USMS Collections.

47. Copy, File Memo to Twomey, September 5, 1980, USMS Collections.

48. Copy, Joel C. Wetherington to Director William E. Hall, ca. September 22, 1980, USMS Collections.

49. "Marshals Pick Up American Prisoners in Cuba," *Pentacle*, November-December 1980, 7.

50. Interview, Joseph Tolson, April 20, 2004, USMS Collections.

51. "Headquarters Spotlight," *Pentacle*, February 1978, 5; "SOG Under-goes Reorganization," *Pentacle*, February 1978, 2; "A Look at the New Prisoner Airlift Program—30,000 Miles in Four Flights," *Pentacle*, June-July 1979, 8; "New Prisoner Transportation Division Opens," *Pentacle*, June-July 1979, 1, 9.

NOTES TO CHAPTER 11

1. "The Capture of Christopher Boyce," *Pentacle*, September/October 1981, 12.

2. Ibid.

3. "Headquarters Spotlight," *Pentacle*, July/August 1980, 6-7.

4. Interview, Chuck Kupferer, September 22, 2008, USMS Collections.

5. Interview, Marvin Lutes, October 2, 2006; "Capture of Christopher Boyce," 12-13; Interview, Dave Neff, May 1, 1991, USMS Collections.

6. Interview, Neff, May 1, 1991, USMS Collections.

7. Ibid.

8. Ibid.;"The Capture of Christopher Boyce," 12-13; Calhoun, *Lawmen*, 309; Interview, Chuck Kupferer, September 22, 2008, USMS Collections.

9. Copy, Enforcement Operations Division, "Operation Noriega," Publication prepared for the Office of Director, United States Marshals Service, 1978. Pablo Noriega was the original appointment for the Southern District of California, on September 30, 1850.

10. Ibid.

11. Ibid.

12. "USMS Fugitive Operatons Come Alive in the 80's," *The Pentacle*, Fall 1982, 18; Interview, Howard Safir, August 1, 2013, USMS Collections.

13. "USMS Fugitive Operatons Come Alive in the 80's," *The Pentacle*, Fall 1982, 18.

14. Interview, Howard Safir, August 1, 2013, USMS Collections; Copy, "Program Initiative FIST Fugitive Investigative Strike Team," Office of the Associate Director of Operations, September 1986, USMS Collections.

15. "USMS Fugitive Operations," *Pentacle*, Fall 1982, 18; "Operation FIST II Concluded," *Pentacle*, Spring 1982, 6; Copy, "Combining Efforts with State and Local Law Enforcement to Combat Violent Crime," ca. 1990, USMS Collections.

16. "USMS Fugitive Operations," *Pentacle*, Fall 1982, 18.

17. Copy, "Combining Efforts with State and Local Law Enforcement," USMS Collections.

18. Ted Gest with Pat Lynch, "As Federal Marshals Round Up Fugitives," *U.S. News & World Report*, December 3, 1984.

19. Ibid.

20. Copy, "Program Initiative FIST Fugitive Investigative Strike Team," Office of the Associate Director of Operations, September 1986, USMS Collections.

21. "USMS Fugitive Operations," *Pentacle*, Fall 1982, 18.

22. Ibid.

23. Marie J.G. du Motier, Marquis de Lafayette Collection, AC 4873, Box 2, Library of Congress, Manuscript Divison; "Service Protects Foreign Diplomats at United Nations," *Pentacle*, November/December 1980, 14.

24. Lyle Denniston, "Hinckley Prosecutors Want Trial Rules Eased," *Baltimore Sun*, April 9, 1982; "Marshals Sweep into Action after Assassination Attempt," *Pentacle*, June/July 1981, 8-9. St. Elizabeth's hospital was founded as the Government Hospital for the Insane.

25. "Marshals Sweep into Action after Assassination Attempt," *Pentacle*, June/July 1981, 8-9.

26. Ibid.

27. Ibid.

28. Louie McKinney with Pat Russo, *One Marshal's Badge: A Memoir of Fugitive Hunting, Witness Protection, and the U.S. Marshals Service* (Washington, D.C.: Potomac Books, 2009), 2.

29. Ibid., 2-3.

30. "U.S. Marshals Foil Suicide Try by John Hinckley Jr.," *Daily News*, November 13, 1981.

31. McKinney, *One Marshal's Badge*, 3.

32. Ibid.; "U.S. Marshals Foil Suicide Try," *Daily News*, November 13, 1981.

33. "Extraordinary Security Measures Mark Hinckley Detail," *Pentacle*, Fall 1982, 24.

34. Ibid.; Interview, Ken Barry, May 8, 2003, USMS Collections.

35. "Extraordinary Security Measures," *Pentacle*, Fall 1982, 24.

36. Ibid.; Copy of Letter, Attorney General William French Smith to Director William E. Hall, April 20, 1981, as printed in *Pentacle*, June/July 1981, 11.

37. Petula Dvorak, "It's Nuts to Spend so Much Time and Money on John W. Hinckley Jr.," *Washington Post*, December 1, 2011.

38. "National Wanted Poster Program Gearing Up," *Pentacle*, Fall 1982, 32-33; Interview, Robert Leschorn, November 20, 2007, USMS Collections.

39. Draft, "15 Most Wanted," Undated, ca. 1983, Courtesy of Robert Leschorn.

40. Ibid.; Copy, "Fifteen Most Wanted Cases Open," April 15, 1986, USMS Collections.

41. Typed Statistical Notes, "Fifteen Most Wanted," December 14, 1987; "Statistical Profile of the 15 Most Wanted Program," in *Fifteen Most Wanted Program*, USMS Publication, ca. September 1989. Official guidelines for the Fifteen Most Wanted were printed in USMS Publication No. 47.

42. "Introduction," in *Fifteen Most Wanted Program*, USMS Publication, ca. September 1989.

43. Ibid.

44. Chart, "Criminal Cases Pending by Offense in the U.S. Attorney's Offices," in *Fifteen Most Wanted Program*, USMS Publication, ca. September 1989.

45. Enforcement Division, *Fifteen Most Wanted Program: Case Submission Guidelines,"* USMS Publication No. 47, September 23, 1994.

46. Ed Maixner, "Tempers Flared before Medina Shootout," *The Forum [Fargo-Moorhead]*, February 15, 1983.

47. Ibid.; Kevin Murphy, "Suspects' History Includes Tax Convictions, Threats," *The Forum [Fargo-Moorhead]*, February 15, 1983; "Dakota Dragnet," *Time*, February 28, 1983, 25; Interview, Chuck Kupferer, September 22, 2008, USMS Collections.

48. Ibid.

49. "No Greater Tragedy," *Pentacle*, March/April 1983, 3-5.

50. Jim Corcoran, "Sources Say Kahl Takes Blame in Letter," *The Forum*, February 17, 1983; Bill Terry, "Death of a Self-Styled Elijah," *Arkansas Times*, January 1984, 47-48.

51. Terry,"Death," *Arkansas Times*, 48.

52. "Nation Recognized Sacrifice of USMS Heroes," *Pentacle*, March/April 1983, 2.

53. Ibid.

54. "President Participates in Day of Honor for Fallen Heroes," *Pentacle*, March/April 1983, 4.

55. Interview, Roger Arechiga, September 22, 2008, USMS Collections; Ed Maixner, "Mrs. Kahl Begs Husband to Surrender," *The Forum*, February 17, 1983; Dennis J. McGrath, "FBI Attacks N.D. Farm, Finds No Fugitive," *Minneapolis Star & Tribune*, February 16, 1983; Jim Corcoran, "Sources Say Kahl Takes Blame in Letter," *The Forum*, February 17, 1983.

56. Interview, Chuck Kupferer, September 22, 2008, USMS Collections.

57. Ibid.; Interview, Roger Arechiga, September 22, 2008, USMS Collections.

58. Ibid.; Copy, Medical Examiner Division Report, State of Arkansas, State Crime Laboratory, Number MEA-275-83. The results from the medical examiner revealed that bullets from Sheriff Matthews' weapon caused Kahl's death.

59. Interview, Chuck Kupferer, September 22, 2008, USMS Collections.

60. "Sheriff Slain in Kahl Shootout Honored Posthumously," *Pentacle*, September/October 1983, 33.

NOTES TO CHAPTER 12

1. "Leaving...," *Pentacle*, Spring 1982, 11; "USMS Director Hall Appointed Assistant Associate AG," *Pentacle*, November/December 1983, 3.

2. Copy, Biographical Sketch, Stanley E. Morris, 1983; "Stanley E. Morris Named as Marshals Service Director," *Pentacle*, November-December 1983, 3.

3. "Message from the Director," *Pentacle*, November/December 1983, 2.

4. Ibid.

5. "Director's Award Ceremony Held at Headquarters," *Pentacle*, Fall 1982, 26.

6. Interview, Henry Ohrenburger, October 6, 2005, USMS Collections.

7. Interview, Ohrenburger, October 6, 2005, USMS Collections.

8. Interview, Stanley Morris, October 17, 2006, USMS Collections; "FIT Program Is Shaping Up," *FYI—For Your Information* 2, no. 4, (December 7, 1984): 12; Interview, Stanley Morris, July 5, 1991, USMS Collections; Stanley E. Morris, "A Celebration for All Americans.

9. "Historic Reruns—The Last Decade of Progress," *Pentacle*, July/August 1983, 6.

10. Ibid.

11. "New Office of Internal Inspections Formed," *Pentacle*, July/August 1983, 9.

12. Ibid., 9-10.

13. "Procurement and Property Management Division," *Pentacle*, July/August 1983, 16-17.

14. Interview, Gary Mead, May 22, 2003, USMS Collections.

15. Ibid.

16. "Proving That Crime Doesn't Pay—The U.S. Marshals Service Tackles Its Latest Mission," *Pentacle*, summer 1986, 3; "RICO Criminal Forfeiture," *Pentacle*, July/August 1983, 10.

17. "RICO Criminal Forfeiture," *Pentacle*, July/August 1983, 10.

18. Ibid.;"Proving," *Pentacle*, summer 1986, 3.

19. "Rewards of Good Police Work," *Pentacle*, Summer 1986, 12-13.

20. "Media Coverage of the Asset Seizure Program," *FYI—For Your Information* 8, no. 4 (May 13, 1991).

21. Ibid.

22. "Threat Analysis Group Established," *Pentacle*, September/October 1983, 25.

23. Ibid. TAG later became the Threat Analysis Division (TAD). This incarnation contained both administrative and operational personnel. In 1995, this concept was dismantled, and replaced by the more administrative Analytical Support Unit (ASU), but placed within the framework of the Enforcement Division. The duties divided in the mid-2000s, essentially replacing ASU with two different units: the Criminal Investigative Branch under the Investigative Services Division, and the Office of Protective Intelligence, under the Judicial Security Division.

24. Dean St. Dennis, "Threat Analysis—Uncovering Hidden Dangers," *Pentacle*, March 1990, 5-7.

25. Ibid.; Interview, Tony Odom, February 21, 1991, USMS Collections.

26. St. Dennis, "Threat Analysis-Uncovering Hidden Dangers," *Pentacle*, March 1990, 6-7.

27. Interview, Tony Odom, February 21, 1991, USMS Collections.

28. Ibid.

29. Ibid.

30. Jay Mathews, "Former Intelligence Officer Backs Report on Mengele," *Washington Post*, January 26, 1984.

31. Copy, "Sightings in South America," Typed Listing, Undated ca. 1985, USMS Collections.

32. Copy, Statement of Howard Safir, Associate Director for Operations, United States Marshals Service, Undated ca. August 1985, USMS Collections; Memorandum, Stephen S. Trott, Assistant Attorney General to Stanley E. Morris, Director, United States Marshals Service, March 12, 1985.

33. Statement of Howard Safir, United States Marshals Service, Undated ca. 1985, USMS Collections.

34. Interview, Ralph Zurita, September 23, 2004, USMS Collections; Copy, Statement of Howard Safir, Undated, USMS Collections.

35. Ralph Blumenthal, "U.S. Marshals Joining Search for Nazi Death Camp Doctor," *New York Times*, April 24, 1985.

36. Ibid.

37. *Washington Times,* March 26, 1985; Copy, Statement of Howard Safir, Undated, USMS Collections.

38. Interview, Ralph Zurita, September 23, 2004, USMS Collections; Copy, Statement of Howard Safir, Undated, USMS Collections. It was said Mengele suffered a stroke or heart attack while swimming, and drowned as a result. There was concern there may have been deception in the letters to throw off investigators, so it was still necessary to search for the body in South America.

39. Copy, Memorandum to File from Arnold Stolz, Mengele Team, "Translations from German Text," July 10, 1985, USMS Collections; Copy, Statement of Howard Safir, Undated, USMS Collection.

40. Copy, Statement of Howard Safir, Undated, USMS Collections; Copy, [To Dr. Romeu Toma, Superintendent, Federal Police in Sao Paulo, Brazil] Preliminary Report, "Examination of the Human Skeletal Remains Exhumed at Nossa Senhora Do Rosario Cemetary [sic], Embu, Brazil on 6 June 1985," USMS Collections. The latter was done by forensic scientists at the Simon Wiesenthal Center.

41. Copy, Statement of Howard Safir, Undated, USMS Collections; Copy, Memorandum to File, "Translations from German Text," July 10, 1985, USMS Collections; Copy, Testimony of Neal M. Sher, Director, Office of Special Investigations, Criminal Division Before Senate Subcommittee on Juvenile Justice Hearing on Josef Mengele, Friday, August 2, 1985, USMS Collections.

42. Ronald J. Ostrow and Ronald L. Soble, "Mengele Slipped Through U.S. Hands, Report Says; Holocaust: But No Evidence Is Found that U.S.

Knowingly Assisted the Auschwitz Doctor," *Los Angeles Times*, October 9, 1992.

43. George Esper, "Jonestown 'Like a Prison Camp,'" *Santa Ana Orange County Register*, December 3, 1978, via AP; "Jones on Eve of Tragedy: 'I Feel Like Dying Man," *Santa Ana Orange County Register*, December 3, 1978, via AP; Wanda Franks and Thomas Powers, "Frustration Fuels Fanatic Stance of the Weathermen," *Kittanning Simpson Leader-Times*, September 18, 1970, via UPI; "SLA Bombing Link?" *Corona [California] Daily Independent*, May 31, 1974, via AP.

44. "Local Chapter in Sedition Saga," *Southwest Times Record*, April 8, 1988.

45. Ibid.

46. "Sedition—To Be or Not to Be," in Copy, Newsletter, "Aryan Nations," No. 67; Wayne King, "10 Named in a Plot to Overthrow U.S.," *New York Times*, April 25, 1987.

47. King, "10 Named in a Plot to Overthrow U.S.," *New York Times*, April 25, 1987.

48. Interview, Dave Neff, May 1, 1991, USMS Collections. See also "High Threat Trials," in *Pentacle* 7, no. 2 (Summer 1987): 2; "Who's Standing Trial?," in *Pentacle* 7, no. 2 (Summer 1987): 7; "Courtroom Drama," in *Pentacle* 7 (Summer 1987): 11.

49. Interview, Dave Neff, May 1, 1991, USMS Collections.

50. "High Threat Trials," *Pentacle*, Summer 1987, 2.

51. Copy, U.S. Marshal Kernan H. Bagley to Director Stanley E. Morris, August 8, 1985, USMS Collections.

52. Lee Zaitz, "25 Years after Rajneeshee Commune Collapsed, Truth Spills Out," *The Oregonian*, April 14, 2011.

53. Ibid.

54. Ibid.; "Guru, Followers Arrested Trying to Flee U.S. in Jets: Believed to Be Evading Indictments," UPI, October 28, 1985; "Rajneesh City Stay May Grow," *Oklahoman*, November 7, 1985.

55. " 'Fleeing' Rajneesh Arrested," *Wichita Eagle-Beacon*, October 29, 1985; Zaitz, "25 Years after Rajneeshee Commune Collapsed, Truth Spills Out," *The Oregonian*, April 14, 2011. The article in the Wichita paper was reprinted from the *Chicago Tribune*.

56. Tex O'Neill and John Wildman, "Lawyers on Both Sides Plot Their Moves in Indian Guru's Case," *Charlotte Observer*, October 30, 1985; "Rajneesh City Stay May Grow," *Oklahoman*, November 7, 1985.

NOTES TO CHAPTER 13

1. See Associated Press, "Newspaper Says Persico Reportedly Boasted That He Killed Anastasia," June 3, 1986.

2. Interview, Robert Leschorn, November 20, 2007, USMS Collections; Copy, "Fifteen Most Wanted Cases Open," Revised February 14, 1986, Courtesy of Robert Leschorn.

3. Interview, Robert Leschorn, November 20, 2007, USMS Collections.

4. Ibid.; Copy, "Fifteen Most Wanted Cases Open," Revised February 14, 1986, Courtesy of Robert Leschorn.

5. Interview, Robert Leschorn, November 20, 2007, USMS Collections.

6. Ibid.

7. Interview, Arthur Roderick, January 30, 2012, USMS Collections.

8. Ibid.

9. Ibid.

10. Ibid.

11. Ibid.

12. Ibid.

13. Ibid.

14. Ibid. Bender's bust is part of the USMS Collections, and will be part of the U.S. Marshals Museum in Fort Smith, Arkansas.

15. Ibid.

16. Ibid.

17. Ibid.; "Suspected Mob Grave Found," *Ellensburg Daily Record*, October 29, 1990; Edmund Mahoney, "Prosecutor Wraps Up Government's Case," *Hartford Courant*, July 16, 1991.

18. Interview, Chuck Kupferer, September 22, 2008, USMS Collections.

19. Copy, *Operation Flagship 12/15/85, Plan of Operation*, undated, USMS Collections.

20. E-Mail, Mark Shealey to Author, January 21, 2013.

21. Ibid.

22. Copy, *Operation Flagship 12/15/85, Plan of Operation*, USMS Collections; Copy, *Operation Flagship, Manpower Distribution and Position Description*, undated, USMS Collections.

23. Ibid.

24. Ibid.

25. Interview, Joe Tolson, April 20, 2004; Copy, *Operation Flagship 12/15/85, Plan of Operation*, USMS Collections; Copy, *Operation Flagship, Manpower Distribution and Position Description*, undated, USMS Collections. See also McKinney, *One Marshal's Badge*, 169; "No Such Thing as a Free Brunch...," *Pentacle*, Winter, January 1986, 25-27.

26. Interview, Robert Leschorn, November 20, 2007, USMS Collections.

27. E-Mail, Shealey to Author, January 21, 2013.

28. Interview, Stan Morris, October 17, 2006, USMS Collections.

29. Ibid.

30. "Organized Crime Drug Enforcement Task Forces," Department of Justice Website, www.justice.gov; Copy, Report, WANT Warrant Apprehension Narcotics Teams-Report to the Organized Crime and Drug Enforcement Task Force National Conference, May 13, 1987, USMS Collections.

31. Elaine Shannon, "Taking a Byte Out of Crime," *Time*, May 25, 1987.

32. Ibid.

33. Ibid.; Copy, Report, WANT Warrant Apprehension Narcotics Teams —Report to the Organized Crime and Drug Enforcement Task Force National Conference, May 13, 1987, USMS Collections. Statistical tracking began on March 3 and ended May 8, 1987.

34. Ibid. Of the 210 total arrests, 166 were WANT-specific (identified by DEA classification).

35. Elaine Shannon, "Taking a Byte Out of Crime," *Time*, May 25, 1987.

36. Copy, Report, WANT, May 13, 1987, USMS Collections; Ronald J. Ostrow, "Marshals Successful; FBI Wants Role; Federal Lawmen Feuding Over Pursuing Fugitives," *Los Angeles Times*, January 12, 1988.

37. Ostrow, "Marshals Successful; FBI Wants Role." WANT was only one area of disputed jurisdiction. The tipping point was over the extradition of Edwin P. Wilson, a former CIA official, from the Dominican Republic. In that case, deputies successfully arrested Wilson once on American soil after he was convinced to fly into jurisdiction.

38. Copy, Report, Warrant Apprehension Narcotics Team, *WANT II —A Cooperative Enforcement Program Sponsored by The United States Marshals Service*, November 14, 1988, USMS Collections.

39. Copy, Release, "Completion of Anti-Drug Evictions District of Columbia; May 15-22, 1989," USMS Collections. The USMS functions as the "sheriff" for the municipal government of the District of Columbia.

40. Ibid.

NOTES TO CHAPTER 14

1. Interview, Stan Morris, October 17, 2006, USMS Collections.

2. Interview, Gary Mead, May 22, 2003, USMS Collections.

3. Interview, Stan Morris, October 17, 2006, USMS Collections.

4. Leslie Maitland Werner, "Same Star, but Marshal Is Updated," *New York Times*, October 18, 1984.

5. Interview, Henry Ohrenburger, October 6, 2005, USMS Collections.

6. Interview, Stan Morris, October 17, 2006, USMS Collections.

7. Interview, Gary Mead, May 22, 2003, USMS Collections.

8. Ibid.

9. Draft Copy Notes, Joseph Briggs, "The USMS in the Modern Era," for use of inclusion in Annual Report material, USMS Collections.

10. "Briefing Sheet: Court Security Officer Program," with Copy, Memorandum, Chief James E. O'Toole to Associate Director for Operations Howard Safir, October 17, 1985; Court Security Officer Orientation Handbook, Undated, ca. 1985; Draft Copy Notes, Joseph Briggs, "The USMS in the Modern Era," for use of inclusion in Annual Report material, USMS Collections; *The Director's Report: A Review of the United States Marshals Service in FY 1990*, 42; Interview, Stan Morris, October 17, 2006, USMS Collections.

11. "EEO Orientation Program Held," *Pentacle*, July/August 1980, USMS Collections. Butler, who was the first African American employee to achieve an executive level rank at Headquarters, was a former U.S. Marshal (Eastern District of New York) and Assistant Regional Director.

12. Interview, Gary Mead, May 22, 2003, USMS Collections.

13. "Director's Message," *Pentacle,* January 1987, 2.

14. Ibid.; "A Difficult and Dangerous Task," *Pentacle,* January 1987, 5; Copy, Draft, "The USMS in the Modern Era," USMS Collections; "Private Detention Facility," *FYI* 7, no. 5 (July 9, 1990): 2. The IGA Program has since been enacted to provide money for the construction of facilities in return for guaranteed bed space for prisoners.

15. "USMS and DEA Located Together—New Law Enforcement Headquarters," *Pentacle*, August 1988, 45.

16. Ibid.

17. Copy, Text of Public Law 100-690, H.R. 5210, Section 7608, "The United States Marshals Service Act of 1988," November 18, 1988. Public Law 100-690 amended 28 U.S.C. 561. Current day organizational jurisdiction places U.S. Marshals as a report to the Deputy Director.

18. Ibid. The Act affected seized assets management to include confidentiality and security during an active investigation. See Copy, "Implementation of the USMS Act of 1988 and Related Legislation," USMS Collections.

19. "Overview of the U.S. Marshals Service," in *The Director's Report: A Review of the United States Marshals Service in FY 1989,* 3. *The Director's Report* for FY 1990 had greater detail in duty descriptions within the overview.

20. Ibid., 5. See also *The Director's Report: A Review of the United States Marshals Service in FY 1990,* 5.

21. Among the many examples are movies such as *Eraser* and *Out of Sight.* References in television dramas, such as *The Sopranos, Law and Order,* and *Criminal Minds,* also bear mention.

22. "Witness Security," in *Director's Report: A Review of the United States Marshals Service in FY 1989,* 47; "Testifying without Reprisal," *Pentacle,* Winter, February 1988, 6; "Witness Security," *Director's Report, FY 1989,* 49.

23. Frederick S. Calhoun, *Hunters and Howlers—Threats and Violence Against Federal Judicial Officials in the United States, 1789-1993*, USMS Publication No. 80, February 1998, 2.

24. Ibid.; Interview, U.S. Marshal Tom Greene, November 30, 1990, USMS Collections.

25. Interview, U.S. Marshal Tom Greene, November 30, 1990, USMS Collections.

26. Greene Interview; Calhoun, *Hunters and Howlers*, 2.

27. Interview, Inspector Henry Ohrenburger, October 6, 2005, USMS Collections; Calhoun, *Lawmen,* 331.

28. Ibid.

29. Peter Applecombe, "Shadowy Bombing Case Is Focusing on Reclusive and Enigmatic Figure," *New York Times,* July 20, 1990; *The Director's Report: A Review of the United States Marshals Service in FY 1990,* 36-37.

30. Calhoun, *Lawmen,* 207-211; "Bob Pate Dies From the Effect of a Wound Received in July," *Arkansas Gazette,* September 29, 1894. Calhoun's *Lawmen* fully covered the Pullman Strike, and noted that the environment was set by train thieves in Coxey's Army. This movement in early 1894 was a demand for employment in public works programs.

31. Copy, Typed and Pencil Notes, "West Virginia Coal Miners Strike," USMS Collections; "Coal Miners Break Tradition, Return to Work Despite Pickets," *New York Times,* September 9, 1975. See also Bill McAllister, "Judge Refuses Use of U.S. Marshals to Identify Miners," *Washington Post,* September 3, 1975. This was based on the Supreme Court case of *In Re Neagle* that gave authority to federal law enforcement.

32. Calhoun, *The Lawmen,* 321; Copy, Time Line (typed), in Affadavit & Deposition, U.S. Marshal Walter Biondi, 1989, USMS Collections.

33. Copy, Letter, U.S. Marshal Wayne D. Beaman to U.S. Marshal Daniel Horgan, February 28, 1990, USMS Collections.

34. Ibid.

35. Philip Nussel, "New Charges Filed against Miners," *Charleston Daily Mail*, October 24, 1989; Copy, Order Modifying Temporary Injunction, Civil action No. 2:89-0851, United States District Court, Southern District of West Virginia, Charleston Division, USMS Collections.

36. Jim Balow, "Marshals to Begin Enforcing Injunction," *Charleston Gazette*, October 25, 1989.

37. Nussel, "New Charge Filed against Miners," *Charleston Daily Mail*, October 24, 1989.

38. Balow, "Marshals to Begin Enforcing," *Charleston Gazette*, October 25, 1989; Jim Balow, "Pickets Arrested in Defiance of Court Order," *Charleston Gazette*, October 26, 1989.

39. Becky Reed, "Federal Marshals Arrest Five More Striking Miners," *Logan Banner*, December 6, 1989; Jim Balow, "Five Pickets Charged with Blocking Trucks," *Charleston Gazette*, December 6, 1989; Copy, Weekly Report—Week of December 17, 1989, Director K.M. Moore to Attorney General, USMS Collections; "Marshals Seize Weapons from Pickets," *Charleston Gazette*, December 7, 1989.

40. Jim Balow, "2 UMW Officials, Massey Worker Arrested," *Charleston Gazette*, January 24, 1990; Copy, Weekly Report—Week of April 29, 1990, K.M. Moore to Attorney General, USMS Collections; Jack McCarthy, "Judge Intends to Limit Picketing at Mine," *Charleston Gazette*, January 12, 1990; Calhoun, *Lawmen*, 328.

41. "Tourists Flee as Chaos Follows Hurricane," *Des Moines Register*, September 20, 1989.

42. Ibid.

43. Drew Wade and Fran Wermuth, "Restoring Order—A Special Operation in the Virgin Islands," *Pentacle,* March 1990, 9-11; "Tourists Flee as Chaos Follows Hurricane," *Des Moines Register*, September 20, 1989.

44. "Hurricane Hugo Relief Project," *FYI—For Your Information* 6, no. 14 (November 28, 1989): 6.

45. Ibid.

46. Ibid.

47. For a more general assessment of law enforcement responses to Hurricane Hugo, see Reuben M. Greenberg, Charles Wiley, Glenn Youngblood, Herbert Whetsell and James H. Doyle, "The Lessons of Hurricane Hugo: Law Enforcement Responds," *Police Chief* 47, no. 9, 26-33.

48. See Calhoun, *Lawmen,* 331-332.

49. Ibid.

50. *United States Marshals: 1789 to Present*; Calhoun, *Lawmen,* 332.

51. Calhoun, *Lawmen,* 332-33; Interview, Tony Perez, August 21, 1990, USMS Collections.

52. Interview, Tony Perez, August 21, 1990, USMS Collections.

53. Copy, Mel McDowell, Account on Operation "JUST CAUSE," USMS Collections.

54. Ibid.

55. Ibid.

56. Calhoun, *Lawmen,* 333. The U.S. Marshals would be involved in the extradition of Noriega to the United States.

57. Interview, Tony Perez, August 21, 1990, USMS Collections.

58. Ibid. Deputy U.S. Marshal Tim Goode was one of those who brought in the former Panamanian leader, and the handcuffs he used were later mounted for preservation.

59. "USMS Historian Appointed," *Pentacle,* Spring 1985, 27; Copy, "Proposed Agenda for the USMS Bicentennial Working Committee,"

1984, USMS Collections; "New Display Available," *Pentacle*, Fall 1982, 7; Copy, Minutes, "First Meeting of the USMS Bicentennial Working Committee," December 6, 1984, USMS Collections.

60. Copy, Minutes, "First Meeting of the USMS Bicentennial Working Committee," December 6, 1984, USMS Collections.

61. Copy, "Section 16: Consolidated Bicentennial Schedule," in U.S. Marshals Service Bicentennial Events and Programs, USMS Collections.

62. Copy, Press Release, "U.S. Marshals/Smithsonian Exhibit Opening at Supreme Court Building Kicks Off year-long nationwide Bicentennial Observance of U.S. Marshals," November 23, 1988; Copy, Itinerary Map, "America's Star: U.S. Marshals, 1789-1989," USMS Collections; Copy, Brochure, "America's Star: U.S. Marshals 1789-1989."

63. Copy, News Release, "AMERICA'S STAR: U.S. MARSHALS, 1789-1989" SITES Exhibition Opens at Supreme Court Building, Office of Public Affairs, Smithsonian Institution, August 25, 1988.

64. Copy, Brochure, "America's Star: U.S. Marshals 1789-1989"; Itinerary Map, "America's Star: U.S. Marshals, 1789-1989," USMS Collections; Copy, Notes, Office of the Historian, USMS Collections.

65. Interview, Henry Ohrenburger, October 6, 2005, USMS Collections; Copy, Weekly Report, Week of October 22, 1989, USMS Collections; Copy, Director Stanley E. Morris to the Attorney General, October 18, 1989, USMS Collections.

66. Copy of Newsletter, "U.S. Marshals National Memorial Dedication," *FYI—For Your Information*, USMS, 6, no. 14 (November 28, 1989): 3.

67. Copy of Newsletter, "The Marshals National Conference—A New Beginning and a Farewell," *FYI—For Your Information*, USMS, 6, no. 14 (November 28, 1989): 2.

68. Ibid.

NOTES TO CHAPTER 15

1. "K. Michael Moore Sworn in as New Director," *Pentacle*, March 1990, Inner Cover; Copy, Fact Sheet, K. Michael Moore, USMS Collections.

2. "K. Michael Moore Sworn in as New Director," Inner Cover.

3. "*Operation Just Cause*: Marshals on Duty in Panama," *Pentacle* 10, no. 1 (March 1990): 17-18; Copy, *Operation Southern Star—A Fugitive Operation Sponsored by the United States Marshals Service August 6-October 17, 1990;* U.S. Marshals Service Office of Congressional and Public Affairs, *U.S. Marshals Service Joint Fugitive Apprehension Operations*, ca. 1992, 1-5; "Trident Nets Record 5,788 Arrests," *Marshals Monitor*, September 1993, 4; Associated Press, "Atlanta Holds Pre-Games Crime Sweep," *Orange County Register*, June 14, 1996; USMS Congressional and Public Affairs, *U.S. Marshals Service Joint Fugitive Apprehension Operations*, 6-12; "Private Detention Facility," *FYI—For Your Information* 7, no. 5, 1-2.

4. "Honoring Marshals," *Pentacle*, March 1990, 35; "U.S. Marshals National Memorial Dedication," *FYI—For Your Information* 6, no. 14 (November 28, 1989): 3-4.

5. "U.S. Marshals National Memorial Dedication," *FYI*, November 28, 1989, 4.

6. "New Deputy Director Positions," *FYI—For Your Information* 7, no. 4 (May 25, 1990): 1.

7. "New Associate Director for Operations," *FYI—For Your Information* 7, no. 7 (October 12, 1990): 1; "Headquarters Reorganization," *FYI—For Your Information* 7, no. 8 (November 26, 1990): 2-3.

8. United States Marshals Service, Associate Director for Administrative Services, Information Resources Management Division, *The Director's Report: A Review of the United States Marshals Service in FY 1991*, 71.

9. Interview, Henry Ohrenburger, October 6, 2005, USMS Collections

10. "Liaison with the Field," *FYI* 7, no. 1 (January 31, 1990): 2.

11. "A Difficult and Dangerous Task," *Pentacle*, January 1987, 5; Copy, Draft, "The USMS in the Modern Era," USMS Collections; "Private Detention Facility," *FYI* 7, no. 5 (July 9, 1990): 2. This public-private partnership still exists today.

12. "The Jail Crisis," *Pentacle*, March 1991, 2.

13. "Searching for Jail Space," *Pentacle,* March 1991, 5; "Personal Sacrifices," *Pentacle*, March 1991, 6.

14. "U.S. Marshals Advisory Committee," *FYI*, October 12, 1990, 5.

15. "Marshals' History," *FYI*, July 9, 1990, 5; "USMS Historian Appointed," *Pentacle*, spring 1985, 27.

16. "Maximum Entry Age For Deputy Marshals," *FYI*, June 28, 1991, 1-2, USMS Collections.

17. Copy, "Fugitive Apprehension Operations, 1981-1990," USMS Collections.

18. Copy of Printed Publication, "Operation Southern Star—A Fugitive Program Sponsored by the United States Marshals Service August 6-October 17, 1990," 1; "Operation Southern Star," *FYI*, November 26, 1990, 4.

19. "Operation Southern Star," *FYI*, November 26, 1990, 4.

20. "Operation Sunrise," *FYI*, November 8, 1991, 1.

21. Copy, Press Release, "Drugs Out the Window—New York City," ca. October 1991, USMS Collections.

22. Copy, Press Release, "Operation Sunrise Targets Major Drug Fugitives—Miami, Fla.," ca. October 1991, USMS Collections; Copy, Press Release, "The Sun Sets on Violent Fugitives—Atlanta," ca. October 1991, USMS Collections.

23. Bio,"Howard Safir," Montfort Academy Website, www.themontfortacademy.org; "New Position for Deputy Director," *FYI*, January 22, 1991, 1; "New Division Chiefs," *FYI*, January 22, 1991, 1.

24. Chronology, in Michael Hedges, "Deal Unlikely as Noriega, Prosecutors Head for Trial," *Washington Times*, September 3, 1991; Copy, Briefing, "Update in Costs in Support of Activity—Manuel Noriega, 6/25/91," USMS Collections; Copy, UPI Press Release, "Noriega Trial Postponed for the Third Time," USMS Collections; Hedges, "Deal Unlikely," *Washington Times*, September 3, 1991.

25. Arnold Markowitz and David Lyons, "Security Boosted—Quietly," *Miami Herald*, September 2, 1991.

26. Warren Richey, "Noriega Given 40 Years," *South Florida Sun-Sentinel*, July 11, 1992.

27. *Roe v. Wade*, 410 U.S.113 (1973).

28. "Wichita Clinic Protests," *Pentacle*, December 1991, 49.

29. Ibid.; Interview, Kent Pekarek, November 7, 1991, USMS Collections.

30. Interview, Kent Pekarek, November 7, 1991, USMS Collections.

31. Ibid. The Pekarek interview incorrectly mentions this case as "Bray v Alexander." The citations are 726 F. Supp. 1483 (EDVA 1989); 914 F. 2d 582 (4th Cir. 1990); 506 US 263 (1993).

32. Interview, Kent Pekarek, November 7, 1991, USMS Collections.

33. Ibid.

34. Ibid.

35. Ibid.

36. Ibid.

37. "A Fond Farewell," *FYI* 9, no. 2 (February 13, 1992): 5. At the time, the Director received unfavorable press about his travel expenses. However, it was not the immediate cause of his resignation. See Michael J. Sniffen, "Director's Travel Costs Scrutinized," *Associated Press, Hutchinson (Kansas) News*, August 27, 1991.

38. "A Fond Farewell," *FYI*, February 13, 1992, 5.

Notes to Chapter 16

1. Copy, Directors and Deputy Directors, ca. 2009, USMS Collections; Copy, Biographical Outline, Acting Director Henry E. Hudson, 1992, USMS Collections; "Organizational Changes Keep Pace With DOJ," *Marshals Monitor*, November 1992, 1; "Introducing Some New Faces...," *Marshal Monitor*, November 1992, 7; Copy, Memorandum from Henry E. Hudson to United States Marshals, Deputy Director, Associate Directors, Assistant Directors, Division Chiefs, Staff Officers, February 1, 1993, USMS Collections. It should be noted Acting Director Hudson was nominated in December 1991 in anticipation of the departure of Director Moore.

2. "Message From the Director," *Marshals Monitor*, November 1992, 2.

3. "Liaison to Increased International Exposure," *Marshals Monitor*, November 1992, 3.

4. Diane Dungey and Laura Januta, " 'Bearded Bandit' Saga Ends in Blood," *Daily Herald*, July 21, 1992; Copy, Acting Director Henry Hudson to All U.S. Marshals Service Offices, July 23, 1992, USMS Collections. He became director on August 12, 1992.

5. Copy, Hudson to All Offices, July 23, 1992, USMS Collections. Quote was within the text of the memorandum. "WAE" means "Wages Actually Earned," a defunct status of specially deputized guard set for term periods or purposes.

6. Matt O'Connor, "Deputy relives escape bid," *Chicago Tribune*, October 30, 2002.

7. Ibid.

8. Interview, Marvin Lutes, October 2, 2006, USMS Collections.

9. Copy, Acting Director Hudson to All U.S. Marshals Service Offices, July 23, 1992; John O'Brien and Matt O'Connor, "Erickson's Guards 'Were Not Remiss," *Chicago Tribune*, July 23, 1992; O'Connor, "Deputy Relives Escape Bid," October 30, 2002.

10. Copy, Press Release, Office of Public Affairs, June 4, 1993, USMS Collections; "Director Awards Service Achievers," December 1992, 7. The award was previously called the "Court Security Officer of the Year Award."

11. Copy, Q & A, Notes, "Bench Warrant," in Ruby Ridge File, USMS Collections; Copy, Q & A, Notes, "Propriety of Indictment," in Ruby Ridge File, USMS Collections. Note these pages were utilized for preparation or in response to Congressional hearings on Ruby Ridge, ca. 1995-97. Source material was heavily drawn from the Office of Professional Responsibility's findings. Specifically, Weaver tried to sell two illegally sawed-off shotguns to undercover BATF agents.

12. Copy, statement and notes of David Allen Hunt, deputy U.S. marshal, Undated, USMS Collections.

13. Ibid.

14. Ibid.

15. Ibid.

16. Ibid.

17. Ibid.; Copy, Statement of Arthur D. Roderick, Undated, USMS Collections; Interview, Art Roderick, January 30, 2012, USMS Collections.

18. Entry of "March 4, 1992," in Copy, Timeline of Events Regarding Weaver Conflict, ca. 1995, USMS Collections; Entry of "April 21, 1992," in Copy, Timeline of Events Regarding Weaver Conflict, ca. 1995; Quotation from *Bonner County Daily Bee,* May 3, 1992; Entry of "May 3, 1992," in Copy, Timeline of Events Regarding Weaver Conflict, ca. 1995.

19. Copy, Statement of Larry T. Cooper, Undated, USMS Collections.

20. Ibid.; George Lardner, Jr. and Richard Leiby, "Standoff at Ruby Ridge," *Washington Post,* September 3, 1995; Copy, Statement of Hunt, Undated, USMS Collections; Copy, Statement of Roderick, Undated,

USMS Collections; Copy, Memorandum, Arthur Roderick to Jim Sullivan, January 4, 1993, USMS Collections.

21. Copy, Statement of Roderick, Undated, USMS Collections; Lardner, Jr. and Leiby, "Standoff at Ruby Ridge," *Washington Post,* September 3, 1995; Copy, "Information Sheet—Randall Weaver Incident," USMS Collections.

22. Copy, Statement of Roderick, Undated, USMS Collections; Copy,"Events Leading Up to Shootout," Questionnaire of Ruby Ridge Events, USMS Collections.

23. Interview, Art Roderick, January 30, 2012; Copy, Statement of Roderick, Undated, USMS Collections; Copy, Statement of Larry T. Cooper, Undated, USMS Collections; Copy,"Events Leading Up to Shootout," Questionnaire of Ruby Ridge Events, USMS Collections.

24. Interview, Art Roderick, January 30, 2012; Copy, Statement of Roderick, Undated, USMS Collections.

25. Copy, Statement of Larry T. Cooper, Undated, USMS Collections; Copy, Statement of Roderick, Undated, USMS Collections.

26. Ibid.; Lardner, Jr. and Leiby, "Standoff at Ruby Ridge," *Washington Post,* September 3, 1995. Accounts position Roderick away from the initial encounter—he was furthest away and down the path. He also reacted to the first melee—which is not initiation.

27. Copy, "Events Leading Up to Shootout," Questionnaire of Ruby Ridge Events, USMS Collections; Copy, Statement of Larry T. Cooper, Undated, USMS Collections; Copy, Statement of Roderick, Undated, USMS Collections.

28. Copy, Statement of Larry T. Cooper, Undated, USMS Collections; Lardner, Jr. and Leiby, "Standoff at Ruby Ridge," *Washington Post,* September 3, 1995.

29. Ibid.; Copy, Statement of Roderick, Undated, USMS Collections; Copy, "Information Sheet—Randall Weaver Incident," USMS Collections.

30. Richard Leiby and George Lardner, Jr., "Siege Guided by Hastily Revised Rules of Engagement," *Washington Post,* September 3, 1995; Copy, "Information Sheet—Randall Weaver Incident," USMS Collections.

N<small>OTES TO</small> C<small>HAPTER</small> 17

1. "Handling the Fury of Hurricane Andrew," *Marshals Monitor,* November 1992, 9.

2. Ibid.; Fact Sheet, United States Marshals Service Mobile Command Center, ca. 1991, USMS Collections.

3. Interview with Larry Mogavero, Nick Prevas, and Leon Roberts, April 17, 2013, USMS Collections.

4. Fact Sheet, United States Marshals Service Mobile Command Center, ca. 1991, USMS Collections.

5. "Handling the Fury of Hurricane Andrew," *Marshals Monitor,* November 1992, 9.

6. "Special Operations Center Opens," *Marshals Monitor,* January 1993, 1, 3; "SOG Center Dedicated to Bill Degan," *Marshals Monitor,* April 1993, 3.

7. "Frontier Marshal Statue," *Marshals Monitor,* April 1993, 12. The author was present when the statue was brought to headquarters and witnessed the entry and placement in the lobby of Lincoln Place. The revolving doors had to be dismantled to provide entry.

8. Daniel B. Wood, "Los Angeles Braces Itself as Federal Civil Trial Opens in the Rodney King Case," *Christian Science Monitor,* February 1, 1993; U.S. Department of Justice, 1992 *Annual Report of The Attorney General of the United States,* 30.

9. Wood, "Los Angeles Braces," *Christian Science Monitor,* February 1, 1993; "Timeline: Rodney King from 1991-2012," CNN.com, July 17, 2012.

10. Copy, "Trials Attracting High Media and Public Interest," ca. 1993, USMS Collections. This appeared to be a page from the copy of an instructional package.

11. Don Hunsberger, "The Village's Detective Stories," *The Village Daily Sun*, December 29, 2005.

12. Ibid.

13. "Will *The Fugitive* Work on the Big Screen?," Intelligence Report, *Parade Magazine*, August 1, 1993, 10. The movie was based on the old television series from 1963-67, starring David Janssen.

14. Interview, Marvin Lutes, October 2, 2006, USMS Collections.

15. Ibid.

16. Ibid.

17. Ibid. The famous "waterfall scene," which featured a long pursuit before Dr. Kimball's character shouted to Deputy Gerard that he didn't kill his wife, and Gerard's response of "I don't care," was explained by Lutes. This particular scene, filmed in North Carolina with McLaughlin advising, was based on the explanation to actor Tommy Lee Jones that deputy marshals carried out their duties no matter the reason or circumstances. It came out somewhat differently on film, but was a landmark scene.

18. "Media Requests to Fly 'Con Air,'" *FYI,* December 12, 1991, 7; Eric Malnic, "When Jailbirds Fly, They Always Use 'Con Air,'" *Los Angeles Times,* August 9, 1993; Roy Hargrove, "'Con Air' Offers a Thrilling Ride," *Texas City Sun,* June 6, 1997; Roger Ebert, "Out of Sight," *Chicago Sun-Times,* June 19, 1998.

19. Maureen Pan, *"M.A.R.S.H.A.L.S. E Mail Speeds Messages," Marshals Monitor*, February-March 1993, 7.

20. Ibid.; Interview, Ron Pautz, December 10, 2004, USMS Collections.

21. Matt Truell, "Man Enters Court Firing Guns, Throwing Bombs; Officer Killed," *Houston Chronicle*, August 6, 1993; Copy of Teletype,

Director Henry E. Hudson to All United States Marshals, "Update to Shooting Incident in Topeka, Kansas," [August 6, 1993], USMS Collections; Associated Press, "Gunman Kills Guard in Courthouse Spree," August 6, 1993. Two other points—McKnight also had a truck that exploded next to the Jefferson County, Kansas Courthouse, about 20 miles to the northeast. Lastly, he left a suicide note, so his final goal was clear. However, the fatal explosion may or may not have been self-detonated.

22. Copy of Teletype, Director Henry E. Hudson to All United States Marshals, "Update to Shooting Incident in Topeka, Kansas," [August 6, 1993], USMS Collections.

23. Copy, Release, "President Nominates Tampa Police Chief as Director of the U.S. Marshals Service," Department of Justice, June 25, 1993, USMS Collections; Copy, Acting Director John J. Twomey to All U.S. Marshals and Suboffices, All Headquarters Divisions and Staff Officers, "Acting Director of the U.S. Marshals Service," October 15, 1993, USMS Collections.

24. Copy, Release,"President Nominates Tampa Police Chief as Director of the U.S. Marshals Service"; Biographical Outline, Eduardo Gonzalez, Dated November 17, 1998, Office of Public Affairs, USMS Collections.

25. "Hunt Is Renewed for Inmates from 1962 Alcatraz Breakout," *New York Times*, November 14, 1993. See also Mike Deupree, "Eastwood and a Good Yarn," *Cedar Rapids Gazette*, July 7, 1979.

26. "Hunt Is Renewed," *New York Times*, November 14, 1993; Copy, Release, "Alcatraz: The Escape," *America's Most Wanted;* Michael Hedges, "'America's Most Wanted' Joins the Hunt for Alcatraz Escapees," *Washington Times*, November 10, 1993.

27. Copy, Biography Fact Sheet, John J. Twomey, USMS Collections.

28. Biographical Outline, Eduardo Gonzalez, November 17, 1998, Office of Public Affairs, USMS Collections; Email Interview, Eduardo Gonzalez, July 30, 2013, USMS Collections. Please note that the email was received on this date, although the information was sent through an undated

attachment. Therefore, the received date will be used for all subsequent entries with this source.

29. Email Interview, Eduardo Gonzalez, July 30, 2013, USMS Collections.

30. Ibid.

31. Ibid.; Interview with Larry Mogavero, Nick Prevas, and Leon Roberts, April 17, 2013, USMS Collections; Copy, Memo, George R. Havens to All U.S. Marshals Employees, July 14, 1999, USMS Collections; Copy, Release, "President Nominates Tampa Police Chief as Director of The U.S. Marshals Service"; "Consultant Comes on Board," *Marshals Monitor*, April 1994, 4; Interview, Mogavero, Prevas, and Roberts, April 17, 2013, USMS Collections.

32. Copy, USMS News Release, November 19, 1993, USMS Collections; Copy, Release, "President Nominates Tampa Police Chief as Director of the U.S. Marshals Service."

33. "Director Faces Challenge of New Agency and Role," *Marshals Monitor,* February 1994, 2.

34. "Director Faces Challenge," *Marshals Monitor*, February 1994, 2. See also Email Interview, Eduardo Gonzalez, July 30, 2013, USMS Collections.

35. "The Reinvention Ride Begins at the Service," *Marshals Monitor,* February 1994, 15; "Director Supports AWS," *Marshals Monitor*, February 1994, 14.

36. Interview, Mogavero, Prevas, and Roberts, April 17, 2013, USMS Collections.

37. "Process Improvement Teams Score Early," *Marshals Monitor,* March-April 1995, 9; "Improved Allocation Process Being Developed," *Marshals Monitor*, September-October 1995, 11; Interview, Mogovero, Prevas, and Roberts, April 17, 2013, USMS Collections.

38. "Budget Challenges Abound for FY 1994," *Marshals Monitor,* February 1994, 4; Interview, Mogovero, Prevas, and Roberts, April 17,

2013, USMS Collections; "USMS Grapevine Proves Thick and False," *Marshals Monitor*, March 1994, 1; "Dispelling Rumors via E-mail Encouraged," *Marshals Monitor*, March 1994, 2.

39. "New Challenges Await our Agency in 1995," *Marshals Monitor*, January-February 1995, 2. He addressed the subject retrospectively in "An Anniversary Full of Challenges and Victories," *Marshals Monitor*, November-December 1994, 2.

40. Copy, Director Eduardo Gonzalez to Executive Director Joseph Wright, National Organization of Black Law Enforcement Executives, March 21, 1994, USMS Collections.

41. Ibid.; Email Interview, Eduardo Gonzalez, July 30, 2013, USMS Collections. See also Leigh Rivenbark, "Political Appointments vs. Career Jobs," *Federal Times,* March 28, 1994.

42. "Service Transfers Tucker Auto to Smithsonian," *Marshals Monitor*, February 1994, 12.

43. Copy, Email, Jim Herzog to Author, June 13, 2013.

44. "Service Transfers Tucker Auto," 12; Email Interview, Eduardo Gonzalez, July 30, 2013, USMS Collections.

45. Email Interview, Eduardo Gonzalez, July 30, 2013, USMS Collections.

46. Ibid. From the opposing viewpoint, some employees felt Director Gonzalez targeted the function for elimination.

47. Patrick Symmes, "U.S. Marshals Service Succeeds in Closing a Division, But Not a Deal," *Legal Times*, March 27, 1995.

48. Interview with Larry Mogavero, Nick Prevas, and Leon Roberts, April 17, 2013, USMS Collections; Symmes, "U.S. Marshals Service Succeeds." The paring down of regional offices began in 1991 from 8 to 3.

49. Ronald J. Ostrow and Jeff Leeds, "Marshals Sent to Offer Abortion Clinic Security," *Los Angeles Times,* August 2, 1994; Associated Press, "Marshals Begin Protecting Abortion Clinics," *Kerrville [Texas]*

Daily Times, August 2, 1994; "Two Lives Represent Extremes," *Elyria [Ohio] Chronicle-Telegram,* March 14, 1993; Bill Kaczor, "Anti-abortion Activist Gets Life for Shooting Fla. Doctor," *Texas City Sun,* March 6, 1994; Christopher B. Daly, "Salvi Convicted of Murder in Shootings," *Washington Post,* March 19, 1996.

50. Interview, Eduardo Gonzalez, July 30, 2013, USMS Collections.

51. Despite the moral objections of the task to some, the deputies were no different. Most cast aside any personal feelings and did the duties as assigned, but others were allowed to refrain if feasible.

Notes to Chapter 18

1. Interview, Jamy Murphy, May 8, 2008, USMS Collections.

2. Ibid.

3. "Marshal Recounts Oklahoma City Bombing," *The Marshals Monitor,* May-June 1995, 1.

4. Ibid.

5. Interview, Jamy Murphy, May 8, 2008, USMS Collections.

6. Ibid.

7. Interview, Director Stacia A. Hylton, August 19, 2013, USMS Collections.

8. Interview, Jamy Murphy, May 8, 2008, USMS Collections.

9. "Marshal Recounts," *Marshals Monitor,* May-June 1995, 1.

10. Ibid.

11. "Spirit of Giving and Sharing Shines Through," *Marshals Monitor,* May-June 1995, 2.

12. Ibid.; "Marshal Recounts," *Marshals Monitor,* May-June 1995, 4; Interview, Jamy Murphy, May 8, 2008, USMS Collections.

13. "Marshal Recounts," *Marshals Monitor*, May-June 1995, 4.

14. Email Interview, Eduardo Gonzalez, July 30, 2013, USMS Collections.

15. "Marshal Recounts," *Marshals Monitor*, May-June 1995, 4.

16. Jo Thomas, 'No Sympathy' for Dead Children, McVeigh Says," *New York Times*, March 20, 2001; "Thoughts and Thanks to Friends and Colleagues," *Marshals Monitor*, July-August, 1995, 7.

17. Copy, Department of Justice, Oklahoma City Bombing Investigation/Prosecution, Actual Costs FY 1995 through 6/30/98, FY 1998, USMS Collections.

18. Interview, Director Stacia A. Hylton, August 19, 2013, USMS Collections. When assigned the task, she was given just 45 days to present a finished account.

19. Report, United States Marshals Service, "Vulnerability Assessment of Federal Facilities-June 28, 1995; Copy, Statement of Eugene L. Coon, Jr., Acting Associate Director for Operations, Before the House Transportation and Infrastructure Subcommittee on Public Buildings and Economic Development, April 24, 1996; "Service Recommends Security Upgrades," *Marshals Monitor*, July-August 1995, 5.

20. USMS Management and Budget Division, *The FY 1996 Report to the U.S. Marshals: A Review of District Office Activities*, January 1997, USMS Pub. No. 44, 7; "USMS Reinvention Continues Its Winding Path," *Marshals Monitor*, September-October 1995, 2; "AirOps Embarks on New Mission," *Marshals Monitor*, September-October 1995, 1; Ibid., 6.

21. "Office of District Affairs Assists Field," January-February 1995, 7; "Deputies LEAP into Workweek," *Marshals Monitor*, March-April 1995, 4. LEAP provided criminal investigators (known as GS-1811s) an additional 25 percent of base pay for commitment to work a minimum of at least two additional hours a day. Essentially investigators already were putting in the hours, especially during long operational initiatives.

22. "Deputies WIN in Every USMS District," *Marshals Monitor,*January-February 1997, 1.

23. Interview, Don Ward, August 9, 2013, USMS Collections; "New General Counsel Named," *Marshals Monitor,* July-August 1994, 7; "Chief Sullivan to Take Lead Post at INTERPOL," *Marshals Monitor,* November-December 1995, 11. INTERPOL was (and is) an international law enforcement agency with 160 member countries in 1995. Among its priorities are tracking fugitives in member countries and coordinating a worldwide network. Sullivan was the first USMS employee chosen for the post, but not the last. In fact, USMS influence has been steady since this time. Tim Williams, another USMS employee, attained this post in recent times.

24. Copy, Memorandum, Director Eduardo Gonzalez to All United States Marshals Service Employees, May 12, 1995, USMS Collections.

25. Interview, Don Ward, August 9, 2013, USMS Collections; "Ruby Ridge Hearing Delay Sought," *Chicago Tribune,* August 17, 1995; George Lardner Jr. and Richard Leiby, "Government Witnesses Cause Case to Collapse," *Washington Post,* September 5, 1995.

26. Email Interview, Eduardo Gonzalez, July 30, 2013, USMS Collections.

27. "Service Called to V.I. after Hurricane Marilyn," *Marshals Monitor,* November-December 1995, 12.

28. "USMS Back to Work after Furlough," *Marshals Monitor,* January-February 1996, 1.

29. Ibid.

30. Interview, Robert Finan, August 11, 2009, USMS Collections; "People on the Move," *Congressional Monitor,* August 5, 1996, 11; Copy, Biographical Outline, Robert James Finan II, August 19, 1996.

31. "New Personnel Officer," *FYI* 8, no. 6, p. 3; Copy, Director Eduardo Gonzalez to All United States Marshals Service Employees, July 18, 1996, USMS Collections.

32. Copy, Memorandum, Director Eduardo Gonzalez to All United States Marshals, Deputy Director, Assistant Directors, General Counsel, Chief Deputy United States Marshals, April 30, 1997. Kris Marcy departed the U.S. Marshals Service for a position at the Immigration and Naturalization Service (INS).

33. Ibid; "Reno Approves Accreditation Request," *Marshals Monitor*, November-December 1997, 1; "Marshals Service Is Primed for a Jump in Stature," *Marshals Monitor*, November-December 1997, 2.

34. Interview, John Marshall, August 9, 2013, USMS Collections.

35. Ibid.

36. Email Interview, Eduardo Gonzalez, July 30, 2013, USMS Collections.

37. Copy, "The United States Marshals Service 1789-1997," Supporting Documents for H.R. 927, *USMS Improvement Act of 1997*, Undated, USMS Collections.

38. Copy, "Marshals Improvements Act Ad Hoc Committee," Supporting Documents for H.R. 927, *U.S. Marshals Service Improvement Act of 1997*, Undated, USMS Collections; Copy, "*United States Marshals Service Improvement Act of 1997* (Passed by the House), *H.R. 927, AN ACT, 105th Congress, 1st Session*, Supporting Documents, March 18, 1997.

39. Ibid.; Copy, "*United States Marshals Service Improvement Act of 1997*," March 18, 1997.

40. Interview, Marvin Lutes, October 2, 2006, USMS Collections.

41. Copy, "Statement of Eduardo Gonzalez, Director United States Marshals Service Before the United States Senate Committee on the Judiciary March 10, 1998," USMS Collections.

42. Email Interview, Eduardo Gonzalez, July 30, 2013, USMS Collections.

43. Copy, "Statement of Gonzalez, Committee on the Judiciary, March 10, 1998," USMS Collections.

44. Email Interview, Eduardo Gonzalez, July 30, 2013, USMS Collections.

45. Ibid.

46. United States Marshals Service, *Marshals Service 2000: The Strategic Plan of the United States Marshals Service 1997 and Beyond*, USMS Publication No. 42, Revised February 14, 1997, 2-5.

47. "United States Marshals Service, Executive Summary, Third Quarter," in *Report to the Attorney General, United States Marshals Service, Third Quarter 1997 Report*, 3, USMS Collections.

48. United States Marshals Service, *Marshals Service 2000*, 8.

49. Ibid., 9.

50. Ibid., 10-15.

51. "Executive Summary, Third Quarter, *Report to the Attorney General*, 3; United States Marshals Service, USMS Publication No. 73, *United States Marshals Service Tactical Plan 1998-2000*, Revised March 1998, 1-2; Interview, Eduardo Gonzalez, July 30, 2013, USMS Collections.

52. *Tactical Plan 1998-2000*, 1-3; Executive Summary, Third Quarter, *Report to the Attorney General*, 3.

53. Copy, Organization Chart, June 10, 1998, USMS Collections; Copy, Director Eduardo Gonzalez to All United States Marshals, Deputy Director, Assistant Directors, General Counsel, Chief Deputy U.S. Marshals, and Staff Officers, July 25, 1997; Interview, Robert Finan, August 11, 2009, USMS Collections.

54. Interview, Mogavero, Prevas, and Roberts, April 17, 2013, USMS Collections; Copy, Talking Points, Director Eduardo Gonzalez, USMS Town Meeting, March 3, 1999, USMS Collections.

55. Eduardo Gonzalez, "A New Way to Choose U.S. Marshals," *Police Chief* 65, no. 10 (October 1998): 8, as permitted by National Performance Review, "Creating a Government That Works Better and Costs Less," Department of Justice Recommendation No. 15, p. i; "Town Hall Meeting

Affords Chance to Look Back," *Marshals Monitor*, March-April 1999, 2-3; David Ignatius, "Failure Should Be Viewed as a Healthy Endeavor," Originally in *Washington Post*, March 3, 1999.

56. "The Director Heads for the Florida Sun," *Marshals Monitor*, May-June 1999, 1.

57. Copy, Biographical Outline, Eduardo Gonzalez, Director, November 17, 1998; Copy, Memorandum, Director John W. Marshall to All U.S. Marshal Service Employees, November 24, 1999. The agency achieved accreditation in November 1999.

58. "Havens Outlines His Primary Leadership Tenets," *Marshals Monitor*, July-August 1999, 2; Press Release, "John W. Marshall New Director of the Marshals Service," November 18, 1999.

NOTES TO CHAPTER 19

1. Copy, Department of Justice Release, "George R. Havens Appointed Acting Director of the U.S. Marshals Service," June 22, 1999, USMS Collections; Copy, Acting Director George R. Havens to All U.S. Marshals Service Employees, July 14, 1999; Copy, Biographical Outline, George Ray Havens, Deputy Director, USMS Collections; Copy, Untitled Listing of Directors and Deputy Directors, USMS Collections; Copy, "Approved Assistant Directors," Director Eduardo Gonzalez to All United States Marshals Service Employees, July 18, 1996.

2. "Havens Outlines His Primary Leadership Tenets," *Marshals Monitor*, July-August 1999, 2.

3. Ibid. LEAP brought in journeymen Grade Series 12 investigators. See Interview, Jeff Stine and Jeff Cahull, June 24, 2013, USMS Collections.

4. Copy, "Report on Conditions and Roles in Vieques," Undated, USMS Collections; Interview, Robert Finan, August 11, 2009, USMS Collections.

5. Copy, "Report on Conditions and Roles in Vieques," USMS Collections.

6. Ibid.

7. Edward Walsh and Roberto Suro, "Marshals Seize Waco Evidence from FBI," *Washington Post*, September 2, 1999; Interview, Robert Finan, August 11, 2009, USMS Collections.

8. Walsh and Suro, "Marshals Seize Waco Evidence." The evidence included videotapes about the use of teargas at Waco. They immediately turned it over upon discovery.

9. Interview, Robert Finan, August 11, 2009, USMS Collections. The described cartoon was by Chip Bok of the *Akron (Ohio) Beacon Journal.*

10. "Marshall Arts," *Washington Post,* June 5, 1999; Copy, Press Release, "President Clinton Names John W. Marshall as Director of the U.S. Marshals Service at the Department of Justice," from whitehouse.gov website, August 5, 1999; Copy, Director John W. Marshall Biographical Outline, USMS Collections.

11. "John W. Marshall New Director of the Marshals Service," USMS Press Release, November 18, 1999.

12. Copy, Email, "A Message from the Director," November 18, 1999, USMS Collections.

13. Interview, John Marshall, August 9, 2013, USMS Collections.

14. Copy, Biographical Outline, Michael R. Ramon, Deputy Director, Office of Public Affairs, USMS Collections.

15. Interview, John Marshall, August 9, 2013, USMS Collections.

16. "CALEA Project Nears Completion," *Marshals Monitor*, September-October 1999, 15; "2000 Director's Honorary Awards Ceremony," *Marshals Monitor*, March-April 2000, 1.

17. Interview, John Marshall, August 9, 2013, USMS Collections.

18. Copy, Media Advisory, USMS Public Affairs Office, January 27, 2000, USMS Collections; Copy, Program Page for Installation of the Director,

United States Marshals Service, February 1, 2000, USMS Collections; Paul Tolme, "Son of Justice Sworn in to Head Marshals," *Arlington Journal Online*, February 2, 2000.

19. Interview, Eduardo Gonzalez, July 30, 2013, USMS Collections. The Installation and Director's Awards were held the same day.

20. "Marshall Arts," *Washington Post*, June 5, 1999; "USMS Director John W. Marshall Talks Security," *The Third Branch* 32, no. 2 (February 2000): 10-12; "Marshall Law," *People Weekly*, April 3, 2000, 100.

21. "USMS Director John W. Marshall Talks Security," 10.

22. Interview, John Marshall, August 9, 2013, USMS Collections.

NOTES TO CHAPTER 20

1. "Elian, Father Relocated from Andrews," *Washington Post*, April 25, 2000. Today, ICE carries on the duties formerly provided.

2. Ibid.; Copy, Notes on Juan Gonzalez Protective Detail, USMS Collections. *Elian Gonzalez, by and through Lazaro Gonzalez v. Janet Reno*, Order in Case No. 00-206-CIV-MOORE (SDFL March 2000). Of interest is that former USMS Director K. Michael Moore was the judge who issued the order; Michael A. Pearson, later an Assistant Director with the USMS, worked at the INS at the time.

3. "Elian, Father Relocated from Andrews," *Washington Post*, April 25, 2000; Copy, Department of Justice, *Elian Gonzalez Case Costs Through April 24, 2000*, USMS Collections; Interview, John Marshall, August 9, 2013, USMS Collections; Interview, Robert Finan, August 11, 2009, USMS Collections.

4. "U.S. Oks Visit by Elian's Playmates," *USA Today*, April 25, 2000.

5. "Life Quieter for Cuban Boy; Elian's Family Lives Comfortably on Bucolic Estate," *Florida Times Union*, May 7, 2000; "U.S. Psychiatrist: Elian 'Doing Well,'" *CNN.com*, April 26, 2000.

6. "Service Called Upon to Protect Elian Gonzalez," *Marshals Monitor*, July-August 2000, 3-5.

7. Ibid.

8. Interview, Mike Pyo, June 24, 2013, USMS Collections.

9. Copy, Form Letter, August 2000, USMS Collections; Copy, E-Mail, Drew Wade to Tom Connor and Dave Turner, May 15, 2000.

10. Ibid.; Drew Wade, Personal Reminiscence.

11. Wade, Personal Reminiscence.

12. Copy, "The Gonzalez Family at Youth for Understanding," Youth for Understanding International Exchange, Press Release, May 26, 2000; "Service Called Upon to Protect Elian Gonzalez," *Marshals Monitor*, July-August 2000, 3.

13. "Service Called Upon to Protect Elian Gonzalez," 3-5.

14. Copy, Director John W. Marshall to All U.S. Marshals Services Employees, June 8, 2000, USMS Collections; "E/CA's Hillman Always Strove to Be the Best," *Marshals Monitor*, May-June 2000, 6.

15. "E/CA's Hillman," *Marshals Monitor*, May-June 2000, 6; Interview, John Marshall, August 9, 2013, USMS Collections.

16. "E/CA's Hillman," *Marshals Monitor*, May-June 2000, 6; Program, Director's Honorary Awards Ceremony, February 28, 2001; "California Interchange Named for Pete Hillman," *Marshals Monitor*, November-December 2001, 9.

17. "Admin. Employees Are Deserving of Praise, Too," *Marshals Monitor*, July-August 2000, 2.

18. Interview, John Marshall, August 9, 2013, USMS Collections; Copy, List of Directors and Deputy Directors of the USMS, Undated, USMS Collections; Copy, Memorandum, Director John W. Marshall to All

Employees, August 1, 2000, USMS Collections; Interview, E-Mail, Michael Ramon, December 2, 2013, USMS Collections. He was assigned closer to his home, so his departure was likely for personal reasons.

19. Copy, List of Directors and Deputy Directors of the USMS, Undated, USMS Collections; Copy, Biographical Outline, Louie T. McKinney, March 6, 2001, USMS Collections; Interview, John Marshall, August 9, 2013, USMS Collections.

20. Copy, Fact Sheet, Associate Director for Administration David F. Musel, USMS Collections. From 2004 to 2009, Associate Director Musel was Deputy Federal Detention Trustee and Acting Federal Detention Trustee. He became Assistant Director of JPATS after a realignment in 2012, then later became Acting Assistant Director of the Prisoner Services Division.

21. "Regional Task Forces Launch New Era," *Marshals Monitor*, December 2003-January 2004, 5. Citation for the Act is Public Law 106-544, 106th Congress; 28 U.S.C. 566, note.

22. Interview, Mike Pyo, June 24, 2013, USMS Collections.

23. Ibid. See also Copy, Memorandum, Assistant Director [Tactical Operations Division] Neil K. DeSousa to United States Marshals, Chief Deputy United States Marshals, Assistant Directors, Deputy Assistant Directors, "Explosive Detection Canine Program," August 5, 2014. In Fiscal Year 2014, the Marshals Service canine program boasted 21 K-9 units in many districts. A unit consisted of a deputy U.S. marshal and an ATF-certified explosives detection canine. The primary mission of the teams was "to search for explosives devices, firearms, shell casings, and post blast materials in support of agency protective and investigative missions."

24. Interview, John Marshall, August 9, 2013, USMS Collections. See "Spotlight: Ed Dolan, UFMS Project Executive, USMS Intranet Document, November 20, 2012.

25. "New Fiscal Year to Bring Salary Decentralization," *Marshals Monitor*, September-October 2000, 2.

26. Press Release, "Deputy Attorney General Holder to Honor Civil Rights Pioneer Ruby Bridges at Ceremony at Corcoran Gallery of Art," August 9, 2000; "Ruby Bridges Becomes Honorary Deputy," *Marshals Monitor*, September-October 2000, 1; Internet Article, "History—Ruby Bridges: Honorary Deputy," www.usmarshals.gov/history/bridges, History Page, USMS website.

NOTES TO CHAPTER 21

1. Interview, John Marshall, August 9, 2013, USMS Collections.

2. "The USMS Helps Rope in the Texas Seven," *Marshals Monitor*, January-February 2001, 1; Ibid., 8; Copy, Memorandum, Assistant Director [Investigative Services Division] Robert J. Finan II to All U.S. Marshals, All Chief Deputy U.S. Marshals, " 'Texas 7' Investigation," January 29, 2001, USMS Collections.

3. "The USMS Helps Rope in the Texas Seven," 8.

4. Ibid., 8-9; "Questions and Answers: Manhunt," *Newsweek* interview with Art Roderick, msnbc.com, January 16, 2001; Finan to All U.S. Marshals, All Chief Deputy U.S. Marshals, "'Texas 7' Investigation," January 29, 2001, USMS Collections.

5. "The USMS Helps Rope in the Texas Seven," 9-11; "FBI Searching for 2 Texas Escapees Still on the Loose," CNN.com, January 22, 2001; Finan to All U.S. Marshals, All Chief Deputy U.S. Marshals, " 'Texas 7' Investigation," January 29, 2001, USMS Collections. The capture operations lasted three days, from January 20-23. The remaining six escapees were all sentenced to death.

6. "Louie McKinney Becomes Acting USMS Director," *Marshals Monitor*, March-April 2001, 2; Copy, "A Farewell Message to All Employees," January 19, 2001, USMS Collections.

7. Ibid.; Copy, Biographical Outline, Acting Director Louie T. McKinney, USMS Collections.

8. Copy, Biographical Outline, Acting Deputy Director Stacia A. Hylton, USMS Collections; Interview, Director Stacia Hylton, August 19, 2013, USMS Collections; United States Marshals: 1789 to Present.

9. See Calhoun, *Lawmen,* 27-34.

10. "Deputies Gently Seize Baptist Church over IRS Tax Dispute," *Marshals Monitor,* May-June 2001, 3; "Feds Seize Baptist Church over $6 Million Tax Debt," *Deseret News,* February 13, 2001.

11. "Deputies Gently Seize Baptist Church," 3. Citation for case is *U.S. v. Indianapolis Baptist Church,* 2000 WL 1449856 (SDIN September 28, 2000) (No. IP 98-0498-C-B/S). The citation for the Supreme Court case is certiorari denied by IBT v. U.S., 531 U.S. 1112 (January 16, 2001).

12. "Feds Seize Baptist Church," *Deseret News,* February 13, 2001. See also Associated Press, "Feds Seize Baptist Church over $6 Million Tax Debt," February 13, 2001; Copy, Release, "Peaceful Takeover by U.S. Marshals Shifts Baptist Temple to Federal Receiver, USMS Collections."

13. "USMS Plays Vital Roles in Federal Executions," *Marshals Monitor,* July-August 2001, 13; Jo Thomas, " 'No Sympathy' for Dead Children, McVeigh Says," *New York Times,* March 29, 2001. The article announced the sale of the book by Michel and Herbeck on April 3, 2001.

14. "USMS Plays Vital Roles in Federal Executions," *Marshals Monitor,* July-August 2001, 13; Web Article, "History—Historical Federal Executions," usmarshals.gov/history/executions, USMS Website. "An Act for the Punishment of Certain Crimes against the United States" (April 30, 1790) and Judiciary Act of 1789 are the historical references for the role of U.S. Marshals in federal death sentences. While both Acts do not explicitly assign the role, the U.S. Marshals began presiding as the law enforcement officials to carry out the duties.

15. "USMS Plays Vital Roles in Federal Executions," *Marshals Monitor*, July-August 2001, 13.

16. Ibid.

17. Ibid.

18. Karen Gullo, "Backup Ordered for Abortion Protests," *Washington Post*, July 12, 2001; Roxana Hegeman, "Abortion Foes Return to Kansas," *Washington Post*, July 10, 2001; Dan Eggen, "U.S. Marshals to Protect Abortion Doctor," *Washington Post*, July 13, 2001.

19. Gullo, "Backup Ordered," *Washington Post*, July 12, 2001; Eggen, "U.S. Marshals to Protect," *Washington Post*, July 13, 2001; Web Article, Alexandra Marks, "In Abortion Fight, Lines Have Shifted," *Public News-Room*, publicbroastcast.net/wnyc/news/content/144617.html. Ms. Marks was noted as staff writer for *Christian Science Monitor*. Citation to statute: public law 103-259 (May 26, 1994); 18 U.S.C. 248.

20. Marks, "In Abortion Fight," *Public NewsRoom*; Stan Finger, "Picketing, Video Start Abortion Foes' Week," *Wichita Eagle*, July 16, 2001; Tim Jones, "Abortion Battle Back in Wichita," *Chicago Tribune*, July 17, 2001.

21. Web Article, "Abortion Doctor Gunned Down at Kansas Church, Suspect in Custody," Foxnews.com, May 31, 2009; Stan Finger, "Court Upholds Scott Roeder's Conviction in George Tiller's Murder but Orders Resentencing," *Wichita Eagle*, October 24, 2014.

22. Copy, Release, "15 Most Wanted Fugitive Clayton Waagner, on Mission from God to Kill Abortion Doctors, Filmed in Harrisburg, Pa., Robbing a Bank," May 18, 2001, USMS Collections; Edith Brady-Lunny, "Waagner Now Marshals' Top Priority," *Bloomington [IL] Pantagraph*, May 24, 2001; Dennis B. Roddy, "Fugitive Keeps Giving the Slip to Fed Agents," *Pittsburgh Post-Gazette*, May 28, 2001.

23. Copy, Release, "15 Most Wanted Fugitive Clayton Waagner, on Mission from God to Kill Abortion Doctors."

24. Ibid.

25. Ibid.

NOTES TO CHAPTER 22

1. Paul Courson, "Judge Rejects Injunction to Stop Vieques Shelling," cnn.com, April 26, 2001.

2. Ibid.

3. "Marshals Service Helps Quell Vieques Uprisings," *Marshals Monitor,* July-August 2001, 16.

4. Ibid.; Ronald O'Rourke, Congressional Research Service, "Vieques, Puerto Rico Naval Training Range: Background and Issues for Congress," December 17, 2001, U.S. Navy Web Site (www.history.navy.mil).

5. "Donald Gambatesa Becomes Deputy Director," *Marshals Monitor,* July-August 2001, 2.

6. "Astronaut Jim Reilly Takes the Star to the Stars," *Marshals Monitor,* September-October 2001, 11-14; Eileen Hawley, Release J01-59, "Astronaut James Reilly to Become Honorary U.S. Marshal," nasa.gov. The first two Honorary U.S. Marshals were President Ronald Reagan and actor James Arness.

7. Julie Mason, "To the Rescue; Texas Lawman Eyed to Aid Troubled U.S. Marshals," *Houston Chronicle,* July 29, 2001; "Reyna Named Head of Marshals Service," *Washington Times,* October 31, 2001.

8. Interview, Gerry Auerbach, May 11, 2005, USMS Collections.

9. Interview, Jeff Cahall, June 24, 2013, USMS Collections.

10. E-Mail Interview, Dominic Guadagnoli to Author, September 18, 2013, USMS Collections.

11. Ibid.

12. E-Mail, John Svinos to Author, August 28, 2013.

13. Ibid.

14. E-Mail Interview, Dominic Guadagnoli to Author, September 18, 2013.

15. "Deputies answer nation's call to help," *Marshals Monitor*, September-October 2001, 1; E-Mail Interview, Guadagnoli to Author, September 18, 2013.

16. E-Mail Interview, Guadagnoli to Author, September 18, 2013.

17. E-Mail Interview, John Svinos to Author, August 28, 2013.

18. Ibid.

19. Ibid.

20. Ibid.

21. Interview, Donald Horton, May 8, 2014, USMS Collections.

22. Interview, William Sorukas, June 30, 2009, USMS Collections.

23. Ibid.

24. Ibid. Then of Technical Operations, Robertson later became Commander of the Special Operations Group.

25. Interview, Robert Finan, August 11, 2009, USMS Collections.

26. Copy, "Briefing Material—Possible Questions-and-Answer's [*sic*] for "Attack on America" Interviews, Office of Public Affairs, USMS Collections.

27. Ibid.; "Deputies answer the call," *Marshals Monitor*, September-October 2001, 18. William Snelson later became the Associate Director for Operations.

28. Interview, Jeff Cahall, June 24, 2013, USMS Collections.

29. Copy, Acting Director Louie T. McKinney to All United States Marshals and Employees, September 12, 2001, USMS Collections.

30. Interview, William Sorukas, June 30, 2009, USMS Collections.

31. Ibid.

32. Ibid.

33. "FAA allows limited flights to resume,"CNN, September 12, 2001.

34. Drew Wade, Personal Reminiscence.

35. Bill Moor, "Ground Zero Was Not at All the Scene for a Postcard," *South Bend Tribune*, September 28, 2001.

36. "Deputies Answer Nation's Call to Help,"*Marshals Monitor*, September-October 2001, 1; Interview, Mike Pyo, June 24, 2013, USMS Collections.

37. Interview, Mike Pyo, June 24, 2013, USMS Collections.

38. "USMS Played Extensive Role in Sept. 11 Terrorism Aftermath," *Marshals Monitor*, November-December 2001, 2. Michael Prout later became Assistant Director of Witness Security.

39. Copy, "Briefing Material," Office of Public Affairs; Interview, William Sorukas, June 30, 2009, USMS Collections.

40. "2002 Director's Honorary Awards Ceremony," Special Section of *Marshals Monitor*, March-April 2002, 5-10.

41. The photograph was featured in the *Monitor*—and in nationwide venues. The continuing popularity of the image has become one of the prominent depictions of any deputy since Norman Rockwell's painting of anonymous deputies escorting young Ruby Bridges to school in 1960.

42. "2001 Anthrax Attacks Timeline: Five Die After Letters Mailed," *WJLA.com*, October 21, 2011.

43. Interview, Mogavero, Prevas, and Roberts, April 17, 2013, USMS Collections.

44. Ibid.; Copy, Acting Director Louie T. McKinney to All United States Marshals Service Employees, October 19, 2001, USMS Collections.

45. Interview, Mogavero, Prevas, and Roberts, April 17, 2013, USMS Collections.

46. Ibid.

NOTES TO CHAPTER 23

1. "Should Airline Pilots Be Armed?" abcnews.go.com, September 25, 2001; John Lott, Jr., "Arming Pilots Is the Best Way to Get Air Security," *Los Angeles Times*, March 11, 2002.

2. Official Biography, Benigno G. Reyna, Office of Public Affairs, December 3, 2005, USMS Collections; Daniel Borunda, "Former Police Chief Takes the Reigns [*sic*]," *Brownsville Herald*, October 31, 2001.

3. "Benigno Reyna Becomes New Director," *Marshals Monitor*, November-December 2001, 1.

4. Draft Copy, Director Benigno G. Reyna to U.S. Marshals Service Employees, November 15, 2001.

5. Ibid.

6. "Benigno Reyna Becomes New Director," 1.

7. Ibid.; Press Release, "Clayton Lee Waagner Named to FBI's Ten Most Wanted Fugitives List," FBI, September 21, 2001, FBI Web Site; Toni Locy, "Marshals Nab Anthrax Hoax Suspect," *USA Today*, December 6, 2001; "Benigno Reyna Becomes New Director," 16.

8. "U.S. Marshals Focus on Security for Moussaoui, Lindh," CNN.com, January 30, 2002; Department of Justice, "Prepared Remarks of Attorney General Alberto R. Gonzales on Zacarias Moussaoui, Friday, April 22, 2005," Justice.gov; Nikki Cobb, "'American Taliban' held in Victorville," *Desert Dispatch*, January 30, 2003.

9. "On Permanent Display in Wyoming: America's Star Exhibit," *The Pentacle,* December 1991, 16-17; *History* Page, "U.S. Marshals Museum," usmarshals.gov; Notes, U.S. Marshals Museum, Office of the Historian.

10. "Long on Athleticism, Short on Security Breaches," *Marshals Monitor,* May-June 2002, 9-11.

11. "Marshals Service Receives Clean Audit Marks," *Marshals Monitor,* May-June 2002, 2.

12. Interview, Mike Pyo, June 24, 2013, USMS Collections; "Beacon Leads the Way to Dangerous Explosives," *Marshals Monitor,* May-June 2002, 7-8.

13. Interview, Mike Pyo, June 24, 2013, USMS Collections.

14. "Beacon Leads the Way," 7-8; Interview, Mike Pyo, June 24, 2013, USMS Collections.

15. "Hazardous Response Unit Is Ready for Action," *Marshals Monitor,* June-July-August 2003, 13-14; Interview, Mike Pyo, June 24, 2013, USMS Collections.

16. Interview, Mike Pyo, June 24, 2013, USMS Collections.

17. "Sniper Investigation Timeline," abcnews.go.com; Interview, William Sorukas, June 30, 2009, USMS Collections. Both Muhammad and Malvo had criminal history in other states, including Alabama and Washington State, for robbery and homicide.

18. Copy, Director Benigno G. Reyna to All United States Marshals, All Chief Deputy U.S. Marshals, All Assistant Chief Deputy U.S. Marshals, October 16, 2002; Interview, William Sorukas, June 30, 2009, USMS Collections; "Sniper Investigation Timeline," abcnews.go.com. USMS investigative efforts were led by Supervisory Deputy Kevin Connolly, Eastern District of Virginia and Supervisory Deputy Ken Plumley, District of Maryland. Bill Sorukas primarily coordinated with the command post.

19. Interview, Mike Pyo, June 24, 2013, USMS Collections.

20. Ibid.

21. Ibid.

22. Interview, William Sorukas, June 30, 2009, USMS Collections.

23. "Sniper Investigation Timeline," abcnews.go.com.

24. Interview, William Sorukas, June 30, 2009, USMS Collections.

25. Ibid.

26. "Sniper Investigation Timeline," abcnews.go.com; "Prosecutors to Map out Sniper Charges," CNN.com, October 25, 2002; Interview, William Sorukas, June 30, 2009, USMS Collections.

27. Jeordan Legon, "Teen Sniper Suspect Remains a Mystery," CNN.com, April 28, 2003; Jeanne Meserve and Mike M. Ahlers, "Sniper John Allen Muhammad Executed," CNN.com, November 11, 2009.

28. "Civil Rights Legacy Endures at Ole Miss," *Marshals Monitor*, January-February 2003, 1; Ibid., 5.

29. Ibid. A committee—headed by Gary Mead, Deborah Rhode (who took over printing and publications after Larry Mogavero retired), Public Affairs Specialist Dave Turner and the author—decided on these symbols.

30. Ibid.

31. Ibid.

32. Ibid.; "Ole Miss Anniversary: A Time to Honor, Reflect," *Marshals Monitor*, January-February 2003, 2.

NOTES TO EPILOGUE

1. "USMS Leads the Fugitive Brigade," *Marshals Monitor*, Autumn 2004, 2; "Regional Task Forces Launch New Era," *Marshals Monitor*, December 2003-January 2004, 5. The citation for the Presidential Threat Protection Act of 2000 is Public Law No. 106-544.

2. Copy, Draft, U.S. Marshal James Plousis and David S. Turk, "The Measure of a Law Enforcement Icon: The History of the New York/ New Jersey Regional Fugitive Task Force," USMS Collections. This was later featured in *New Jersey Police Magazine*; Interview, Robert Finan, August 11, 2009, USMS Collections; "USMS Leads The Fugitive Brigade," 2; "Regional Task Forces Launch New Era," 5; Fact Sheet, "Gulf Coast Regional Fugitive Task Force," Investigative Operations Division, February 2015; Fact Sheet, "Florida/Caribbean Regional Fugitive Task Force," Investigative Operations Division. The USMS cooperated with A&E on a 3-year program (2008-11) based on the New York/New Jersey Regional Fugitive Task Force called *Manhunters*.

3. "USMS Leads the Fugitive Brigade," 5.

4. Ibid. Many fugitives are career criminals, and apprehending them enhances public safety. Since 2009, Marshals Service-led fugitive task forces annually have arrested more than 86,000 state and local fugitives, on average.

5. Release, "U.S. Marshals and Jamaican Authorities Apprehend 17-Year-Old Female Cobb County Murder Suspect," Southeast Regional Fugitive Task Force, March 13, 2008; Interview, Robert Finan, August 11, 2009, USMS Collections. The origins of these offices go back to 1998, when a pilot program in Mexico achieved great success. See House of Representative Subcommittee on Crime Hearing, July 13, 2000. Coordination with the State Department and Embassies are vital to its success.

6. Interview, Elizabeth Howard, January 29, 2013, USMS Collections. Elizabeth Howard joined in 1974.

7. "USMS pioneered the Air Marshal Program," *Marshals Monitor,* January-February 2002, 1; Ibid., 12; "Hijacking Controls That Worked," *Tampa Tribune,* September 28, 2001, relayed through TBO.com; E-Mail, Gene Coon to Author, July 15, 2014.

8. Jim Malone, "29 Honored for U.S. Civil Rights Bravery," *VOA News,* July 16, 2003; Copy, "Timeline for 40th Commemorative Ceremonies,

Washington, D.C. July 15, 2003," USMS Collections; Copy, Script, "40th Commemoration Symposium Observance," July 15, 2003, USMS Collections; Copy, Media Advisory, "Attorney General Ashcroft to Deliver Remarks at Event to Commemorate 40th Anniversary of Ole Miss Integration," Department of Justice, July 14, 2003.

9. "First-ever Fugitive Task Force Turns 20," *Marshals Monitor*, December 2003-January 2004, 1; Copy, Flyer, Announcement of Event, Unknown Date, USMS Collections. The Honorary U.S. Marshals are different from Honorary Deputy U.S. Marshals, which are usually bestowed by U.S. Marshals or other officials. The known Honorary U.S. Marshals are: Ronald Reagan (1983); James Arness (1987); Robert Dole (1988); John Warner (1988); Bob Hope (1991); Tommy Mottola (1997); James F. Reilly (2001); Jed Erickson (2001); John Walsh (2003); and Paul J. McNulty (2007).

10. Copy, Organizational Chart, "United States Marshals Service," December 22, 2003, USMS Collections; Copy, Organization Chart (Unsigned), "United States Marshals Service." As of April 9, 2001,USMS Collections.

11. "SOG Bolsters Iraqi Court System," *Marshals Monitor*, Autumn 2006, 1.

12. "SOG Bolsters," *Marshals Monitor*, Autumn 2006, 1-4.

13. "'Seeing Daylight' at the Cowtown Rodeo," *Marshals Monitor*, January-February 2005, 4; "Marshals Honored at Cowtown Rodeos," United States Marshals Service District of Delaware Newsletter, March 2005, 2.

14. David Heinzmann and Jeff Coen, "Federal Judge's Family Killed," *Chicago Tribune*, March 1, 2005.

15. Heinzmann and Coen, "Federal Judge's Family Killed"; Amanda Paulson and Brad Knickerbocker, "In Harm's Way? Chicago Slayings Spotlight Risks Judges Can Face," *Seattle Times*, March 3, 2005.

16. Francie Grace, "Suicide Note: I Killed Judge's Kin," *CBS News*, March 10, 2005; "Revenge Likely Motive in Judge Killings Case," CNN.com, March 11, 2005.

17. Ibid.

18. Paulson and Knickerbocker, "In Harm's Way?"; "Judges Plead for Improved Judicial Security," *Third Branch*, June 2005.

19. "Judges Plead for Improved Judicial Security."

20. Ibid.

21. Carol D. Leonnig, "Judges Seek to Oust Chief of Marshals," *Washington Post*, May 16, 2005; Time Line of Directors and Deputy Directors, ca. 2012.

22. Mary Schmich, "Life Goes on, 8 Years Later," *Chicago Tribune*, March 10, 2013; Interview, Donald Horton, May 8, 2014, USMS Collections; "New Threat Assessment Center Provides Immediate Response to Threats," *Third Branch*, December 2007.

23. "FALCON Snatches 10,000 Fugitives," *Marshals Monitor*, Autumn 2005, 1.

24. Copy, Fact Sheet,"Fugitive Safe Surrender—Cleveland, Ohio— August 3-6, 2005," USMS Collections; Entry, "Wayne Leon," Officer Down Memorial Page, odmp.org

25. E-Mail, U.S. Marshal Peter Elliott to Author, May 19, 2014.

26. Copy, Fact Sheet,"Fugitive Safe Surrender—Cleveland, Ohio— August 3-6, 2005," USMS Collections; E-Mail, U.S. Marshal Peter Elliott to Author, May 19, 2014. Douglas Weiner, of DC Strategic Partners, was a key partner in bridging to the community.

27. Copy, Fact Sheet,"Fugitive Safe Surrender—Cleveland, Ohio— August 3-6, 2005," USMS Collections.

28. Copy of Bill, S. 2570, 109th Congress, 2D Session, April 6, 2006. Community bonds were also strengthened by outreach efforts such as U.S. Marshal David Gonzales' Citizens Academy in the District of Arizona.

29. "USMS Efforts Brought Relief, Order to Gulf," *Marshals Monitor*, Autumn 2006, 8; Copy, After Action Report, "Hurricanes Katrina and Rita, September-October 2005," USMS Collections.

30. "USMS Efforts Brought Relief, Order to Gulf," 8.

31. "USMS Efforts Brought Relief," 8-9; Copy, After Action Report, "Hurricanes Katrina and Rita, September-October 2005," USMS Collections.

32. Copy, Director and Deputy Director Time Line, 2012, USMS Collections; Mavis DeZulovich, "Trono Continues Long Standing with USMS," *Marshals Monitor*, Autumn 2006, 7. The timeline was a formal collaboration between the Office of Public Affairs and the Office of the Director's Lisa Griffin that compiled a full listing of Directors and Deputy Directors from 1970.

33. David A. Turner, "John Clark: Comfortable in the Shoes," *Marshals Monitor*, Autumn 2006, 5.

34. Copy, H.R. 4472, 109th Congress, 2D Session, Adam Walsh Child Protection and Safety Act of 2006, January 3, 2006; "Adam Walsh Child Protection and Safety Act," U.S. Marshals Service Web Site, usmarshals.gov.

35. "U.S. Marshals Choose Fort Smith for Museum, *Arkansas Business*, January 5, 2007; Mary L. Crider, "No. 7: Marshals Museum on Track for 2014 Groundbreaking," *Southwest Times Record*, December 25, 2013; Jill Rohrbach, "Hundreds Celebrate Groundbreaking for U.S. Marshals Museum," Arkansas.com. The USMS Museum Site Selection Committee existed from 2004-07. Director Clark appointed ten members: Assistant Director Michael A. Pearson (Chair); U.S. Marshals John Moore (E/TX) and Richard Wingert (D/NV); Senior Counsel Joseph Band; Inspector

Quintella Downs; Chief Deputy U.S. Marshals Rich Knighten (W/KY), Rick Long (D/DE), and Kelly York (N/MS); Budget Chief Jim Murphy; and the Author.

36. *In Re: Edward & Elaine Brown—Time line at a glance*, in Notes, Office of Public Affairs, USMS Collections; U.S. v. Gerhard, 615 F.3d 7 (7/30/10).

37. Ibid.

38. Ibid.;"Talking Points: Ed & Elaine Brown Following Their Capture," USMS Collections. According to 615 f3d 7, Elaine was at the trial, but Edward stopped showing up on the fourth day. In US v. Brown, 669 f3d 10, court says: Edward, who had stopped attending trial after only a few days, was convicted in absentia. Both Edward and Elaine were sentenced to just over five years in prison. Neither Brown attended the sentencing.

39. Ibid.; Draft,"Talking Points: Ed & Elaine Brown Following Their Capture," USMS Collections.

40. Ibid.; Copy, Topical Photograph, Brown Residence, Top View, USMS Collections.

41. Copy, Draft, U.S. Marshal Stephen R. Monier to Edward and Elaine Brown, April 24, 2007, USMS Collections.

42. *In Re: Edward & Elaine Brown-Time line*, Notes, Office of Public Affairs, USMS Collections; Margot Sanger-Katz, "Marshals Tried to Nab Brown in June," *Concord Monitor*, April 2, 2008; Copy, Statement to the Media, June 7, 2007, USMS Collections.

43. Interview, Bill Sorukas, June 30, 2009, USMS Collections.

44. Kathryn Marchocki, "Lessons of Waco, Ruby Ridge Applied at Plainfield," *New Hampshire Union Leader*, June 10, 2007; Margot Sanger-Katz, "Ruby Ridge Figure Coming to Browns Standoff Survivor to Advise Tax Protestors," *Concord* Monitor, June 16, 2007; Margot Sanger-Katz, "Browns: Dog Walker Saved Lives Supporter Claims Marshals Chased Him," *Concord Monitor*, June 9, 2007; Kristen Senz, "Browns' Bash Draw

about 200," *New Hampshire Union Leader*, July 15, 2007. The mid-July "Live Free or Die Concert" at the Brown compound featured musical acts such as "Poker Face," "Blue-Eyed Fools," and "Paperback Radio." The local police, watching from helicopters, informed deputies about activities below. See also Kristen Senz, "Browns Say They Will Either Walk Free, or Die," *New Hampshire Union Leader*, June 19, 2007.

45. "Tax Evading Browns Lose Federal Appeal of Convictions Following NH Stand-off," *New Hampshire Union Leader*, January 20, 2012; Interview, Bill Sorukas, June 30, 2009, USMS Collections.

46. Interview, Bill Sorukas, June 30, 2009, USMS Collections.

47. Ibid.

48. Copy, Director and Deputy Director Time Line, 2012, USMS Collections.

49. Copy, Fact Sheet, U.S. Marshals Operation FALCON 2009, USMS Collections.

50. Interview, Sylvester Jones, August 20, 2013, USMS Collections.

51. Interview, Robert Finan, August 11, 2009, USMS Collections.

52. Copy, Director and Deputy Director Time Line, 2012, USMS Collections; Interview, Christopher Dudley, 2009, USMS Collections.

53. Copy, Director and Deputy Director Time Line, 2012, USMS Collections.

54. Interview, Christopher Dudley, 2009, USMS Collections.

55. Interview, Director Stacia Hylton, August 19, 2013; Copy, Director and Deputy Director Time Line, 2012, USMS Collections; Copy, Memorandum, Director Stacia A. Hylton to United States Marshals Employees, July 13, 2011; Copy, Director Stacia A. Hylton to United States Marshals Employees, October 17, 2012.

56. Interview, Director Stacia Hylton, August 19, 2013.

57. Ibid.

58. Ibid.

59. Ibid.

60. Ibid. Isaac G. Hylton, Sr. was U.S. Marshal of the Eastern District of Virginia from 1969 until 1982.

61. Ibid.

62. Ibid.

63. Ibid.

64. Ibid.; *The United States Marshals Service Monitor,* March 2012; "History—Roll Call [of Honor]," U.S. Marshals Service Web Site. The six Task Force Officers were: Fermin Archer (July 13, 2011); Roger Castillo (January 20, 2011); Amanda Haworth (January 20, 2011); Warren B. Lewis (June 9, 2011); Brent Long (July 11, 2011); and Kyle David Pagerly (June 30, 2011). The commemorative issue of the *Monitor* was meant to be a one-time addition. Regular circulation ended in 2006.

65. Investigative Operations Division, U.S. Marshals Service, "Risk Mitigation Can Lead to Fewer Officer Fatalities," *Police Chief* 80 (May 2013), 28-30; U.S. Department of Justice, *United States Marshals Service Strategic Plan: 2012-2016,* 35; Email, "Message from Director Hylton—Re: Law Enforcement Safety Training Program (LESTP)," Undated, USMS Collections.

66. Investigative Operations Division, U.S. Marshals Service, "Risk Mitigation Can Lead to Fewer Officer Fatalities," *Police Chief* 80 (May 2013), 28-30; "USMS Completes Largest Operational Training Initiative in Agency History," Training Division, USMS Collections. This was a web-based article.

67. Copy, Director and Deputy Director Time Line, 2012, USMS Collections; Program, Charles Christopher Dudley, July 19, 1966-November

23, 2012, George Washington Masonic Memorial, Alexandria, Virginia, November 28, 2012.

BIBLIOGRAPHY

PRIMARY SOURCES

USMS Collections

As this is an official Federal Government publication, the most plentiful primary source material is comprised as the "U.S. Marshals Service Collection," also denoted in endnotes as "USMS Collections." These are primarily copies of internal documents, such as memoranda, correspondence, and reports, that were located at agency offices. Most have not been published or noted previously. Within the framework of the "USMS Collection" are several sub-units of collected papers. These are miscellaneous memoranda, reports, and other internal notes. Some have been denoted as part of a former employee's papers. Detailed descriptions of each are below.

Collection Subsets by Name or Operation

Bowser, Paskal D Papers. 1964-1969. Copies of Notes, Memoranda, and Assignment Files, including George Rockwell Funeral.

Brown, Ed and Elaine Case. 2007-10. Copies of Letters, Memoranda, Talking Points, Timeline, Topical Photo, Various Related Note on Court Cases.

Cameron, John "Jack" Papers. 1956-1985. Copies of Notes, Memoranda.

Chattanooga File [Hoffa Trial]. 1964. Copies of Notes, Memoranda.

Hoffa File Assignment File. 1964-67. Copies of Notes, Memoranda.

Marcello Trial File. 1965. Copies of Letters, Procedures, and Notes.

Nashville Evidence File (Hoffa Trial). 1964-65. Copies of Notes, Memoranda.

"New Orleans File." Contains Copies of Reports, Memoranda and Notes.

Partin File [Eddie Partin, Witness in Hoffa Case] 1964-67.

Ruby Ridge File. Contains Notes, Memoranda, Questionnaires, Statements, Time Line of Events.

"Tuscaloosa File." Contains Copies of Reports, Memoranda and Notes.

Interviews

Arechiga, Roger. September 22, 2008. Conducted by author.

Auerbach, Gerald. May 11, 2005. Conducted by author.

Banta, Bill. September 21, 2008. Conducted by author.

Barry, Ken. May 8, 2003. Conducted by author.

Brake, Bennie. June 25, 2008. Conducted by author.

Buckheim, Michael. 1991. Telephone Notes. From author.

Butler, Clarence (Al). January 31, 2007. Telephone Interview. Conducted by author.

Butler, Clarence (Al). August 30, 2011. Conducted by author.

Campbell, Judge Gordon. August 20, 1993. Conducted by Ted Calhoun.

Courtright, Robert. October 6, 1993. Conducted by Ted Calhoun.

Dudley, Christopher. 2009. Conducted by author.

Finan, Robert. August 11, 2009. Conducted by author.

Garner, Herschel. July 8, 1985. Conducted by Ted Calhoun.

Gonzalez, Eduardo. July 30, 2013. E-Mail Interview. Conducted by author.

Greene, Tom. November 30, 1990. Conducted by Ted Calhoun.

Grider, Jesse. July 12, 1985, and September 20, 1991. Conducted by Ted Calhoun.

Guadagnoli, Dominic. September 18, 2013. E-Mail Interview. Conducted by author.

Haislip, Robert. November 6, 1985. Conducted by Ted Calhoun.

Hall, William (Bill). April 6, 2005. Conducted by author.

Hall, William (Bill). January 25, 2005. Telephone Notes by author.

Hall, William (Bill). July 30, 1986. Conducted by Ted Calhoun.

Horton, Donald. May 8, 2014. Conducted by author.

Howard, Elizabeth. January 29, 2013. Conducted by author.

Hylton, Stacia A. August 19, 2013. Conducted by author.

Jones, Sylvester. August 20, 2013. Conducted by author.

Kash, Reis. February 7, 1985. Conducted by Ted Calhoun.

Kupferer, Chuck (Thomas C.). September 22, 2008. Conducted by author.

Leschorn, Robert. November 20, 2007. Conducted by author.

Lutes, Marvin. October 2, 2006. Conducted by author.

Marshall, John. August 9, 2013. Conducted by author.

McArdle, Willard, and Clarence "Al" Butler. October 1, 2003. Conducted by author.

McShane, Michael J. June 13, 2003. Conducted by author.

Mead, Gary. May 22, 2003. Conducted by author.

Messa, Ronnie. September 22, 2003. Telephone Notes by author.

Miller, Cecil. July 8, 1985. Conducted by Ted Calhoun.

Mogavero, Larry, Nick Prevas, and Leon Roberts. April 17, 2013. Conducted by author.

Morris, Stanley. October 17, 2006. Conducted by author.

Murphy, James (Jamy). May 8, 2008. Conducted by author.

Musquiz, Ray. November 29, 1990. Conducted by Ted Calhoun.

Neff, Dave. May 1, 1991. Conducted by Ted Calhoun.

Oczkowski, Ralph. January 31, 2003. Notes. From Author.

Odom, Tony. February 21, 1991. Conducted by Ted Calhoun.

Ohrenburger, Henry. October 6, 2005. Conducted by author.

Parish, Carl. June 20, 2003. Conducted by author.

Pautz, Ron. December 10, 2004. Conducted by author.

Pekarek, Kent. November 7, 1991. Conducted by Ted Calhoun.

Perez, Tony. August 21, 1990. Conducted by Ted Calhoun.

Prevas, Nick. June 29, 2007. Notes. From author.

Pyo, Mike. June 24, 2013. Conducted by author.

Ramon, Michael. December 2, 2013. E-Mail Interview. Conducted by author.

Roderick, Arthur. January 30, 2012. Conducted by author.

Safir, Howard. August 1, 2013. Conducted by author.

Shoemaker, William. August 30, 2011. Conducted by author.

Sorukas, William. June 30, 2009. Conducted by author.

Staple, Denzil "Bud." Undated. Conducted by author.

Stine, Jeff, and Jeff Cahall. June 24, 2013. Conducted by author.

Tolson, Joseph. April 20, 2004. Conducted by author.

Vandegrift, Frank. July 10, 1985. Conducted by author.

Waite, Donald. August 30, 2004. Conducted by author.

Ward, Donald. August 9, 2013. Conducted by author.

Williamson, Billy. January 12, 2003. Notes. Conducted by author.

Zurita, Ralph. September 23, 2004. Conducted by author.

Printed or Published Primary Sources

"America's Star: U.S. Marshals 1789-1989." Brochure.

Becker, E. Norris, Editor. *Year Book National Association of Deputy United States Marshals.*Baltimore, Maryland: French-Bray Company, 1950.

"Charles Christopher Dudley, July 19, 1966-November 23, 2012." George Washington Masonic Memorial. Alexandria, Virginia, November 28, 2012. Program.

Congressional Record. A6083, 1965.

Court Security Officer Orientation Handbook. ca. 1985.

Deputy United States Marshals' News of the National Association of the Deputy United States Marshals. Newsletter. 1947-ca. 1975. Executive Office for United States Marshals.

Deputy U.S. Marshal Training Program. Copy of Program, ca. 1959.

Director's Honorary Awards Ceremony, February 28, 2001. Program.

Director's Report: A Review of the United States Marshals Service in FY 1989.

Director's Report: A Review of the United States Marshals Service in FY 1990.

Director's Report: A Review of the United States Marshals Service in FY 1991.

Enforcement Division. *Fifteen Most Wanted Program: Case Submission Guidelines.* USMS Publication No. 47, September 23, 1994.

Enforcement Operations Division. "Operation Noriega." 1978.

Fifteen Most Wanted Program. Copy of Publication, ca. September 1989.

FYI—For Your Information. Newsletter Publication, 1988-1992.

"History-Historical Federal Executions." Web Article, U.S. Marshals Service Website.

"Hurricane Katrina and Rita, September-October 2005." Copy of After Action Report.

Management and Budget Division. *The FY 1996 Report to the U.S. Marshals: A Review of District Office Activities.* USMS Pub. No. 44, January 1997.

Marshals Monitor. Publication, 1992-2006. Various Issues.

Marshal Today. Publication, 1973-78. Various Issues.

Mississippi State Jr. Chamber of Commerce, Inc. *Oxford: A Warning for Americans.* Jackson, Mississippi: Electronic Building, October 1962.

Office of Congressional and Public Affairs. *U.S. Marshals Service Joint Fugitive Apprehension Operations.* Publication, ca. 1992.

"Operation Southern Star—A Fugitive Program Sponsored by the United States Marshals Service August 6-October 17, 1990." Publication.

Pentacle. Publication, 1978-1991. Various Issues.

Register of the Department of Justice and the Courts of the United States, 42nd Edition. Washington, D.C., 1955.

Report to the Attorney General, United States Marshals Service, Third Quarter 1997. Copy of Report.

Turk, David S. "History—A Visit to Chief Deputy U.S. Marshal Helen Crawford, Retired." Web Article, U.S. Marshals Service Website.

United States Marshals: 1789 to Present [1989].

United States Marshals Bulletin. Newsletters, 1946-1970.

United States Marshals Service Newsletter. 1971-1973.

United States Marshals Service Strategic Plan: 2012-2016.

United States Marshals Service. *Marshals Service 2000: The Strategic Plan of the United States Marshals Service 1997 and Beyond.* USMS Pub. No. 42, February 14, 1997.

United States Marshals Service. *United States Marshals Service Tactical Plan 1998-2000.* USMS Pub. No. 73, March 1998.

United States Marshals Service. *Vulnerability Assessment of Federal Facilities, June 28, 1995.*

WANT Warrant Apprehension Narcotics Teams-Report to the Organized Crime and Drug Enforcement Task Force National Conference, May 13, 1987. Copy of Report.

Warrant Apprehension Narcotics Team. *WANT II—A Cooperative Enforcement Program Sponsored by The United States Marshals Service, November 14, 1988.* Copy of Report.

National Archives and Records Administration Sources

Barnett, [Governor] Ross and Robert F. Kennedy. Copy, Phone Call Conversation Transcript. R12 (B3). John F. Kennedy Library, Boston, Massachusetts.

Department of Justice, May 20, 1961. Copy of Communication re: Montgomery, Alabama. Record Group 60. College Park, Maryland.

Holtzoff, Alexander to Attorney General. Copy of Letter, October 8, 1936. Record Group 60. College Park, Maryland.

Faupel, Edward L. to S.A. Andretta, September 4, 1937. Copy of Letter, Record Group 527. College Park, Maryland.

Rosenberg, Ethel. Receipt of Prisoner, April 11, 1951. Records of U.S. Attorneys, Record Group 118. College Park, Maryland.

"Statement By Attorney General on Behalf of the United States in Support of Petition for Rule Making." Docket No. MC-C-3358, *In the Matter of Discrimination in Operations of Interstate Motor Carriers of Passengers.*Interstate Commerce Commission, in Records of Burke Marshall, Attorney, Civil Rights Division. Record Group 60. College Park, Maryland.

"Statement by the Honorable Robert F. Kennedy Attorney General of the United States Issued At 11:00 A.M., May 24, 1961." Files of W. Wilson White, Civil Rights Division. Record Group 60. College Park, Maryland.

SECONDARY SOURCES

Books

Arsenault, Raymond. *Freedom Riders: 1961 and the Struggle for Racial Justice.* New York: Oxford University Press, 2006.

Baldwin, James. *The Fire Next Time.* New York: The Dial Press, 1963.

Berrigan, Daniel. *The Trial of the Catonsville Nine.* Boston, MA: Beacon Press, 1972.

Burton, Arthur T. *Black, Red, and Deadly.* Austin, TX: Eakin Press, 1991.

Calhoun, Frederick S. *Hunters and Howlers: Threats and Violence Against Federal Judicial Officials in the United States, 1789-1993.* USMS Publication No. 80, February 1998.

———. *The Lawmen: United States Marshals and Their Deputies, 1789-1989.* New York: Penguin Books, 1991.

———. *The Trainers: The Federal Law Enforcement Training Center and the Professionalization of Federal Law Enforcement.* Brunswick, GA: Federal Law Enforcement Training Center, 1996.

Clauss, F.J. *Alcatraz: Island of Many Mistakes.* Menlo Park, CA: Briarcliff Press, Inc., 1981.

Cornell, Julien. *The Trial of Ezra Pound.* New York: John Day Company, 1966.

Day, James M. *Captain Clint Peoples: Texas Ranger Fifty Years a Lawman.* Waco, TX: Texian Press, 1980.

Earley, Pete, and Gerald Shur, *WITSEC:Inside the Federal Witness Protection Program.* New York: Bantam Books, 2002.

Fortunate Eagle, Adam. *Alcatraz! Alcatraz!* Berkeley, CA: Heyday Books, 1992.

Huck, Susan L.M. *Renegades: The Second Battle of Wounded Knee.* Belmont, MA: American Opinion, 1973.

Jimenez, Janey. *My Prisoner.* Mission, KS: Sheed Andrews and McMeel, Inc., 1977.

Kobler, John. *Capone: The Life and World of Al Capone.* New York: Putnam Publishing Group, 1971.

McKinney, Louie, with Pat Russo. *One Marshal's Badge: A Memoir of Fugitive Hunting, Witness Protection, and the U.S. Marshals Service.* Washington, D.C.: Potomac Books, Inc., 2009.

Mailer, Norman. *The Armies of the Night.* New York: New American Library, Inc., 1968.

Nelson, Jack, and Ronald J. Ostrow. *The FBI and the Berrigans.* New York: Coward, McCann & Geoghegan, Inc., 1972.

Nix, Evett D. *Oklahombres.* St. Louis, MO: Eden Publishing House, 1929.

Sherrard, Ray, and George Stumpf. *Badges of the United States Marshals.* Garden Grove, CA: RHS Enterprises, 1991.

Thrapp, Dan L., Compiler. *Encyclopedia of Frontier Biography.* Three Volumes. Glendale, CA: Arthur H. Clark, 1988.

Wexley, John. *The Judgment of Julius and Ethel Rosenberg.* New York: Cameron & Kahn, 1955.

Periodicals

"2 Seize Hostages at Court." *Washington Post.* July 12, 1974.

"40 Indians Accept Amnesty and End Plant Occupation." *New York Times.* March 4, 1975.

"201 Viet Refugees Start Return Trip." *Washington Post.* July 4, 1975.

"1,546 Vietnamese Go Home on a Vessel from Guam." *New York Times.* October 17, 1975.

"2001 Anthrax Attacks Timeline: Five Die after Letters Mailed." *WJLA.com.* October 21, 2011.

"Abortion Doctor Gunned Down at Kansas Church, Suspect in Custody." *Foxnews.com.* May 31, 2009.

"AIM Defense to Watch Possible Jurors Closely." *Minneapolis Tribune.* January 8, 1974.

"Ambush Prompts Police to Guard Judge, Lawyer." *Sandusky [Ohio] Register.* November 23, 1978.

Anspacher, Carolyn. "Patty, Judge and Jurors Visit the Scenes of Her Captivity." *San Francisco Chronicle.* February 17, 1976.

Applecombe, Peter. "Shadowy Bombing Case Is Focusing on Reclusive and Enigmatic Figure." *New York Times.* July 20, 1990.

"Armed Forces: The Military Mafia." *Time.* October 17, 1969.

"Army Prevents Rockwell Burial with Nazi Rites in Culpeper Grave." *Washington Post.* August 30, 1967.

"As Marshal, Smith Part of History in Making." *Greenville News.* February 14, 2001.

"Assassin Transferred from Gallinger to District Jail." [*Washington*] *Times Herald.* November 10, 1950.

"Assassin's Bullet Fatal for Huey P. Long." *Monroe [Louisiana] News-Star.* September 10, 1935.

Associated Press. "Anastasia of Murder, Inc.—Overlord of Crime Slain." *Syracuse Herald-Journal.* October 25, 1957.

———. "Atlanta Hold pre-Games Crime Sweep," *Orange County Register.* June 14, 1996.

———. "Feds Seize Baptist Church over $6 million Tax Debt." *Deseret News.* February 13, 2001.

———. "Gunman Kills Guard in Courthouse Spree." August 6, 1993.

———. "I Feel Like a Dying Man." *Santa Ana Orange County Register.* December 3, 1978.

———. "Kennedy Extremely Critical." *Findlay [Ohio] Republican Courier.* June 6, 1968.

———. "Kennedy Is Dead from Killer Shot." *Southern Illinoisan.* June 6, 1968.

———. "Marshals Begin Protecting Abortion Clinics." *Kerrville [Texas] Daily Times.* August 2, 1994.

———. "Newspaper Says Persico Reportedly Boasted That He Killed Anastasia." June 3, 1986.

———. "Racial Clash Threatens in Alabama City." *Lowell Sun.* December 5, 1955.

———. "SLA Bombing Link?" *Corona [California] Daily Independent.* May 31, 1974.

———. "State Police and Treasury Agents Break Up Meeting of 65 Leading Members." *[Helena, Montana] Independent Record.* November 15, 1957.

———. "Top Marshal Dies." *Tucson Daily Citizen.* December 25, 1968.

Badhwar, Inderjit. "Caviar and Champagne? U.S. Marshals Picked Up Huge Tab for Tongsun Park." *Federal Times.* September 4, 1978.

Badhwar, Inderjit. "Let Them Eat Cake." *Federal Times.* October 23, 1978.

Baker, Donald P. and Raul Ramirez. "Officials, Indians Parley on Protest." *Washington Post.* November 5, 1972.

Balow, Jim. "2 UMW Officials, Massey Worker Arrested." *Charleston Gazette.* January 24, 1990.

———. "Five Pickets Charged with Blocking Trucks." *Charleston Gazette.* December 6, 1989.

———. "Marshals to Begin Enforcing Injunction." *Charleston Gazette.* October 25, 1989.

———. "Pickets Arrested in Defiance of Court Order." *Charleston Gazette.*October 26, 1989.

"'Bat' Masterson Is Dead" *Kansas City Star.* October 21, 1921.

"'Big Six' Henderson Retires." *Gimlet Edmonson News.* October 2, 1975.

Blumenthal, Ralph. "U.S. Marshals Joining Search for Nazi Death Camp Doctor." *New York Times.* April 24, 1985.

"Bob Pate Dies From the Effect of a Wound Received in July." *Arkansas Gazette.* September 29, 1894.

Bok, Chip. *Akron [OH] Beacon Journal.* Copy of Cartoon. September 1999.

Borunda, Daniel. "Former Police Chief Takes the Reins." *Brownsville Herald.* October 31, 2001.

Brady-Lunny, Edith. "Waagner Now Marshals' Top Priority." *Bloomington [IL] Pantagraph.* May 24, 2001.

Brown, Dee. " 'Lightning Crash' at Wounded Knee, 1890." *Journal [Hamilton, OH] News.* August 14, 1971.

Butler, Caroline Kleiner. "Down in Mississippi." *Smithsonian.* February 2005.

"Californian Named Chief of Marshals." *Washington Star.* January 12, 1970.

"Carlton Beale Named D.C. Postmaster." *Washington Evening Star.* December 2, 1958.

Cartwright, Gary. "The Last Posse." *Texas Monthly.* Web article. Undated.

Cassano, Dennis. "Marshal Testifies He Found 'Trip-bomb.'" *Minneapolis Tribune.* February 28, 1974.

"Charlie Chaplin's Women." *Sunday Mail.* April 9, 1989.

Clancy, Paul. "Fired Up: Catonsville Files Plus Nine Hearts; 25th Anniversary of 'Suffering Love.' May 17, 1968 Burning of Selective Service

Records in Catonsville, Maryland." *National Catholic Reporter*, May 21, 1993.

Clark, Ramsey. "Watergate: A Brush with Tyranny." *Nation*. June 4, 1973.

Clayton, James E. "Marshal McShane Freed After Arrest in Ole Miss Rioting." *Washington Post*. November 22, 1962.

"Clinton Grants More than 100 Pardons." *The Sunday [Annapolis, MD] Capital*. January 21, 2001.

"Coal Miners Break Tradition, Return to Work Despite Pickets." *New York Times*. September 9, 1975.

Cobb, Nikki. "'American Taliban' Held in Victorville." *Desert Dispatch*. January 30, 2003.

"Collazo in Plot at Blair House." *Washington Post*. November 11, 1950.

"Colburn Due for Job of U.S. Marshals." *San Diego Union-Tribune*, January 11, 1970.

Comerford, Gary. "S.C. Marshal to Oversee Viet Security on Guam." *Columbia Record*. July 17, 1975.

Corcoran, Jim. "Sources say Kahl takes blame in letter." *[Fargo-Moorhead, ND] The Forum*. February 17, 1983.

"Cost of Cellblock Takeover Already Exceeds $300,000." *Washington Star-News*. July 18, 1974.

Courson, Paul. "Judge Rejects Injunction to Stop Vieques Shelling." CNN.com. April 26, 2001.

Cox, Richard. "The Growing Role of the U.S. Marshal." *Los Angeles Herald-Examiner*. September 24, 1971.

Crider, Mary L. "No. 7: Marshals Museum on Track for 2014 Groundbreaking." *Southwest Times Record*. December 25, 2013.

"The 'Crime' of a Good Dinner." *Manchester Union Leader*. June 20, 1969.

"Dakota Dragnet." *Time*. February 28, 1983.

Daly, Christopher B. "Salvi Convicted of Murder in Shootings." *Washington Post*. March 19, 1996.

"Dave Beck to Start 5-Year Federal Prison Term Today." *Toledo Blade.* June 20, 1962.

Davis, Robert. "The Chicago Seven Trial and the 1968 Democratic National Convention." *Chicago Tribune,* September 24, 1969.

Deane, Daniela. "H Street NE, the Next Hot Spot." *Washington Post.* June 12, 2004.

"Death Will Postpone Sentencing of Hearst." *Washington Post.* June 15, 1976.

"Defendants Call Trial Focus of Indians' Struggle." *Minneapolis Tribune.* January 8, 1974.

"Defense Rests in Trial of 2 AIM Leaders." *Washington Post.* August 17, 1974.

Denniston, Lyle. "Hinckley Prosecutors Want Trial Rules Eased." *Baltimore Sun.* April 9, 1982.

"Deputy Marshal's Daring Plan Enable 7 to Slip to Freedom." *Washington Post.* July 15, 1974.

Deupree, Mike. "Eastwood and a good yarn." *Cedar Rapids Gazette.* July 7, 1979.

DeVine, Terry. "Wounded Knee Seige [*sic*] Ends." *Estherville [IA] Daily News.* April 6, 1973.

Dobbs, Michael. "Koreagate' Figure Tied to Oil-for-Food Scandal." *Washington Post.* April 15, 2005.

Dries, Bill. "Judge Brown Dies; Ordered School Integration." *Memphis Commercial Appeal,* October 7, 2004.

Duff, Edward. "Why Are You Not Here? Bearing the Burden of the Berrigan Brothers." *New Republic,* March 6, 1971.

Dungey, Diane, and Laura Januta. "'Bearded Bandit' Saga Ends in Blood." *Daily Herald.* July 21, 1992.

Dunleavy, Steve. "Patty Hearst Jailer Signs $1m Book Deal." *The Star.* September 7, 1976.

Dvorak, Petula. "It's Nuts to Spend so Much Time and Money on John W. Hinckley Jr." *Washington Post.* December 1, 2011.

"'Dynamite' Ruse Backfires." *Las Vegas Sun.* July 5, 1968.

Ebert, Roger. "Out of Sight." *Chicago Sun-Times.* June 19, 1998.

Eggen, Dan. "U.S. Marshals to Protect Abortion Doctor." *Washington Post.* July 13, 2001.

"Elian, Father Relocated From Andrews." *Washington Post.* April 25, 2000.

Emerine, Edward. "You Should Know Louisiana." *Farmington Times-Hustler.* March 1, 1946.

Esper, George. "Jonestown 'Like a Prison Camp.'" *Santa Ana Orange County Register.* December 3, 1978.

"FBI Battles with Indians." *Santa Fe New Mexican.* February 28, 1973.

"FBI Searching for 2 Texas Escapees Still on the Loose." CNN.com January 22, 2001.

"Feuger Quiet on Trip Back to Iowa Prison." *Dubuque [Iowa] Telegraph Herald.* March 6, 1963.

Finger, Stan. "Court Upholds Scott Roeder's Conviction in George Tiller's Murder but Orders Resentencing." *Wichita Eagle.* October 24, 2014.

———. "Picketing, Video Start Abortion Foes' Week." *Wichita Eagle.* July 16, 2001.

"'Fleeing' Rajneesh Arrested." *Wichita Eagle-Beacon.* October 29, 1985.

"For Prosecutors, Wood Slaying a Crime that Had to be Solved." *The Paris [Texas] News.*May 29, 1989.

"For U.S. Marshal Grider, a Job at Home." *Louisville Courier-Journal.* August 25, 1975.

"Former U.S. Marshal Honored." *Taylorsville [North Carolina] Times.* August 27, 2003.

Franks, Wanda and Thomas Powers. "Frustration Fuels Fanatic Stance of the Weathermen." *Kittanning Simpson Leader-Times [UPI],* September 18, 1970.

Garlington, Lela. "Versatile, Busy Cato Ellis Was once U.S. Marshal." *Memphis Commercial Appeal.* September 22, 1995. Courtesy of son of Cato Ellis.

Gest, Ted with Pat Lynch. "As Federal Marshals Round Up Fugitives." *U.S. News and World Report.* December 3, 1984.

Glass, Andrew. "Castro Launches Mariel Boatlift, April 20, 1980." *Politico.* April 20, 2009.

Gonzalez, Eduardo. "A New Way to Choose U.S. Marshals." *Police Chief.* October 1998.

"Gorham Trial Opens Here." *Washington Star.* April 9, 1975.

Grace, Francie. "Suicide Note: I Killed Judge's Kin." *CBS News.* March 10, 2005.

Greenberg, Reuben M., Charles Wiley, Glenn Youngblood, Herbert Whetsell and James H. Doyle. "The Lessons of Hurricane Hugo: Law Enforcement Responds." *Police Chief* 47.

"Guam Wants to Isolate Repatriates." *Washington Star-News.* September 8, 1975.

"Guardsmen Called Out after Louisville Rioting." *Washington Post.* September 9, 1975.

Gullo, Karen. "Backup Ordered for Abortion Protests." *Washington Post.* July 12, 2001.

Hageman, Roxana. "Abortion Foes Return to Kansas." *Washington Post.* July 10, 2001.

Hall, Tom. "San Mateo Paid $599 a Day for Patty's Safe-keeping." *San Francisco Examiner.* November 5, 1975.

Hargrove, Roy. "'Con Air' Offers a Thrilling Ride." *Texas City Sun.* June 6, 1997.

"Hearst's Final Sentence Is Delayed." *Washington Post.* April 13, 1976.

"Hearst Released on $1.5 Million Bail." *Washington Post.* November 20, 1976.

Hedges, Michael. " 'America's Most Wanted' Joins the Hunt for Alcatraz Escapees." *Washington Times.* November 10, 1993.

———. "Deal Unlikely as Noriega, Prosecutors Head for Trial." *Washington Times.* September 3, 1991.

Heinzmann, David, and Jeff Coen. "Federal Judge's Family Killed." *Chicago Tribune.* March 1, 2005.

"Hijacking Controls That Worked." *Tampa Tribune.* September 28, 2001.

Himaka, Mitch. "3 Women Become First U.S. Deputies." *San Diego Union-Tribune.* August 10, 1971.

"Hiss in Handcuffs on Way to Jail." *Coshocton [Ohio] Tribune.* March 23, 1951.

Hodge, Paul. "Another 'Wounded Knee' Was Feared Friday Night." *Washington Post.* November 5, 1972.

"Hoffa Is Sentenced to 5 Years, $10,000." Undated News Clipping.

"Hoffa Sentenced to Five Years." *Arizona Republic.* September 23, 1967.

"Hoffa's Shadow Puts New Strain on Probe." *Washington Evening Star.* September 14, 1964.

Hunsberger, Don. "The Village's Detective Stories." *The Village Daily Sun.* December 29, 2005.

"Hunt Is Renewed for Inmates from 1962 Alcatraz Breakout." *New York Times.* November 14, 1993.

Ignatius, David. "Failure Should Be Viewed as a Healthy Endeavor," *Washington Post.* March 3, 1999.

"Indians and Supplies Pouring into Alcatraz." *Oakland Tribune [Sunday].* November 30, 1969.

"Indians, Historians Criticize Army Report on Wounded Knee." *The Daily [Fergus Falls, MN] Journal.* December 30, 1975.

International News Service, "O'Dwyer Goes Before Grand Jury in Brooklyn Today." *Lowell Sun.* March 26, 1951.

"J. Jefferson Bennett." Obituary. *Tuscaloosa News.* 2001.

Jones, Tim. "Abortion Battle Back in Wichita." *Chicago Tribune.* July 17, 2001.

"Judges Plead for Improved Judicial Security." *Third Branch.* June 2005.

Kaczor, Bill. "Anti-abortion Activist Gets Life for Shooting Fla. Doctor." *Texas City Sun*. March 6, 1994.

Kelly, G. Milton. "Teamster Boss to 'Talk.'" *Nashua Telegraph*. November 16, 1957.

Kelly, Orr. "How U.S. Blends Endangered Witnesses into the Landscape." *Washington Star*. April 25, 1975.

———. "U.S. Appeals Indian Case." *Star-News*. December 20, 1974.

King, Glen D. "Guidelines Issued by FCC for Air Security." *Police Chief*. May 1971.

King, Wayne. "10 Named In A Plot To Overthrow U.S." *New York Times*. April 25, 1987.

Kupferer, Thomas C. Jr. "Offensive Column." *Federal Times*. December 4, 1978.

Landauer, Jerry. "Culebrians Fire Back: Islanders Seek to End Role as a Navy Target—Shells Fall Close to Governor of Puerto Rico." *Wall Street Journal*. June 10, 1970.

Lardner, George Jr., and Richard Leiby. *Washington Post*. September 3, 1995.

"Last of Guardsmen Set to Exit Louisville Today." *Boston Globe*. September 16, 1975.

"Lawyers for 2 Indians Seek Curbs on Marshals." *New York Times*. August 19, 1974.

"Lawyers for Means, Banks to Seek Dismissal of Charges." *Minneapolis Tribune*. January 8, 1974.

Legon, Jeordan. "Teen Sniper Suspect Remains a Mystery." CNN.com. April 28, 2003.

Leiby, Richard, and George Lardner, Jr. "Rules of Engagement Siege Guided by Hastily Revised." *Washington Post*. September 3, 1995.

Leonard, George B., T. George Harris, and Christopher S. Wren. "How a Secret Deal Prevented a Massacre at Ole Miss." *Look*. December 31, 1962.

Leonnig, Carol D. "Judges Seek to Oust Chief of Marshals." *Washington Post.* May 16, 2005.

"Life Quieter for Cuban Boy Elian's Family Lives Comfortably on Bucolic Estate." *Florida Times Union.* May 7, 2000.

"Local chapter in sedition saga." *Southwest Times Record.* April 8, 1988.

Locy, Toni. "Marshals Nab Anthrax Hoax Suspect." *USA Today.* December 6, 2001.

Lott, John Jr. "Arming Pilots Is the Best Way to Get Air Security." *Los Angeles Times.* March 11, 2002.

"Louisville Busing off to Violent Start." *Chicago Tribune.* September 5, 1975.

McAllister, Bill. "Judge Refuses Use of U.S. Marshals to Identify Miners." *Washington Post.* September 3, 1975.

McCarthy, Jack. "Judge Intends to Limit Picketing at Mine." *Charleston Gazette.* January 12, 1990.

McElroy, Pat. "Congressmen Talk to Refugees." *Pacific Daily News.* August 7, 1975.

McGrath, Dennis J. "FBI Attacks N.D. Farm, Finds no Fugitive." *Minneapolis Star & Tribune.* February 16, 1983.

"Mace Fired in Wounded Knee Trial." *Washington Post.* August 24, 1974.

Macomber, Frank. "Wounded Knee Impasse Hurts Tribe's Economy." *Colorado Springs Gazette.* April 12, 1973.

Mahoney, Edmund. "Prosecutor Wraps Up Government's Case." *Hartford Courant.* July 16, 1991.

Maixner, Ed. "Mrs. Kahl Begs Husband to Surrender," *[Fargo] The Forum.* February 17, 1983.

———. "Tempers Flared before Medina Shootout." *[Fargo-Moorhead, ND] The Forum.* February 15, 1983.

Malnic, Eric. "When Jailbirds Fly, They Always Use 'Con Air.' " *Los Angeles Times.* August 9, 1993.

Malone, Jim. "29 Honored for U.S. Civil Rights Bravery." *VOA News.* July 16, 2003.

Mansfield, Stephanie. "Park Visits His Seized Belongings." *Washington Post.* October 20, 1978.

Marchocki, Kathryn. "Lessons of Waco, Ruby Ridge Applied at Plainfield." *New Hampshire Union Leader.* June 10, 2007.

Marder, Murrey. "U.S. to Let 1,600 Return to Vietnam." *Washington Post.* October 1, 1975.

Markowitz, Arnold and David Lyons. "Security Boosted—Quietly." *Miami Herald.* September 2, 1991.

Marks, Alexandra. "In Abortion Fight, Lines Have Shifted." *Public News-Room. [Christian Science Monitor]*, Undated [ca. 2001].

"Marshal Is Shot at Wounded Knee." *Stars and Stripes.* March 28, 1973.

"Marshall Arts." *Washington Post.* June 5, 1999.

"Marshals Seize Weapons from Pickets." *Charleston Gazette.* December 7, 1989.

"Marshals to Police Busing Orders." *Washington Star.* July 31, 1975.

Maslin, Janet. "Eraser." *New York Times.* June 21, 1996.

Mason, Julie. "To the Rescue; Texas Lawman Eyed to Aid Troubled U.S. Marshals." *Houston Chronicle.* July 29, 2001.

Mathews, Jay. "Former Intelligence Officer Backs Report on Mengele." *Washington Post.* January 26, 1984.

"Md.'s New U.S. Marshal Takes Heat, Keeps Cool; He Once Delivered Watergate Tape Subpoena to Nixon." *Baltimore Sun.* October 23, 1995.

Meserve, Jeanne and Mike M. Ahlers. "Sniper John Allen Muhammad Executed." CNN.com. November 11, 2009.

Meyer, Eugene L. "Indians Seize Files as Some Go Home." *Washington Post.* November 8, 1972.

"Meyer Takes Office as Federal Marshal." *Arizona Star.* April 13, 1954.

"Military Funeral for Raoul Dorsay." *The [San Francisco] Recorder.* November 27, 1937.

"Miss Hearst Transferred to San Diego for Mental Tests." *Los Angeles Times.* April 28, 1976.

"Miss Hearst Was Set to Flee, Report Says." *Los Angeles Times.* March 29, 1976.

"Miss Hearst's Trial Put Off 6 Months but Her Lawyer Doubts He'll Find Jury." *New York Times.* July 27, 1976.

Mitchell, Grayson. "Indians Find Living in BIA 'Miserable.' " *Washington Post.* November 8, 1972.

Mohbat, Joseph E. "Order Halts Rockwell Rites." *Petersburg [Virginia] Progress Index.* August 29, 1967.

Mollenhoff, Clark R. "Behind the Plot to Assassinate Robert Kennedy." *Look.* May 19, 1964.

Moor, Bill. "Ground Zero Was Not at all the Scene for a Postcard." *South Bend Tribune.* September 28, 2001.

Murphy, Kevin. "Suspects' History Includes Tax Convictions, Threats." *[Fargo-Moorhead, ND] The Forum.* February 15, 1983.

"Nazi Leader Rockwell Shot Down by Sniper." *Harrisonburg [Virginia] Daily News.* August 26, 1967.

"New Threat Assessment Center Provides Immediate Response to Threats." *Third Branch.* December 2007.

Nussel, Philip. "New Charges Filed Against Miners." *Charleston Daily Mail.* October 24, 1989.

O'Brien, John, and Matt O'Connor. "Erickson's Guards 'Were Not Remiss.' " *Chicago Tribune.* July 23, 1992.

O'Connor, Matt. "Deputy Relives Escape Bid." *Chicago Tribune.* October 30, 2002.

Olivers, Deputy U.S. Marshal Stanley. "Hard to Believe." *Federal Times.* November 13, 1978.

O'Neill, Tex and John Wildman. "Lawyers on Both Sides Plot Their Moves in Indian Guru's Case." *Charlotte Observer.* October 30, 1985.

Osmos, Peter, and Raul Ramirez. "500 Indians Here Seize U.S. Building." *Washington Post.*November 3, 1972.

Ostrow, Ronald J. "Marshals Successful; FBI Wants Role; Federal Lawmen Feuding Over Pursuing Fugitives." *Los Angeles Times.* January 12, 1988.

Ostrow, Ronald J., and Jeff Leeds. "Marshals Sent to Offer Abortion Clinic Security." *Los Angeles Times.* August 2, 1994.

Ostrow, Ronald J., and Ronald L. Soble. "Mengele Slipped Through U.S. Hands, Report Says; Holocaust: But No Evidence Is Found That U.S. Knowingly Assisted the Auschwitz Doctor." *Los Angeles Times.* October 9, 1992.

"Owensville Resident Recognized for Part in 'Ole Miss' Integration." *Gasconade County Republican.* October 1, 2003.

"The Park Patrol." *Newsweek.* March 13, 1978.

Parsons, Gena. "Marcotte Recalls Days of Mariel Boatlift." *The Citizen.* November 11, 2014.

"Paskal Bowser, Ex-deputy Marshal, Dies." *San Diego Union.* February 14, 1985.

"Patty Arraigned in L.A." *Star News.* March 29, 1976.

"Patty's Fate Rests in Hands of Jury." *San Francisco Herald-Examiner.* March 19, 1976.

Paulson, Amanda, and Brad Knickerbocker. "In Harm's Way? Chicago Slayings Spotlight Risks Judges Can Face." *Seattle Times.* March 3, 2005.

Pearlstine, Norman. "Refugees Trying to Return to South Vietnam Wait on Guam and Blame U.S. for Long Delay." *Wall Street Journal.* August 28, 1975.

Pearson, Richard. "Retired Army Carl C. Turner Dies." *Washington Post.* January 1, 1997.

"People on the Move." *Congressional Monitor.* August 5, 1996.

Petrick, Jane Allen. "Lynchburg Woman Was Child Model for Rockwell Painting." *Lynchburg News and Advance.* October 9, 2011.

"Progress in War on Skyjackers." *U.S. News and World Report.* August 9, 1971.

"Prosecutors to Map out Sniper Charges." CNN.com. October 25, 2002.

"Rajneesh City Stay May Grow." *Oklahoman.* November 7, 1985.

Ramirez, Raul. "Indians Continue Occupation of BIA." *Washington Post.* November 4, 1972.

Ranson, Edward M. "Our United States Marshal." *The Nevada Peace Officer.* Vol. 11 (1948).

Reed, Becky. "Federal Marshals Arrest Five More Striking Miners." *Logan Banner.* December 6, 1989.

Reed, Steven R. "Deal with Feds Got Chagra in Witness Program; Official Sees 'Rank Injustice' in Plot Figure's Plea Bargain." *Houston Chronicle.* April 23, 1989.

"Refugees to Be Flown to Guam." *Washington Star-News.* September 17, 1975.

Renteria, Ramon. "Daughter Writes Manuscript About El Paso Personality Jimmy Chagra." *El Paso Times.* January 19, 2014.

"Revenge Likely Motive in Judge Killings Case." CNN.com. March 11, 2005.

"Reyna Named Head of Marshals Service." *Washington Times.* October 31, 2001.

Richey, Warren. "Noriega Given 40 Years." *South Florida Sun-Sentinel.* July 11, 1992.

Rivenbark, Leigh. "Political Appointments vs. Career Jobs." *Federal Times.* March 28, 1994.

Robbins, Maro, and Guillermo Contreras. "Judge Wood's Assassin Dies of Heart Attack." *San Antonio Express-News.* March 21, 2007.

Roddy, Dennis B. "Fugitive Keeps Giving the Slip to Fed Agents." *Pittsburgh Post-Gazette.* May 28, 2001.

Rohrbach, Jill. "Hundreds Celebrate Groundbreaking for U.S. Marshals Museum." *Arkansas.com.* September 2014.

Rutherford, Glenn. "Marshal Makes Lone Stand at Building." *Louisville Courier-Journal.* September 5, 1975.

"Saigon to Accept Refugees." *Washington Post.* October 27, 1975.

"Same Hotel for Zebra, Patty Juries." *San Francisco Examiner.* March 12, 1976.

Sanger-Katz, Margot. "Browns: Dog Walker Saved Lives; Supporter Claims Marshals Chased Him." *Concord Monitor.* June 9, 2007.

———. "Marshals Tried to Nab Brown in June." *Concord Monitor.* April 2, 2008.

———. "Ruby Ridge Figure Coming to Browns—Standoff Survivor to Advise Tax Protestors." *Concord Monitor.* June 16, 2007.

Schmich, Mary. "Life Goes on, 8 Years Later." *Chicago Tribune.* March 10, 2013.

"The Schoolhouse Door." *[Pasadena, California] Independent.* June 13, 1963.

Senz, Kristen. "Browns' Bash Draw about 200." *New Hampshire Union Leader.* July 15, 2007.

———. "Browns Say They Will Walk Free, or Die." *New Hampshire Union Leader.* June 19, 2007.

Shannon, Elaine. "Taking a Byte Out of Crime." *Time.* May 25, 1987.

Shaw, Gary. "Nixon Aide Fights Ex-SB man over Wounded Knee." *[Chula Vista, CA] Star-News.* October 9, 1975.

"Should Airline Pilots Be Armed?" abcnews.go.com. September 25, 2001.

"Slayer Sent to Hospital." *San Francisco News.* February 24, 1938.

Smith, J.Y. "Charlie Chaplin, Comic Actor Famed for Role as 'Tramp,' Dies." *Washington Post.* December 26, 1977.

Snell, David. "Spies Take Secrets to Grave." *New York World-Telegram Sun.* June 20, 1953.

Sniffen, Michael J. "Director's Travel Costs Scrutinized." *Hutchinson [KS] News [Associated Press].* August 27, 1991.

"Sniper Investigation Timeline." Abcnews.go.com.

"Subpoena for Nixon Awaiting 'Time and Place,' Officer Says." *Los Angeles Times.* August 21, 1974.

"Suspected Mob Grave Found." *Ellenburg Daily Record.* October 29, 1990.

Symmes, Patrick. "U.S. Marshals Service Succeeds in Closing a Division, But Not a Deal." *Legal Times.* March 27, 1995.

"Tax Evading Browns Lose Federal Appeal of Convictions Following NH Stand-off." *New Hampshire Union Leader.* January 20, 2012.

Terry, Bill. "Death of a Self-Styled Elijah." *Arkansas Times.* January 1984.

Thomas, Jo. "'No Sympathy' for Dead Children, McVeigh Says." *New York Times.* March 20, 2001.

Thomas, Robert McG. Jr. "Mitchell Goodman, Antiwar Protest Leader, Dies at 73." *New York Times.* February 6, 1997.

"Threat to Kill Valachi at Hearings Revealed." *Milwaukee Journal.* October 8, 1963.

"Timeline: Rodney King from 1991-2012." *CNN.com.* July 17, 2012.

Tischler, Gary. "James Gandolfini: More than Tony Soprano, and Yet." *Georgetowner.* June 20, 2013.

"Tocks Island Facts." *New York Times.* March 23, 1974.

"Tocks Island Niceties." *Evening Bulletin [PA].* March 4, 1974.

"Tocks Squatters Were Lawless." *Philadelphia Inquirer.* March 16, 1974.

Tolme, Paul. "Son of Justice Sworn in to Head Marshals." *Arlington Journal Online.* February 2, 2000.

Tompkins, Stephen G. "Army Feared King, Secretly Watched Him." *Memphis Commercial Appeal.* March 21, 1993.

"Tongsun Park Booked to Leave for Washington." *Washington Post.* February 22, 1978.

"Tourists Flee As Chaos Follows Hurricane." *Des Moines Register.* September 20, 1989.

"The Trial of the Boston Five." *Eugene Register-Guard.* September 14, 1969.

Truell, Matt. "Man Enters Court Firing Guns, Throwing Bombs; Officer Killed." *Houston Chronicle.* August 6, 1993.

"Two Lives Represent Extremes." *Elyria [Ohio] Chronicle-Telegram.* March 14, 1993.

Unnamed Article. *Bonner County Daily Bee.* May 3, 1992.

Unnamed Article. *Federal Times.* ca. October 18, 1973.

Unnamed Article. *Federal Times.* October 29, 1975.

Unnamed Article. *Milwaukee Sentinel.* August 17, 1970.

Unnamed Article. *New York Times.* April 19, 1974.

Unnamed Article. *New York Times.* August 16, 1974.

Unnamed Article. *New York Times.* August 17, 1974.

Unnamed Article. *New York Times.* August 28, 1974.

Unnamed Article. *Time.* November 29, 1948.

Unnamed Article. *Washington Post.* November 3, 1972.

Unnamed Article. *Washington Times.* March 26, 1985.

"U.S. Deputy Marshal Slain Making Arrest." *San Francisco Examiner.* November 25, 1937.

"U.S. Oks Visit by Elian's Playmates." *USA Today.* April 25, 2000.

"U.S. Marshal Is Shot in Chest in Wounded Knee Gunfire." *Rocky Mountain News.* March 27, 1973.

"U.S. Marshals Choose Fort Smith for Museum." *Arkansas Business.* January 5, 2007.

"U.S. Marshals Evict Dam Squatters." *Pittsburgh Post-Gazette.* February 28, 1974.

"U.S. Marshals Evict Squatters." *Pocono Record.* February 28, 1974.

"U.S. Marshals Evict Squatters from Tocks Island." *Philadelphia Inquirer.* February 28, 1974.

"U.S. Marshals Focus on Security for Moussaoui, Lindh." CNN.com. January 30, 2002.

"U.S. Marshals Foil Suicide Try." *Daily News.* November 13, 1981.

"U.S. Marshals Injured by Viets." *Los Angeles Herald.* September 1, 1975.

"U.S. Marshal Still Leads Exciting Life." *Crocker-Anglo Bank Notes*. San Francisco, California. September 1963.

"U.S. Marshal Wounded in Gunfight at 'Knee.'" *Indianapolis News*. March 27, 1973.

U.S. Marshals Service [Investigative Operations Division]. "Risk Mitigation Can Lead to Fewer Officer Fatalities." *Police Chief*. May 2013.

"USMS Director John W. Marshall Talks Security." *The Third Branch*. February 2000.

"U.S. Psychiatrist: Elian 'Doing Well.'" *CNN.com* April 26, 2000.

"U.S. Spent $70,000 on Tongsun Park During Visit to U.S." *Washington Star*. October 6, 1978.

"U.S. to Pay Costs in Indians' Trial." *New York Times*. January 15, 1974.

UPI. "Guru, Followers Arrested Trying to Flee U.S. in Jets: Believed to Be Evading Indictments." October 28, 1985.

———. "Noriega Trial Postponed for the Third Time." Copy of Press Release, Undated.

———. "Valachi: Hoodlums could buy into Cosa Nostra for $40,000." October 3, 1963.

———. "Wallace Prepares to Surrender to Armed Might of Federal Govt." *Redlands [California] Daily Facts*.June 11, 1963.

Vizenor, Gerald. "Those Searches at the St. Paul Trial." *Minneapolis Tribune*. January 30, 1974.

von Hoffman, Nicholas, and Dan Morgan. "Rally of 12,000 Ends Jackson March." *Washington Post*. June 27, 1966.

Waldron, Martin. "Dismissal Urged in Indians' Trial." *New York Times*. September 16, 1974.

———. "Indians in Take-Over Free As Judge Criticizes F.B.I." *New York Times*. September 17, 1974.

———. "Witness Testifies No Firearms Were Found at Wounded Knee." *New York Times*. February 28, 1974.

Walsh, Edward, and Roberto Suro. "Marshals Seize Waco Evidence from FBI." *Washington Post.* September 2, 1999.

Watson, Elmo Scott. "When Tombstone, Ariz. Was 'Helldorado.'" *Blockton News.* April 4, 1929.

Welkos, Robert W. "Scripting a Scandal in Hollywood." *Toronto Star,* August 27, 1992.

Werner, Leslie Maitland. "Same Star, but Marshal Is Updated." *New York Times.* October 18, 1984.

Wheatley, Ralph. "Death of Long Leaves Regime Without Rudder." *Monroe [Louisiana] News- Star.* September 10, 1935.

"Wilkerson Denies Kidnap in July Cellblock Siege." *Washington Star-News.* December 5, 1974.

"Will *The Fugitive* Work on the Big Screen?" *Parade Magazine.* August 1, 1993.

Wills, Denise Kersten. "'People Were Out of Control'; Remembering the 1968 Riots." *Washingtonian.* April 1, 2008.

Witherspoon, Tommy. "Century of Law-Enforcement Tradition Riding Off into Sunset." *Waco Tribune-Herald.* May 6, 2003.

Wood, Daniel B. "Los Angeles Braces Itself as Federal Civil Trial Opens in the Rodney King Case." *Christian Science Monitor.* February 1, 1993.

Zaitz, Lee. "25 years after Rajneeshee Commune Collapsed, Truth Spills Out." *The Oregonian.* April 14, 2011.

Other

"Aryan Nations." Copy of Newsletter, Undated [1986].

Department of Justice. "Organized Crime Drug Enforcement Task Forces." Website Description.

Federal Judiciary Center. Entry of John Howland Wood, Jr. *Biographical Directory of Federal Judges.* Web biography on fjc.gov.

"Joseph Valachi." Entry in *Encyclopedia Britannica,* found online at www.britannica.com.

Minnesota Historical Society Library. "American Indian Movement (AIM)." Copy of Research Guide. Undated.

Montfort Academy. "Howard Safir." Website Biography.

"Questions and Answers: Manhunt." *Newsweek* Interview with Art Roderick, on msnbc.com January 16, 2001.

INDEX